THE SOVIET ECONOMY

THE SOVIET ECONOMY

Howard J. Sherman
University of California, Riverside

LITTLE, BROWN AND COMPANY Boston

to my daughter
LISA

PREFACE

There are many good books on specific aspects of the Soviet economy. Most of these studies are listed in the selected references following each of the chapters of this book. The present book, however, is an attempt at a detailed coverage of *all* of the main aspects and approaches to the Soviet economy.

For this reason, Part One contains not only an introduction to Soviet geography and political-economic institutions, but also a lengthy inquiry into the Marxist ideology currently promulgated in the Soviet Union. In Part Two the evolution and performance of the Soviet economy from the situation at the 1917 Revolution to the reforms of 1965 is investigated. Soviet institutions and problems, including the organization of central planning, labor and managerial behavior, agricultural incentives, and international trade and aid are discussed more systematically in Part Three.

The author himself is most fascinated by the problems of Soviet central planning. In Part Four these problems are presented far more fully than in any previous book discussing the Soviet economy as a whole. The problems of growth, full employment, and inter-industry balance are explored in two chapters. Then the most difficult problem — achieving optimal efficiency — is examined in two more chapters. First the possibility of achieving optimal efficiency is questioned, then the methods for calculating optimal efficiency are analyzed.

Relatively unexplored areas — the history and possible impact of the recent decentralization reforms in the Soviet Union and Eastern Europe — are investigated in Part Five. In the final chapter the comparative advantages of decentralized versus centralized socialist economies are considered.

All of these are highly controversial subjects, and — in spite of every effort at objectivity — the author's own biases must surely intrude. As a check on this tendency, not only have all the available facts been presented without any intentional omissions, but both sides of each issue are equally developed. Thus wherever available, *both* Soviet and Western estimates and interpretations of data are considered at every point.

Finally, it was felt that the subject is complex enough without giving the reader additional language problems. Therefore, all terms were translated into English, with only a few of the most important also given in Russian. Moreover, all references and most footnotes are to works in English. It is easy to compile an erudite list of references in French, German, Russian, and Eastern European languages, but this serves only to frustrate the average reader. A plentiful literature is now available in English, including a vast and increasing flow of translations.

ACKNOWLEDGMENTS

The author owes an immense debt of gratitude to Professors Robert Campbell and Gregory Grossman for a very careful initial training in this field. In addition, Professor Benjamin Ward gave many hours both in conversation and in a written review of the manuscript to the difficult task of clearing away my confusions. Another extensive and very useful review of the whole manuscript was given by Professor Lynn Turgeon. Most of all, however, this book was improved beyond measure by the detailed comments of Professor Franklyn Holzman on three different drafts of the manuscript.

A small amount of the material in this book previously appeared in three articles by the author: "Marxist Economics and Soviet Planning," in *Soviet Studies* (October, 1966); "The 'Revolution' in Soviet Economics," in Alex Simirenko, ed., *Contemporary Soviet Social Thought* (Chicago: Quadrangle Books, 1968); and "Planned Socialism versus Market Socialism," *Jahrbuch der Osteuropaischen Wirtschaft* (Munich: Osteuropa-Institut, 1969). Thanks are due in these cases to the publishers for permission to use parts of those articles, suitably rewritten, in the present book.

This book benefited greatly from the extremely valuable research assistance of Mr. Dennis A. Cohen, Mrs. Eliza Nash, and Mr. Kent Mason. Several points on Eastern Europe were clarified through valuable discussions with the late Czech economist, Pavel Eisler, whose untimely death took from the world a courageous and very warm human being. I have tried to inject into this book the spirit of hope and tolerant understanding that he transmitted to all who came into contact with him.

Advice on some of the mathematical points was gratefully accepted from Professors Robert E. Manning and Ramesh Bhardwaj. A grant from the Center for Slavic Studies, University of California, Berkeley, was much appreciated. Sincerest gratitude is also given for the prompt and accurate typing of the manuscript by Mrs. Elizabeth Korber, Mrs. Cheryl Fischer, Mrs. Jean Golden, and Miss JoAnne Graybill. Lastly this book was made possible only by the efforts of my wife, who managed to keep two young children out of my hair for an unbelievable number of hours. Of course, no one but the author can take the blame for all of the remaining mistakes in this book.

TABLE OF CONTENTS

PART ONE BACKGROUND

xi

PART THREE   INSTITUTIONS OF CENTRAL PLANNING

PART FOUR   PROBLEMS OF CENTRAL PLANNING

PART FIVE　REFORMS AND COMPARATIVE EVALUATION

LIST OF TABLES

LIST OF FIGURES

xxi

THE SOVIET ECONOMY

PART ONE
BACKGROUND

BASIC SOVIET INSTITUTIONS
AND ENVIRONMENT

Before starting a more detailed analysis, this chapter provides the reader with a thumb-nail sketch of Soviet geography, Soviet political institutions, and Soviet economic institutions. It begins with the geographical and resource base of the economy. Next, it turns to a discussion of Soviet political institutions, their present organization and their previous history. Then, more briefly because it is the subject of most of the rest of the book, the Soviet and U.S. economic institutions are contrasted. The basic differences are listed, such as Soviet public ownership versus U.S. private ownership of producer goods, followed by some important similarities, such as private ownership of consumer goods.

Geography of the Soviet Union

In speaking of the Soviet Union, one must realize that it is an immense country, three times the size of the United States, and comprising one-sixth of the entire land surface of the world outside of the permanent ice caps. The Soviet Union has common borders with Norway, Finland, Poland, Czechoslovakia, Hungary, Rumania, Turkey, Iran, Afghanistan, China, Mongolia, and Korea. The accompanying map reveals the size of the U.S.S.R. as well as the regional distribution of its manufacturing (which is discussed in the next section).

Transportation and Location. The enormous distances of the Soviet Union make transportation and communication real problems for Soviet planners. Although mountains cover only one-fifth of Soviet territory, and high mountain ranges occur only in border areas,

Distribution of Manufacturing in U.S.S.R.

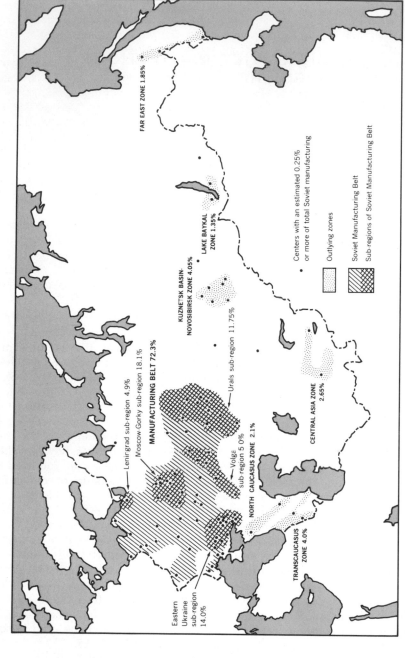

FAR EAST ZONE 1.85%

LAKE BAYKAL ZONE 1.35%

KUZNE'SK BASIN-NOVOSIBIRSK ZONE 4.05%

Urals sub-region 11.75%

CENTRAL ASIA ZONE 2.65%

Leningrad sub-region 4.9%

Moscow-Gorky sub-region 18.1%

MANUFACTURING BELT 72.3%

Volga sub-region 5.0%

NORTH CAUCASUS ZONE 2.1%

Eastern Ukraine sub-region 14.0%

TRANSCAUCASUS ZONE 4.0%

• Centers with an estimated 0.25% or more of total Soviet manufacturing

Outlying zones

Soviet Manufacturing Belt

Sub-regions of Soviet Manufacturing Belt

Adapted from Paul E. Lydolph, *Geography of the U.S.S.R.*, John Wiley and Sons, Inc., New York, 1964 land transport has not been well developed. Tsarist Russia had neither extensive railways nor extensive paved roads. Although some 40,000 miles of railways were built in the last 50 years of the Tsarist period, the railway network was still inadequate for a country of such size and there were almost no paved roads. Wars, the high capital requirements of developing a transport system, and the small number of passenger automobiles have kept the Soviet Union from developing land transport as rapidly as most other nations. They have made up for lack of investment in transport by using what they had much more intensively. For example, in the early 1950's, Soviet traffic density per mile of railroad was three times that of the United States. Further, Soviet freight cars covered two and one-half times as many miles per day as U.S. cars despite the fact that they traveled at lower speeds. And freight car turn-around times had been reduced to 5.8 days in comparison with a U.S. figure of approximately 15 days.[1]

In contrast with the United States, the Soviets have placed much more emphasis on railroads than on auto or truck transport. In 1957, 90 percent of their freight went by rail in comparison with less than 40 percent in the United States. Transportation by water is normally a cheaper means of moving goods, and should be of great importance to the Soviet Union, considering the number and lengths of its rivers. Unfortunately, many of the waterways are frozen during part of the year, and most rivers run north and south, whereas the great need is for all-year transport east and west across the Soviet Union. An increasing part of the transport burden is being undertaken today by air. It is noteworthy that the Soviet Union had the first commercial jet passenger plane in service.

Partly as a result of transportation difficulties and partly as a result of other historical factors, industry in the old Russian Empire was concentrated mainly in the western areas. The rich coal and ore producing Donbas-Dnieper region (called Eastern Ukraine in the map) was the center of heavy industrial production. This region, along with the Krivoi Rog region, accounted for almost nine-tenths of the coal mining and three-fourths of the iron smelting. Ninety-seven percent of all oil production came from the Caucasus. Electric power production and engineering were centered mainly around the large western cities, especially Moscow and St. Petersburg. In fact, two-thirds of all Russian large-scale industry in 1914 was to be found in these few western regions. The vast areas of the east and southeast had little population, and even less urban and industrial development. It is estimated that Siberia, Central Asia, and Kazakhstan, which together composed three-fourths of the Tsarist territory, had only 6 percent of all large-scale industry.[2]

[1] See Holland Hunter, *Soviet Transportation Policy* (Cambridge: Harvard University Press, 1958); and E. Williams, "Some Aspects of the Growth and Structure of Soviet Transportation," in Joint Economic Committee, U.S. Congress, *Comparisons of U.S. and Soviet Economies* (Washington, D.C., 1959).

[2] See Maurice Dobb, *Soviet Economic Development Since 1917* (London: Routledge and Kegan Paul Ltd., 1966), Chapter 16.

The reasons for the disproportion lay in certain political influences as well as in the virtual absence in the eastern "colonial" areas of any population centers, markets, transportation, or credit facilities. In this respect, a remarkable change has been wrought by the Soviet government, so that the center of gravity of industry has shifted toward the eastern regions. The map shows as of 1960 the great expansion of manufacturing in the Urals, in Kuznetsk and Novosibirsk, and even the beginnings of a significant industry in the Far East. These changes will be the object of more detailed discussion in later chapters.

Land and Resources. In view of the size of the country, Soviet agriculture is able to utilize a surprisingly small land area. One problem is that a vast area of the Soviet Union lies very far north, much of it at the same latitude as Canada, and a large percentage actually north of the Arctic Circle. On the other hand, in large parts of the area where there is sufficient warmth, there is very little rainfall. In addition to the mountainous and desert areas, there are also large areas of poor soil, especially clay-like and excessively acidic soils.

A Soviet geographer, Prasolov, summarized the situation in the 1930's as follows: "26½ percent of the land is either too cold or too dry; infertile soils comprise another 29 percent; still another 29 percent are covered by forests; this leaves only 15½ percent available for agriculture, of which 4 percent is suitable only for grazing."[3] This appraisal may have been overpessimistic. In the late 1950's, Khrushchev put into cultivation some 100 million acres of land in Western Siberia which had been considered climatically marginal. Whether these lands will be productive enough to continue in cultivation is still a debatable question. Further, to combat inadequate rainfalls, the Soviet Union under Stalin embarked on major irrigation and afforestation programs, although his successors cut back on some of the more extravagant projects.

At the same time, Soviet resources for industrial use are particularly abundant. As late as 1939 almost one-third of the entire Soviet area was covered by forests — about a fifth of all the forest areas of the world. In addition, the Soviet Union's water resources are among the greatest in the world, their potential hydroelectric power being estimated as high as six times that of the United States.

Furthermore, intensive geological prospecting has revealed sufficient amounts of most necessary metallic and non-metallic raw materials. Soviet writers claim that their coal supply will be adequate for the next five or six thousand years. The Soviet Union also claims to have more than half of the known iron ore reserves of the world. Soviet oil resources are very large and are also calculated to be among the highest known reserves in the world. The Soviet Union produces more of the vital element manganese than any other country in the world. It produces also large amounts of copper, lead, zinc, bauxite, nickel, uranium, and gold. In addition, it produces sufficient amounts of such non-metallic minerals as salt, kaolin, asbestos, corundum, and various borates.

[3] Quote cited in A. Bergson, ed., *Soviet Economic Growth* (Evanston, Illinois: Row, Peterson and Co., 1953), pp. 252–253.

Finally, it has a very large supply of natural gas. The only major mineral in which it is not self-sufficient is tin. The Soviet Union is also self-sufficient in most agricultural inputs into industry, although it does import natural rubber and part of its cotton requirements.

Population Trends. In recent years, Soviet population has been rising rapidly. In 1950, the population amounted to 179 million persons; by 1966, the total had reached 231 million. Normal death rates are very low, even lower than those in the United States. This is a result largely of improvements since the Revolution in public health, sanitation, and education, but also may reflect the fact that many of the weak, sick, and aged died prematurely during World War II. Death rates were abnormally high during both the World Wars — and also in the interwar period as a result of famines and internal strife. The legacy of these high death rates is a population (in 1966) with 19 million more women than men.

The Soviet birth rate was, before the Revolution, one of the highest in Europe; but continued industrialization and urbanization has brought declining birth rates, with a particularly rapid drop in recent years. This decline is perhaps aided somewhat by the general Soviet policy of free and legitimate abortion, and a slow change in recent years toward more liberal publicity about birth control devices. In the case of births, also, the Second World War had a very drastic effect, lowering the births during the war years by about one-third. The lower births and higher deaths of those years show up in a much reduced supply of new workers in the present period. It is estimated that the Soviet population is 40 to 45 million persons below the level which would have been reached had the U.S.S.R. not been involved in World War II.

The increasingly urbanized Soviet population signifies a trend which has remarkably accelerated in the Soviet Union, due to rapid industrialization. In spite of the Second World War, the Soviet urban population in the four decades from 1926 to 1966 more than quadrupled. In 1926 only 18 percent of the population lived in urban areas; today, the percentage of city dwellers has reached almost 55 percent.

In studying the Soviet Union one must also keep in mind the enormous variety of ethnic groups in the population. While Great Russians still constitute a majority of the population, there are also very large numbers classified as Ukrainians, White Russians, Jews, Uzbeks, Tatars, Kazakhs, Moldavians, Azerbaidzhans, Georgians, Estonians, Lithuanians, Armenians, Latvians, Mordovians, Chuvaski, and Tadzhiks. In addition to these major groupings, there are over one hundred other identifiable minor ethnic groups.

Soviet Political Institutions

Political Dictatorship. The United States is formally a political democracy. It has the secret ballot, and elections in which any adult citizen may vote (with, in practice, some exceptions). It has two or more opposing political parties, and any view may be represented on the ballot (except that the Communist Party has been outlawed to a large degree at times). In the next chapter, there is an analysis of the Soviet view that democracy in the United States is fundamentally restricted by the fact that U.S. enterprises and wealth are privately owned and highly concentrated in a relatively few hands. They contend that such economic power gives these few individuals *effective* control over United States propaganda facilities (newspapers, TV, radio), political parties (Democrat as well as Republican), election campaigns, and elected officials.

The Soviet Union claims to be a "purer" political democracy because its enterprises are publicly owned and its wealth more evenly divided (a claim investigated below). More concretely, it does have the secret ballot and universal suffrage in elections. *But* there is only one legal political party, the Communist Party! By Western standards, this one restriction justifies calling the Soviet Union a political dictatorship.

Although all other parties are prohibited, nominations may be made by trade unions and other "non-political" organizations. The single candidate is then usually nominated in an enormous public meeting; the democratic content of this procedure is open to serious question. As a general rule (with exceptions in recent years), there is only one candidate in the final elections. A new election must be held if that candidate fails to get a majority of the votes. *Within* the Communist Party, there are theoretically free and democratic elections, but in practice (as will be shown) the General Secretary of the Party has usually controlled the nominations and elections at every level of the Party.

Present Soviet Political Organization. The Soviet Union has at least three different organizational structures at local and regional levels, which converge only at the top national level. It has, like all countries, a governmental structure; but it also has an economic hierarchy because it is centrally planned; and it has an all-important political party structure, representing the one legal party in the society. These three lines of power are all pictured in Figure 1–1, and are described in detail in the following paragraphs (with letters referring to this figure).

The Communist Party is the most important decision-making body because it holds ultimate power over both the economy and government. The Party's highest official is its General Secretary (*A.* — called just Secretary for some years). The General Secretary (Stalin, then Khrushchev, now Brezhnev) controls the Secretariat (ten to fifteen members), which has the power to assign all Communists to any job in the country and to transfer them to other jobs at any time. The General Secretary also presides over the Politbureau (*B.* — called Presidium for some years), a small group of five to fifteen members who make all important decisions in the Soviet Union. The Politbureau is elected by the Central Committee (*C.*), which has about one hundred or more members. The Central Committee has the power to overrule the Politbureau, but the Central Committee only meets a few times each year.

The supreme body, in theory, is the Party Congress (*D.*), but it meets at most once every two years (and usually less frequently). When it is in session, the Congress can overrule any past acts of the Central Commit-

Figure 1–1

Organization of the Soviet Union

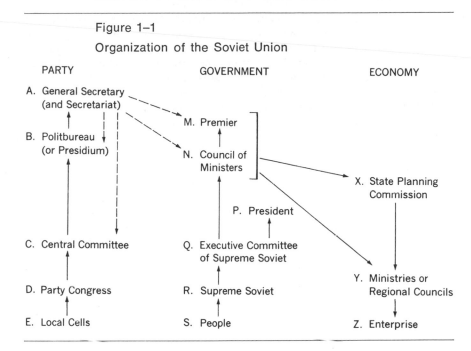

tee or Politbureau, and the Congress elects a new Central Committee. The Congress delegates are elected in turn by Party cells (*E,*) all over the country, each containing ten to a hundred members. Thus, in theory, the Party structure is democratic, but in practice most elections within it have been controlled from higher levels. In fact, the General Secretary has usually controlled the "election" of a pre-selected Politbureau, as well as the "election" of the Central Committee, and even the "election" of Congress delegates.

Parallel to the Party apparatus is the governmental structure, which is controlled by the Party. Each locality has a Soviet (the Russian word for council), theoretically elected by all the inhabitants. At one time, the local (city and village) Soviets elected the regional or Republic Soviets, which then elected a Supreme Soviet (*R.*). It should be noted that the Soviet Union is formally a federation of Republics, though it is quite centralized in practice. Since 1936, however, the Supreme Soviet has been elected by direct election by the universal suffrage of all citizens. The Supreme Soviet is divided into a Soviet of Nationalities (about a thousand members representing different nationalities — from Russian to Uzbek to much smaller groups) and a Soviet of Union (about a thousand members representing equal numbers of population by areas).

The Supreme Soviet meets once or twice a year to pass (or rubber-stamp) laws, to give vent to local grievances, and to elect its Executive Committee (*Q.*), composed of two to three hundred members. The Executive Committee meets more often, and it elects a Council of Ministers

(N.), composed of 30 to 100 members who act daily on all government matters. The Executive Committee also elects a President (P.) of the Soviet Union, who is a figurehead with only ceremonial power (and the right to hand out medals). The Council of Ministers is the functioning executive body, making everyday decisions in all areas from industrial sectors to foreign affairs to health and welfare. The Council of Ministers elects the highest government official, the Premier (M.).

At every level of government, however, the Party can issue orders to all Communists; and all top leaders are Communists. Thus, the Party has its own men in office and can interfere with their actions at any time. Furthermore, lest there be any doubt, the Soviet Constitution allows only one political party in elections, the Communist Party. On lower levels, however, the single slate of candidates includes a higher percentage of approved non-Party people, who are sometimes referred to as non-Party Communists. Only since 1956 has there been some experimentation with more than one (approved) candidate in some districts.

The General Secretary of the Party not only has extra-legal power to control Party elections, but also has ultimate power through Party discipline to control the Premier and Council of Ministers. In the period immediately after Stalin's death and again in the period since Khrushchev was deposed, it appears that power has been exercised much more collectively or equally by all the members of the Politbureau. The Premier, who is also a member of the Politbureau, appears now to be almost equal in power to the General Secretary. In turn, the Premier and Council of Ministers exercise control over the top economic bodies. They appoint both the State Planning Commission (X.) and the heads of Ministries (Y.) and the heads of Regional Councils (Y.).

The economic plan is designed by the State Planning Commission, and is then enacted into a formal law by the appropriate government bodies. The Plan is carried into operation at the top level by either Ministries (one minister for each industrial sector) *or* by Regional Councils (one council for each main territorial division). There are usually also several intermediate bodies, all of which give orders to the basic economic unit, the enterprise (Z.). The Soviet enterprise is a factory or farm run by a manager, who usually has sole authority within it and sole responsibility for its performance.

Soviet Political Evolution. Pre-revolutionary Russia was an absolute autocracy for most of its history, headed by the Tsar, strongly military and imperialist in nature, and supported by a feudal landowning nobility. Ideas of political democracy came very late to Russia, and for some time after the French Revolution they influenced only the few intelligentsia. A small degree of parliamentary political democracy existed only from the peasant uprising of 1905 until the Revolution of November, 1917; and, even in that period, the Russian Duma or parliament was neither very popular nor very effective. There was thus very little theoretical or practical experience with democracy among the Russian people.

Furthermore, the Russian Marxists were forced to illegal conspiracy by the repressive laws of the Tsarist government. In theory, the Communists (called Bolsheviks) were in favor of "democratic centralism," which meant democratic election of central officers plus strict obedience to orders from the elected officers. In practice, the Party was not always able to hold elections for top officers, but it still enforced orders from the top down in an atmosphere of strict discipline. This tradition, by which the Party led the masses, and the top leaders directed the Party, was understandable and in general harmless before the 1917 Revolution. Since anyone could leave the Party without harm, the Party could only lead by persuasion, and Party discipline could only be voluntary self-discipline. Few revolutionaries thought about how differently this system might operate when the Party became the all-powerful ruling party of the government, with "persuasion" changed to censorship and coercion, while "voluntary discipline" became external control or opportunistic fawning on leaders.

The Russian Revolution of 1917 resulted in a government of "Soviets," or Councils of Workers, Peasants, and Soldiers, led by the Communist Party. At first, the Communist Party ruled in alliance with the Left Socialist Revolutionary Party, which mainly represented the poorer peasants. Within a month after the Revolution, the first step against political democracy was taken when all the parties (and all the newspapers) advocating capitalism or monarchism were banned. This was partly explained as a temporary measure during the violence of the revolution and attempts at counterrevolution. Yet it was also given more dangerous theoretical meaning as a "natural act of proletarian dictatorship."

Then a few months later the elected Constituent Assembly was dispersed because, it was said, the attitude of the people had changed so quickly that the elections to the Assembly were now outdated. This seems like a reasonably democratic argument, except that new elections to the Assembly were not called then or ever. The further argument was given that the Soviets were more democratic in nature than a parliamentary Assembly. Of course, in the Soviets the Communists had a majority. The Soviets were councils representing soldiers, industrial workers, and farmers. Since the owning classes were to be dispossessed, they too would eventually also be part of the working classes, so eventually everyone could vote for the Soviets (as has been the case since 1936). Furthermore, all socialist parties participated in the Soviets; and some non-Communist parties were represented for a time in the central government. Therefore, except for the exclusion of the capitalist and monarchist parties (who anyway represented only a very small minority by this time), it could be argued the Soviets would turn out to be the same kind of democratic instrument as an Assembly.

Within a few more months, however, as the Civil War grew in intensity and bitterness, the other socialist parties were also largely prohibited. Even so, it appears that they continued to function to some degree in the trade unions and the Soviets. In fact, those who proved loyal to the government were tolerated all the way through the Civil War and into the early 1920's. It was only in 1921 or 1922 that the last remnants of the other socialist parties were outlawed, apparently out of fear generated by the anti-Communist revolts of the period (especially at Kronstadt). The banning of bourgeois parties was the first step against political democracy. The banning of all other socialist parties was the second step against political democracy.

The dictatorship of the proletariat was narrowed in practice from the rule by a majority of all people down to the majority among socialist "working-class" people, and then further down to the members of the Communist Party. The ideology of a single revolutionary truth known to the faithful and embodied in the "dictatorship of the proletariat" was already gaining powerful momentum. In fact, the next step was already beginning within the Communist Party. By a resolution of its 1921 Congress, the Party prohibited all factions within itself. At first this was not at all meant to strangle free speech in the Party, but merely to halt all actual organizational splitting (especially secret factional caucuses). It was, however, a sign of things to come. As long as Lenin lived, open and lively conflict continued within the Party. Then occurred the most violent factional fight in Party history, that of Trotsky versus Stalin versus Bukharin from 1924 to 1928. Increasingly, the rule against factions was used first to oust members from the Party, then to deport them to Siberia, and finally to send Trotsky into exile. After 1928, only Stalin's faction existed openly in the Party. Thus, the third step against political democracy progressed from the outlawing of non-Communist socialists to the outlawing of non-Stalinist Communists.

Finally, after 1928 and up through 1936 the Stalinist faction itself was narrowed. After the purges of 1936 and 1937, only Stalin held power. Thus was completed the fourth and final retreat from democracy with power moving from the Stalinist faction to Stalin alone. After excluding advocates of capitalist parties, loyalty to the Soviet state was defined first as loyalty to any of the socialist parties, then more narrowly as loyalty to the Communist Party, then as loyalty to the Stalinist faction of the Party, and finally as loyalty only to Stalin. To follow any other view was to be a traitor, and to be a traitor meant to be jailed or executed.

The Post-Stalin Change. In 1956, at the 20th Congress of the Soviet Communist Party, Khrushchev pointed out that the situation since 1917 had greatly changed with respect to "counter-revolutionary" violence. Because of the power of the Soviet Union and China, he held that in those countries with a long democratic tradition there may occur in the future a peaceful transition to socialism through a parliamentary majority. The power of the Soviet Union and China makes a difference (according to Khrushchev) because most of the violence of civil war in modern times can be attributed to foreign intervention. The 1917 Revolution in Russia was brief and largely peaceful before the intervention of foreign powers. The mildly socialist Spanish government of 1936 might have quickly overcome Franco but for his powerful Italian and German backing. The right wing might have been unable to make a counter-revolution in Brazil in 1964 without foreign support. There-fore, he argued, if foreign intervention is prevented, in many countries socialism may come into power and remain in power in a peaceful and fully democratic manner.

Mao Tse Tung, on the contrary, continues the dogmatic argument that any movement toward socialism is bound to run into reactionary violence with foreign imperialist support. The example given is the South Vietnam dictatorship, which he claims is operating obviously against the will of the majority, but existing on military violence fi-nanced and led by the United States.

The present Soviet leaders also completely distinguish the democratic perspective in some of the advanced countries from that in most of the underdeveloped countries. In the Congo, as in Cuba earlier, democratic elections appear to them to be a farce since there is no long meaningful democratic tradition, and violence lurks close to the surface. Even with-out foreign intervention, Asia, Africa, and Latin America contain coun-tries where feudal chiefs and landowners fight with the poor peasant masses, with both sides ready for violence and neither strongly at-tracted to middle-class democratic processes. In West European coun-tries such as Italy, on the other hand, there is a long tradition of de-mocracy, though with some vacillations toward fascism. There is also a strong industrial working class committed to active advocacy of *both* democracy and socialism. The more liberal Marxists look to the assump-tion of power by West European Communists and their Socialist allies as the only possible road to a democratic and socialist world.

Although their steps have been slow and hesitant, the post-Stalin So-viet leadership has liberalized Soviet politics. First, there is some evid-ence that, in addition to the General Secretary and the Politbureau, the more numerous Central Committee members are now more fully involved in the decision-making process. Second, even the Supreme Soviet has shown a little more life, and elections to it have involved more than one candidate in some instances. Third, Stalin's police terror has been de-nounced, the number of political prisoners reduced from hundreds of thousands to a few, due process has increased, and there have been no political executions since the execution of the secret police chief, Beria. Of course, progress is not smooth, and there have been some terrible re-gressions to Stalinist methods — the most important instance being the tragic invasion of Czechoslovakia.

Backwardness and Dictatorship. One important view has been argued by the liberal Marxist, Isaac Deutscher, in his many books on the Soviet Union.[4] When socialism came to the Soviet Union, that country was exceedingly backward in its economic development, as China is today. Deutscher argues that dictatorship was one result of the curse of backwardness, but that the Soviet Union will slowly liberalize and achieve political democracy as it achieves advanced economic de-velopment.

[4] See, e.g., Isaac Deutscher, *Russia in Transition* (New York: Coward-McCann, Inc., 1957).

In this view, many countries today are prone to both socialism and political dictatorship because *both* are results of the economic backwardness of these countries. These countries are filled with an intense desire for rapid economic growth, to achieve both national prestige and individual welfare. Yet they are poor, agrarian countries with little modern industry, and lack buildings, equipment, skilled workers, and experienced managers.

Socialism is viewed as the necessary instrument of industrialization. The most important reason is that the desperate lack of capital in the underdeveloped countries is most easily remedied by governmental control of resources. The government could tax the rich and gather the small savings of the poor in order to invest by itself in new factories and equipment, as did the government of the Soviet Union. This makes it possible to do without the accumulation of capital by landlords or commercial speculators, who make very few industrial investments in any case. It also makes it possible to do without investment by foreign capitalists to some extent, which is a welcome development because many effects of foreign investment are not liked by the leadership of the underdeveloped countries.

It is thus explained why backwardness may generate socialism, but why does it unfortunately also generate one-party dictatorship? According to Deutscher's argument, the reason lies within exactly the same set of circumstances. Both the revolutionary leadership and the masses of the people may agree on the desirability of rapid economic growth, as they did in the Soviet Union. Yet the Soviet leadership and their economic planners soon found that there is a conflict between rapid long-run growth and immediate consumption. Concretely, they found that to gather the resources necessary to build industry meant to take food away from the mouths of the farm population. Excluding foreign investment, there was simply no other major source of capital. It was necessary to take from the farms the food and raw materials for export, for the feeding of the new industrial working class, and as the basis for the manufacturing processes themselves.

In the Soviet Union (as will be seen in detail in a later chapter) Stalin coerced the peasantry into collective farms, from which the government could extract the entire surplus over minimum consumption. At the cost of low or even declining living standards, Stalin succeeded for many years in putting a fourth to a third of national income into investment in heavy industry as a firm base for Soviet economic development. Since most of the population was still on the farm and carried the burden of this policy, the extraction of the farm surplus met the most violent and bloody opposition from millions of people. Obviously, the unpopular policy of overcoming backwardness by such extremely high investments at the cost of years of severely restricted consumption would not be voted voluntarily by any people on earth, especially in a country beginning with consumption levels just above starvation. It follows that such a very rapid economic development cannot be achieved under democratic institutions, but only by a dictatorship like Stalin's; though it is arguable that a somewhat slower industrial development *might* be achieved with democratic consent.

Today in the more developed Soviet Union, according to Deutscher's view, there are new tendencies toward liberalization and eventual political democracy. China, on the other hand, is still in the earlier stage of rapid industrial construction at the expense of present consumer needs, and thus still finds a need for rigid dictatorship. The Soviet Union has now progressed to the stage where it has a large industrial base capable of generating sufficient surplus within itself to facilitate continued rapid growth of production as well as the increased satisfaction of consumer needs both in cities and on the farm. Furthermore, its intensive education of a large population has now provided that population not only with scientific knowledge, but also with a liberal arts education, which results in the capability for democracy and the demand for a wider democratic process.

Deutscher concludes that dictatorship resulted in the Soviet Union from economic backwardness, not because of socialism, but in spite of socialism. He argues that in an advanced economy a socialist system would provide a better environment for political democracy than capitalism. Of course, it would require institutions such as a multi-party election system, the legal right of the opposition to certain amounts of time or space in government-run newspapers or television (like B.B.C. in England), and the allowance of non-profit cooperative ownership of some newspapers and television (like the Pacifica radio stations in the United States). With these safeguards, he argues, the greater equality of income, and the elimination of private control of large productive enterprises, means that socialism would actually be more conducive to political democracy than capitalism has been. These are, of course, still hypothetical and as yet unprovable assertions.

Soviet Economic Institutions: Differences from the United States

Socialist Ownership of Industry. One of the basic differences between the Soviet Union and the United States lies in the ownership of productive facilities. In the United States, most land and factories are privately owned. In the Soviet Union, most land and factories are publicly owned. The public ownership, of course, tends to mean public direction, and therefore usually means planning. The principal type of household income in the Soviet Union is wage income for labor. On the other side, in the United States income consists not only of wages, but also profit, rent, dividends, and interest. These latter incomes are derived basically from private property; thus most U.S. planning is necessarily limited in scope to the confines of single enterprises, in which decisions reflect the search for private profit.

Even in the Soviet Union, there are some exceptions to socialist production. One *can* work for oneself in the Soviet Union. Thus, there are some people, a large absolute number but an insignificant percent of the whole, who do not work for the government. They produce goods or services privately by themselves, and they can sell them; this category includes some doctors, lawyers, and handicraftsmen. No one, however, can employ someone else for a wage for private profit — this is viewed as exploitation.

Most Soviet industrial enterprises are owned and operated by the "public," represented by the Soviet government. The only exceptions are a very small percentage of enterprises that are cooperatives, mainly composed of handicraft workers. In the public enterprises, the government, or some agency of the government, appoints a manager. He is solely responsible for the performance of the factory, and his bonus is based on how well it performs. His performance and his conduct are checked by numerous agencies, and he may be promoted, transferred, or fired at any time. In turn, he hires and fires all the other workers at the enterprise.

The government grants the enterprise its plant and equipment and initial working capital, though they are now beginning to charge interest on capital. After the initial grant of capital, however, the enterprise is then made financially independent. It must meet all costs of wages and materials out of current revenue. It must also replace or repair depreciated and broken capital out of its revenues from sales. And it is normally expected to show a profit above all of its costs.

Socialist Ownership of Agriculture. Most farming constitutes an exception to pure socialist production. Most Soviet farms are theoretically cooperative. The government owns the land; however, it leases the land to the farm for 99 years. The profits are supposed to be split among the farmers. These units are the "collective farms," so called. Collective farming means that the farmers pool their resources, work the land together, and divide the profits among themselves. It is required, of course, that a great deal of income must be set aside for communal consumption and reinvested for further expansion. Furthermore, until recently, there were obligatory deliveries of crops to the government at low prices, in effect a tax in kind, which cut sharply into collective farm profits.

There are also some "state farms" in the Soviet Union. These farms are run essentially like factories. The state (or government) owns the farms, and simply hires farmers to work on them. This is easiest to do with a mass-production type crop like wheat. In recent years the amount of land under state farms has been increasing absolutely and relatively, partly because the huge new areas in Western Siberia recently brought under cultivation have been largely committed to grain, and partly because of discontent with the collective farm as a form of economic organization.

The government is the sole purchaser of most of the collective farm products. By law the collective farms have to give a certain percentage to the government, after which they can dispose of the rest as they see fit. The farmers have a contract with the government, which includes a set price and a set amount of what they have to deliver. Beyond that amount, one finds in all Soviet cities bazaars or so-called "collective farm markets" where the farmers sell all the produce that remains over and above the deliveries required by the government, the amounts necessary for feed and seed, and the farmers' own consumption. It may be brought to market either by the collective farm or by individual farmers. They can then sell it for whatever price the market will bear. These prices are almost always considerably above the prices that one finds in government stores. This is partly because of the existence of chronic excess spending power (or repressed inflation), but also reflects the fact that the food brought in by the farmers to these markets is definitely somewhat fresher and of better quality.

While the collective farm served well its original function of getting grain out of the countryside and putting the burden of the industrialization on the backs of the peasants (see Chapter 3), agriculture has been the major "drag" in the Soviet economy over the past 40 years. The collective farm embodies (or embodied until very recently) some of the weakest points of both capitalism and socialism. As a socialist form of organization, it suffers from the fact that many farmers did not wish to "cooperate" and had to be forced to do so. This is in sharp contrast, for example, with the Israeli "kibbutz" which is similar in form to the collective, but, for historical reasons, is totally different in spirit. Further, the collectives have always been burdened by heavy-handed bureaucratic intervention from above. This happened because the planners have forced compliance with their agricultural output plans, plans which often did not make much sense for reasons of climate, soil, and profit.

Possibly the weakest feature of the collectives, until a few years ago, was the worker incentive system. The farmers were paid on a so-called work-day basis. For a day of work at different jobs on the farms, a person received work-day credits — the greater the skill required, the larger the credits. After the crop was sold and all expenses paid, the funds which remained were divided up among the collective farmers in proportion to the number of work-day credits they had accumulated.

This system provided little incentive to effort on the farms for the following reasons. First, until very recently, there were various excessive operating expenses. These included paying high fees in kind for rental of state-owned farm machinery and for wages to its operators, borrowed from the so-called Machine Tractor Stations. They also included the large obligatory deliveries to the state (the tax in kind). These expenses left the average farm with very little to divide up among its members. Second, even if a member was anxious to "put in time" in order to accumulate work-day credits, he had no incentive to exert himself on the job. For under the system as it existed until recently, the extra output produced by him as a result of extra effort accrued not to him personally but was divided up among all members. In the last few years, this has been partly corrected by the introduction of bonuses to individuals or groups of individuals. Third, the collective farmers have an alternative and more profitable pursuit open to them — the cultivation of the little private plots which surround their dwellings. In these are usually planted garden vegetables. These vegetables are either consumed by the farmers, or else they are sold in the bazaars or "collective farm markets" at much higher than regular retail prices. While the state requires the collective farmers, by law, to put in so many days of work on the collective farm, the farmers work on the collectives as little as possible, and devote all their spare time to this more lucrative labor. The intensity with which they cultivate the plots is evident from the fact that while the plots aggregate a very small fraction of the total land cultivated, produce from them averaged about one-third of the total sold in the 1950's and livestock more than one-half.

Central Planning. In a later chapter devoted solely to economic organization, the analysis will include in detail not only the types of enterprises, but also the chain of command from above. The most important orders originate from the U.S.S.R. Council of Ministers, but additional orders to the enterprise may come from regional or local government bodies. Further orders may originate in or be transmitted through the agency directly supervising the enterprise, whether that agency is associated with a regional governing body or with the Ministry directing some industrial area. Finally, all of these orders from governmental or supervisory bodies are supposed to be in accord with the Plan, which emanates from the Central Planning board or its subordinate agencies. The enterprise manager is solely responsible for the performance of the factory, then, only in the sense that he must execute all of the orders he has received within the constraint of the resources allocated to him.

The Central Planning Commission (as will be seen in detail in a later chapter) first collects information up the ladder of agencies from the enterprise in order to evaluate the last year's performance and the present conditions and possibilities. Then the Commission is told by the Council of Ministers what goals it must strive to meet. On these bases, it draws up a general plan for the whole economy, though details of production and allocation are provided only for a couple of thousand commodities. The draft plan is then shown to all agencies on down the ladder to the enterprise. After all of these units have added their detailed modifications and suggestions, the Central Planning Commission draws up the final draft.

The Plan is supposed to provide sufficient investment for the desired rate of growth, guarantee balance among all the industrial needs and outputs, and choose the "best" assortment of goods. Later chapters examine just how the planners must calculate so as to achieve balanced growth and optimal choices of assortments of goods and technologies. At any rate, the Central Planning Commission hands the Plan over to appropriate government bodies to enact into law, and it is then passed on with detailed expansions at each intermediate level till the enterprise receives a formidable document. This document is supposed to tell the enterprise for a year — or some other period — exactly what to produce, how to produce it, what prices to charge, and what funds it may use.

Again, the manager is judged on how well he follows these commands, though it will be shown in Chapter 7 that he has more room for maneuver than appears on paper.

Government Taxes and Spending. The Soviet government levies very low income taxes, with a maximum rate of only 13 percent on the highest-paid workers and salaried employees, and it is preparing to abolish the income tax altogether in the near future. This does not mean that the Soviet Union collects low taxes, but that it collects them in forms other than the income tax. Almost all profits of enterprise, plus all of a very high sales tax (which averages 60 percent on goods sold to the public), go to the Soviet government. This means that the Soviet government actually collects and spends a much higher proportion of the national income than does the U.S. government, perhaps higher than that of any Western government.

The Soviet government *must* collect a larger percentage because it also spends a much larger percentage of the national income than does the U.S. government. In the first place, the Soviet government has very large defense expenditures (of course, no government has "offense" expenditures). Defense is a smaller percentage of the Soviet budget than of the U.S. budget, but only because the Soviet budget expenditures include some large items not included in the U.S. budget. However, it is approximately as large a percentage of Soviet national income as it is of U.S. national income; this implies a greater relative (though smaller absolute) effort on the part of the Soviets since U.S. defense spending comes out of a much larger national income.

In the second place, the Soviet budget also finances very large welfare expenditures in the form of socialized medicine, free education, other subsidized services, pensions, and free aids to the population — a relatively much larger expenditure by the government than in the United States. In statistical terms, the Soviets claim that what we would call fringe benefits, distributed freely by the government as the only employer, amount to between a quarter and a third of the total real wage. This is one of the things that makes it very difficult to compare wages between the Soviet Union and the United States.

Finally, unlike the United States government, the Soviet government needs funds to run state enterprises. The Soviet government finances most of the new investment in industry, trade, transport, communications, and other productive areas. Expenditures on "Financing the National Economy" is the largest single item in the budget, and presently amounts to almost 40 percent of total expenditures.

Public Health, Education, and Housing. One of the basic areas of difference between the Soviet Union and the United States lies in the Soviet practice of providing completely free health service, largely subsidized education, and largely subsidized housing. There is no tuition so education is free to the average student. In addition, the student with high grades is paid a fellowship adequate to buy textbooks, pay for room and board, and have some left over. Students work under great competitive pressure for grades, not only for higher fellowships, but because of the superior opportunities available to those who graduate near the top of their class. Large resources are put into education, including good educational facilities and high salaries to professors.

For a while the Soviet Union switched into a system by which the student, upon graduating from high school, would work for a couple of years. The political leadership believed it good for the student's general understanding of life to go to work for a time in an ordinary industrial job before attending college. Now the Party is compromising with other goals, so work experience is merely one of several factors in gaining admission to higher education.

In addition to the general ideology, in the recent past students were sent to work for a couple of years before beginning college simply because of the rising pressure of college applicants for advanced education. So many students were getting through high school, and these students were under such pressure to obtain an advanced education, that the inflow could not be handled with the facilities at hand. The bottleneck, apparently, was not primarily in teaching staff, but rather in building and equipment and other general university facilities. In addition, a national labor shortage, reflecting the population losses of World War II, existed. This problem was eased, at least temporarily, by diverting high school students away from higher education. In the past few years the situation has improved and it has become feasible again to allow a much higher percentage of students to go directly to the University from high school (discussed further in Chapter 9).

A great deal of money is spent on the free health services of the Soviet Union. That U.S. citizens still have to *pay* money for medical services is considered extremely barbaric by Soviet citizens, who often question U.S. tourists quite incredulously on this point. Of course, the Soviet taxpayer is paying for health services indirectly.

Housing is an area of striking difference between the United States and the U.S.S.R. — it is the sphere of consumption in which Soviet inferiority is greatest. True, rent charges are almost negligible in the Soviet Union, but this low rent is paid for terribly inadequate housing. By law not more than a very small percentage of a citizen's income may go for rent. Whereas the average U.S. citizen spends 25 to 30 percent of his income for rent, the average Soviet citizen spends less than 5 percent. All rental units are, of course, rationed and subject to price control. It is necessary to ration them because people would be willing to pay a great deal more than 5 percent of their income for a decent place to live.

Why are Soviet housing facilities so inadequate? There are several explanations. The construction of housing requires a vast amount of capital goods — more per dollar of annual output than any other good or service. Since the Soviets have always been very short of capital, because they have needed it for other things, housing has been far down on the priority list. In addition, in the Tsarist period very little housing was built for the common man. Furthermore, 30 or 40 million people have migrated into the cities over the past 40 years. Finally, during the

Second World War, the Germans destroyed six million buildings, or something like a third to a half of all Soviet housing. As a result, the housing situation is miserable. There is very little privacy as we know it. It is the rule rather than the exception for a whole family to live in a room and to share a kitchen and bathroom with several other relatives. If there is an apartment with four or five rooms, very likely the mother and father have one room, a sister and brother another, a grandmother and grandfather the third, and maybe an uncle and aunt the fourth room. All these people will, of course, use one kitchen and one bathroom. It was only in 1957 that the Soviet planners announced the construction of apartments with bathroom and kitchen designed for one family, and this was a tremendous advance.

Advertising and Propaganda. Striking, though less important, is the fact that there is no private advertising in the Soviet Union. The tourist walking down the street in the Soviet Union does not see private brand advertising for any product. If one looks at Soviet television, there is little advertising. The only kind of product advertisement a traveler sees in Moscow is the neon sign which says: "Drink tomato juice." No brand is indicated. The Soviet Union and the Eastern European nations have only recently begun to introduce brands based on the factory in which the product is made. The object is to achieve some consumer control over quality. If a consumer has been sold an umbrella that leaks in the first rain, he will know on whom to put the blame.

While the Soviet Union has very little product advertising, there is no lack of public propaganda. All of the newspapers, radios, and television are owned by the government, and, of course, are used for government propaganda purposes as well as for disseminating factual information. In contrast with the United States, the Soviet newspapers contain no sensationalism at all, or, at least, no sensationalism of the private sort that is found in the U.S. press. The Soviet press is generally full of long grey columns with few pictures, though they have lately been trying to put a little more life in their format. All newspapers are, of course, published by the government, which receives the income from sales (but no advertising income). The low price at which Soviet papers are sold suggests that they are subsidized by the state.

Soviet Economic Institutions:
Similarities to the United States

In everyday activities, there are also many obvious similarities between Soviet and U.S. economic life.

Privately Owned Consumer Goods. While the Soviets do not allow private ownership of the means of production, this prohibition does not apply to consumer goods. The consumer goods market in the U.S.S.R. appears little different from its American counterpart. In every town and city, stores line the streets and individuals can buy everything from tomatoes to television sets providing they have the money — more expensive items can even be bought on the installment plan. Consumer goods are the private possession of those who buy them. Consumer goods as well as cash can even be passed on by their owners to relatives or friends when they die. Land is not considered a consumer good; it is possible, however, to own one's own house.

Work for Money Wages. A second important point of similarity between the everyday economic life in the Soviet Union and in the United States is that in both countries the majority of people work for money wages. In the industrial sector of the Soviet Union, this is the only form of income, with some slight exceptions. "Wages" is used broadly here to include monthly salaries, bonuses and commissions, time wages (paid by the hour, day, or week), and also piece-work wages (according to the number of pieces one produces). In the past, the Soviet Union has relied very heavily on piece-work for incentive reasons. More recently, piece-work has been deemphasized. The basic principle according to which wages are supposed to be paid is that of socialism, namely, "from each according to his ability, and to each according to the work that he produces."

The communist principle, "to each according to his need" is clearly not operative in the Soviet economy. This is one explanation of why the Soviets call their economy "socialist" rather than "communist." Wage and salary scales of the average employees within and between industries are also strikingly similar in the Soviet and U.S. economies. The greater the skill or effort required to do a particular job, the higher the pay. And the higher the pay, the more commodities one is able to buy in the retail markets. This is the "carrot" which motivates capitalist and socialist workers alike. It is the overriding principle of labor allocation and income distribution under both systems. Distribution according to "need" has proceeded a long way in the Soviet Union *only* in the areas of medical care and education, areas in which the U.S. economy has also taken a few strides in the same direction.

While the distribution of wage and salary payments is similar in the two countries, the overall income distribution is more unequal in the United States. This is due primarily to the high incomes received in the United States in the form of profits and dividends, interest and rent — incomes from ownership of firms and property. Incomes from these sources have been abolished, of course, in the U.S.S.R. The highest paid individuals in the U.S.S.R. are the dancers, artists, writers, composers, and others in the fine arts. Not only are they paid high wages, but they receive large income from royalties. Also near the top of the pay pyramid are the scientists and leading university professors. As already noted, a very high premium is placed on education in the U.S.S.R. It is probably as difficult to get into the average Soviet college as it is to get into one of our top universities. The Soviet system is very much a merit system in which education is one of the major stairways to the top. This is not to deny the unofficial importance in the job market of political pull, of being the right nationality, and so forth.

Interestingly, the medical profession does not rate very high in the

Soviet pay hierarchy, a sharp contrast with the situation in the United States. The very high returns to the medical profession in the United States are partly explained by a coincidence of several extraordinary circumstances. First, there is no other profession in the United States in which the training and apprenticeship period is so prolonged and poorly compensated. Second, for reasons which cannot be dealt with here, the number of doctors trained and available in the United States has not expanded significantly for decades despite the tremendous increase in demand for their services. The U.S.S.R. presently has one and one-half times more doctors per person than the United States, despite the fact that Tsarist Russia had very few doctors. The high pay of American doctors is undoubtedly partly a compensation for long apprenticeship and partly a reflection of the shortage which exists.

Worker Mobility. Another major area of similarity is the ease with which workers can change jobs. Soviet workers are now completely free to move from job to job, though they are discouraged from doing so. In fact, a major problem has always been excessive labor turnover, far greater than that which characterizes the U.S. labor market. In the 1930's, labor turnover in industry reached a peak of over 150 percent — on the average each worker changed jobs one and one-half times a year. This implies almost a whole new work force in each factory each year. People were simply looking for better situations, and moving to higher paying jobs. Before 1956, many administrative devices were used to try to reduce the turnover, and severe penalties could, in theory, be imposed for transgressions. However, because of the extreme labor shortage which has always existed in the Soviet industrial sector (the reasons for which are discussed in Chapter 9), managers of enterprises trying to hire workers have been willing to collude with those seeking new jobs and penalties have rarely been applied. In 1956, most of these penalties were abolished. At present, a worker is free to move as long as he gives two weeks notice.

The labor shortage has been particularly serious among skilled workers, though the supply of skilled workers has been increasing rapidly and the situation is now relatively much better than ever before. There apparently is no shortage of unskilled labor. Workers interested in changing jobs can get information on openings in the central labor exchanges which are found in all Russian cities, something like our state employment offices. Workers may also go to the labor exchanges when they are unemployed. However, they cannot expect to get unemployment checks for two reasons. First, the Soviet Union as a planned economy claims to have abolished unemployment, and therefore unemployment insurance. Second, any unemployed worker seeking a job at one of the exchanges could immediately be directed to unfilled jobs even though these might be unacceptable to him. It should be noted that workers needing retraining can usually obtain it at government expense.

Another major labor market problem is the housing shortage. While workers are quite free to change jobs within a city or locality, they are not in practice free to take jobs in other cities because of the great difficulty in securing adequate housing. The need to provide housing for workers has been a factor which the planners have had to take into serious consideration in planning the location of new industry.

SELECTED REFERENCES

1. A very critical introduction to the Soviet Union may be found in John Gunther, *Meet Soviet Russia: Land, People, Sights* and *Meet Soviet Russia: Leaders, Politics, Problems* (both, New York: Harper and Row, 1962).

2. A more sympathetic and more thorough introduction is in William Mandel, *Russia Re-examined: The Land, The People, and How They Live* (New York: Hill and Wang, rev. ed., 1967).

3. Two Western works critical of Soviet political institutions are: Merle Fainsod, *How Russia is Ruled* (Cambridge, Mass.: Harvard University Press, rev. ed., 1963), and John N. Hazard, *The Soviet System of Government* (Chicago: University of Chicago Press, third ed., 1964).

4. More sympathetic works on Soviet politics are by the liberal Marxist, the late Isaac Deutscher, especially his biographies of *Stalin* and *Trotsky*.

5. A standard work containing much information on Soviet resources is A. Bergson, editor, *Soviet Economic Growth* (Evanston, Illinois: Row, Peterson and Co., 1953).

6. An interesting recent report on population is: James W. Brackett and John W. DePauw, "Population Policy and Demographic Trends in the Soviet Union," in Part III of Joint Economic Committee of Congress, *New Directions in the Soviet Economy* (89th Congress, 2nd session, U.S. Printing Office, 1966).

2

THE SOVIET IDEOLOGY

In order to understand the present policies of the Soviet Union, it is necessary to know the beliefs of her leaders. Of course, their actions are not determined solely by Marxist theory, although they profess to be motivated by it. It will be shown that Marxist theory is flexible enough so that it may often be interpreted in different ways. Exactly what interpretation will be used depends, among other things, on the needs of factional struggle, on the tensions of world politics, and even on the national background of the particular interpreter. For example, Stalin's course of action was certainly shaped to some extent by his Russian (or Georgian) background as well as by the specific circumstances in which he assumed control of the former Tsarist Empire.

Main Characters of the Marxist Drama

Karl Marx. Karl Marx (1818–1883) was born in Trier, Germany.[1] Marx took a Ph.D. in philosophy, and carried the imprint of the predominant 19th century German philosophy, that of Hegel, throughout his life. First denied an academic post for his political views, Marx was later exiled to France for republicanism. There he learned the views of the French revolutionary socialists. After the failure of the 1848 revolutions, Marx was expelled to England. Here he spent several decades studying British political economy, specifically the Classical school from Adam Smith onward. Thus the intellectual heritage of Marxism was derived from three main sources: German philosophy, French revolutionary socialism, and English Classical economics. On this basis, Marx

[1] The classic biography of Marx is by Franz Mehring, *Karl Marx* (Ann Arbor: University of Michigan Press, 1962, first published in German in 1918).

25

turned out the many volumes which constitute the core of Marxist thought, each aspect of which is discussed in detail in later sections of this chapter.

Marx was also an active revolutionary in the 1840's. After the collapse of the 1848 Revolution, Marx led the inactive life of the political exile for many years. In 1864, however, he joined with British trade unionists and some French and Belgian unionists, as well as certain sects of syndicalists and anarchists, to form the International Working Men's Association (known also as the First International).

In 1871 socialist Paris rebelled against the central government and formed a democratic city government or Commune. The Paris Commune lasted but a few months, and then was drowned in blood by the more conservative French government. All of Europe was aghast at the red Commune of Paris, and equally horrified were the merely reformist, business-like British unionists who formed the base of the International in England. When Marx wrote a flaming defense of the Commune, these respectable unionists and non-revolutionary socialists deserted the International. Since the International was already badly split by Marx's fight with Bakunin's Anarchist movement, this was the effective end of the First International. The First International lingered on until it formally died in 1876. Marx continued working and writing until his death in 1883.

V. I. Lenin. The early 1880's witnessed the beginnings of strong Socialist parties in France, Germany, and much of Western Europe. In spite of much initial persecution, the German Social Democratic Party eventually came to be a very large and very law-abiding party. The various Socialist parties together formed the Second International in 1889. Although the Second International continued to use revolutionary Marxist language, its actions grew less and less revolutionary as its member parties grew more and more an accepted part of the parliaments and cabinets of Europe. During the late 1890's and 1900's the chief spokesman of orthodox Socialism was Karl Kautsky, who used suitably revolutionary language while defending a peaceful evolutionary view of Socialism.

Kautsky was challenged from the Right by Edward Bernstein, who admitted that he wanted to revise Marx to accord with the newer non-revolutionary practice of the Socialist parties. Henceforth, any Socialist who wanted merely to reform capitalism gradually and to revise the revolutionary ideals of Marx was called a "revisionist."

Kautsky was also challenged from the Left. The most important of his leftist critics was V. I. Lenin (1870–1924), who wished to add revolutionary action to revolutionary verbiage. In 1917, when the Russian Revolution broke out, Lenin put his theories into practice. The first Russian Revolution of March, 1917, put the parliamentary democrats and democratic socialists into power. In November, 1917, Lenin led the socialist Revolution of the Bolshevik Party, which had constituted the left faction of the socialist movement in the cities, and which later was to be called the Communist Party. Under the leadership of Lenin, the Bolsheviks attempted to transform Russia into a socialist country. Lenin formed the new Third International or Communist International (Comintern) of the Communist Parties of the world in 1919.

Stalin. After Lenin died in 1924, a struggle for power began within the Communist Party. From 1924 to 1928 the struggle raged between Trotsky on the Left against Bukharin on the Right and Stalin[2] 1879–1953) in the Center. By a sly use of the right against the left, and then of the left against the right, Stalin won undivided power. Trotsky was exiled and later murdered in Mexico in 1940. The other old Bolshevik leaders continued under Stalin's direction until the purge trials of 1936 and 1938. After that, Stalin ruled completely alone until his death in 1953. After the Second World War, Stalin attempted to continue his rule as a dictator, not only over the Soviet Union, but also over Communist Parties elsewhere, including especially Eastern Europe (with the exception of Yugoslavia, where Tito split with Stalin in 1948).

In early 1956, Premier Khrushchev, who was by then the leader of the Soviet Union, achieved considerable popularity with the Russian people by denouncing the evils and murders of Stalin's day and promising a new era of freedom. De-Stalinization did not proceed as smoothly as Premier Khrushchev had anticipated. First there was a fight within the Soviet Communist Party in which Khrushchev narrowly defeated Malenkov and Molotov. Then Eastern Europe took Khrushchev's teachings to heart and showed a restless independence. In late 1956 the pot boiled over in Hungary and in Poland in the form of open revolts against the Governments. In consequence, a more liberal and independent Communism came to stay in all of Eastern Europe (even in Hungary, where Soviet troops ousted the extreme liberals, but still had to install the moderately liberal Kadar).

The dragons of independent thought, moreover, once set free, were not easily restrained. The Italian Communist leader, Togliatti, voiced the thoughts of many when he said that this was to be an era of polycentrism, or of many divergent national paths to socialism. The many rumblings within the Communist movement were kept under cover for some years, but finally in 1963 an open break came between the revolutionary and more aggressive Chinese Communists and the now conservative Russian Communists. This schism now dominates the Marxist movement, and finds almost all of the Communist Parties divided into a "right" and "left" wing, with more or less formal splits occurring in many of the Parties. Thus, in the following pages will be found not one, but a variety of interpretations of Marxism by Soviet, Chinese, and other Marxists.

Perhaps the most promising new interpretation was the development of a movement in the Czech Communist Party in early 1968 to make both certain radical political and economic reforms in their country. The economic reforms, which favored decentralization of decision-making

[2] Perhaps his most famous biographer is Isaac Deutscher, *Stalin* (New York: Vintage Books, 1960).

to the enterprise level, are discussed in Chapter 14. The political reforms were intended to bring political democracy by an end to censorship, an end to controls on opposition groups, abolition of the secret police, and democratization of the Communist Party. These fragrant blossoms of a new democratic Communism were crushed by Soviet tanks in August, 1968.

Marx and Philosophy

Marx identifies all religions, all theologies, and all philosophies which recognize any supernatural phenomena or any beings free from natural laws as "idealism." Marx opposes this idealism to his doctrine of "materialism," which recognizes the existence only of a material world which follows natural laws. The material world exists whether we are aware of it or not. Our scientific activity gains for us more and more knowledge of it, though that knowledge can never be complete.

Materialism. Marx's materialism is evolved from the thought of the early British empiricists, such as Hobbes and Locke. It thus emerged from the long struggle of European science against religious superstition and mystification. Materialism says that we must base our activities solely on our empirical and sensual knowledge of the world. It must be understood in this light, and must not be confused with ethical materialism (or "hedonism"), which is the desire to become rich, accumulate material objects, and live the "sweet life."

Marxism finds no evidence for the idealist belief in supernatural beings. It is less easy for Marxists to defeat the agnostic scepticism of Hume and of the modern positivists, who deny that there is any more empirical evidence for the belief in a material world than for the belief in a God. The dogmatic Marxist (like the dogmatic religious believer) finds it sufficient to re-assert his faith. The more progressive Marxists[3] admit that materialism is only an assumption, but point out that the practical consequences of accepting the opposite idealist assumptions are catastrophic. If the world does not really exist (or if the supernatural world is the only reality), then why should one take any action at all? The progressive Marxist therefore asserts materialism not as a dogma, but as a necessary *assumption* for any constructive action, as a necessary basis for scientific inquiry.

Dialectic Method. One of Marx's most interesting contributions is his combination of materialism with Hegel's theory of the "dialectic." For Marx, "dialectics" means thinking about the world in terms of evolution and change, processes rather than things, and interrelated flows rather than isolated objects.

Hegel[4] developed a comprehensive view of a changing universe, which he called the dialectic process or outlook. Like the medieval philosophers, however, he saw the whole complex process of evolution that he de-

---

[3] See, e.g., Maurice Cornforth, *Science and Idealism* (New York: International Publishers, 1947).

[4] See the excellent account in Bertrand Russell, *A History of Western Philosophy* (New York: Simon and Schuster, 1945), pp. 730–745.

scribed as being directed by and encompassed by the Absolute (or God). Hegel saw a general pattern, which revealed change and evolution through conflict. The conflict of "thesis" and "antithesis" — two opposing forces arranged by God — brings about a harmonious "synthesis" in all the universe, leads society to the predetermined end of the harmonious state, and leads the categories of thought to the idea of the Absolute.

Marx claimed to have taken the dialectic out of the realm of mysticism and to have shown that this pattern of change is due instead to the nature of the material world, and that it applies to this world as well as to abstract ideas. Marx did not spell out his approach, but some of his Soviet followers state rigid "laws" of how the world changes, as well as a "logic" of change and contradiction. Their three most important laws are: (1) the Unity of Opposites, which states that opposites (thesis and antithesis) are united in strife, and their tension produces change (synthesis); (2) the transformation of Quantity into Quality, which states that small quantitative changes eventually produce major qualitative jumps; and (3) the Negation of the Negation, which states that at a later stage any developmental process returns to many features of an earlier stage, but at a "higher" level, as in an ascending spiral.[5]

One example of a dialectic process would be the Darwinian description of biological evolution from amoeba to man through survival of the fittest by constant adaptation of animal (thesis) to environment (antithesis). The classic Marxist example is the rapid development of the productive power of capitalism (thesis) opposed by the barrier of the vested interests of the ruling capitalist class in preserving the economic institutions of capitalism (antithesis). This opposition leads ultimately to the socialist revolution, which produces a qualitatively new socialist society (synthesis).

If one takes seriously the official Soviet position that dialectics states the most general laws of all movement, this position seems to conflict with their own materialist outlook. Materialism rejects any super-scientific or "metaphysical" dogma, yet here are universal laws unrecognized by science. Perhaps it could be argued that Marx and Engels derived these laws from their own wide scientific knowledge of the material world. Yet, certainly in Hegel, but also in Stalin and in much of current Soviet philosophy, the dialectic laws are stated as absolute propositions, applying always and everywhere without the usual scientific qualifications and limitations. Furthermore, these absolute laws are so vague that they do not meet the pragmatic or operationalist criterion accepted by most modern Western scientific research.[6] In other words, there is

[5] The dialectic is expounded by Frederick Engels in Part I of *Herr Eugen Dühring's Revolution in Science* (New York: International Publishers, 1939, first published 1885, some parts written by Marx). A concise modern exposition of the Marxist view is Maurice Cornforth, *Materialism and the Dialectic Method* (New York: International Publishers, 1953); and a comprehensive criticism of the Marxist position is in Z. A. Jordan, *Philosophy and Ideology* (Dordtecht, Holland: D. Reidel Publishing Company, 1963).

[6] See, e.g., Anatol Rapoport, *Operational Philosophy* (New York: Harper and Brothers, 1954).

no indication of how to measure or test or refute these laws in the material world. Nor can one apply them like any other scientific law to make specific predictions from specific facts.

To get around these criticisms of dialectics as universal laws, many Soviet philosophers have interpreted dialectics not as laws of the world, but as a new logic to replace the traditional Aristotelian or formal logic. This interpretation does fit Hegel's work in some sense and it does find apparent support in some statements of Engels. Yet it runs into completely devastating criticisms.[7] If we take "logic" very broadly as a correct or useful way of thinking, then all kinds of propositions may be called logic. This approach, however, would have dialectics replace "formal logic," which is the science of consistency in the use of the forms of our language. Yet if dialectics is accepted as a logic in this sense, it leads to inconsistent thinking. It would be necessary to argue the logic of "contradiction," that both a proposition A and its opposite, not A (or –A), are true, and rely on "synthesis" to resolve the contradiction that results. In other words, if any proposition is true, so is its opposite. By this nonsensical logic, however, it is very easy to prove absolutely anything, and no argument can be brought to a rational conclusion.

The more progressive or undoctrinaire Marxists (called "revisionists" by their more dogmatic opponents) have moved to meet the critics by means of a third interpretation of dialectics, much less pretentious, but perhaps more useful. They see dialectics as a part of scientific method, not as a replacement of science, and not as a replacement of formal logic. Elements of this approach have been discerned by some Marxist theoreticians in Engels and Lenin. In fact, Stalin himself refers to the dialectic as a "method." The problem is that while many orthodox Marxists refer to the dialectic "method," they often seem to revert in practice to its interpretation as a system of universal laws or a new logic (or all three at once, which is very "dialectic").

In the progressive Marxist outlook the dialectic is simply an approach or orientation toward scientific method. It cannot conflict with formal logic because it discusses only method, and not logic. The dialectic method is only opposed to the "static" approach to method. This "static" or two-valued orientation evolves its method as if the world were composed of isolated and unchanging objects. Thus, the static orientation considers it easy to give exact characteristics to an object, to say whether it is white or black, solid or liquid, alive or dead; and to maintain that it continues to have these characteristics over time. The dialectic or dynamic or multi-valued orientation produces a method appropriate to a world in which there are assumed to be not static things, but interconnected and changing processes.

The dialectic approach thus looks for a whole spectrum from black to white, at things changing from solid to liquid, and at the whole process of development from birth to death. It should be most useful in the study of functional relationships in connections such as between man

[7] See, e.g., Z. A. Jordan, op. cit.

and nature, or between worker and employer, or between teacher and student. It may also be especially useful in considering an evolutionary process, such as the development of the planet Earth, or the evolution of biological species, or the changes in organization of human society, or the development of an individual from child to adult to old age. This view of interaction and conflict always provides the framework for any Marxist analysis of economic development, whether in the United States or in the Soviet Union.

Marx and History

All social problems are approached by Marxists in their historical context. Moreover, the greatest impact of Marx on Soviet, as well as on Western academic social scientists, has been in history. Therefore, it is most important to study carefully the Marxist view of historical processes.

Basic Marxist Views. The Marxist approach to history is called "historical materialism." The essential feature of historical materialism is its belief that the ideas of men are shaped by the life of men. Ideas do not come from a vacuum, but are created in the maelstrom of human activity and out of the needs of human beings. This is true of all ideas, whether in the arts, in philosophy, or in history itself. When Marxists speak of environment, however, they do not refer primarily to the physical surroundings, but to the social environment, and most especially to its "economic base" or "mode of production." The mode of production — the way that man earns his daily bread — comes of necessity for the Marxist before he thinks about religion or other nonessentials.

The mode of production is divided into two parts, the "forces of production" and the "relations of production." The "forces of production" constitute all of the present plant and equipment, all of our acquired scientific knowledge and the total available supply of workers. The "relations of production" are the ways of organizing men economically, answering the questions of who shall own the means of production, who shall work with them, and who shall own the product. The economic base as a whole, including both means and relations of production, determines the "super-structure" of society = the political institutions, the type of culture, and the total ensemble of the ideology of society.

In this view the economic base determines everything. To discover why Barry Goldwater was the Republican nominee for President of the United States in 1964, one should examine the latest stage of U.S. economic development. To know why the Roman Empire fell, one should examine the economic base of slavery. To understand the bitterness of a James Joyce, one should eventually go back of Irish politics to Irish economics.

The essence of politics in the Marxist view is the "class struggle," which is directly related to the economic base of society. The class struggle is the conflict of economic classes, where classes are defined in relation to ownership of and work with the means of production. Thus Marxism does not see history as determined by the clash of a few extraordinary individuals, but by the more prosaic everyday way of life and economic struggles of whole classes of men.

Of course, economic developments, such as the invention of atomic power, are reflected in the rest of society neither immediately, directly, nor automatically. On the contrary, new developments in the forces of production only slowly clash with the old relationships of production, and only win out after a long period of conflict. The old relations of production and the entire super-structure of society are geared to the old forces of production; the ruling economic classes have a vested interest in the old relations of production. A significant change in the forces of production, such as the discovery and use of agriculture, may be held back by the old productive relations. If the ruling class attempts a defense of the old relationships, then only a *revolution* can bring new relations of production, which will allow the full and unfettered development of the new forces of production. Similarly, for example, automation of industry meets strong resistance in present economic relations, whereas a different type of economy could greet automation as a pleasant relief from man's labors.

Critics of the Marxist Historical View. The critics[8] of the most dogmatic Marxism protest that there is more in life than economics. Economic factors may be an important determinant of history, but they are not the only factors. The art of a Picasso must be explained by more than the French economy or even all of modern socio-economic institutions; his art is also the result of previous artistic developments, of the new ideas of cubism and abstractionism, and of the unique psychology of Picasso. The fall of the Roman Empire is connected not only with the institution of slavery, but with the migration of certain Germanic tribes and with the new ideas of Christianity as well as the factional strife within Christianity.

An endless number of examples may be given to show that most historical events are not solely and directly determined by economic development. In fact, many economic events seem to be determined by new ideas. Thus, Max Weber makes a weighty case for the belief that the Protestant Reformation was a necessary prerequisite to the growth of capitalism. Moreover, many research scientists are notoriously isolated from the economic world, yet their inventions — the product of their ideas — certainly change the economic base. Thus, there appear to be cases where the mode of production is changed by the super-structure, rather than the other way around.

Progressive Marxist View of History. The more progressive Marxists do not speak of one factor or another as dominant in history. They rather consider society as an organism, its parts interrelated, to be explained by the functional relations of all its parts. Of the traditional historical materialism, they retain the basic thought that no ideas spring

8 See, e.g., A. James Gregor, *A Survey of Marxism* (New York: Random House, 1965).

from the void, that all of our ideas arise from our social environment. They argue strongly that simple economic determinism is much too crude and is not good Marxism.[9]

In a static sense, that is to say in a cross-section of society at any one time, the progressive Marxists assert only that all the components of society have a functional purpose in terms of each other — in the same way as the parts of our bodies. If the parts do not function in a unified way, the society is unstable and must change. For example, religion may sometimes support rebellion, as early Christianity did, but in the majority of societies religious ideas appear to have played the role of a pacifier. They reconcile the believer to his social order by telling him that it is divinely ordained and, anyway, that his suffering on earth is merely a brief prelude to his eternal pleasure in paradise. Similarly, the arts may convey the religious message; or a message that the society, be it good or bad, is too powerful to be changed; or that the inner psychological life is the only really important thing; or may merely drench the audience in complacency-producing pleasure.

The progressive Marxists also emphasize that the relations of production will ordinarily correspond to the forces of production. For example, slavery does not exist where a man cannot produce a surplus above his own needs. Moreover, the super-structure normally does correspond to the mode of production in essential points. Thus, most philosophers living under the slave system rationalized a defense of its essential goodness.

Progressive Marxism asserts that when a basic component of society changes so much that its relationship with other, less basic components is altered, then conflict arises and — eventually — the less basic components change. The changing element usually is the technological aspect of the mode of production. Technological change itself is a function of a certain technological and social environment. A change in the forces of production does not, however, automatically change the rest of society. Rather, the changing technology and forces of production come into conflict with the existing relations of production and the whole super-structure.

The change in society will be only gradually prepared, though it may come to fruition with some suddenness. Thus, the beginnings of the Industrial Revolution found a France that was still ruled by an absolute monarchy in league with a very conservative landowning nobility. This political structure imposed many artificial industrial restrictions, which held back the enterprises of the rising class of merchants and businessmen. Eventually the conflict was reflected at the most abstract levels of the super-structure, for example, in the critical writings of Voltaire and Rousseau. Finally, the new political ideas led to a revolution, and the sudden emergence of new political institutions, which inaugurated

[9] See, e.g., Maurice Cornforth, *Historical Materialism* (New York: International Publishers, 1954); or V. Gordon Childe, *History* (London: Cobbett Press, 1947).

new economic relations, which allowed the new forces of production to reach their full potential.

After the change, society is again a more or less smoothly functioning unit in all its parts. Eventually its own rapid growth and development, with new vested interests holding back any change in the relations of production, lead to new conflicts and new sudden changes. If society is able some day to set up relations that eliminate all vested interests, then, even though there would still be changes in the means of production, the changes in the rest of society would be slow and peaceful rather than violent and sudden. Marx believed that this would be the case under socialism.

At any rate, Marxists argue that if the functional relations of the different elements are sufficiently understood, and the relative weight of the different elements is estimated well enough, then the overall direction of the next change can be scientifically predicted. Since, however, the whole process starts over on a new basis after the main change, it may be possible to make a general prediction of a new society, but the detailed forms of the new society are hard to predict.

Marx and Economics

Marx spent most of his life investigating the economic functioning of capitalism. He had very little to say about the functioning of socialism except to claim that it is better in every way than capitalism. Therefore, his ideas on capitalism are discussed here, but their relevance to the Soviet economy is left to a later chapter.

Value. Marx argued that the exchange value of any commodity (which is expressed in its price) is determined by the total amount of labor necessary in the present society for its production. This total labor includes both current living labor, and the past labor that is congealed in the production of machinery and in the extraction and preparation of raw materials. Labor expended on useless articles, however, creates no exchange value. Neither is exchange value created by unnecessary labor which fails to make use of available technology — for example, the production of a standard automobile by hand without using machinery.

The most dogmatic Soviet interpretation of the labor theory insists that it excludes the Western theory of marginal utility, which attributes all value to the consumer demand for useful commodities (or "utilities"). Yet Marx himself stated that a commodity must have a subjective use-value or utility to *some* consumer, or else it would have no value.

On the other side, the more stringent Western critics of Marx's labor theory of value argue that it is only a supply or cost theory, and completely ignores demand or utility. Some even argue that it is circular reasoning to pin all exchange value to labor time because the exchange value of labor time itself can only be determined by demand. At any rate, the more dogmatic writers on both sides agree that Western marginal utility theory and Marxist labor theory are completely opposed.

The more tolerant views of a minority of economists see no analytic contradiction between the two theories.[10] In the first place, Marx himself explains that he limits his law of value to the *long-run* situation in which supply is exactly adjusted to demand. But Western economics agrees that in the long run, if each additional unit is supplied at the same constant cost per unit, then the price simply equals the "cost of production," including an average "profit." By definition, in this long-run situation, an increase in consumer demand will only dictate an equal increase in supply, leaving the price exactly as it was before the change in demand.

Both economic views thus agree that demand determines the level of output, but that long-run price is determined by the "cost" of supply, including a "profit." For price theory, therefore, there is at least a minority opinion that the Marxist labor theory is merely one very particular case of Western marginal utility analysis. The argument becomes much more spirited, however, when the two sides explain what they mean by "costs" and "profits."

Surplus Value. Suppose there are only two elements used in the productive process: (1) capital owned by the enterprise and (2) hired labor, ignoring for present purposes both land and borrowed capital. In that case Marx argues that labor is paid a wage equal only to its "value," namely, the necessary cost of keeping workers healthy and alive and well-trained. Yet a worker in a day's labor will produce a value higher than his own necessary cost of living. In Marx's terms, the labor producing his own necessities is called necessary labor; the rest of his labor is called surplus labor. The product of the surplus labor is called surplus-value by Marx. He argues that this surplus over necessary labor is the source of all capitalist profit (and rent and interest); and, furthermore, he considers it a measure of "exploitation."

Marx's critics claim that he ignores the value of capital's contribution to output, because this gives him an intellectual basis for advocating worker's revolution. Even some non-Marxist socialists would admit that capital has a value and deserves a return, but that only the people as a whole are entitled to it. The usual Western view is that profit is the return on capital, which is itself "productive." In this view, capitalists (owners of capital) deserve their profits because of their "sacrifice," "abstinence," "waiting" for the return on their capital, or "giving up liquidity" for a time. Notice that all of these terms apply to the subjective state of mind of entrepreneurs, so they describe only that aspect of the situation.

Note that both sides agree that (1) the productive process combines raw materials with labor and capital; (2) the result is a market value far beyond the value of the raw materials; (3) that added value is on the average and in the long run equal to the wage cost of labor plus an average rate of profit proportionate to the amount of capital. Suppose

[10] See further discussion and citations in Howard J. Sherman, "Marxist Economics and Soviet Planning," *Soviet Studies*, Vol. 18 (October, 1966), pp. 169–188.

one asks *why* there is a profit? There still might be agreement on the minimum statement that, given the institution of capitalism or private enterprise, only profit will induce a holder of capital to invest in production. Since, under pure private enterprise, all capital is privately owned, it follows that there will be no production if there is no profit.

A Marxist, however, would emphasize that mere investment of capital does not "justify" the profit, because the profit, like all of the product, is actually produced in the sweat of labor's brow. Marxists note that even the capital goods employed were produced by labor at some previous time. The most doctrinaire Western economists, on the other hand, emphasize the subjective sacrifice and waiting. They point out that, since no one would invest or innovate without an expectation of profit, profit plays an essential social function. The Marxist will answer that the social system could be changed so as to eliminate the need for private investment.

One (highly controversial) view is that the really profound differences do not lie primarily in the economic analysis of how the system operates.[1] The basic difference is over the ethical evaluation of whether the system as a whole (including private ownership and private profit) operates to the greatest good of the greatest number — or according to whatever ethical criteria one uses. Is there maximum output and maximum employment? Are costs kept to a minimum? Is there the most equitable distribution of income according to the observer's ethical criterion? These are some of the particular questions on which an overall evaluation of economic systems is based.

Although Marx discussed value and profit theory only for capitalism, Soviet economists have been concerned with applying his theories to their own "socialist" economy. In later chapters of this book, the question arises as to whether his value theory applies at all in an economy that is not competitive, but planned. Yet if Marx's labor theory does not apply, and if "bourgeois" marginal utility theories do not apply, then what theory should be used by Soviet planners? For example, how should prices be set? Should "interest" be charged on capital to socialist enterprises? Should "rent" be charged to socialist farms? Should managers be urged to make a "profit," and should they be judged on how much "profit" their firm makes? We shall see that the Soviets have interpreted (or misinterpreted) Marx's theory to apply to all of these questions.

Evolution of Capitalism. Marx spends much time discussing value and surplus value, and the division between total wages and profits at a given time. Marx and his followers, however, have been at least as much concerned with the evolution of capitalism, especially the alleged problems of cyclical depressions and their increasing severity, the trend toward economic concentration and monopoly, and the imperialist and military urges of capitalist countries. It is vital to have at least a brief look at each of these theories if we are to understand how the So-

[1] See citations in *ibid.*

viet leaders view the rest of the world. Many of their policies from Vietnam to international trade to rapid industrialization are based on these
views.

Cyclical Unemployment. Marx says that underconsumption
or the inadequacy of mass consumer demand is the "ultimate cause"
of all depressions and periods of mass unemployment.[12] Suppose we begin with a period of "prosperity" or mounting income and employment.
Why should it come to an end? The underconsumption strand in Marx's
cycle theory (though he stated several other theories at times) might be
stated systematically as follows: As output and income rise, a larger and
larger proportion goes to profits, while an ever-smaller proportion goes
to wages. Since profit recipients consume a much smaller percentage of
their income than wage earners, this means that the proportion of income spent for consumer demand must be falling. When consumer demand is restricted, however, Marx argues that this will lower expected
profit rates. Finally, when the profit perspective is dimmed, investment
and production will fall off and a depression will begin. During a depression, the whole process is slowly reversed (that is, wages do not
fall as rapidly as profits, consumer demand is stabilized, and so investment eventually recovers, and expansion begins).

Marx saw a constant cyclical up and down as the usual form of movement of capitalism. Nevertheless, he believed that innovations and rapid
investment would raise each prosperity phase far above the previous
highest level. Therefore, capitalism would continue to show growth,
even though it would be in fits and starts. Marx did expect that a completely unregulated capitalism would lead to more and more violent
fluctuations (like the 1929 depression, perhaps), but he still did not predict a complete end to growth.

Monopoly. So far we have considered Marx's analysis only
in the situation of a pure and perfect capitalism. Marx, however, was
one of the first to predict a vast increase in the concentration of capital
ownership. He predicted that most business assets and overwhelming
economic and political power would be held by a relatively small number of capitalists. He specifically noted that his analysis would have to
be modified in several respects to make allowances for the operation of
monopoly power.

In the first place, by restricting competition a monopoly may make a
profit rate far higher than the average long-run rate of profit. But how
is this possible if surplus value must still be produced by some particular
labor? Marx and his followers have answered that monopoly profit
comes from: (1) lower real wages, because unions lack sufficient power
to resist monopoly price increases; (2) a part of the profits of small business and small farmers, because monopolies are able to charge them
higher prices as suppliers and pay lower prices as buyers; (3) extra
profitable contracts and subsidies from government, which in turn extracts surplus value in the form of taxes; and (4) above average profits

[12] See Karl Marx, *Capital* (Chicago: Charles H. Kerr, 1909), Vol. III, p. 568.

from investments in foreign countries, which we investigate in the section on imperialism.

Some less revolutionary Marxists have argued that monopolies could at least help stabilize the economy because they plan the investments for a whole industry over a long period. Lenin and his followers, however, have argued the opposite. They believe that monopolies actually make the economy less stable: (1) by intensifying the severe competition between industries and internationally between countries, (2) by making small business still weaker and more sensitive and more prone to losses and bankruptcy in depressions, and (3) by depressing the gain in real wages so as to lower consumer demand as a proportion of income. Marxists also emphasize the role of monopoly price manipulation in causing a certain degree of inflation.

Finally, from Marx onward, the role of monopoly has been emphasized as a depressing factor on the rate of economic growth. First, monopoly is under no competitive pressure to replace old machinery, so may keep it long after new inventions have made available more productive machinery. Secondly, Marxists charge that highly concentrated industries are notorious for high levels of wasteful spending on purely persuasive advertising and excessive sales forces. Thirdly, as we shall see, Marxists argue that monopolies are the main instigators of that much larger area of wasteful and unproductive government spending, the outlay on military goods. To the degree that these allegations are true, they would certainly reduce the rate of growth below that which competition would maintain if it were able to ensure full employment.

Imperialism. Marx described a capitalist economy subject to periods of mass unemployment and large amounts of excess savings or unutilized capital. Marx also emphasized the concentration of capital ownership in the hands of a small number of monopolies. His follower, Lenin, made these two alleged facts the cornerstones of his theory of "imperialism."[13] He argued that the monopolies are politically powerful enough to pressure their governments into a policy of colonialism and the domination of foreign lands. The old colonialism, he said, was based simply on the policy of plunder and control of trade. The new colonialism is based on imperialist investment and control of production in the colonies — and in those "independent" countries that are actually under the thumb of imperialism.

The essential feature of modern imperialism, he says, is the export of capital to the colonies, and the return of profits to the imperial country, mostly in the form of raw materials. The export of capital gets rid of the excess saving that cannot profitably be invested in the imperial country. It also raises the monopoly rate of profit because of the very high profits made from the low-paid colonial labor. Thus, he argued that the monopolies may be in favor of imperialism, even though it is very costly in resources and lives to the imperialist country as a whole. The Soviets

---

[13] V. I. Lenin, *Imperialism, The Highest Stage of Capitalism* (New York: International Publishers, 1939, first published in Russian in 1917).

argue that the Vietnam war has cost both money and blood to most citizens of the United States, but has been highly profitable to a few corporations producing war supplies and owning investments in South East Asia.

The alleged facts that (1) imperialism extracts a large flow of profits from the colonial countries, and (2) imperialism forces the colonial countries to concentrate solely on agriculture and raw materials production, lead Marxists to conclude that imperialism is the root cause of underdevelopment. In the modern world they argue that a sort of "neo-colonialism" has continued the same conditions in the newly independent countries.

Finally, Lenin argued that imperialism is also the basic cause of wars in the modern world. He pointed out that different imperialist countries, such as England and Germany, have developed their own industry at very different speeds. They divided the world between them (as Africa was divided in the 1890's) according to their industrial power at the time of division. At a later time, however, their relative power changed as German industry began to overtake British industry. Then the newer powers want to redivide the world, but the older powers will not consent to do this peacefully. The result is a war between the various imperialist powers, of which the First World War was said to be the classic case. In addition, Lenin foresaw many conflicts between imperialists and colonial peoples.

Socialist Revolution. Marxists like Lenin predict that the result of periodic mass unemployment, monopoly control of the economy, and imperialist warfare is an inevitable revolution of the workers in the imperialist countries (as well as the peoples of the colonial or neo-colonial areas). Marx predicted that the workers' revolution would result in the establishment of a "socialist" economy. By socialism he meant that all of the means of production, all capital goods, would be owned by the public as a whole, thereby eliminating private profit. Socialism is desirable and inevitable, Marxists argue, because it is the only way to guarantee a just distribution of income; to ensure the end of cyclical fluctuations, since public planning produces steady growth; and to provide equality and cooperation among nations so as to end wars.

Beyond explaining that socialism would inevitably result when workers came to realize the evils of capitalism, and that socialism would end these evils, Marx had very little to say about the details of socialism. In fact, he condemned all such detailed schemes as utopian dreaming. He did distinguish the socialist system from the communist one. He said that in socialism it would still be necessary to pay workers a wage according to the amount of work accomplished. Only after achieving a high degree of material abundance and a much more unselfish cultural attitude could mankind proceed to the communist economy, in which people would voluntarily work to their best ability and take from society whatever amount they may "need." Since Marx said so little about it, Soviet economists really developed their own ideas about a socialist economy, though they often quote (or misquote) anything from Marx that they think may conceivably apply to socialism. For several decades, a quotation from Marx was used as the best "proof" of any proposition in Soviet economics — this was unfortunate for Soviet economics because it prevented any original thought or research. For a long time, the Soviets paid little attention to developments in Western economics or Western criticisms of Marx's economics.[14]

Marx and Political Science

The theory of government (or "the State," if one prefers the older usage) was formulated most fully by Lenin, in his *State and Revolution,* and we follow here his exposition of Marxist views. He argues that the theory of the State follows naturally from the Marxist theory of class struggle. It was observed in the discussion of history that classes are defined by Marx in terms of their relations to the means of production. "Slaveowners" own all of the means of production in slavery, including land, implements, and slaves. The "slaves" do all the work, but they own nothing, though they must be given a minimum subsistence ration. Similary, "capitalists" own all the means of production as well as the product, though they must pay a wage to the "worker," who does all the work to create the product.

The government, according to Lenin, represents the economic ruling class, for politics and economics are two sides of the same coin. Thus, in ancient Egypt the government did perform certain service functions — for example, defense (and aggression) and control of the Nile — but it was primarily devoted to upholding law and order, which meant protecting the privileges and property of the priests, nobility, and Pharaoh. Similarly, in the United States the government is primarily devoted to provision of "law and order," which means safeguarding the property and interests of capitalists, though in form it also protects the property of an unemployed worker on Skid Row or a non-white tenant farmer. Thus, in Leninist theory, a capitalist government is considered to be in essence a "dictatorship" of the economic ruling class, regardless of whether it is in form a political democracy or a political dictatorship.

Of course, says Lenin, the form of government may make a great deal of difference in practice. Under a capitalist democracy, the workers may be able to exert pressure to get many reforms in their favor; the workers may be better able to organize for the socialist revolution; and, in very extraordinary circumstances, the transition to socialism may be peaceful. Furthermore, the capitalists in a democracy must exercise their control in an indirect manner through their ownership (and advertising pressure) on all newspapers, radio, and other expensive means of electioneering. Without censorship, socialists may express their views in some small newspapers and may be able to publish a few books. Universities may be outlets for some new ideas that are not taboo.

[14] A classic criticism of Marxist economics is to be found in Joseph A. Schumpeter, *History of Economic Analysis* (New York: Oxford University Press, 1954).

Leninists also agree that everything is quite different in a Fascist dictatorship, such as that of Hitler, Mussolini, or Franco. No working-class organization is allowed, whether unions or political parties. Socialists are imprisoned or executed. No socialist views are allowed in any newspaper, radio, or university. Votes do not count for anything, so the working class cannot peacefully pressure for reforms. Socialism would become possible only through violent revolution.

Personal Power and Economics. The critics of the Marxist-Leninist theory of government point out that some people want power for the sake of power, and not merely for protection of economic exploitation. They also point out that society is not completely polarized into capitalists and workers. Besides independent farmers and craftsmen, there is a large and even growing middle class. Thus, the Marxist view is not only oversimplified, but leaves out certain vital factors.

The modern progressive Marxists have attempted to answer these charges. They admit the desire for personal power in people such as Hitler or Stalin, but they conclude that it is nevertheless the class situation which determines the overall governmental policies. Hitler determined much of the form of the Nazi political dictatorship, yet Nazi Germany never deviated from capitalism. Hitler imposed certain regulations, and his friends in the Nazi government took over certain major businesses for their own, yet the bulk of German business remained private enterprise reaping high private profits from Hitler's war spending. The Nazis even denationalized some of German industry. Likewise, Stalin determined some of the forms of his violent and bloody dictatorship, yet he maintained and developed socialist ownership on the basis of the 1917 workers' revolution.

Other neo-Marxist writers, such as C. Wright Mills, have discussed the evolution of classes in modern capitalism in terms of a "power elite."[15] Mills identifies the power elite in the United States to be the militarists, bureaucrats and politicians, and corporation executives. He also discusses the rise of the middle class. He points out that in the United States the "old middle class" (consisting of small farmers, professionals, and small craftsmen who hire no labor but their own) has indeed drastically declined in numbers. But a "new middle class" has arisen, composed of white collar employees and salaried professionals, such as teachers and engineers. It is true that the attitudes of much of the new middle class are the same as the old, but a Marxist still must consider them only highly paid, and still exploited, workers. In the long run they may even be organized as workers, as are large numbers of teachers in their own union. Since economic concentration is still very high (and possibly increasing, at least in Western Europe), Marxists argue that the polarization of a ruling economic class and an exploited working class has persisted in the capitalist United States, whether or not it is commonly recognized.

[15] See, e.g., C. Wright Mills, *The Power Elite* (New York Oxford University Press, 1959).

Government under Socialism. Marx said that the government under socialism would take the form of a dictatorship of the proletariat. The "dictatorship of the proletariat" is perhaps an unfortunate name for Marx's conception of a more democratic government than that which can exist under capitalism. The idea is that even with formal political democracy, the government in a capitalist country must in practice be a dictatorship of the minority of capitalists, who control all economic and political power. In socialism all economic and political power must pass to the working class (or "proletariat"), so until the former capitalist class has been economically eliminated, the proletarian majority must exercise its "dictatorship." Thus, the latest program of the Soviet Communist Party says: "The dictatorship of the proletariat is a dictatorship of the overwhelming majority over the minority; it . . . is aimed at abolishing all exploitation of man by man."[16] At a minimum, Marx assumed this "dictatorship" would mean complete political democracy *within* the proletarian majority.

Specifically, during Marx's lifetime he was able to point to the Paris Commune as an example of the "dictatorship of the proletariat." In this "dictatorship" there were a large number of conflicting political parties, with the full structure of democratic elections, right of recall, freedom of speech, and so forth. The capitalist representatives *voluntarily* withdrew from the Commune, but this still left a large number of socialist parties, of whom the Marxists were a very, very small minority. Thus, Marx certainly did not expect a one-party dictatorship over the workers as the form of the "dictatorship of the proletariat."

In the Socialist parties of Europe immediately after Marx's death, and while Engels was still alive, the "dictatorship of the proletariat" came to mean simply a majority vote for the Socialist party in competition with various capitalist parties. Their main problems in this field were seen to be the establishment of democratic republics to replace the monarchies then ruling most of Europe, the legal entry of Socialist parties into elections, and the extension of the franchise to the entire population. Under the leadership of Karl Kautsky, socialists assumed that the majority of the population was the working class, and that all of the working class would eventually vote Socialist. Therefore, *if* the capitalists would give up peacefully, the advent of full political democracy would mean the peaceful election of a Socialist majority to carry out the "socialist revolution." No one ever dreamed that a socialist movement could be in favor of political democracy under capitalism, and then against it under socialism.

This basic position was common to all Socialists before 1917. On the one side, however, the reformists such as Edward Bernstein believed that the capitalists *would* peacefully give up power. Thus the whole "class struggle" would be peaceful, and the "socialist revolution" would

<hr />

[16] Quoted in Harry Shaffer, *The Soviet Economy* (New York: Appleton-Century-Crofts, 1963), p. 80.

be a very slow and gradual accretion of gains for the workers through a long series of political compromises. This would be so because the "working class" majority would include a large section of middle-class persons, such as skilled workers, professionals, and farmers.

On the other side, the radicals such as Lenin believed that the capitalist class would resist with violence a socialist majority. Thus the socialist revolution could only be carried out through a civil war. In this connection the radicals often cited the American Civil War as a case in which the owners (slaveholders) would not peacefully give up their property (slaves) in spite of the democratic election of progressive forces (Lincoln, even though Lincoln was still not definitely abolitionist in 1860). Yet after the revolution Lenin also foresees the "dictatorship of the proletariat" as a government by the working-class majority operating through democratic processes. Though civil war might automatically outlaw the capitalist political parties, Lenin specifically endorses the example of the Paris Commune with its multiplicity of "socialist" parties. He writes that in the Commune, "Representative institutions remain. . . . Without representative institutions we cannot imagine democracy, not even proletarian democracy."[17]

Stalinist and Post-Stalin Concepts of Dictatorship. When Stalin had consolidated his power in the 1920's, there was a sharp break with past socialist practice, and an insidious change in socialist ideology. Instead of a political democracy of the working class, the "dictatorship of the proletariat" came to mean a dictatorship over the working class by the Communist Party and over the party by one man (Stalin). We leave for later the question of why this happened. Here we are concerned with the "arguments," if they may be dignified by that name, in favor of the Stalinist position presented by Stalin and his followers.

The Stalinists did in practice glorify the single leader (the "cult of personality"), but they never really argued for this in theory because it is so blatantly opposed to the whole Marxist tradition. They did, however, present arguments in favor of one-party rule. First, they claimed that even after the civil war is ended, the class struggle becomes ever more violent under socialism; and, therefore, a multi-party system is a luxury that cannot be afforded. Apparently, the defeated capitalists still have so much strength that they can sneak back into political power if other political parties are allowed. When it was pointed out that the capitalists quickly grew weaker and almost non-existent in the Soviet Union, it was claimed that they would make up for weakness by all-out desperation. In addition, Stalin raised the potent specter of foreign help for the capitalist side.

The second Stalinist argument was the reverse of the first. It is said that there is no class struggle in socialism and no opposing interests, therefore, no need for more than one political party (why even one?). The working class is the only class left in society, and the Communist

[17] V. I. Lenin, *State and Revolution*, p. 41.

Party represents the working class, and Stalin (or Khrushchev or Brezhnev) represents the Communist Party. One of the faithful Stalinists in the United States, W. Z. Foster, wrote:

> The existence of many political parties in capitalist countries . . . merely signifies that the class struggle is raging. . . . In a fully developed socialist country, inasmuch as all the people's interests are fundamentally harmonious, there is a proper place for only one political party, the Communist Party.[18]

Of course, the perfect harmony and the increasing disharmony arguments do seem to contradict each other. If there are no more opposing interests, then why does the Soviet Constitution have to prohibit other parties? If there are still opposing class interests, there is not perfect harmony — though Stalin tried to answer this by claiming that all of the hundreds of thousands of Communists executed were "foreign agents." In fact, the myth is widely propagated in the Soviet Union that the other socialist parties of revolutionary Russia, the Socialist Revolutionaries and the Menshevik Socialists, *voluntarily* went out of existence some years after the revolution. On the other hand, if the class struggle is getting more intense, then there certainly are opposing interests for political parties to represent.

Khrushchev officially repudiated the Stalinist idea that the class struggle grows more intense under socialism, thus doing away with the reasons for government terrorism. Yet Khrushchev still clung to the one-party dictatorship, presumably because there are now no opposing class interests, and *therefore* no need for opposing political parties. It is true, if we accept the Marxist definition of a class as a group in relation to the means of production, that there is only one class legally possible in the Soviet Union today. Excluding a certain percentage of farmers (and intellectuals), everyone else is supposed to be a "worker" with no individual ownership interest in the means of production.

On the contrary, the critics of the Soviet system, such as Djilas in *The New Class*,[19] do contend that the top bureaucracy constitutes a new type of owning or controlling class. To find opposing interests in socialism, however, one need not ask the extreme critics, but may refer to such a pillar of Marxist orthodoxy as Mao Tse Tung in his pamphlet famous for the slogan: "Let a hundred flowers bloom."[20] Mao argues that even in socialism there are conflicts or "contradictions" between farm workers and industrial workers, between manual workers and intellectuals, and between individuals and the government bureaucracy. He adds, however, that these conflicts are *not* antagonistic, meaning that there is no permanent opposition of vested interests, and that the conflicts may be resolved without violence.

[18] William Z. Foster, *History of the Three Internationals* (New York: International Publishers, 1953), p. 271.

[19] Milovan Djilas, *The New Class* (New York: F. A. Praeger, 1957).

[20] Mao Tse Tung, *On the Correct Handling of Contradictions Among the People* (New York: New Century Publisher, 1957).

One would think, from reading Khrushchev and Mao, that Marxists were now ready to endorse political democracy, but that was certainly not the case in practice. Khrushchev did use his arguments in order to end the Stalinist practice of open police terror, large-scale concentration camps, and widespread executions of political opponents. The Soviet leadership, however, in the early 1960's has severely limited political controversy to a few safe topics; and criticism is still limited to specific acts of minor officials (or leaders who have already lost power). The Soviets still maintain the one-party dictatorship, even though their own theory seems to call for an end to it.

Progressive Marxist View of Democracy. Many Communists in other countries, from Togliatti in Italy to Dubchek in Czechoslovakia, have developed much further the ideas of political democracy in a socialist country. These progressive Marxists (called "revisionists" by their enemies) believe that political democracy is a good thing, and that it is more likely to operate under socialism than under capitalism. This latter idea is critically examined in a later section.

They are still Marxists, so they do not argue that political democracy is good because God commands it nor because there is any other supernatural ethical imperative. It is merely the best means towards the end of the greatest happiness for the greatest number of people. The socialist humanist position is that political democracy serves a very useful function in improving society. Since the position is not an absolute one, they are quite willing to admit that there may be periods of war or revolution in which political democracy is difficult or impossible. But they can never agree with those more dogmatic Marxists who argue that *all* elections are "phony," and theorize that *all* elections are a mask for reaction.

Leaving aside such special circumstances as foreign pressure, the progressive Marxists argue that political democracy can at least serve certain minimum functions to make socialism work better with than without it. We may assume for the moment that there are only two political parties, both equally devoted to socialism. Suppose, for example, that in Czechoslovakia one party would agree with the liberal Dubchek, while another party would agree with the Stalinist Novotny. These two parties, if they were free to contest elections, would, in the first place, guarantee a peaceful succession to power, unlike the bloody conspiratorial fighting of Stalin and Trotsky or Khrushchev and Beria. Leadership in that period was selected by the physical elimination of all opponents. In the post-Stalin era physical violence has gone out of fashion, but rival leaders are still eliminated by a power struggle within the narrow confines of the Central Committee, a body small enough to be subject to personal bribery and self-perpetuating recruitment procedures.

Second, and closely related to the first point, is the necessity for political democracy to help restrict excesses of personal corruption. Socialist bureaucracy is by nature all-powerful, and there are many officially documented cases of extreme personal corruption in the Soviet Union at the local and regional levels as well as in national administration. Since a bureaucracy in socialism is so all-important, the free criticism of it up to the very highest officials is more important than ever. This principle is recognized by official Soviet Communism in theory, but not in practice. The top Soviet leadership is never open to criticism of its way of life; and criticism by an organized opposition is strictly prohibited.

Third, it is necessary to have a non-violent process for criticism of tactical and strategic errors made by the leadership, even if they are honest errors, and not due to corruption. In theory the Soviet Union is very much in favor of criticism, but in practice the Stalin era witnessed a process that was inevitable once begun. Criticism was allowed, but not criticism of socialism; politics was allowed, but only by the Communist Party. In the end, any criticism of Stalin was considered a crime against the Soviet state or against socialism. Yet no leadership is perfect, and this process has undoubtedly cut down the efficiency of the Soviet administrative apparatus. Some of the issues that might be open for public debate in Soviet society include the degree of economic decentralization, the structure and forms of wages, collective versus state farms, educational policies, foreign policies, and many others. That the present leadership still prohibits dissent on foreign policy is evident in the harsh treatment of Soviet citizens who opposed the invasion of Czechoslovakia (though the lack of executions or even life sentences emphasizes the progress from the Stalin era).

Finally, there are objective clashes of interest even in socialism, which should be expressed in the political process. Assume even that all remnants of capitalism, including individual handicraft workers and individual or cooperative farmers, have been replaced by complete public ownership. The short-run interests of the individual worker may still conflict with the long-run interests of the state. For example, all state planners taking a long-run view will favor the expansion of the means of production rather than goods for immediate consumption. Individual Soviet citizens should have some voice concerning the division of new investment between producer goods and consumer goods; but this influence can only come through the political process in a centralized socialist economy.

Stalinists may object that government (and therefore democracy!) is unnecessary under full communism, because no one owns any private property, so that government will wither away. Eventually, it is said, the individual bureaucrat will have neither need nor opportunity for personal aggrandizement. This may be so, but a socialist economy is not yet a full communist economy. Realistically, a communist utopia of equality based on abundance does not appear to be around the corner in any country. So long as socialism exists in the Soviet Union, individuals are able to gain through politics extra amounts of wealth and privilege, and these may be far beyond their contribution to society.

Just as the older Marxists argued that there are "contradictions" (or conflicts) with capitalism, so the modern progressive Marxists point to many contradictions within socialism. Under socialism commodities must be bought by people with money, and workers are paid different wages. Therefore, in socialism there are still rich and poor, as well as opposed and vested interests, not to speak of opposing opinions from people with the same interests. It follows that there is plenty of need for discussion and majority decision. For example, an entrenched socialist bureaucracy may talk about achieving communist equality. In practice, however, they may do everything possible to prevent the coming of communism in order to retain their privileges. Thus political democracy even seems to be a necessary prerequisite to communism!

Denial of the Possibility of Democracy in Socialism. Many critics of socialism have argued that any attempt at marriage between socialism and democracy can only end in violent divorce, that socialism is only compatible with political dictatorship. The critics now argue on the basis of experience that in most areas of socialism there is also dictatorship. Thus the USSR, Eastern Europe, Cuba, and China all claim to have socialist economies, and they are all considered by the critics to be one-party political dictatorships. Can all of these areas be shown to have other or special characteristics such that their dictatorships may not be the results of socialism?

The critics have also argued, long before the present world situation, that the functioning of a socialist economy is such as to make dictatorship more likely. In the first place, there is the physical difficulty of disseminating ideas in opposition to the government. If the government owns all radio, television, newspapers, and book publishing, how can ideas contrary to the government ever get a hearing? In a capitalist democracy at least everyone may have the formal right to spread any ideas *if* the individual has the money to do so. Then even a whole group of very poor people might together find enough money to publish a book or print a newspaper on a modest scale.

In the second place, and more profoundly, under the heading of functional problems comes the fact that the ruling party must control, not only the means of propaganda, but the whole economy. This enormous economic power may, to take a leaf from Marx's writings, be used to achieve complete effective political control. It means the power to hire and fire individuals, or to prevent an individual from getting any job. This is a much greater control over livelihoods than the most powerful group of capitalists could have in view of the millions of other corporations and businesses that may offer jobs. Such economic power also means that the vast resources of the nation may be diverted into the treasury of the ruling party for all-out advertising and influencing of all individuals.   *Socialism = monopoly*

The Socialist Answer on Democracy in Socialism. Before 1917 it seems that almost all socialists from Marx to Kautsky argued or assumed that democracy is quite compatible with socialism. In fact, they believed that one of the main arguments for socialism is that it constitutes economic democracy, a necessary extension of political democracy, and an addition of effective freedom to the "merely formal" freedom of a capitalist democracy. Actually, the early socialist parties were all closely tied to the fight against monarchy or for the extension of political democracy; for example, they fought against Prussian and Tsarist autocracy and fought for the extension of voting rights to all citizens including women. They argued that effective freedom of the press in capitalism is limited to the few newspaper magnates who control these very big businesses.

In socialism, public ownership would mean more equal economic power for everyone, would guarantee everyone the job security and leisure time to participate in politics, would mean there could be no millionaires to buy votes, and would somehow mean an equal access of everyone to the means of propaganda. The majority of the people would extend their control to the economy through their majority control of the political process.

The Soviet Union has had the longest experience with a socialist economy, but it has been saddled with a political dictatorship for the entire period. *Is* the one the "cause" of the other? Currently, there are three different answers deriving from three basically opposed interpretations of Soviet history. The critics of socialism argue that there has been one of the world's worst dictatorships in the Soviet Union, and that dictatorship is the necessary result of socialism. The Stalinists argue that the Soviet Union has had the world's most wonderful democracy, and that perfect democracy is the necessary result of socialism. The progressive Marxist view is that the Soviet Union suffered from a terrible dictatorship, but that this was due to unique circumstances and was not caused by socialism. The official Khrushchev view was a very mild and hesitant form of progressive Marxism. It admitted that Stalin was a noxious dictator, but it argued that this was due solely to Stalin's personality.

Of course, no "iffy question" in history can be answered with much certainty, but we can attempt to pick out the various ideological and objective factors that produced and maintained the Soviet dictatorship. Among the pertinent factors to be considered are: (1) the traditional attitude toward democracy in Tsarist Russia, (2) the Marxist outlook toward democracy, (3) the effect of civil war, (4) the effect of foreign encirclement and wars, and (5) the realities of economic backwardness and illiteracy.

Concerning the first point, we saw in Chapter 1 that the theory of political democracy spread to Russia very late in history, while the practice of political democracy began even in a limited way only in 1905. Concerning the second point, we have seen that Marxists were usually more concerned with economics than with political democracy. Specifically, the Russian Marxists were engaged in all-out war with the Tsarist government under conditions of severe repression, and had no room for the niceties of political democracy even within their own parties.

In the third place, political democracy really flourished to some extent in Russia only during the brief period of March to November 1917. After the Communist Revolution, there was a chaotic situation, which blossomed into full-scale civil war by the middle of 1918. Even the democracy of 1917 was limited by the Russian participation in the First

World War, while all democratic forms must fall by the wayside during any violent and rapidly changing civil war.

Fourth, to make matters much worse, a large number of foreign countries not only intervened militarily against the Communists, but continued their blockade for many years. Foreign threats never ceased until they culminated in the devastating Nazi invasion, followed by the Cold War and the threat of the bomb. All of this foreign pressure gave strong support to the Soviet variety of Cold War fighters.

Fifth and last, we noted at length in Chapter 1 the progressive Marxist argument that backwardness and the grim realities of enforced rapid industrialization were a major factor in Stalin's dictatorship. To raise a whole nation in a short period by its own bootstraps requires immense and unpopular economic sacrifices. People must not be allowed to vote for an easier program, but must be kept at fever pitch by constant propaganda and pressure. As confirmation, these Marxist writers point to the clear — but painfully slow — liberalization of the Soviet Union since about 1956. They claim that greater affluence has allowed more consumer satisfaction to accompany continued economic growth. Finally, they maintain that increasing satisfaction of the average citizen (as well as increased education and a more secure place in the world) has changed the Soviet atmosphere, so that political democracy becomes slowly more probable — as well as more useful.

SELECTED REFERENCES

1. The briefest authoritative summary of Marxism is V. I. Lenin, *The Teachings of Karl Marx* (New York: International Publishers, 1964 edition).

2. A brief criticism of all aspects of Marxism may be found in Sidney Hook, *Marx and the Marxists, The Ambiguous Legacy* (Princeton, N.J.: D. Van Nostrand Company, Inc., 1955).

3. A detailed and sympathetic statement of Marx's economics is Paul Sweezy, *The Theory of Capitalist Development* (New York: Oxford University Press, 1942); also see Maurice Dobb, *Political Economy and Capitalism* (New York: International Publishers, 1945).

4. The most famous attack on Marx's economics is by Eugen von Bohm-Bawork, *Karl Marx and the Close of his System*, edited and introduced by Paul Sweezy (New York: A. M. Kelley, 1949, first published 1896).

5. A full-length history of socialist and Marxist thought from a critical viewpoint is George Lichtheim, *Marxism, An Historical and Critical Study* (New York: Frederick Praeger, 1961).

PART TWO

ECONOMIC HISTORY

3

ECONOMIC DEVELOPMENT FROM 1917 TO 1928

To understand the changes in the economic structure and development of Russia since the Revolution in 1917, it is useful to begin by reviewing conditions prior to that date. What were the persistent trends that acted in such a way as to cause those revolutionary changes?

Russia Before 1917

Although the serfs were emancipated in 1861, the Russian class structure some forty years later was still basically feudal. That is, the majority of the population was tied to the land, and consisted of either "lowly peasants" or aristocratic landlords. The middle class was still negligible. The ruling elite continued to be the coalition of the Tsar, the military officers, and the landlords. The emancipation reform despite its liberal appearance was essentially a victory for the aristocracy. Every serf was given his freedom as well as the right to an allotment of land. The terms which fixed the conditions for the transfer of land to the peasants, however, were very harsh.

The landlord was to lose both land and services, but he was to be compensated by annual money payments for forty-nine years. The terms of the compensation were in effect determined by the landlord himself within limits set by the State. The landlord could choose between granting a larger allotment of land in exchange for a larger redemption payment, or a smaller amount of land with a smaller redemption payment. After the terms were decided upon, the responsibility for collection was assigned to the village commune (known as the *mir*), which was to distribute the burden equally among its members. Thus, each peasant came under the jurisdiction of the village commune, and as a member of the commune he was obliged to contribute his share of the redemption payments.

A major principle of life in the village commune was economic equality. To assure equality, the village practiced periodic repartitioning of the land, so that no one family would be any more favored by the different qualities of land than any other. This system of repartition was not practiced everywhere. It was almost universal in the poorer northern regions, where the amount given to the peasants was greater; but it was almost nonexistent in the richer black-earth region of the Ukraine, where the landlord gave only the minimal amount.

The drive for equality was implemented in still another unique, and perhaps even more dramatic way. Since the land occupied by each commune was not always uniform with regard to fertility, availability of water, hills, rockiness, location, and other natural factors, equality was achieved by dividing up each qualitatively different piece of land among all the families in the village. In areas in which the land was of very uneven quality, each farmer sometimes found himself cultivating not one solid lot but as many as 30 or 40 narrow strips, sometimes only a few feet in width.

The economic consequences of this agricultural system were:

The Immobilization of the Peasant. Since the village allocated tax charges on the basis of the number of workers per household (regardless of whether they stayed there or moved elsewhere), the peasant could not leave the commune without increasing the burden on the rest of the family. Thus, in those areas where the land was held in common and the taxes paid in common, the peasant was effectively immobilized. This system prevented the peasant from moving to the cities to try other occupations. Therefore, it reduced the extent of the division of labor in Russia, and also reduced the possibility of the formation of an urban middle class. Only after the Stolypin Reforms of 1906 were the peasants encouraged to get private plots and withdraw from the commune. These Reforms, which were promulgated as a result of the uprising of the peasants in 1905, abolished the redemption payments and ended the commune's collective responsibility for tax payments.

The Extremely Low Level of Agricultural Productivity. In the areas where the commune periodically repartitioned land, there was little incentive to raise the productivity of the land, since the gains would only be reaped by the next user of the land after the next partitioning. The parcelization of land into narrow strips also had a disastrous impact on efficiency for obvious reasons: it was impossible to use any but the most primitive implements on the strips; each farmer had an enormous amount of walking to do to get from strip to strip; and it has been estimated that in some regions about one-seventh of the land went into "boundaries."

About 80 percent of the people worked in agriculture, but at a very low standard of living because of the low productivity. Tsarist Russia's yield per worker in wheat was on a level with Asiatic countries, such as India, and was considerably below even the poorest European countries, such as Serbia and Italy. Primitive wooden ploughs were still used by a majority of all peasants.

It was basically because of the low agricultural productivity that the Russian national income per person in 1914 was less than 25 percent of England's and less than 15 percent of that of the United States. More-over, we should keep in mind the extreme variations in living standards resulting from variations in ownership among the peasantry. The rich-est 10 percent of the peasantry owned 35 percent of the land. On the other hand, the poorest 17 percent of the peasantry owned only about 2.5 percent of the land. This means that the average among the 10 per-cent richest peasants owned 14 times as much land as the average among the 17 percent poorest peasants.

Another feature of Tsarist Russia was the continued predominance of foreign investors in industry. The lack of entrepreneurship and lack of a middle class left the direction of industry to the ruling elite, who invited foreign investors to establish heavy industry (since it was needed for military purposes). As a result, the most important Russian industry was to a considerable extent in the hands of British, French, and German investors.

Foreigners owned nearly half the capital in the coal industry, and more than 80 percent in the oil and steel industries. In a typical colonial pat-tern, Russia exported raw materials and agricultural products, and im-ported mostly finished manufactured goods. Since most Russian indus-try was established either by the government or by large foreign in-vestors, enterprises were usually built on a very large scale. One finds the paradoxical situation that although Russia had comparatively little industry (because of the extra-long survival of serfdom), the industry which did exist was quite modern and consisted of very concentrated units. In fact, a majority of workers worked in factories which employed more than 500 workers. This high degree of concentration further re-duced the size of the middle class, thereby limiting political support for the existing economic system and making the subsequent change to socialism easier.

In the 1890's and 1900's Russian industrial output grew rapidly, espe-cially due to the great investment in railway construction. Between 1890 and 1914, industrial output almost quadrupled. Nevertheless, intensive industrialization occurred primarily in the limited regions around Mos-cow and St. Petersburg. More than 85 percent of the population still lived in the rural countryside. Of the 10 percent who actually worked in "industry," a very large number were employed in handicraft work rather than in mechanically powered factories (though we have seen that the few factories were quite large and concentrated). At the same time, the living conditions of the Russian urban worker were described as a hundred years behind those of West Europe. Although the Russian working class was numerically very small, the fact that it had a miserable standard of living and was concentrated in large factories in a few areas made it a potentially strong base for revolutionary movements.

In addition to these economic trends, certain political trends may be noted. These political movements and ideas first came to the surface in 1905, and then culminated in the Bolshevik Revolution of 1917. The most important revolutionary factor was the growing aspiration of the peasants, goaded by their hunger for land, to expropriate the large landed estates. This was most emphatic in the black earth regions where the allotments were too small to enable the dense population to eke out an existence.

There was also an increasing bitterness against the militaristic policies of the Tsarist regime. This strong anti-war sentiment was the natural consequence of Russia's humiliating defeats in several wars. The sentiment was reinforced by the fact that the peasantry had to carry the main burden of any war effort, both through the payment of taxes and the bearing of arms.

Furthermore, there was an increasing political consciousness among the workers, who felt that they were being "exploited" by the government and by foreign entrepreneurs. The fact that workers were highly concentrated in the centers of industry helped to crystallize this consciousness, and made their organization much easier. Trade unions and socialist parties spread among the industrial workers in the early 1900's. The lost war against the supposedly "inferior" Japanese in 1905 brought the situation to a boiling point.

The 1905 rebellion was a nation-wide attempt by the peasants as well as the workers to redress their grievances against the Tsarist regime. It failed because it lacked enough organization to unite the country against the Tsar. An organization was created, however, by the striking workers of St. Petersburg in 1905, which was called a council or "Soviet" of all the workers. The soviets were at first merely propaganda bodies, but even in 1905 they began to exercise some governing functions. The 1905 Revolution failed, but the greatly worsened conditions in Russia which resulted from her participation in World War I led to another attempt in March 1917. The so-called March Revolution succeeded in overthrowing the Tsarist regime.

The revolutionary movement and the Soviets, which immediately assumed some government powers, both were controlled at first by liberals and moderate socialists. By April of 1917 the peasants as well as the soldiers had joined the workers in creating Soviets to express their wishes. The war, however, was continued by the new government, and this created a further worsening of the conditions that had brought the revolt against the Tsar. The inefficient agricultural sector, controlled in part by absentee landlords, produced very little after the best part of its labor force had been drafted into the army. During 1917, the remaining peasant producers withheld much of their food from the market because they were paid in rubles whose value was rapidly declining as a result of severe inflation. The effects of these agricultural deficiencies were terrible food shortages both in the cities and at the front.

In the towns, the relatively small Russian industry (acting under directives of a highly inefficient bureaucracy) could not produce even sufficient ammunition, let alone maintain rapid communications or transport of supplies. As the economy further deteriorated and the power of authority declined, the peasants began illegally to confiscate the landlords' estates. For example, in September, 1917 the landowners in just one small province (Tambov) complained that twenty-four estates were burned by the peasants in just three days, while the local government did nothing about it. The burnings and confiscations accelerated in October and November. At the same time the local workers' Soviets began to take over control of industrial enterprises.

Gradually, in these circumstances, the Soviets began to swing to the Left — first the Workers' Soviets in the cities, then the Peasants' Soviets on the land, and finally the Soldiers' Soviets at the front. The Soviets everywhere took on more and more of the functions of government. When the Bolsheviks (later called Communists) achieved a majority in the Soviets, they were able to launch a successful revolution; they took power on November 7, 1917.

War Communism.[1]

The conditions faced by the Bolsheviks were far from ideal. They took over in the gravest of economic crises, and soon were to face the gravest of political crises: civil war. The Bolshevik program called for "peace" for the soldiers, "land" to the peasants, and "bread" for the workers. They did achieve a peace with the Germans, though at an enormous cost in land and population. Landlord estates were confiscated and divided into twenty-five million individual farms. Similarly, in industry the local workers' councils or Soviets were soon given authority to take over the management of the factories.

The Bolshevik program originally called only for a strict regulation or "control" of capitalism by a worker-directed government, and not for immediate confiscation or nationalization of capitalist enterprises. They envisioned on the economic side (after the seizure of power) a long and slow transition toward a socialist economy. In 1918, however, further considerations of long-run, peace-time economic policy were halted by the eruption of the Civil War. From an already faltering economy, destroyed and exhausted by war and revolution, the Bolsheviks had to mobilize resources for their own defense. To understand the economic measures that followed, we must look at the entire situation.

In addition to civil war, there was foreign intervention against the Communists by the armies of Britain, France, Japan, and the United States. As a result of the war with the Germans, the Civil War, and the foreign invasions, by 1920 Soviet industrial production had fallen to

[1] The political events (and much economic background) from 1917 to the mid-1920's is detailed most thoroughly in the monumental, multi-volume work of E. H. Carr, *History of Soviet Russia* (London: MacMillan and Co., 1950).

from 10 to 20 percent of the pre-war level of 1913. The major coal and iron-ore producing area, the Donetz Basin, which supplied the industrial centers of the North, was in the hands of anti-Bolshevik Russians and foreigners for most of the Civil War. Furthermore, the stoppage of oil supplies from Baku drastically reduced industrial fuel supplies, and the lack of coal from the Donetz necessitated an almost complete transfer to wood fuel on the railways. Moreover, many factories ceased operating because of desertions and lack of food in the cities. The managers deserted to the West, and workers went back to the cities (where there was at least some food). Leningrad, previously a city of some 2½ million persons, became a ghost town of only 800 thousand. In fact, there were only half as many workers in industry in 1920 as in 1914, and the productivity per worker in 1920 was only about a third of what it had been in 1914. Consequently, industrial production was estimated at only 14.5 percent of the 1914 level.

All the usual sources of finance were blocked. The government lacked the machinery for tax collection. External loans and financing became politically impossible as the Western nations enforced an embargo on the new Communist nation. The only recourse to cover government expenses was to continue the inflationary policy of printing more money (in the face of restricted supplies of products). In fact, after 1918, inflation proceeded at a disastrously accelerated pace. By October 1920 the purchasing power of the ruble was no more than 1 percent of what it had been in 1917.

The production of agricultural products for the market began to contract. The farmer (former peasant, now the owner of land) found little incentive to produce for the market when the industrial goods for which he wished to exchange his own products were either not available or else were sold for fantastically inflated prices. He preferred to hoard his surplus food, or simply reduce production and exchange it for leisure. The Russian farmer, for the first time in history, possessed the product of his own land; and he would consume it himself if he could not sell it at a high price in real terms.

In such a situation the Soviet government could not obtain the resources it needed through the market. Yet military needs somehow had to be filled. Soldiers needed, at a minimum, food and rifles and ammunition. Squads of men were sent into the countryside to "requisition" (or just take) supplies of food from the rich and middle farmers, who might have a surplus over and above the needs of their own families.

To obtain military supplies from industry was just as difficult as to obtain food from farmers in the early months of Communist rule. No sweeping nationalization proposals were made by the new Communist government; the government authorized only local workers' "control" or supervision over factory owners. Yet private owners and managers closed their factories and fled the country. The local workers' councils, which took control after the flight of private owners, were inexperienced and were unresponsive to the central government's wishes and needs. Managers who stayed were at first responsible only to the workers' councils.

because of military or because workers were impatient

Although it was agreed by the middle of 1918 that managers should be responsible to higher economic bodies in order to avoid chaos, such responsibility did not become a fact in non-essential industries until 1920. Yet the Civil War became acute in the summer of 1918. Thus, *as a necessary military measure*, by the end of 1918 all large-scale factories had been nationalized and put under central control. By 1920 all middle-sized and even many small factories had been nationalized as well.

Since inflation had ended the usefulness of money, all supplies from farm and factory were requisitioned by the Government and then reallocated primarily in terms of military requirements. And so there came into existence War Communism, in effect, a centralized substitute for the market in the determination of income distribution and resource allocation. Although in theory the government not only owned, but also directed, every single industrial enterprise, there was in reality no comprehensive planning or coordination of economic activity. It was true that *government* ran every detail of the economy, but it was mostly *local government*. There was no overall central output plan, and most of the vast number of *ad hoc* central directives were ignored by local authorities. Central interference was expressed only from time to time in emergencies, and then only in brief campaigns or "shock tactics" (which are discussed further below).

A central feature of War Communism, and key to the whole system, was the requisitioning of food supplies from the peasants. The allocation of the food surplus extracted from the countryside went to two users. On the one hand, it went to the industrial enterprise in the form of primary raw materials. In return, industry was expected to produce the goods needed by a war-time nation. The very scarcity of resources required the strictest control over them.

The second recipient of the food was the industrial worker. The workers were paid their wages "in kind" (in goods rather than money), which generally meant no more than bare subsistence food portions. This had serious consequences. For one thing, the reduction of "income" to the barest levels did not leave any incentive for labor to work in the factory. Furthermore, wage differentials are the usual means of allocating labor to its most productive employment. Since wage differentials were very much reduced by the food-ration wages, which varied little from job to job and industry to industry, labor itself had to come under the administrative control of the government. Labor was "militarized" or conscripted for peaceful work into so-called "labor armies" and allocated by the central government to the best of its ability.

Some loyal ideologists tried to create a virtue out of necessity and applauded the features of this system of War Communism as bearing the hallmarks of Full Communism. The use of money and market relations had been eliminated by the physical allocation of goods and services. There was public ownership of means of production and relative equality in income distribution. Obviously, this was a communism based on equality in poverty, and was very far from the abundance which could free man from toil.

editorialization

The extreme centralization of decision-making led to a great deal of administrative delay. To break the bottlenecks, use was made of the "shock" system of planning. This simply meant (in lieu of a comprehensive plan, which did not exist) that all-out effort was centered on the success of a few enterprises, which happened to be militarily important at that moment. Unfortunately, this approach tended to persist in modified form, throughout much of subsequent Soviet history. Furthermore, in these early years few loyal workers knew much about administration, while few good administrators felt any loyalty to the Soviet government.

By the end of the Civil War in 1921, the recklessness of continuing such a course became clear to almost everyone. The peasant, estranged from the system by the policy of requisitioning, simply cut production to just that amount necessary for subsistence consumption for his family. Why should he produce for a government which was hostile to his desires and unwilling to pay for his goods? Furthermore, the whole political alliance with the peasantry was falling apart because of the harsh economic measures and conflicts. For the nation, this could now mean only starvation, and the eventual downfall of the party in power.

In addition to peasant dissatisfaction, the urban working class itself was frustrated and angry with the system, partly for its inefficiency and partly for alleged injustices in distribution. Workers were suspicious of government-sponsored trade unions as well as all higher economic agencies. By the end of 1920, there were strikes, protest demonstrations, and protest resolutions by whole factories. Then Kronstadt, the naval base where the Communist revolution had received its strongest support, rebelled in favor of Soviets *without Communists*. This was the final blow to War Communism. The Communist leadership, and especially Lenin, decided that the time was ripe for a complete economic reform.

The New Economic Policy

As we have seen, the farmer's reaction to government requisitioning was simply to hoard more and produce less. Unless the government could provide the farmer with an incentive to produce more, the towns would starve. To remedy this situation, Lenin introduced the New Economic Policy (NEP). First, the government abolished requisitioning, and reintroduced a free market in agricultural goods. Second, as a substitute for requisitions, a single tax consisting of a set percentage of his output was levied on the farmer. This would be his only responsibility to the government, and was payable in goods rather than money. Any other surpluses could be sold on the open market for money or exchanged for industrial goods. Third, even some of the large nationalized industrial units were allowed to respond to the demand registered on the market by deciding independently of the Central government what and how much to produce. Fourth, most small businesses and handicraft enterprises were denationalized. Fifth, middlemen or private traders (called NEP men) were allowed to bring the wholesale goods to retail markets, and collect any windfall gains. In this way, the period of requisitioning, central allocation of material supplies, and in-

structions to producers was over for the time being with the exception
of a few of the most important industries.

Some have seen the period of the NEP as a successful experiment in
Market Socialism.[2] This view, however, fails to recognize the persistent
failure of heavy industry to make very rapid progress during this period
and the inability of the system to cope with this shortcoming. For it was
exactly this problem — that is, how to spark the development of heavy
industry — which later became the subject of bitter controversy cul-
minating in the introduction of full-scale central planning in 1928. At
the other extreme were those foreign commentators who declared that
NEP was the beginning of the end of the socialist experiment and pre-
saged an eventual return to capitalism. This theory ignored the fact
that NEP fitted perfectly Lenin's view of a long, smooth transition period into socialism (whereas War Communism had been an unexpected
and forced interruption of the process). To really understand the work-
ings of the NEP, one must review the changes in each sector and in central economic policy, as well as the problems which arose and the attempts of the government to solve them.

Beginnings of NEP (1921–1923)

Agriculture. In the early days of NEP, agricultural goods
were a scarce commodity relative to industrial goods and sold at first at
high prices on the market (because 1921 was a year of crop failure and
famine in some regions). These favorable prices for agriculture provided an additional incentive for the farmer to produce as much as he
could for the market. In fact, the government retreated even further
and allowed the richer farmers to lease land and even to hire for
wages the poorer farmers. In succeeding years, agricultural production
did increase in response to the new measures of the NEP. Indeed the
recovery was rapid and resulted in real gains to the farmer, and especially to the larger-scale farmers.

Industry. The New Economic Policy toward industry was to
make enterprises independent both financially and operationally. Small
government-owned businesses were leased out for private independent
management (though government-managed enterprises still produced
92 percent of output in 1923). Furthermore, each large government-run
enterprise was expected to make its own production decisions, to be financially responsible, and to be economically efficient. Financing of
enterprise activities from the government budget was abolished by
1922 (with the major exception of the railroads). The firm could now
obtain funds only from its own revenues or through bank credit. The
immediate result of the introduction of competition among the different
industrial producers was a relative decline in industrial prices. This only
reinforced the favorable "terms of trade" for agriculture versus industry
(that is, one unit of industrial good A could "buy" less and less of agri-

[2] See V. N. Bandera, "The NEP as an Economic System," *Journal of Political Economy*, Vol. 71, No. 3 (June, 1963).

cultural good B). But industrial cartels or "trusts" were soon formed to collaborate on fixing prices at artificially high rates. Each trust could plan the output and prices of its own factories, merely submitting the plan to the government for final sanction.

Trade. Private trading organizations expanded rapidly and soon controlled nine-tenths of the retail trade. Many of the gains from the NEP were reaped by the notorious middlemen (NEP men) who cashed in on the difference between a low price paid to the farmer and a high price received from the city dweller for food. Furthermore, small businesses and retail traders were allowed to hire up to ten or twenty workers, and to sell the products of their labor at a profit. It was in this area of small business and trade that capitalism flourished under NEP.

Labor. Under the NEP, restrictions on labor mobility were abolished. The laborer was free to change his job. Wages were no longer centrally distributed on an equalitarian basis, but were differentiated by the "market" according to productivity. Trade unions were formed, partly to negotiate wage contracts for the worker, but also to increase the general culture and welfare of the working class. Actually, however, the Communist Party kept firm control of the unions as well as the enterprises with whom they were supposed to negotiate. The right to strike existed in theory, but was not often exercised in practice.

Finance. Government financial policy during the first part of the NEP was conservative in outlook. An attempt was made to return monetary and fiscal policy to what was considered "safe, healthy" orthodoxy — though in practice money was still being printed at a great rate. Bank deposits were supposed to be secured against government requisitions. For the ideal future, a balanced budget was envisioned with government expenditures eventually to be covered by tax revenues from industry and agriculture. Actually, by the end of 1923 only two-thirds of state expenditures were yet covered by tax revenues. This situation was still highly inflationary — prices were still rising at more than 50 percent per month in 1923 and the price index stood at, roughly, *1 billion* times the 1913 level. It was nevertheless a great improvement over the situation at the end of 1921 when 90 percent of all government expenditures were financed by the printing press. Inflation was not finally brought under control until the Monetary Reform of the spring of 1924.

Planning. Central planning went into eclipse. It came to be thought of as strictly contradictory to the spirit of NEP, which was itself partly a reaction to the overcentralized attempts at planning under War Communism. The mood of the central government leadership was to give every encouragement to NEP, to stress its stability, and to strengthen the farmer's and merchant's confidence in it. The theoretical rationale behind this was the economists' notion that private demand and market forces would encourage economic development. The demand for durable consumer and light industrial goods generated by a prospering agricultural sector would spur growth in those industries. They in turn, by demanding more inputs (machines and raw materials), would spur a response in the heavy industry which furnished supplies to them.

Investment policy was clearly in line with this approach as credits were more readily given to high profit, quick turnover industries. Only Trotsky and a few of his followers called for central planning to "control" the market, though even he did not call for planning to replace the market. He warned the Party of the consequences of neglecting heavy industry and called for planning to redress the growing imbalance between light and heavy, private and socialized, sectors of industry. But he stood alone and was ignored at this time. Most of the other Party leaders justified the lack of planning under NEP as part of the necessarily long transition period from capitalism to communism.

The Scissors Crisis (1923–1924)

During 1923 and 1924 a crisis arose which can be seen as a turning point in the NEP period. As we have said, in the first days of NEP, in 1921 and in 1922, the terms of trade favored agriculture relative to industry. Yet agriculture soon made a complete recovery and, as industrial supply lagged behind, the terms of trade began to change against agriculture. Food prices dropped drastically relative to prices of industrial goods, which remained in short supply *despite* the increased demand, in part due to a slower recovery and in part due to the fact that the industrial cartels were consciously acting to restrict competition. Thus, at the beginning of 1923 industrial production had risen only to about a third of the 1914 level, but agriculture had almost reached the 1914 level. Furthermore, by the end of 1923 about 190 of the 360 industrial trusts had joined syndicates for the explicit purpose of preventing competition.

Whereas agricultural prices had previously risen relative to industrial prices, they now fell further and further behind. These price movements resembled a scissors when drawn graphically, and this crisis has been aptly called the "scissors crisis." During 1923 the price ratio moved three to one in favor of industry and against agriculture. This situation was of grave portent. The farmer was able to buy less and less with the meager returns he received from the sale of his products. What incentive would he have to produce for the market if the goods he desired were priced far out of his reach? The economy was again threatened with a contraction in agricultural output. The NEP was thus plagued by the same disease that had helped bring War Communism to an end. The problem was far from solved.

The various leaders of the Soviet Union saw the problem in different ways. There were those on the Right (Bukharin and others) who viewed it essentially as a problem internal to the agricultural sector. They prescribed "remedies" that would increase the motivation of the private farmer by offering him additional incentives, that is, the freedom to accumulate wealth or "enrich themselves." Others, those on the Left (Trotsky, for example), claimed that the problem lay in the industrial sector, in its inability to recover, to expand supply at lower costs, and thus to reduce prices.

At this time Bukharin, the spokesman for the Right, was able to win support for his view from a majority of the Party. Bukharin attacked the monopoly position of industry and its artificially high prices. His argument was that the well-being of the town depended not upon the 26 million small farms which barely produced enough for themselves, but upon the few richer farmers (*kulaks*) who produced primarily for commercial sale. The larger farmer was willing to sell his goods since he was eager to grow wealthy. Hampered by restrictions on the sale and renting of land and on the employment of labor, he began to sell less. It was this trend that had to be reversed. Therefore, the government decided to support the well-to-do farmer, and enacted new laws which permitted him to hire labor and to lease land.

In the Fall of 1923 the Soviet government took action against the high industrial prices. The government reduced the flow of bank credit to the trusts, forcing them to unload excessive inventories of finished products in order to get the funds to continue operating. In addition, maximum price ceilings were set on some goods, and cheaper foreign goods were imported in a few cases. Finally, less efficient plants were closed, so production costs could be decreased (and industrial costs were indeed lowered almost 20 percent by the end of 1924). On the other hand, efforts were made to raise farm prices. The government paid more for its own grain, and encouraged the export of grain.

The "scissors" did begin to close to some degree in 1924, and for the rest of the NEP the price spread was never again quite so acute. Nevertheless, the scissors never fully closed and the peasants never again had the same incentive to sell their surpluses that they had in 1921–22. In the years following 1924 there were increasing doubts and misgivings about the NEP. Farm production increased very slowly, and the share brought to market continued to decline because of the relatively high prices of industrial goods and heavy taxes.

The End of NEP (1924–1928)

Agriculture. In agriculture, the richer farmers took advantage of their newly won powers to expand at the expense of the poorer farmers. Many of the poorer farmers lost their land and became hired workers. The increasing differentiation of the farming population that resulted was so antithetical to socialist ideology that repercussions soon appeared in a growing resentment by the Communists toward this "capitalist" farmer class. While the Right wing of the Party wanted to placate the richer farmers as a necessary evil in agricultural development, the Left wing wanted to capitalize on the growing resentment in order to restrict and heavily tax richer farmers.

In spite of the surface agitation, however, it was a fact that most of Soviet agriculture resembled too closely for comfort the situation under the Tsars. The Russian villager remained an extreme individualist, very conservative technically as well as politically, and still using the primitive methods of his ancestors. Since agricultural productivity was so low and had such poor prospects of improvement, Soviet industry would certainly not make any rapid progress if it were constrained to an advance no more rapid than that of agriculture. In the late 1920's, a considerable flow of tractors and other machinery did begin to reach the villagers. Yet most of the peasant holdings were much too small to utilize efficiently such heavy equipment.

As early as 1925–26 (the harvest year runs from October 1 to September 30) the total agricultural area reached 95 percent of the pre-war average while the gross harvest was even higher than pre-war. Since industry was not to reach the pre-war level until the end of 1927, agriculture seemed to be in a good condition, although its prospects for the future were not very bright. Yet one critical agricultural problem remained which had to be confronted at once: although agricultural output had reached the pre-war level, the *agricultural surplus available to be marketed* outside of the village was still far from the pre-war level. It had, in fact, reached only 70 percent of the pre-war level in 1925–26. Yet this agricultural surplus was needed (a) to feed the growing urban working population, (b) to provide the exports to be exchanged for machinery, and (c) to be sent to other areas of the Soviet Union which produced specialized food stuffs and increasing amounts of industrial raw materials. Clearly, it was an essential ingredient in any rapid industrialization program. In effect, the agricultural surplus had to be the "savings" upon which investment for rapid industrialization depended.

Why was the marketable surplus of agriculture much smaller in the 1920's than it had been in pre-revolutionary Russia? Even the Communist Party found it hard to put all the blame on the rich peasant or kulak, since the kulaks produced only 15 percent of the total output (though they had produced about 50 percent before the war). The kulak did exert an additional restraining influence over the market through his role as a middleman, trader, and speculator in the grain market; but just how much harm this speculation did is hard to document.

On the contrary, it is quite clear that the problem lay with the behavior of the great mass of poor and middle peasants, who now produced some 85 percent of the total grain. Generally speaking, the problem was simply that the relatively equal distribution of land achieved by the peasants was itself the main reason for the decline of the marketable surplus. The agrarian revolution of 1917 and the modest monetary tax on the peasants introduced during NEP had resulted not only in peasant control, but in the ability of the peasant to actually keep much of the harvest for his own consumption (which had previously been at or sometimes below subsistence level).

In order to see the problem more concretely, a table is presented below comparing the pre-revolutionary period with the Soviet agriculture of the mid-1920's.

The table shows that in both periods the largest production units (land owners' estates and, later, collective and state farms) produced a small part of the total grain, but each marketed almost half of their total. One problem was simply that state and collective farms owned only one-sixth as much land and produced only one-sixth as much total grain as had the large land owners before the revolution. The next largest pro-

Table 3–1

The Grain Market Problem, 1914 and 1927

Type of Farm	Total Grain Production (in %)	Ratio of Marketed Grain (outside of village) to total production (in %)
Pre-Revolution: in the year 1913–14		
Landowners	12	47
Kulaks (or rich peasants)	38	34
Poor and Middle Peasants	50	15
Average	100% (total grain)	26% (average % marketed)
TOTAL	5,000,000,000 poods	1,300,000,000 poods
Soviet: in the year 1926–27		
State and Collective Farms	2	47
Kulaks (or rich peasants)	13	20
Poor and Middle Peasants	85	11
Average	100% (total grain)	13% (average % marketed)
TOTAL	4,749,000,000 poods	630,000,000 poods

Source: The Central Statistical Department of the USSR, cited in Stalin, in International Press Correspondence (June 14, 1928).
Note: 1 pood equals 36 pounds avoirdupois.

duction units (those held by the kulaks or rich peasants) declined in land area and production by over half since the revolution; and it may be noted that they also declined considerably in the percentage of grain marketed. Nevertheless, the table reveals clearly that the major source of the problem lay with the smallest land holdings (of the poor and middle peasants), whose share of land and production rose from 50 to 85 percent, but who marketed only 15 percent of their grain before the revolution and now marketed only 11 percent.

The great equalitarian advance in land ownership — an unfortunate advance from the viewpoint of development planning — proved to be the greatest barrier to rapid industrialization by reducing the marketable agricultural surplus. This land reform had the further disadvantage of reducing the size of the average land holding to such an extent that it was unprofitable to buy and use efficiently more modern agricultural machinery. In addition, the marketable surplus was reduced even further because of the continued high industrial prices and the successful attempts to hold down agricultural prices. As a result of these continued and ever worsening terms of trade, grain collections by the government in 1927–28 were about 14 percent lower than the previous year, although the total grain production had fallen only a little more than 7 percent. The downward trend in collections continued into the year 1928–29.

Industry. During the period 1924 to 1927 industrial production rose rapidly. Official data for the period are probably biased upward, but they do indicate well enough the general trends in production. Notice that these are percentages of 1913 rather than the higher 1914 level. The pre-war, 1913 level was probably not reached again until some time in 1927.

Table 3–2

Volume of Industrial Output in the USSR, 1913–1927

Year	Output (as % of 1913)
1913	100
1917	71
1921	31
1925	73
1926	98
1927	111

Source: Central Statistical Board of the USSR, *National Economy of the USSR* (Moscow: Foreign Languages Publishing House, 1957), p. 41.

Most of the increase in industrial production, however, consisted of output from reconstructed facilities, rather than the building of new plant and equipment. By 1927, reconstruction was complete and the more demanding job of capital expansion loomed ahead. Moreover, the emphasis during this period had been on light industry, rather than on the heavy industry which required so much larger and longer-term commitment of resources. The Party came to agree on the need for rapid industrialization, and began to devote more and more resources to it. The main issue under discussion was how and where to get the resources for further industrial investment. Yet Trotsky was still being attacked for overestimating the importance of rapid industrialization, and the tempo and methods of industrialization remained vague. We shall return in detail to the issues of the great debate over industrialization in a later section.

Labor. Wage policy was designed to increase productivity, piecework wages had become the predominant mode of payment, and the earlier theories of income equality were severely attacked. Under the direction of the Party, unions ceased their fight for higher wages, and redefined their aims as the bringing of a communist cultural outlook to the masses and the increasing of workers' productivity. The official unions remained mostly quiescent in the face of very low money wages, made still lower in real buying power by some continued inflation (though less than in the early 1920's), and also by the existence of significant unemployment. The workers, however, did react by means of many unofficial or "wildcat" strikes in the years from 1924 through 1926.

Trade. During the latter years of NEP, the government and cooperatives became dominant in the wholesale trade. In retail trade, however, private traders were still quite important. Finally, in foreign trade in the early 1920's, in addition to the government trading agency, there had been some trade by industrial "trusts" and even by individuals. Now, a complete monopoly of foreign trade was given to one government agency, a condition which has persisted ever since. Yet foreign trade was not as useful to industry as expected, partly because of barriers set up by foreign countries, and partly because of a lack of grain collected for export. In the earliest years of the Soviet regime many anti-Communist countries joined in the *"cordon sanitaire,"* an attempt to cut off all trade with the Soviet Union — even in medical supplies. By the late 1920's, however, a gradual increase in the number of countries willing to trade with the "Bolshevik menace" had resulted in a substantial recovery in foreign trade — though a few nations have maintained special political barriers against Soviet trade to this day (as we shall see in a later chapter).

Finance. The hyperinflation was finally ended by a monetary reform in the spring of 1924. All outstanding cash currency, 800 quadrillion of so-called *sovznaks,* were called out of circulation and redeemed for 15 million new rubles, that is, at a rate of roughly 50 billion *sovznaks* per ruble. The Treasury was no longer allowed to finance budget deficits by printing notes — deficits had to be covered by bank credit. Since the Bank was a creature of the government, however, this restriction may have been more semantic than real. Direct income taxes, collected mostly from the farm population, had been the most important source of government revenue in the first few years of NEP. Sales and excise taxes, however, were becoming more important all the time, especially after the Right wing managed to have the income tax on farmers reduced in 1925. The importance of sales taxes meant that the increased expenditure on heavy industry fell as a burden, no longer on the rich farmers alone, but on all groups of the population. Meanwhile, inflationary deficit spending also continued and excess demand developed, but price control held prices fairly stationary. Still the inflationary pressure was enough to force the Soviet Union off the international gold standard. This meant that rubles were no longer redeemable in gold, but this had little or no operational effect because of the government monopoly of international trade.

Planning. Serious attempts at planning did begin by 1924 or 1925, but they were limited to the segments of heavy industry most closely controlled by central authorities. Actually, the most ambitious earlier planning was the plan for electrification of the whole country, begun in 1920 by the State Commission for Electrification, known as GOELRO. Electrification was given priority at Lenin's insistence, and we are reminded of his aphorism: "Soviets *plus* Electrification equals

Communism." In 1921, the GOELRO was merged into the State Planning Commission (or *Gosplan*).

More general planning first developed out of attempts at control of the soaring industrial prices. Some general planning was also necessary to eliminate the heavy unemployment that had resulted from the flood of the rural population into the more attractive towns (now that the urban-rural difference had been brought back to the pre-revolutionary ratio of conveniences available). The combination of rising urban population and a lack of capital for plant and equipment presented the early Soviet government with a type of unemployment problem common to many other underdeveloped countries.

The first thing that might be called an attempt at overall planning of the whole economy was the document issued by the State Planning Commission, which was known as the *Control Figures for 1925–26* (though there were a few control figures issued as early as 1923–24)[3] This little hundred-page booklet was epoch-making as the first pioneering effort to formulate a rational and unified plan, rather than a mere collection of the proposed projects of different government departments. It was very sketchy, however, and had little practical effect, though it greatly stimulated further efforts. It was more in the nature of a trial run and was not really meant to be operational.

From 1926 to 1928 the government attempted to formulate the First Five Year Plan. Besides the argument over the practical content of the Plan (to be discussed in the next section), Soviet leadership was held back by more theoretical uncertainties. The most eminent Communist theoreticians (Bukharin, Trotsky, and others) all agreed that a socialist economy needs no value theory nor theory of political economy because these relate only to "capitalism." Under socialism the economy would do whatever the planners wanted it to do without regard for economic laws, since "economic laws" only apply to the unregulated operation of a market economy and do not restrict the freedom of planners. This view leaves little room for a scientific approach to planning, except for engineering details. Those who held this view, that planners are completely free to set any goals, were called the "teleologists."

On the other side were the "geneticists," who insisted that planning was rigidly bound by the present state of things, and had only limited room for maneuver within existing trends. An example of the genetic approach was Kondratiev's argument that "planning work must avoid a fetishism of oversize calculations; which must bow before an understanding of those processes which are in actual motion in the economy; we must grasp these basic processes which confront us."[4]

[3] The earliest recorded effort was by P. I. Popov and others, *Balance of the National Economy of the USSR in the year 1923–24*, published in Russian in 1926; its introductory chapter was translated in Nicolas Spulber, ed., *Foundations of Soviet Strategy for Economic Growth: Selected Essays* (Bloomington: Indiana University Press, 1964).

[4] Cited in M. Dobb, *Soviet Economic Development Since 1917* (London: Routledge and Kegan Paul, rev. ed. 1966), p. 353.

Thus, he believed that planning must passively subordinate industrial growth to whatever development rate agriculture is likely to show. Another example of this line of thought was the argument by Bazarov and many others that the rates of growth in economic development would unavoidably follow descending curves according to the laws of diminishing marginal productivity. These writers were mostly older technical economists, who believed that the planners could only observe the "empirical regularities" of the past, and then predict the "objective tendencies" of the future on that basis. Once again, this left little room for understanding how to construct a plan for the way economic development should take place. Even more defeatist were those (such as Rykov) who were just plain skeptical of man's ability to really construct a workable plan of any kind.

Obviously, in practice the planner must first know the existing conditions and past trends, but he then does have some freedom to choose among alternative roads of future development. The planner can use only existing resources, but may use them in a large number of possible ways, some perhaps very different from the ways that have been used in the past. Eventually, the Soviet debaters came to realize that the practical questions were which methods of development to use, how fast to develop, and in what possible directions the economy might develop.

The Great Debate

It is now time to turn to the political and economic debates of the period concerning the best road to a further growth of the economy. There are two different aspects to the problem of growth in a socialist economy. First, there is the question of the *initial* construction of socialist industry, especially in a country with only an underdeveloped agricultural economy. The second question is the rate of growth of an *established* socialist industry (considered in a later chapter of this book).

The whole period of the 1920's in the Soviet Union was witness to a violent debate on methods of rapid initial development.[5] The Left wing of the Communist Party, led by Trotsky in the 1920's, took the view that NEP must be quickly ended and a transition made to the rapid growth of socialist industry. They considered it necessary to build largescale industry on the basis of modern technology, but also considered it necessary for such modern technology to be extended into the countryside by the fullest encouragement of agricultural cooperatives to replace the tiny peasant farms. Yet Trotsky considered that the international political situation would prevent such a development until the revolution could spread to more advanced economies, capable of furnishing political support and economic aid to Soviet Russia. In this context, he denied "the

[5] For a comprehensive discussion, see Alexander Erlich, *The Soviet Industrialization Debate, 1924–28* (Cambridge, Mass.: Harvard University Press, 1960).

possibility of socialism in a single country." Trotsky argued instead
that:

> ... the contradiction inherent in the position of a workers' govern-
> ment functioning in a backward country where the large minor-
> ity of the population is composed of peasants, can only be liqui-
> dated on an international scale in the arena of a worldwide
> proletarian revolution, [and that] the real growth of the socialist
> economy in Russia can take place only after the victory of the
> proletariat in the more important countries of Europe.[6]

Although Trotsky was the main proponent of the notion that socialist
industry could not really expand rapidly in the Soviet Union until after
the revolution triumphed in Europe, he nevertheless was also the main
proponent of the attempt to industrialize as rapidly as possible, while
recognizing the difficulty of accomplishing this under the existing conditions. (In fact, it seems that Trotsky later came to believe that economic growth was possible under these conditions, but that such forced
industrialization would lead to harsh political dictatorship *over* the proletariat.) The argument in favor of the all-out expansion of industry at
the expense of agriculture came to be the principal plank of Trotsky's
opposition faction in the Party. He conceived that it was unfortunate
but true that rapid industrialization under the existing circumstances
could only come at the expense of the peasantry. Furthermore, Trotsky
argued strongly that such industrial expansion could be achieved only
by detailed and comprehensive economic planning under the direction
of the State Planning Commission.

The more systematic economic analysis of the Left wing position was
most clearly stated by the very original Soviet economist, Preobrazhensky.[7] Preobrazhensky spoke of the need for "primitive socialist accumulation." Marx had described "primitive capitalist accumulation"[8] as the
period in which "capitalist" countries first acquire the initial capital for
rapid industrialization. They acquire most of it by piracy or colonial
plunder or the slave trade, or some other means of extraction from other
countries.

Primitive socialist accumulation means the accumulation of capital
for socialist industry from "the surplus product of all pre-socialist economic forms." Of course, when socialism comes to an advanced private
enterprise economy, the primitive accumulation will be completed by
the revolutionary acquisition of all large firms. In a relatively underdeveloped economy, however, there is little to take over, so the problem is
one of constructing industry from scratch.

Where could capital be obtained? The Soviet Union in the 1920's had

[6] Cited in Dobb, *op. cit.*, p. 178.
[7] See E. A. Preobrazhensky, "On Primitive Socialist Accumulation," (written 1926) translated in Nicholas Spulber, *Foundations of Soviet Strategy
for Economic Growth: Selected Soviet Essays, 1924–1930*. (Bloomington:
Indiana University Press, 1964).
[8] See *Capital*, Vol. I, Part VIII.

neither the desire nor the strength to engage in the imperialist plundering of other countries. It was also impossible to obtain large foreign loans or investments. Most foreign governments still backed the return of the pre-Soviet government or even the Tsars. Moreover, they feared that the Soviets might confiscate any new loans and investments just as they had done the old. At any rate, they were more willing to hinder Soviet development than help it.

Thus the Soviet Union would have to develop solely from its own meager resources. Preobrazhensky argued that up to a half of all the profits of Soviet trade and industry were going into private hands under the NEP. He advocated nationalizing these enterprises so as to increase the profits available for government investment in industry. Yet Preobrazhensky pointed out that Soviet industry was still so small that — even including private profits — the internal reinvestments of its surplus product (above workers' wages and replacement costs) would mean only minute amounts of new capital each year. A "big push" in investment was necessary, however, to create new factories in the many related industries all at once. Without this initial surge of capital creation, development could never get off the ground, let alone gain momentum.

Since sufficient capital could not be obtained from foreign countries nor from the infant Soviet industry, the only remaining possibility was to extract it from agriculture. In agriculture pre-socialist private ownership prevailed. In fact, in 1928 there were still twenty-six million private farms in the Soviet Union. The Left wing urged that the agricultural surplus be extracted by high taxes, and by setting high monopoly prices on the industrial goods that farmers must buy (which amounts to the same thing as taxation of the product of the private farmers).

The Right wing of the Communist Party, led by Bukharin,[9] criticized this policy on several grounds. First, they argued that it would not succeed because the farmer would either cut back production or use his ingenuity to hide his products, and either consume them himself or sell them on the black market. Second, Bukharin argued that such a harsh policy would break the vital political alliance between the workers and farmers.

Third, Bukharin presented his own policy, which he believed would reach the same goal more easily. He had been impressed by the results of the NEP, which had allowed freedom for private trade and private agriculture. Under the NEP, large-scale industrial output had tripled from 1920 to 1924, though this was reconstruction and not new expansion. So Bukharin recommended more of the same, allowing the farmer to prosper and grow rich. Eventually he would use moderate taxes on the farmer to build industry, while very gradually forming voluntary farmer cooperatives to end the rule of rich farmers. In his own words, Bukharin wrote:

> . . . the ideologists of Trotskyism believe that a maximum annual transfer from peasant agriculture into industry secures the max-

---

[9] See, e.g., N. I. Bukharin, "Notes of an Economist" (first published in 1927) in Spulber, *op. cit.*, pp. 258–265.

imum rate of development of industry in general. But this is clearly incorrect. The maximum continued rate of growth will be experienced . . . when industry will advance on the basis of rapidly growing agriculture.[10]

Another Right wing writer, Rykov, expressed the idea that industry would eventually acquire the capital for expansion simply out of the continually increasing turnover of goods traded between agriculture and industry.[11]

Preobrazhensky and Trotsky countered with two arguments. The political argument was given that the Right wing policy would strengthen the rich farmers and thereby weaken the Communist political base. Furthermore, the Left argued that their own policy of rapid industrialization would eventually result in an increased flow of manufactured consumer goods to the villages, which would finally solve the "scissors" problem and peasant dissatisfaction once and for all. Finally, they claimed that small amounts of resources drawn very gradually from agriculture would *never* get industry moving on a basis of self-sustaining expansion (because of the necessity for an initial "big push" to development).

Stalin, leading the Center faction, first joined with the Right to defeat the Left and to exile Trotsky. Then he swung over to an ultra-Left program, and used the remnants of the Left to help defeat the Right wing. Finally, when Stalin became sole ruler, he "solved" the problem.

This political evolution may be traced most clearly through the record of the Congresses of the Communist Party of the Soviet Union during the 1920's. At the Tenth Party Congress in 1921 Lenin introduced the New Economic Policy, based on a temporary retreat to more private capitalism and more use of the market. The Eleventh Party Congress in 1922, still under Lenin, endorsed the NEP, but called for no further retreats from socialism. At the Twelfth Party Congress in 1923, with Lenin sick and unable to attend, the Right wing policy became evident in the enthusiastic arguments for the continuation of NEP and for further strong alliances with all of the peasantry. The Thirteenth Party Congress, in 1924 after the death of Lenin, attacked Trotsky's policies, alleging that they meant rapid industrialization only with impossible sacrifices by the peasantry. Instead, Stalin — supported by the other main leaders, Kamenev, Zinoviev, and Bukharin — supported the Right wing policy of relying on the rich peasants to build up agriculture as a base for eventual industrial expansion. Some important concessions were made to the rich peasant at this time, as was noted earlier.

In 1925 at the Fourteenth Party Congress, Stalin and the Center faction fully supported the Right wing policies, of which Bukharin had become the major spokesman. They continued to call for conciliation with the rich peasant, and a policy of "balanced growth," which meant (according to the Left) that industrial development would continue to be limited by the snail's pace of agricultural development. Now, however, Kamenev and Zinoviev had joined Trotsky in the Left opposition.

[10] Bukharin, *op. cit.*, p. 260.
[11] Dobb, *op. cit.*, p. 187.

They emphasized that industry must be rapidly developed, even if it meant taking resources from agriculture. Bukharin replied that NEP was not so much a retreat as "a regrouping of forces and an advance upon a reorganized front line." On the contrary, he called for an end to the last remnants of War Communism, that is, an end to any hostility toward the rich peasant. The Left feared the policy of letting the rich peasants lease land and hire workers; even more, they feared that the whole peasantry was gaining economically at the expense of industry and the urban worker. Stalin replied that the rich peasant and the private trader were really not doing as well as the Left opposition thought they were. He stated that in internal trade the share of the private trader had declined to 25 percent, while the share of the government had risen to 50 percent, and the share of the cooperatives had risen to 25 percent. He generally avoided, however, specific figures on agriculture, where concentration in favor of the rich peasant was continuing at a fair pace.

In 1926 and 1927 the Right wing (led by Bukharin, Rykov, and the trade union leader, Tomsky) continued to argue loudly for the encouragement of peasant agriculture, even at the risk of restoring petty capitalism in the countryside. Bukharin argued that agriculture must be given top priority for a long time, during which government-owned industry would develop parallel to peasant agriculture, each helping the other. The rate of growth of industry would, presumably, have to be held back to the slow rate of agricultural growth. Bukharin even made a political *faux pas* once by saying to the peasants (in a speech in April, 1925), "enrich yourselves." As late as 1928, Bukharin was still arguing that the lack of food and consumer goods was mostly caused by the fact that industry was expanding too rapidly, and its rate of growth should be lessened accordingly. A follower of his (Frumkin) wrote in November, 1928, that "we should not hinder the *kulak* undertakings in their production," state farms should not be expanded too rapidly, and less should be invested in industry than had been planned.[12]

Against this continued Right wing outpouring, the Left argued that as a result of lenient government policies the rich peasants were growing in power. In various regions, the rich peasant farms numbered from 15 to 25 percent of the total, had 25 to 45 percent of the total cultivated land, and owned 40 to 60 percent of the agricultural machinery. Stalin's answer to the Left opposition was to expel all of them from the Party in October, 1927, two months before the Fifteenth Party Congress. Trotsky was exiled to Siberia and then out of the country.

The Stalinist Solution

The interesting and thoroughly unexpected development (certainly unexpected by Bukharin and the Right) was that Stalin then at the Fifteenth Party Congress immediately adopted the Left policies and attacked the Right. Stalin claimed that industry had recovered the

[12] Dobb, *op. cit.*, p. 205.

pre-war level by 1926, and had surpassed it by 18 percent in 1927. While industry was doing well, in agriculture the total harvest was barely above pre-war. Thus, the crucial grain production was only 91 percent of pre-war, and the marketed surplus of grain was only 37 percent of pre-war. He concluded that collectivization was necessary: "The way out is to unite the small and dwarf peasant farms gradually and surely, not by pressure but by example and persuasion, into large farms based on common, cooperative cultivation of the soil, with the use of agricultural machines and tractors and scientific methods of intensive agriculture."[13] He defended this sudden policy shift by arguing that conditions had changed considerably since the last Party Congress, that now the peasants were in a mood favorable to collective farming, that the Party was now strong and capable enough to lead the change, and that industry was now enough developed to supply the new collective farms with sufficient machinery and tractors. Whether this argument was true or merely politically convenient, the Fifteenth Party Congress (packed with Stalin's supporters) agreed "to build the industrialization program upon the introduction of large-scale farming on cooperative lines as its cornerstone."

Stalin's solution to economic development was bloody and costly, but it did accomplish his objectives. He "persuaded" the unwilling farmers (and not only the small farmers, but especially the richer farmers) to give up their private farms and livestock and to join collective farms. These collectives were supposed to be cooperative ventures, but were actually under strict central control. It should be noted that the earlier proposals by Bukharin had only casually mentioned peasant cooperation and collectives, and even Trotsky had thought of the process as a very long and gradual one, not an overnight collectivization. Thus, until Stalin acted in favor of collectivization in 1928, no one else had seriously considered it as more than a minor component in raising the marketed agricultural surplus. Even Stalin started very slowly, and only intensified the program in later years as a result of unforeseen emergencies (see next chapter).

Stalin's "persuasion" to collectivize, which began in earnest in the fall of 1929, was marked by a civil war in which large numbers of peasants were killed or exiled to Siberia for resisting collectivization. Livestock were slaughtered by the farmers, and crop production fell. Yet Stalin succeeded in three objectives. First, he eliminated the rich farmer and strengthened socialism politically. Second, the large size of collectives *eventually* allowed the introduction of machinery and efficient farming (though they were anything but efficient in the first few years). Third, and this was most important, in spite of the lower total production, he greatly increased the amount of grain actually marketed and available for government use as "capital."

That Stalin succeeded in increasing grain collections is clear from Table 3–3.

[13] Stalin quoted in Dobb, *op. cit.*, p. 222.

Table 3–3

Output, Procurement, and Exports of Grain, 1928–1932
(millions of tons)

	Output	Collections	Exports
1928–29	73.3	10.8	.1
1929–30	71.7	16.1	4.8
1930–31	83.5	22.1	5.1
1931–32	66.0	22.8	1.7

Sources: Jasny, *Soviet Russian Agriculture*, Appendix. Also U.S.S.R. Central Statistical Agency, *Foreign Trade Handbook*.

Procurements of grain doubled from 1928–29 to 1930–31. Then, despite the terrible famine in 1931–32, procurements actually increased slightly. This would have been impossible to achieve had peasants not been collectivized. But in collective farms and under strict government control, they were no longer in position to withhold grain either for speculation or for their own use. The Government levied upon the farms so-called "obligatory deliveries" — in effect, a tax in kind — which had first claim on whatever output was produced. The amount of deliveries was based on the number of acres owned by the farm or in cultivation. Thus, it did not matter how much the farm produced, or whether or not there was a famine; the state's share remained stable since it was based on acreage, not output. The state did pay the farms for these deliveries — but at a fraction of their true cost of production, not to mention the high prices at which grain products were eventually sold in state stores. In effect, then, the mass collectivization combined with the obligatory deliveries was Stalin's technique for institutionalizing the NEP scissors — turning the terms of trade against the peasant by a greater amount than ever before — but forcing him to sell to the state nevertheless. It was this tax in kind which provided the bulk of the "capital" for the industrialization drive of the first two Five Year Plans.

The Soviet leaders wanted collective farms rather than state farms at this point because the collective farms enabled them to institutionalize the scissors with obligatory deliveries. Under the collective farm system, if output falls, returns to peasants fall, but deliveries remain stable. Under the state farm system, farm workers are paid wages which remain stable in the face of falling output — so the government loses *or* has to raise consumer prices and collect the surplus through inflation. The Soviet leaders preferred not to raise prices, since they were always afraid of the use of inflationary processes. They are now (in the mid-1960's) willing to do away with collective farms in favor of state farms because the farm sector is now relatively much smaller, and it is no longer necessary to finance industrialization on the backs of the peasants.

How can farm products become "capital"? First, note that some farm products, such as industrial crops and raw materials, are directly useful in industry. Second, farm products can be exported in exchange for machinery. Third, and most important, farm products can be used to feed industrial workers while they build new factories and basic utilities (or infra-structure). Fourth, food must be sent to those other rural areas which specialize in the production of non-edible industrial crops and raw materials.

Farmers then constituted the majority of the Soviet population, as in most underdeveloped countries. Stalin's solution therefore amounted to keeping most of the population at a very low level of consumption, while using their "surplus" product for investment purposes. Since investment reached 25 to 35 percent of national income, this naturally resulted in a very rapid economic growth. Once industry got under way, the problem became a little easier since more of industry's own resources could be reinvested for further expansion. This meant high profits and restriction of wages, again postponing the increase of current consumption, though this time at the primary expense of the urban worker.

Obviously, this model of economic development not only presumes heroic sacrifices in present consumption initially and for many years to come, but it also continues to reinforce the arguments for one-party dictatorship. No people will freely vote for such unpopular and drastic development measures. Only a one-party dictatorship allowing no opposition could possibly enforce these "temporary" measures for the development of an "infant" economy. This situation was surely a basic ingredient prolonging the Stalinist dictatorship in its protection of the "infant" U.S.S.R. against the temptations of its own populace (who were in favor of more present consumption). But, one wonders, who decides when the infant is grown up enough to restore democracy?

Recently, many critics have argued that it is possible to have such rapid development without socialism. Thus Jan Prybyla[14] says that Soviet strategy consists of a high allocation of current output to investment rather than consumption, concentrating investment in "heavy industry," and the use of the latest (very capital-using) technology. The Soviet tools, he says, are central planning, socialization of industry and agriculture, and a one-party dictatorship. He argues that the strategy is possible without the tools. But this argument overlooks the main point that probably only public taxation and public ownership could mobilize such a high percentage of national resources for capital investments. And if the forced saving is very unpopular, then political dictatorship may be the only way to enforce it. Of course, a more moderate rate of development might be maintained under public or "socialist" ownership with popular acceptance and without political dictatorship. This political question, while interesting, is beyond the scope of this book.

[14] Jan S. Prybyla, "Competitive Coexistence and Soviet Growth," *Pennsylvania Business Survey* (July, 1962), p. 5.

SELECTED REFERENCES

1. For detailed discussion of 1861 to 1917 development see Alexander Gerschenkron, "Problems and Patterns of Russian Economic Development," in Cyril E. Black, ed., *Transformation of Russian Society* (Cambridge, Mass.: Harvard University Press, 1960).

2. A critical account of Soviet economic policies is in Alexander Baykov, *The Development of the Soviet Economic System* (Cambridge: The University Press, 1947).

3. A sympathetic account of the whole Soviet period is in Maurice Dobb, *Soviet Economic Development Since 1917* (London: Routledge and Kegan Paul, Ltd., rev. ed., 1966).

4. A critical analysis of the Soviet debates appears in Alexander Erlich, *Soviet Industrialization Controversy* (Cambridge, Mass.: Harvard University Press, 1960).

5. The Soviet leaders and economists speak for themselves in the translations in Nicolas Spulber, editor, *Foundations of Soviet Strategy for Economic Growth: Selected Soviet Essays, 1924–1930* (Bloomington: Indiana University Press, 1964).

6. The definitive history of the Soviet economic and political developments of the early 1920's is E. H. Carr, *History of Soviet Russia* (London: Macmillan and Co., Ltd.). This has appeared in several volumes with several subtitles.

4

ECONOMIC DEVELOPMENT
FROM 1928 TO 1950

The First Five Year Plan (1928–1932)

The need to develop heavy industry as a foundation for future economic progress was agreed upon early in the industrialization debates. In 1926 at the Fifteenth Party Conference the country was told that "every effort must be directed in the coming periods towards an enlargement of the country's stock of capital equipment and of the reconstruction 'of the whole economy on a higher technical basis.'" The year, 1926–27, was designated as the first year in which the net expansion of the economy over the pre-war level must begin. The work of restoring production levels on the basis of existing capital was to be completed by October, 1926; and the question of enlarging the capital equipment of industry by new construction would then become imperative. (We may note that, in this early period, the planning year for the whole economy was always from October 1 to September 30 — for example, from October 1, 1926 to September 30, 1927 — because the harvest period made this sensible timing for agricultural planning, and agriculture was the major economic activity of the U.S.S.R.)

By 1927–28, the Plan for the volume and form of capital development became the backbone of economic policy, and had a predominating influence over all branches of economic life. This is because investment decisions must be coordinated and related to a consistent picture of development sketched over a longer period of time. This investment planning was the prelude to the First Five Year Plan, which began in 1928–29.

The delay in the final drafting of the Plan reflected the political dis-

Table 4–1

The Planned Collectivization

	1927–28 (actual)	1932–33 (plan)	1933–34 (plan)
Rural Population (calculated in million of peasants)			
Collectivized	1.1	12.9	18.6
Private	122.0	121.0	116.9

Source: Naum Jasny in Franklyn Holzman, *Readings on the Soviet Economy* (Chicago: Rand McNally & Co., 1960).

pute which we have already examined in the great industrialization debate. Several detailed plans were put forward. The plan of the State Planning Commission (representing the Right wing philosophy) assumed that the pace at which industry could develop was strictly limited by conditions in agriculture, that is, "by the meager ability and readiness of the peasant economy to supply produce to the market."[1] The rival plan submitted by the National Economic Council gave a much greater emphasis to heavy industry, and it was accused by the Planning Commission of "building castles in the air." Several more drafts of the Plan were presented and rejected during 1928.

Industry. The production targets which were finally accepted in 1929 for the period 1928–1933 were based on the following three optimistic assumptions: (1) no serious failure in harvests would occur during the five year period, (2) an expansion of exports and imports would occur, and (3) there would be increases in productivity throughout the economy, such as rising labor productivity and rising grain yield per acre. *Consumption was planned to increase by a "slight" 75 percent over the five year period, but net investment in heavy industry was to increase by more than three times.* The Five Year Plan called for a fourth to a third of national income to be put into net investment (whereas net investment in Tsarist Russia had averaged only about a tenth of national income). The *share* of consumption in national income was to fall from 77 percent to 66 percent; though we have noted that its absolute value was planned to increase about 75 percent in real terms as a result of the projected growth in output.

Collectivization of the peasant was to proceed at an extremely conservative pace. Jasny presents the initial planned rate of collectivization of peasants in terms of the number of peasants as shown in Table 4–1. If this planned pace of collectivization had been followed, there would have been no large-scale disruption of agriculture.

In the second year of the Five Year Plan, 1929–30, it was decided to revise upward the plan targets, and thus effect an increase in the tempo of development. As a side effect, an intensive collectivization drive be-

[1] Quoted in Maurice Dobb, *Soviet Economic Development Since 1917* (London: Routledge and Kegan Paul, Ltd., 1966), p. 233.

gan. It was found necessary to force the pace in agriculture if the main drive in industry was to be successful. The point was that a much greater surplus of food was needed to feed the rapidly growing urban working class, and only collectivization could insure this flow from country to town. In other words, the Communist government was unable to extract more grain from the peasants without collectivization. One important indication was the decline in grain exports, which were used to pay for vital imports of machinery. In 1913 Russia had exported 9.2 million tons of grain, but by 1928–29 grain exports had declined to .1 million tons. Moreover, the Soviets now needed more rather than less grain because the world depression had worsened their terms of trade (grain prices fell faster than machinery prices), so that it took more grain than planned to buy the same amount of machinery.

To some extent, the acute difficulties of the next three years — the slaughtering of livestock, the accentuated shortages of supply on the retail markets, the unanticipated enlargement of the labor force — can all be attributed to this forcing of the pace in agriculture. In addition, all of the three conditions postulated above as prerequisite for plan fulfillment turned out to be less than favorable. We shall see in detail that (1) there *were* harvest failures, (2) the terms of international trade moved drastically against the Soviet Union, and (3) productivity did not rise very much, mostly because of the disorganization caused by the vast transition from rural to urban life. All of the shortage in output below planned levels came out of consumption rather than investment. The result was that production of investment goods (according to somewhat biased official Soviet figures) did increase two and a half times, but at the expense of consumption and current output. After a further look at industrial results, we shall examine each of the three conditions individually to see what went wrong, and how the plan was affected.

The First Five Year Plan was officially described as successfully completed in December, 1932, just four and a quarter years after it began. According to official claims, planned investment targets were exceeded, though consumption fell far below the targets (and actually declined significantly according to Western estimates). In fact, investment in heavy industry was 50 percent higher, and investment in all industry 33 percent higher, than the planned targets for the whole five years! The production capacity of the iron and steel industry was increased by nearly two-thirds, and the beginnings of two entirely new metallurgical complexes were established at Kuznetsk in Western Siberia and at Magnitogorsk in the Urals. The machine-tool stock in the engineering industry was increased by nearly 100 percent and electric power generating capacity was also doubled.

According to official Soviet data — which are especially misleading in this period — while investment goods were increasing two and a half times, industrial consumer goods (not agriculture, which declined) increased their output by only 87 percent. Most U.S. estimates place the rise in investment goods at considerably below the Soviet claim, and do not concede that production of industrial consumer goods rose at all or find that they rose only slightly.[2] One problem with Soviet statistics (as we shall see) is that they include only socialized industry; yet in this period there was still a sizeable amount of small-scale, private, handicraft production of consumer goods. This small-scale consumer goods production was probably declining as fast as socialized large-scale production of consumer goods was rising. Moreover, and more important, in the last years of the First Five Year Plan output of food products for the Soviet consumer declined catastrophically. This large decline in agricultural output undoubtedly left the consumer much worse off on balance.

On the other hand, an important long-run gain was registered in the improvement in the quality of labor. Thus, there was a 250 percent increase in the number of "specialists" in the economy, meaning persons with some kind of technological education at the university or secondary school level. It is true that the inexperience and lack of familiarity of most workers with machinery prevented any significant increase in productivity in this period. In later years, however, an important economic gain was reaped from the investment in human beings, both in schools and in on-the-job training.

Agriculture. In the years 1928 and 1929, the Plan seemed to be proceeding better than expected on all fronts. Thus, industrial production rose rapidly in the first two years — according to both Western and official data. In fact, Soviet data claim a rise of 24 or 25 percent per year, considerably above the planned rate. Moreover, agriculture showed modest but steady advances. For example, the cultivated area rose by about 5 percent in the first two Plan years. By the Plan year 1929–30 the Soviet leadership was optimistic, but generally had a "now or never" feeling. This was felt to be the crucial or "spinal" year of the Plan, and development now had to be very rapid if the whole industralization effort was to be a success. Politically, a campaign was fought against the Right opposition, and their final surrender was accepted (they were "liquidated" politically, though not yet bodily). Thus, at the Sixteenth Party Congress in 1930 Stalin spoke of "the sweeping offensive of Socialism along the whole front, of the elimination of the *kulaks* as a class, and of the realization of solid collectivization."[3] Then industrial targets were raised considerably for 1929–30 and even more for 1931–32. In this context an all-out farm offensive was considered vitally necessary to bring in the agricultural surplus for the use of industry.

Specifically, the collective farms were ordered to more than double the Plan for both their cultivated area and their total production. In order to double their area, it was necessary to expand these farms by the in-

---

[2] See Norman Kaplan and Richard Moorsteen, "An Index of Soviet Industrial Output," *American Economic Review* (June, 1960), p. 235. Other Western estimates by Seton, Hodgman, Jasny, and Nutter are cited in Table 4–2 below. Statistical problems are further discussed there and in the Appendix to Chapter 5.

[3] *History of the Communist Party of the Soviet Union* (published by the Central Committee of the Party, 1949 English edition), p. 382.

clusion of many private farms; so the order went out to collectivize agriculture. In theory this was to be by persuasion and voluntary desire for admission. In practice, however, the mass of conservative peasantry could not be persuaded to join collectives at the pace of the revised Plan. They were "conservative" not only in resisting innovations, but because they wanted to keep their own farms — which they had obtained in 1917 after centuries of serfdom and struggle. Therefore, teams of young Communists from the cities came to help push them into collectives, and the situation soon approximated civil war in the rural areas.

Only the poorest peasants were happy to join the collectives; the middle and rich peasants (*kulaks*) resisted bitterly. Yet the rich peasants held almost all the capital equipment and livestock, so the collectives could not be successful without their participation. Thus, the period of tolerance of the *kulak* suddenly ended — many were killed or exiled. The Right wing policy of letting them lease land and hire other peasants for wages was forbidden forever. On the contrary, the village Soviets were allowed to take by force their livestock and capital equipment and all property above a certain minimum, and to give it to the collective farms.

The collectivization drive which occurred in 1929–30 touched off violent peasant resistance. The slaughtering of privately-held livestock drastically reduced the number of draught animals and cattle. By 1931, the number of cattle had fallen by one third, sheep and goats by one half, and horses by one fourth. (Even by the end of 1939, the 1929 level had scarcely been regained in the case of cattle, had not yet been reached in the case of sheep and goats, and only half reached in the case of horses.) On October 1, 1929, only 4 percent of peasant households had been collectivized. By March 10, 1930, the accelerated drive had forced the collectivization of 58 percent of the peasant households and the countryside was in a state of civil war.

To prevent further disasters, Stalin reduced the pressure for collectivization in March, 1930. People were allowed to leave the collective farms, and by May, 1930, the percentage of collectivized households fell to 28 percent; by September, to 21 percent. Strong economic preferences given to the collective farmer and more gradual and judicious use of force, however, soon "persuaded" many to return. Thus, by a year later, in June of 1931, there were again 52 percent of the peasants in collective farms. In fact, by 1936, 90.5 percent of the peasantry was collectivized;[4] this included virtually all the peasants located in heavily populated rural areas.

The slaughter of draught animals left a gap in animal-power used for cultivation, which the small though rapidly growing number of machines was unable to fill (one reason for the small harvests of the early years of collectivization). Low grain yields and bad harvests contributed to a decline in product per acre. Yet government collections were main-

---

[4] Naum Jasny, "Early Kolkhozy and the Big Drive," in Franklyn Holzman, *Readings on the Soviet Economy* (Chicago: Rand McNally & Co., 1960).

tained by the increase in sown area under collective farms. By the end of 1932, sown area under state and collective farms had increased eightfold over the 1928 level. Even more important, collectivization gave the government control of whatever output was produced, so the grain supply available to the state markedly increased (see Table 3–3). Thus the principal aim of the planners — to increase marketed agricultural surpluses — had been accomplished.

In addition to the collective farms, the years 1929–30 and 1930–31 saw some effort to create gigantic state farms, to be run as government-owned factories. The collectives, we may recall, were supposed to be run as cooperatives with all profits and losses accruing to the members (though, in fact, their management was closely controlled by the central government until the reforms of the mid-1960's, so that in effect most of the profits really went to the state). The state farm was thus more "socialist" in character, and the Soviet government sank a very large investment into the state farms. They were mechanized as far as possible and run on a gigantic scale. They did increase their production in these years, but *not* to a degree commensurate with the investment in them.

The state farms were therefore subsequently reduced in number, and played a very minor role. This was in part due to peasant resistance to the idea of giving up any ownership: they preferred the collectives where at least they retained a cooperative form of ownership. Perhaps more importantly, the Soviet government could not provide enough of either the capital equipment or the skilled managers to successfully run the state farms as "factories in the fields" (and it was only in the 1950's that the economic situation made such large farms more feasible). Finally, in Chapter 3 we mentioned the most important reason for using collective rather than state farms at the time: the state farms had to pay steady wages, so the government absorbed the losses in bad years. The collective farms were obligated to deliver to the government a certain fixed quota of output at low, fixed prices; and the quota was based on acreage, regardless of bad harvests. The collectives thus provided the steady minimum amount of agricultural surpluses necessary for the industrialization drive, with the extra burden of bad crops falling automatically on the peasants.

The same problems of the lack of skilled agronomists and sufficient machinery partially account for the poor performance of the collectives in increasing crop yields. The increased machinery they did obtain made possible higher output per worker (which released workers for industry), but did not succeed in raising output per acre or total output for some years. In fact, it was not until 1938 or 1939 that the flow of agricultural machinery made good the power deficit which resulted from the loss of horses during collectivization. Nevertheless, we repeat that the government's objective of raising the amount of agricultural surplus marketed in the cities was achieved.

One additional means both of achieving more control and of rationing more effectively the limited supply of agricultural machinery was the establishment of Machine Tractor Stations. All farm machinery was concentrated in the hands of these Stations, which rented it or sent operators to run it on the collective farms. The claim was that in this way the machinery got a great deal more use, and that repairs were more effectively carried out. Also, a small number of politically reliable directors of these Stations could ensure that the farms carried out the agricultural plans of the government (or else they would have no machinery made available to them!). Finally, the "agricultural surplus" was augmented since the farms paid the Stations for their services.

Foreign trade was a crucial link in the industrialization plans of the First Five Year Plan. The Soviets hoped to import vast amounts of machinery and equipment in order to get off to a fast start. In addition, they had to import almost all of their nonferrous metal requirements. These imports were to be financed by exports of grain, lumber, and other raw materials. The Great Depression dealt them a serious blow as the price of grain fell to one-third of its 1929 level, whereas the prices of the commodities the Soviets wished to import fell much less catastrophically — for example, machinery and equipment by only 20 percent. Nevertheless between 1929 and 1932, the volume of imports rose fourfold. Producer goods and raw materials constituted 94 percent of these imports; the machinery and equipment alone amounted to 55 percent in 1932. The significance of these imports is highlighted by the fact that roughly half of the new machinery introduced in Soviet factories in the First Plan period was imported. Figures for specific industries are: machine tools — 66 percent; tractors — 81 percent; metal cutting machines — 59 percent; turbines, generators, and boilers — 78 percent. Of the machinery and equipment imports, 93 percent were machines which produced other machines, whereas only 7 percent were machines which produced final products. It is clear that exporting grain and importing machinery was a process of investment for the future at the expense of the current standard of living of the people.

Productivity. Not only did the grain-yield index fail to rise, labor productivity also failed to reach its planned target. This had serious consequences. The original plan had anticipated an increase of 30 to 40 percent in the number of wage and salary earners. Instead the industrial work force *doubled* in four years. Obviously, since the expected increases in labor productivity were not forthcoming, more workers were required to meet the Plan targets. The wage bill also far exceeded its plan. The money wage rate was supposed to rise only half as fast as productivity; instead it rose several times faster than productivity.

Wages rose for several reasons. On the demand side, the Plan called for more production than was possible with the given labor force at the actually achieved level of productivity. Therefore, there was always a labor "shortage" compared with what was needed to meet the production plan. The result was a bidding for workers and a consequent inflationary rise of wages. Factory managers could afford to bid high because it was easy to get credit from the State Banks, credit which led to a large increase in cash in circulation. Furthermore, heavy industry (or producer goods industry) was assured and actually received large subsidies to cover any losses incurred, so it could bid labor away from the rest of the economy at even higher wages. On the supply side, workers were under pressure to produce more, and had the incentive to do so because of the highly progressive or differential wage policy. Thus, the higher production may have resulted in higher real wages to some workers. On the whole, however, the wage increase was purely monetary. Indeed, the government was happy to utilize the monetary illusion whereby workers worked harder because they thought they were earning more for their work, even though the increase in wages was counterbalanced by an even more rapid rise in consumer goods prices.

Financial Problems. With wages rising rapidly and the amount of consumer goods available declining, the result was inflation; consumer prices rose rapidly. In spite of his rising money wages, the worker-consumer — as well as the peasant-consumer — received lower real wages, that is, was made to bear the brunt of the industrialization drive. The situation in consumer goods was particularly bad in 1932 because of a poor harvest caused by drought conditions in many areas. The general lack of consumer goods (relative to wages) throughout the First Five Year Plan made it necessary to introduce rationing.

Prices, though rising very rapidly, were simply not raised fast enough to adjust the more rapidly rising wage levels to the declining volume of goods, so rationing was essential to preserve some equity in distribution. As early as 1929, bread was rationed in the major cities. By 1931 and 1932, almost half of all manufactured consumer goods and almost all agricultural consumer goods were on the ration list. If anything extra was produced, it was sold "off the ration" in special stores, but at very much higher prices. The fact that one could buy at least some goods beyond the ration at high prices gave some meaning to the high wages that could be earned by hard work. Yet this was a compromise which increasingly dulled the edge of the incentive wage policy. Higher wages and wage differentials were of less and less importance as rationing encompassed a wider sphere.

Although lack of consumer goods was a major cause of the inflationary problem, the Soviet political leadership felt that existing financial and banking institutions made the problem worse by encouraging industrial waste of resources. In industry, about a quarter of new investment during the first Five Year Plan came from direct reinvestment of profits; but about three-quarters was funneled from the government through the Industrial Bank. This development Bank no longer gave long-term credit repayable with interest as in pre-revolutionary days, but — acting as an agent of the State Budget — handed out interest-free grants to government enterprises. This free disbursement of long-term investment credit led to a wasteful maldistribution of capital goods, since all enterprises sought funds for investment whether economical or not. This has been a chronic problem to which we shall return, especially in Chapter 13.

The problem considered urgent in the first Five Year Plan period, however, was not the use of too much long-term credit, but the excessive use of short-term credit by enterprises in the purchase of supplies and labor. All government enterprises had accounts with the State Bank, and could obtain short-term credit from it or, in some instances, from other enterprises. The majority of industrial enterprises, however, had no financial resources of their own, but relied completely on their account with the Bank for funds. They drew on it not only for expenses covered by their deposits, but rather too freely by overdrafts, thus going into debt. These were in effect loans, which were inflationary to the extent that, in the aggregate, they exceeded the deposits in the Bank resulting from the usual State Budget surplus. An excess of loans relative to budget surplus usually involved lending by means of currency creation. A further evil of this credit from the Bank or from other enterprises was that the money was often invested in excessive inventories of materials or in employing a reserve group of skilled workers. In this way the individual manager insulated himself against the chronic shortages which occurred all too often. The aggregate effect, of course, was to worsen all the shortages, to further increase the pressure for higher prices in raw materials and skilled labor, and to divert resources into those channels without highest priority in the Plan.

To meet this problem, credit reforms were introduced during 1930, 1931, and 1932. In essence, each enterprise was henceforth to finance its own "normal" spending for current production needs out of receipts from sales; all credit for additional needs was to be strictly planned and governed by the State Bank. More precisely, no enterprise could grant credit to another; only the State Bank could grant credit; and the State Bank could grant credit only if it was specifically ordered to do so within the national plan. All of the "planned credits" together constitute the Credit Plan. The State Bank must make sure that all of these credits are used only for the planned purposes; and in fact the debts of the Bank are presumably liquidated just exactly to the extent that the planned output-quotas are met. The State Bank must also regulate the exact amount of currency to be circulated according to the Cash Plan. This plan specified exactly how much cash was to be paid out to individuals (mostly in the form of wage payments from government enterprises), and how much would return to the government in the form of taxes or as spending in government shops.

The State Bank is still a true central bank which does try to implement the credit and cash plans. It makes loans to enterprises for short-term credit needs, such as financing goods in transit, seasonal credits, and other short-term working-capital requirements of enterprises. To the extent that these credits to enterprises increase faster than deposits from the budget (from surpluses) as well as deposits of other enterprises, then there is net credit creation. To the extent that funds are needed for wages, this credit creation may result in printing of notes and an increase of cash in circulation. Since wages rose by unplanned amounts during the 1930's, so did cash in circulation (so the reforms were not entirely successful).

The long-term industrial or investment banks were even more sharply curtailed in their lending activities. After the credit reforms, the invest-ment banks no longer resembled the older kind of credit-making insti-tutions at all; they were now primarily bookkeepers of the Credit Plan and financial controllers of the Credit Plan. These banks were supposed to disburse (as agents of the state budget) only those moneys approved to supply capital for specific projects in the form of long-term invest-ment credit. Financing was to play only its planned role, with no inde-pendent influence. In fact, although the situation improved somewhat, Soviet enterprises continued to obtain credit above their plans and for unplanned uses (both through the State Bank and the investment banks). The reason was that, until 1965 at least, there was very little penalty on the enterprise for excess spending, *and* the output targets re-mained all important.[5]

Finally, the year 1930 saw a reform of the taxation system, abolish-ing a large number of antiquated taxes, and substituting the turnover tax (or sales tax) as the main instrument of government revenue. Dur-ing the 1930's, there were to be just two main kinds of taxes: (1) taxes on enterprises and (2) taxes on individuals. The taxes on enterprises included (a) the turnover or sales tax, (b) the tax on profits of govern-ment enterprises, and (c) taxes on profits of cooperative enterprises and collective farms. The taxes on individuals included income and in-heritance taxes and minor licenses, stamp, and customs duties. The in-come tax was very low, its maximum rate on workers and salaried em-ployees being only 13 percent (in fact, in May of 1960 it was announced that it would be gradually abolished). Individuals not in the socialized sector (private doctors or lawyers, priests, handicraft workers) were subject to tax rates that exceeded 50 percent for high incomes. It was argued that income taxes are not necessary under socialism (in the so-cialized sector) in order to redistribute income because income is al-ready equitably distributed by the publicly-determined wage scales. In fact, of course, wide income differentials were encouraged to provide strong work incentives, and the Soviets were not about to negate this policy by introducing large progressive income taxes.

A major form of taxation which does not appear explicitly in the budget is the tax in kind on the collective farms and individual farmers. As noted earlier, the government preempts a substantial share of all crops and livestock output and pays for these a much below-cost price. These products are then processed and sold to consumers at far higher prices. The difference between the price the government pays the collec-tives for grain (plus processing and distribution costs) and the price at which it sells to the final consumer is collected in the form of the turn-over tax. Thus, part of the turnover tax represents a tax in kind on the agricultural sector — and in the 1930's it was a very substantial levy.

The Soviets also introduced, in this period, the so-called mass sub-scription bonds. These bonds, which were sold to workers and peasants

[5] See further detailed discussion in Gregory Grossman, "Soviet Banking," in Benjamin H. Beckhart, ed., *Banking Systems* (New York: Columbia Uni-versity Press, 1959).

at their places of work, withdrew about as much money from the population as the income tax, and were deducted from the workers' salaries by withholding in exactly the same way. Because the subscriptions were taken under great social pressure, and the bonds almost never redeemed, one can in fact treat them as constituting a more or less hidden form of income tax.

In summary we can say that in spite of all the unforeseen calamities and in spite of some gross inefficiency and wastefulness, the first Five Year Plan was successful in building the basis of future industrial production — the primary objective of the planners. Because of unforeseen difficulties, however, consumption did not rise by the planned 50 to 75 percent, but actually fell. In effect, an industrial base was built at the expense of the current consumption of the workers and peasants. A more precise statistical evaluation of growth in the entire 1930's is presented later in this chapter.

The Second Five Year Plan (1933–1937)

The Second Five Year Plan (covering the five years from 1933 through 1937) was devoted to the "completion of the reconstruction of the whole economy on a higher technical basis." The official idea was to advance not quite so rapidly, but to really learn the new technologies and to solidify the industrial structure already erected. There was a strong effort to improve labor productivity both on the farm and in the new factories. A small decrease in the investment ratio was envisioned (down from 25 percent to 20 percent of national income), and the emphasis was placed on consolidation and qualitative improvement. There was to be a relative increase in investment in consumer goods, and consumer goods output was *planned* to grow more rapidly (18½ percent a year) than capital goods (14½ percent a year). These figures simply reflect the need to redress the imbalance of the previous Plan. In fact, three-quarters of total investment was still in heavy industry, particularly in iron and steel, machine tool production, and nonferrous metal industries. Yet the overall trend to slightly more conservative planning was exemplified by the fact that the final draft of the Second Five Year Plan actually had lower targets than its initial draft.

Financially, the lessened pressures for investment and the fact of greater consumer goods production (partly the fortuitous result of bumper crops in 1935 and 1937) were reflected in the achievement of stable retail prices in 1936 and 1937.

Transportation problems loomed as a major bottleneck during this period. For example, the length of railway track had risen by only 50 percent since 1913, but the volume of railway freight had risen by 500 percent. A very great burden was thus laid on all kinds of existing transport facilities. *Why* did industrial transportation needs evolve so much faster than transport facilities?

For one thing, the shift of population from village to town required movement of foodstuffs from the country to urban consumers. Also, the new industrial centers required the transportation of building materials over long distances. In other words, one effect of industrialization was to increase considerably the volume of interchange of products between different regions of the country. During these years the demands of industrial construction and of railroad construction upon the scarce supplies of iron and steel were sharply competitive. As a result, until the output capacity of the iron and steel industries had expanded considerably, the possibility of any large scale expansion of the transport system was very slender.

One very important reason why the Soviets did not want to increase railroad construction is that the output-capital ratio in railroad transport is lower than in any other activity except housing. When short of capital, there is a temptation to avoid, if possible, low output-capital ratio enterprises.

Another more ideological reason for the overextension of transportation was the tendency of the planners (based on a dogmatic interpretation of Marx) to glorify bigness, so-called "gigantomania." With just a few big plants producing each type of commodity, there are greater distances involved in transporting raw materials to the plants, and finished products to markets. This situation imposed the necessity of choosing the location of new plants in such a way as to economize to the maximum extent the use of transport. In the western industrial areas, Soviet planners were forced to utilize local high-cost lignite and peat as suppliers of fuel to avoid longer shipments of better quality fuel. At the same time it forced a minor shift in industrial production toward the eastern areas, where more plentiful supplies of raw materials and power were available. This accorded with the announced Soviet political intention of rapidly bringing to a level of equality all the former "colonial" and economically backward national areas, mostly located in the east.

The link between agriculture and industry improved during the Second Five Year Plan, when supply deliveries became obligatory and were regularized as much as possible. Quantities of agricultural goods were contracted for and paid for in advance at official purchase prices. These prices were so low as to constitute another form of taxation, especially when certain minimum quotas became obligatory in 1933. This guaranteed a certain minimum supply to the towns, on the basis of which industrial plans and forecasts could be made. Surpluses above the minimum quotas could be sold to the state at "State purchasing prices" (which were higher than the obligatory delivery prices) or could be sold on the free market. After more dislocations and disproportions in the first year of the Second Five Year Plan, supplies of food to the cities did indeed improve markedly. By 1938, the agricultural surplus procured by the state was actually 250 percent higher than it had been in 1928.[6]

By 1935 the improved supply had made it possible to abolish rationing.

[6] A very careful Western estimate of Soviet agricultural performance in the 1930's with annual data is presented in the article by Gale Johnson in the book edited by Abram Bergson and Simon Kuznets, *Economic Trends in the Soviet Union* (Cambridge, Mass.: Harvard University Press, 1963).

The end of rationing meant an end to the "on"-rationing and "off"-rationing stores, and an end to the two (or three if we include privately run collective farm markets) separate sets of prices. The end of rationing also meant that wage differentials assumed a much greater importance in determining actual differences in consumption. By the same token, wage differentials became a more effective instrument to stimulate work incentives.

In fact, the productivity of labor rose *faster* in the Second Plan than the planners had assumed. This was due in part to the greater incentives, and in part to the fact that workers (who had formerly been farm workers) were finally learning how to use machinery. At the same time, productivity was improved by the fact that many of the new, modern plants built in the First Plan period were just now being put into use and were reaching full capacity; and were being manned by workers who had eventually learned their jobs after several years of what amounted to on-the-job-training. Although the labor force doubled in the First Plan, it rose only gradually in the Second Plan, so industry had time to absorb further arrivals in an orderly manner.

The period of the Second Plan was generally a period in which the sacrifices of the First Plan were belatedly reflected in significant economic gains. By the end of the Second Plan, the Soviet Union surpassed all Western European countries in absolute production, though not in per capita production. By 1937 some 80 percent of all industrial output came from brand new or completely renovated factories built during the Five Year Plans, since 1928. Specifically, the capacity to produce iron and steel increased 400 percent between 1928 and 1938. The production of tractors and railway locomotives grew till the Soviet Union was the world's largest producer. Furthermore, during the Second Plan period alone — according to somewhat biased Soviet official figures — the output of machinery rose by 300 percent, though its target had been only 200 percent (but Western observers estimate that it actually only doubled).[7] On the other side, some consumer goods — especially textiles — fell far, far behind their planned goals, though they did rise somewhat in this period.

One indicator of the epochal changes in Soviet economic and social structure are the population figures for those years. According to the censuses, the urban population doubled from 1926 to 1939, while the rural population actually fell by 5 percent in those years, thus reflecting a vast internal migration from country to city, and from agriculture to industry. From 1928 to 1938, the number of wage and salary earners had grown from only 10 percent to more than a third of the labor force (most of these being urban workers); while cooperative producers (mostly collective farmers) grew to a full 55 percent of the whole. In the same period, the self-employed peasants, handicraft workers, landowners, and "capitalists" had shrunk from about 90 percent to little over 10 percent of the occupied population.

[7] See Kaplan and Moorsteen, *loc. cit.*

A cloud on the horizon was the noisy hostility of Hitler's fascist Germany. It was to meet this threat that plans were changed and resources were shifted to military goods. At first, in the years 1935 to 1937, not only consumption, but even investment growth rates declined — because investment and military spending were competitive for the same resources. By 1938, however, there was renewed stress on investment in heavy industry as the necessary economic base for military production. Thus, during the Second Five Year Plan, without very much diminution of investment spending, armaments grew unexpectedly from 5 percent of the government budget in 1932 to 20 percent of the budget in 1938. This again meant a further shift of workers to the production of goods that they could not consume. In order to soak up the excess household income, or to bridge the gap between the production costs and the necessary prices of consumer goods, the turnover tax rose steadily (and continued to rise into the war period).

Finally, one disappointing aspect of the economy during the Second Five Year Plan was the international trade sector. Foreign trade largely shriveled up in this period. By 1937, exports and imports were each down to only ½ percent of Gross National Product. One reason was that the Soviets had now developed an industrial base, so further machine imports were not quite so crucial to development. Another set of reasons lay in the hostility of Western nations and the impact of the Depression on their trade policies. These factors made it difficult to reach profitable trade agreements, and those concluded usually provided adverse terms of trade for the Soviet Union (relatively low prices for Soviet exports, and relatively higher prices for desired imports). Only in 1939–40 did trade increase somewhat, mainly as a result of the huge increase in exchanges with Germany after the German-Soviet pact of 1939. (Further discussion of international trade will be found in Chapter 8.)

The Third Five Year Plan (1938–1941)

The Third Five Year Plan was formulated under the threat of war, and was terminated after three and one-half years by the outbreak of war. Industrial growth targets were set at only 14 percent a year, much below the goals of the first and second Plans. The reason for the lower planned pace of economic development lay in the diversion of increasing amounts of resources to armaments. Not only were new plants built for military production, but existing plants — especially agricultural machinery factories — were converted to military uses. Thus, not only consumption but even investment in productive facilities was curtailed by the defense effort.

By 1940 investment plus defense spending together took at least half the Soviet national income. Defense spending alone was by 1940 twice the 1938 figure, and at least equalled investment. By 1941, defense spending had risen to three times the 1938 level, and was far higher than productive investment. As a result, living standards declined again after 1937–38.

Most of the new industrial construction of these years was in the eastern areas. These areas were obviously safer from German attack, and did become the home of millions of refugees and the main source of industrial output after the Germans occupied the western centers of production. In June, 1941, the German invasion put an end to the constructive activity of the Third Five Year Plan, reversing economic growth by the waste and devastation of war.

Size and Location of Industry in the 1930's

In order to understand some of the war and post-war developments, we must look briefly at Soviet decisions concerning the size and location of new enterprises in the 1930's. We saw in earlier chapters that Russian industry before the revolution was mainly located in the western areas of Russia. Specifically:

> About half of the industry of Tsarist Russia was concentrated in the central industrial regions (Moscow and Leningrad) and some 20% in the Ukraine. In the vast remaining expanses of Russia, industry either had not developed at all, or, at best, was in an embryonic form. Thus less than 10% of all Russian industrial production came from all the eastern regions of the country, with 4.7% in the Urals, 2.4% in Siberia, and 1.8% in Turkestan.[8]

The Soviets argue that this disproportional development was due to the semi-colonial condition in which the eastern areas were kept in the Tsarist period, and that this overconcentrated development was "far from rational according to any of the usual criteria."[9] The usual criteria include nearness to raw materials, to power and fuel sources, and to markets. Clearly, much of the raw material and power base was located in the East, and involved long and costly transportation to western industrial centers. For example, cotton, wool, and linen were generally shipped 2,000 miles from Kazakhstan and the Trans-Caucasus in Central Asia to the textile mills around Moscow.

Of course, markets for most goods were mainly in the western areas, so one might argue that this could make the location of industry there a rational decision. This conclusion does not follow, however, because of the weight-losing principle which applies to most industries. For example, when 100 tons of copper ore are processed, they may yield as little as one ton of copper, thus losing 99 tons of their original weight. Since most raw materials lose so much weight in refining, it pays to have the processing factories located as close to the mining areas as is possible, thereby saving an enormous amount in transportation costs. This principle of locating factories close to their mines is always relevant to planning, except to the extent that the planners may also have to take into consideration their own future decisions to develop mines in different

---

[8] S. S. Balzak, V. F. Vasyutin, and Y. G. Feigin, *Economic Geography of the USSR* (New York: The MacMillan Co., translated from Russian, 1961), p. 122.

[9] See Dobb, *op. cit.*, p. 426.

areas (as well as non-economic considerations, such as the avoidance of urban congestion or the avoidance of concentrated military targets).

In the aftermath of its Civil War, the Soviet Union was very busy rebuilding industries which had been destroyed in the western areas. Little or no effort was spent in the early 1920's on the task of developing the East. With the First Five Year Plan, however, a small beginning was made toward the more rapid development of the East, a trend which has continued and gathered speed ever since. Yet even then the older industrial districts received most of the investment in electric power development. Likewise, in coal production there was very little shift in weight toward the eastern regions. Heavy industry, however, was developed in some degree in this period in both the Urals and in the Kuznetsk basin of western Siberia. The result was that, by the end of the First Five Year Plan, industrial production in these two areas was outrunning the fuel and power capacity.

In the Second Five Year Plan, Soviet attention was therefore concentrated on the twin objectives of (a) establishing a new and powerful complex of iron and steel production in the eastern areas of Kuznetsk and Magnitogorsk, and (b) developing the necessary coal production at Kuznetsk and Karaganda in Central Asia. Until these coal and iron supplies were actually developed, there was an enormously long haulage of raw materials and fuel to these new plants in Siberia. In the mid-1930's, the gigantic and very modern new factories in Magnitogorsk and Kuznetsk required an average of only two man-days to produce a ton of steel, compared with 12 man-days per ton of steel in the antiquated Urals Works. On the other hand, the Urals Works required an average of only 100 ton kilometers of freight haulage of raw materials and fuel, whereas the Magnitogorsk and Kuznetsk complexes required an average of 4,500 ton kilometers of freight haulage to their factory per ton of steel production.

This excessive transport was the cost paid for these very large and modern Siberian plants, a cost which was reduced somewhat in the late 1930's when they were able to meet part of their requirements out of their own local coal and iron deposits. Further excess costs were incurred in the shipment of metallurgical products from the eastern U.S.S.R. to the markets in the western U.S.S.R. Most non-Soviet observers consider that the gigantic size and high transport costs of these plants resulted in part from the Soviet planners' gigantomania as well as from pure miscalculation — and that they were saved from the worst consequences only by the occurrence of World War Two (which unexpectedly added a great military benefit to the Siberian location).[10]

In the late 1930's, the desperate situation in transportation made it necessary for the Communist Party itself to attack gigantomania in the construction of new factories at a great distance from their fuel and

[10] See Franklyn Holzman, "The Ural-Kuznetsk Combine," *Quarterly Journal of Economics* (August, 1957).

materials bases or from their markets. For example, at the 18th Party Congress in 1939 Molotov emphasized:

> In keeping with the best interests of the state, industry should be brought nearer to the sources of raw material and the consuming districts. This will help to do away with irrational shipments and shipments carried over inordinate distances.[11]

This policy of balancing the regional production of industrial goods with the fuel and resource base was somewhat successfully pursued in the late 1930's. For example, the proportion of iron and steel production in the Urals and Siberia grew rapidly till it was 29 percent of all Soviet production by 1937. By the same year, moreover, the Urals, Siberia, and Kazakhstan came to produce 28 percent of the total Soviet coal output. In fact, coal production in the new central Siberian area of Kuznetsk challenged the old traditional coal producing region of the western U.S.S.R., the Donbas, and seemed likely to surpass it in the future. Indeed, Kuznetsk has five times the coal reserves of the Donbas, and its reserves are second only to those of Appalachian fields of the United States.

Is that really true

It was no accident, of course, that steel production and coal production in the East were the same percentage of total output. In fact, this was set up to be a metallurgical complex and it had to work that way.[12] But if coal production and ore production in the East were equalled by iron and steel production in that area, they were still far ahead of iron and steel *consumption* in that area. We find the big (and relevant) imbalance in the fact that most of the iron and steel was being shipped west to its users at a very high expense in transport.

On the steel and iron bases of Kuznetsk and Magnitogorsk, Siberia also began to turn out finished goods at the same sites, thus eventually saving on transport costs (a much slower and later development). One of the Siberian cities which was quickly becoming a complete scientific and industrial center was Novosibirsk. Novosibirsk grew from a population of 5,000 in 1900 to 500,000 by 1939. Similar growth was taking place in many eastern regions.

It had always been the announced policy of the Soviet government to locate light industry and consumer goods production in each region in proportion to population. This principle, however, was violated to a considerable extent in the First and Second Five Year Plans when even these goods tended to be produced in a few very large-scale factories, and then transported at great cost to distant areas. The Third Plan reversed this trend because of transport problems and emphasized local production of consumer goods consonant with local needs, a policy which especially benefited the new Siberian centers.

[11] *In the Land of Socialism Today and Tomorrow*, Reports and speeches at the 18th Party Congress (Moscow: Foreign Languages Publishing House, 1939), p. 134.

[12] See Holzman, *op. cit.*

At the same time as fuel, resource, and production complexes were growing in the East, the older industrial areas were instructed to reduce their dependence on long hauls of eastern fuel and raw materials. Leningrad, for example, which had long been a center of engineering and shipbuilding, now began to produce its own finished metal supplies. These in turn required iron ore, which was increasingly mined in the nearby Kola peninsula, and coal supplies, for which the coal fields at Vorkuta in the northern Urals were developed.

Growth in the 1930's

Before leaving the 1930's, we must summarize the record of Soviet growth in this period. Let us first examine industry alone, leaving aside other sectors of the economy. Table 4–2 shows the whole range of estimates of industrial growth by the Soviet government and by British and U.S. specialists.

Table 4–2

Indexes of Growth of Soviet Industrial Production,
1928–1940 (the indexes are all set at 100 for 1928)

Year	Official Soviet	Seton	Hodgman	Jasny	Nutter	Kaplan-Moorsteen
1928	100	100	100	100	100	100
1932	202	181	172	165	140	154
1937	445	380	371	287	279	249
1940	583	462	430	350	312	263

Sources: Official Soviet figures from Central Statistical Board of the U.S.S.R., *National Economy of the U.S.S.R.* (Moscow: Foreign Languages Publishing House, 1957), p. 41. Seton data from Francis Seton, "The Tempo of Soviet Industrial Expansion," *Manchester Statistical Society* (January, 1957), p. 30. Hodgman data from Donald Hodgman, *Soviet Industrial Production, 1928–51* (Cambridge, Mass.: Harvard University Press, 1954), p. 89. Jasny data from Naum Jasny, *The Soviet Economy during the Plan Era* (Palo Alto, Calif.: Stanford University Press, 1951). Nutter data from G. Warren Nutter, *Growth of Industrial Production in the Soviet Union* (Princeton, N.J.: Princeton University Press, 1962), p. 158. Kaplan-Moorsteen data from Norman Kaplan and Richard Moorsteen, "An Index of Soviet Industrial Output," *American Economic Review* (June, 1960), p. 235.

Table 4–2 shows the indexes of Soviet growth from various estimates, but it may be clarified by converting these to *rates* of growth for each of the time periods (which correspond roughly with the periods of the first three Five Year Plans); these rates are shown in Table 4–3.

Some interesting observations can be made about this table. First, the very high Soviet figures are not quite so incredible when we note that — for each of the Plan periods — the highest non-Soviet estimates are much closer to the Soviet estimates than to the lowest estimates of their Anglo-American colleagues (though the Soviets' data are certainly higher than *any* foreign estimates). Secondly, *all* observers estimate very high growth rates for the first two Five Year Plans, all averaging well over 10 percent for the 1928–1937 period. At that time, correctly or incorrectly,

Table 4-3

Rates of Growth of Soviet Industrial Production,
1928–1940 (in percent per year)

Period	Official Soviet	Seton	Hodgman	Jasny	Nutter	Kaplan-Moorsteen
First Five Year Plan 1928–1932						
	19.2	16.0	14.5	13.3	8.8	11.4
Second Five Year Plan 1933–1937						
	17.1	16.0	16.6	11.7	14.8	10.1
Third Five Year Plan 1938–1940						
	9.4	6.7	5.0	6.8	3.8	1.8

Source: Table 4-2.

the rest of the world was impressed by the contrast with the United States, which was in a great depression and had a zero rate of industrial growth from 1929 to 1939. Third, all estimates show a severe decline in the growth rate in the Third Plan, reflecting the dislocation caused by war preparation (and also, perhaps, the purges of managerial personnel). Finally, one observer finds the same rate of growth in the First and Second Plans, and two find a *higher* growth rate in the Second Plan than in the First Plan! This is a sensible result since many factories that were constructed in the First Plan only came into operation in the Second Plan.

This still leaves the question as to why there is such a great range among these estimates of growth. Certainly, political bias plays some role, but we must look more carefully to understand how the same data can be used to reach such different estimates. To begin with, the U.S.S.R. did not publish much data during the 1930's, so some later estimates are based on more complete statistics than earlier ones. The lack of availability also meant that each investigator had to provide a (different) method to fill in the gaps.

These statistical difficulties were magnified in the 1930's because the Soviet economy did not merely grow quantitatively, but was completely transformed from a rural, agricultural economy to an urban, industrial economy. How can such a transformation be adequately measured? One unique problem was that village handicrafts were being replaced by urban factory production. In the official figures, the rural handicraft production had not been recorded, whereas all factory production was recorded (one reason for the high official estimates). Secondly, in this period of political repression and dictatorship (especially after the purges of 1936 and 1937), Stalin used his control to keep some figures hidden and to issue some exaggerated claims by the use of peculiar definitions. Really abundant and reasonably defined Soviet economic statistics only became available after Stalin's death (though quite a bit of data were available until 1937). The third problem created by the rapid transformation was rapid changes in the quality of old products and the introduction of many new products, each of which involves arbitrary decisions on weighting in the construction of output indexes.

Lastly, the simple fact of a change in the composition of the national product caused a difficult statistical problem. For example, let us say that the whole national product consisted in 1928 of shoes and steel. Suppose that far more shoes than steel were produced in 1928, so that shoes were *relatively* abundant and cheap while steel was scarce and expensive (that is, the price of steel was relatively high compared to the price of shoes). Finally, let us assume that from 1928 to 1937 the production of shoes increased by 10 percent, whereas the production of steel increased by 1,000 percent. As a result, in 1937 steel was relatively more abundant and its price was much lower relative to the price of shoes than it had been in 1928.

Changes of almost this magnitude did occur in the First and Second Five Year Plans. But then what can we say about the growth of the total shoes-plus-steel national product? Was it 10 percent or 1,000 percent or some number in between? The estimate will depend on the weight or "importance" of steel versus shoes, which in turn depends on the relative prices we attach to the two goods. Valued in 1928 prices (when steel was very high priced), the growth would be very high, reflecting the 1,000 percent growth of steel. Valued in 1937 prices, however, when steel was already less high priced and carried less weight, the growth of the total product would be much lower, reflecting the 10 percent growth of shoe production. This qualitative change in the composition of Soviet output is one fundamental reason for the vast range of statistical estimates of growth for the period; each observer used his own price-weights, and each system was equally valid on its own assumptions (a numerical example of this problem is presented in the Appendix to Chapter 5). It should perhaps be noted here that in the years following 1937, the broad industrial composition of Soviet output changed somewhat less rapidly, so estimates for the period after the Second World War fall within a much narrower range.

So far we have been speaking only of industrial production, but the economy includes several other sectors, which may move at very different rates. In fact, we have seen that in the 1930's agriculture had a poor growth record and other sectors of low priority, such as services, also grew slowly. Therefore, the Gross National Product (GNP) grew more slowly than industrial production. There are few good studies of Soviet GNP in the 1930's, but there is one very thorough one by Bergson.[13]

This study by Bergson indicates very clearly the importance of one's statistical methods. He finds that, if 1928 price-weights are used, the Soviet GNP grew 11.9 percent per year between 1928 and 1937. On the

---

[13] Abram Bergson, *The Real National Income of Soviet Russia Since 1928* (Cambridge, Mass.: Harvard University Press, 1961); also see Abram Bergson and Simon Kuznets, *Economic Trends in the Soviet Union* (Cambridge, Mass.: Harvard University Press, 1963).

other hand, if 1937 price-weights are used, the Soviet GNP grew only 5.5 percent per year between 1928 and 1937. Of course, even 5.5 percent is a very high rate of GNP growth, achieved by very few countries for a period as long as ten years. But the 11.9 percent rate — calculated by this careful U.S. observer — is truly an exceptional rate of GNP growth. The political impact of the rapid Soviet growth rate on the rest of the world was especially magnified by the fact that the rest of the world was in depression with mass unemployment in that period. In fact, at the time the important political point about the Soviet system was not its growth rate, but the mere fact that it could prevent depression.

The Second World War (1941–1945)

At the beginning of the invasion of the U.S.S.R. in 1941, German output alone was greater than Soviet output; Germany plus her allies and occupied countries produced twice the Soviet output. Moreover, in the very important coal, iron, and steel industries Germany alone produced more than the U.S.S.R. The Soviet Union, however, was able to convert her production very rapidly, so that a huge percentage of all her resources was soon devoted entirely to the war effort.

Nevertheless, Soviet production declined very sharply because Hitler swiftly took over an area which had contained one-half of Soviet prewar capacity. The invaded area included up to 70 percent of Soviet coal mining, 60 percent of iron ore production, and over 50 percent of steel capacity. It included an important "bread basket" of the U.S.S.R., containing a third to a half of the area sown in grain. In addition, the Germans ultimately killed at least twenty million Soviet citizens.

The main economic salvation of the Soviet Union was achieved by an amazing mass evacuation of skilled workers and whole factories to the eastern regions of the U.S.S.R. Over half the populations of Kiev and Kharkov were evacuated. More than 70 percent of the capital equipment of Leningrad was evacuated. And whole factories were evacuated from many other areas. In addition, there was much new construction in the eastern areas during the war. Civilian consumption was, of course, cut to the bone. External assistance during the war, largely from the United States via lend-lease, totaled some $12 billion.

When the Soviet Army retreated, it pursued a scorched earth policy, attempting to destroy all productive facilities that could not be evacuated. Subsequently, when the Germans retreated, they also destroyed everything in sight, especially Soviet factories and housing. The result was a great decline in production by the end of the war. This is also one explanation for the fact that Soviet housing is still very poor. Thus, official Soviet figures claim that the war destroyed the homes of 25 million people, and leveled about 2,000 towns and about 70,000 villages. In summary, the Soviet government calculated that "the war retarded our industrial development for eight or nine years, that is, approximately two five-year plans."[14]

[14] Malenkov, cited in Dobb, *op. cit.*, p. 313.

Reconstruction (1945–1950)

Immediately following the war, a large number of plants producing war goods were converted to civilian use. Then the process of reconversion to peacetime uses and reconstruction of devastated factories was formalized in the Fourth Five Year Plan, running from March, 1946, through 1950. The main task of the plan was to rebuild and re-equip the destroyed enterprises. Therefore, the emphasis was on investment in the western regions that had been laid waste by the war.

Industry. The emphasis was also inevitably on producer goods and investment in heavy industry so as to restore and surpass the pre-war level. In fact, industrial output was supposed to rise by 1950 to 48 percent above the pre-war level. Thus, there was little room for consumer goods or housing, and consumers had to remain in terrible circumstances for this period. In addition, the problems of reconversion and movements back to the western areas put a tremendous pressure on transport facilities in the Urals and Siberia. Hence, a large amount of resources also had to be invested in the transport system there.

In the period from 1946 to 1950 the Soviet economy succeeded in reconstructing the productive capacity destroyed by the war. It was officially claimed that the pre-war production level was reached by 1948 (partly by the addition of the new facilities built in the East), but pre-war factories and equipment were not all restored until 1950. Housing was restored at a still slower pace, because housing uses up a great deal of capital per unit of output (about 15 rubles of capital to one ruble of housing). The Soviet planners attempted to divert the largest part of the scarce capital resources to reconstruction of factories in the immediate post-war period, and did succeed in this way in restoring the economy.

The much too rosy official figures[15] published in 1951 indicated that the Fourth Five Year Plan was completed in much less than five years. Specifically, by 1950 total industrial output was supposed to have risen 73 percent above 1940. This included a 200 percent increase of producer goods above 1940, though even the official figures admit that industrial consumer goods rose only 23 percent above pre-war. Agriculture again grew far more slowly. Western observers recognize that Soviet recovery to the pre-war level was completed in the aggregate by 1949 or 1950, but question strongly the official claims on the magnitude of the further advance up to 1950.

Financial Reforms. During the war large numbers of workers had been shifted from agriculture and consumer goods to military production or to the army. This drastically reduced the amount of food and other goods available to the consumer, while the money wage bill was actually increasing — due to high wage rates and overtime in military production. This imbalance led to inflationary pressures, higher prices of consumer goods, and the necessity for rationing of food and other items. At the same time, by sales of food in the private and collec-

---

[15] Quoted in Dobb, *op. cit.*, p. 316.

tive farm markets at soaring prices (where rationing and price control did not apply), many farmers amassed huge hoards of rubles.

By the end of 1947, agricultural production had improved enough so that food rationing could finally be ended. At the same time a monetary reform was put into operation. The object was to replace the old ruble whose value had fallen during the war (when rubles in circulation had probably increased by at least 250 percent), and to do so primarily by soaking up the excess buying-power and money hoards of those who had made profits by wartime speculation. To that end, the reform was designed so that it would hit disproportionately those with large hoards of cash, especially those held by the farmers.

The 1947 reform, therefore, allowed the exchange of *cash* at the rate of only one new ruble for ten old ones. *Bank* deposits, on the other hand, were given one new ruble for one old one up to 3,000 rubles. Bank deposits over 3,000 rubles were exchanged at progressively lower ratios down to the one-for-ten ratio for very large deposits. This reform (coupled with increasing production of consumer goods) was successful in ending the inflationary spiral. Thus, the following years saw the successful implementation of a policy of money wages rising slower than labor productivity, and the accomplishment of price-*reductions* once a year. By 1954, State retail prices which had tripled during the war, were back down to only 20 percent above the 1940 level, implying that real wages had risen very significantly from the war-time low.

SELECTED REFERENCES

The five year plans are discussed from a sympathetic view in Maurice Dobb, *Soviet Economic Development Since 1917* (London: Routledge and Kegan Paul, Ltd., 1948, rev. ed., 1966); and from a more critical view in Alexander Baykov, *Development of the Soviet Economic System* (England: Cambridge University Press, 1947). Also see Naum Jasny, *Soviet Industrialization, 1928–52* (Chicago: University of Chicago Press, 1961).

Thorough statistical studies of Soviet growth are found in Abram Bergson, *The Real National Income of Soviet Russia Since 1928* (Cambridge, Mass.: Harvard University Press, 1961); and in Abram Bergson and Simon Kuznets (eds.), *Economic Trends in the Soviet Union* (Cambridge, Mass.: Harvard University Press, 1963).

5

GROWTH AND PERFORMANCE
FROM 1950 TO 1965

We use the word "development" to describe the initial transformation of the Soviet Union from a predominantly agrarian to a predominantly urban, industrialized economy. In the 1950's and 1960's we
speak of the quantitative "growth" of the Soviet economy, and compare
it with the growth of other advanced economies. The emphasis of this
chapter is on the overall comparison of U.S. and Soviet growth rates and
the levels of productivity of resources achieved by each. For that reason,
there is far less detailed description of particular areas in this chapter
than in Chapters 3 and 4. Detailed description of developments in the
1950's and 1960's in Soviet organizational, labor, managerial, agricultural, international trade, and planning problems will be found in Chapters 6 through 13.

Soviet Growth (1950–1965)

After 1950, the U.S.S.R. planned for long-run peacetime
industrial expansion, beginning with the Fifth Five Year Plan, 1950–
1955. The Fifth Plan was to have a slower, less demanding overall rate
of growth, especially because consumer goods were to begin their own
long-delayed rapid growth. Producer goods grew twice as fast as consumer goods in the 1930's according to official Soviet data (though Western observers estimate a very much wider gap). By contrast, the Fifth
Plan called for only an 80 percent rise in producer goods and a 65 percent rise in consumer goods, that is, producer goods were to grow only
about 23 percent faster than consumer goods.

Then at Stalin's death in 1953 his successors quickly revised the Plan
still further toward agriculture and consumer goods. This was the first

102

time ever that a revision had been favorable to the consumer. The net result was that from 1951 to 1954 producer goods and consumer goods grew at the same rate. For the whole Plan period, 1950 to 1955, the Soviets claim that the Plan was overfulfilled. The compounded rates of growth *per year* during the period were supposed to be 13 percent for total industrial production, including 14 percent for producer goods and 12 percent for consumer goods. (Later in this chapter the official claims are contrasted with the much lower Western estimates.)

During the Fifth Five Year Plan, however, agriculture ran into further severe problems. The poor performance of agriculture led to much talk of an "agricultural lag" and to some concrete measures for improvement (most of them initiated by Khrushchev). In 1953 and 1954, agricultural incentives were increased both by lower taxes on farmers' incomes and by higher government procurement prices for farm goods. In 1955 and 1956, not only were there further increases in farm prices; there was also considerably more investment in agriculture, a campaign to increase the production of corn used for forage in order to increase output of livestock, and the famous campaign to extend grain production into very large areas of "virgin lands" in central Asia. All of these measures paid off in the significant rise in grain production in 1955–1960 of perhaps 50 percent over 1950–1955.

In the Sixth Five Year Plan, 1955–1960, the growth rate of consumer goods was set even closer to the growth rate of producer goods, while — in consequence — the aggregate growth rate was expected to decline somewhat. Thus, the planned five-year increases were to be 65 percent in the aggregate, 70 percent for producer goods, and 60 percent for consumer goods. The Sixth Five Year Plan, however, ran into many unforeseen problems, witnessed a declining growth rate, and was terminated before it ran its course.

The Sixth Plan was dropped in 1958, and was replaced by a Seven Year Plan for 1959–1965. The new Plan called for an even lower rate of industrial growth in the 1960's, only 8.6 percent per year compared with official claims of more than 10 percent in the 1950's. The reasons stated (or implied) for this lowering of planned goals included (1) still further attention to the growth of consumer goods, (2) a higher minimum wage, (3) drastic increases in pensions, (4) the need for major shifts among industries (for example, a decreasing growth in steel but a 300 percent increase in chemicals and mineral fertilizers), and (5) a reduction in working hours from forty-seven or forty-eight to forty or forty-one per week. The reduction of working hours was an especially significant welfare measure if we consider that it was taken just at the time when the annual increment to the labor force dropped very drastically as a result of the decreased birth rate of 1941–1945. Some of these reasons for lower growth rates are examined in detail in later sections.

Official Soviet data[1] claim an annual growth rate of about 8.6 percent

---

[1] Central Statistical Agency of the U.S.S.R., *Narodnoe Khozaistvo S.S.S.R. v 1966 godu* (Moscow, 1966).

in gross industrial output from 1960 through 1965. U.S. observers place the Soviet rate at only about 7 percent during this period.[2] But even the officially claimed rate was much below the claimed 10 or 11 percent rates of the 1950's, which in turn were far below the 16 or 17 percent claimed average rate of the 1930's. The question of whether the lower rates of the early 1960's were temporary or will persist in the future cannot be answered definitively at this time, but we shall refer to the general problem of predicted rates further in Chapter 8 on growth.

Many of the important changes in the late 1950's and early 1960's were inaugurated by the very important Twentieth Congress of the Soviet Communist Party in 1956. In Chapter 1, we described Khrushchev's attack on Stalinism, which took place at this Congress. Some economic policies were also decided there which were obviously closely related to the political line taken. First, there were the improvements in welfare mentioned above, including the turn toward consumer goods and lessened emphasis on producer goods, the very considerable reduction of hours worked, higher wages, and higher pensions. Second, the rejuvenation of Soviet trade unions can be mentioned, with a new emphasis on their role as defenders of the rights of individual workers (though they had always done some of this), and increased attention to their function of bargaining for better working conditions.

Third, the Twentieth Congress sanctioned more open and rational discussion of economic planning. On the one hand, this led to immediate proposals for major changes in the composition of output to reflect the latest technological developments — for example, the shift from steel to chemicals. In the long run, this spirited discussion led to the more radical proposals of Soviet economists for the use of several Western mathematical planning techniques (discussed below in Chapters 10, 11, and 12). On the other hand, the discussion led in 1957 to the reorganization of the planning and industrial administration. In 1957 the 30 to 40 Ministries in Moscow were abolished, and replaced by over one hundred regional councils responsible for different geographical areas. This change is discussed in Chapter 6; the far more radical and meaningful decentralization reforms of 1965 are discussed in Chapter 13.

Finally, the Twentieth Congress launched further programs to increase agricultural production. There were additional reductions in taxes on farmers, and some decentralization of agricultural planning from the central Ministry of Agriculture to provincial administrations. In 1958 the Soviets abolished all compulsory procurement-quotas of farm goods, which previously had to be sold to the government at a low fixed price. In 1958, Khrushchev also abolished Stalin's Machine Tractor Stations, and allowed the collective farms to buy and have ownership of their own machinery. These changes in agriculture are further discussed in Chapter 7.

[2] See U.S. Congress, Joint Economic Committee, *Current Economic Indicators of the U.S.S.R.* (Washington, D.C., 1966).

*Comparison of U.S. and
Soviet Growth Rates, 1950–1965*

After this very brief and general review of events in this period, a detailed comparison of U.S. and Soviet growth rates can be made. The whole period from 1950 through the present is as close as we can come to a long-run picture of "normal, peacetime" growth in the Soviet Union and in the United States. Their respective growth rates are compared for the whole period (to the extent available) and for two sub-periods in Table 5–1.

Table 5–1

U.S. and U.S.S.R. Annual Growth Rates
of Gross National Product, 1950–1963

Period	Official U.S. Data of GNP of U.S.	U.S. Estimates of GNP of U.S.S.R.	Official U.S.S.R. Data of GNP of U.S.S.R*
1950–1958	2.9%	7.0%	10.5%
1958–1963	4.1%	4.5%	7.1%
Average of both periods	3.5%	5.8%	8.8%

* Note: The closest Soviet equivalent to GNP is called the Combined Social Product, and is defined somewhat differently. The great difficulties in any comparison are discussed in the Appendix to this chapter.
Sources: The official U.S. data and the U.S. estimates of Soviet data both come from U.S. Congress, Staff Report of the Joint Economic Committee, *Current Economic Indicators for the U.S.S.R.* (Washington, D.C.: U.S. Government Printing Office, 1965), p. 13. The official Soviet data are from Central Statistical Agency of the U.S.S.R., *Narodnoe Khozaistvo S.S.S.R. v 1962 godu* (published in Russian, Moscow, 1965), p. 65.

A number of interesting points emerge from these figures. According to both official U.S.S.R. and U.S. estimates, the period 1950–1958 was much better for the U.S.S.R. than was the period 1958–1963. What caused this decline in the growth rate? First, growth was probably much easier in the early 1950's because some of it was still due to reconstruction of partly destroyed capacity. Second, it appears, as we shall see, that agriculture fared considerably better in the earlier years than in the later period. Third, the incredible number of young adults killed in the Second World War — and the consequent lowering of the number of children born — began to express itself in the late 1950's and early 1960's in the form of fewer entrants into the labor force. Fourth, there may have been some reduction in the new investment proportion of national income, because of the competing pressure of consumers for more goods (even though growth of consumer goods also slowed considerably). Fifth, the Soviet economy was becoming more and more

Table 5–2

Comparison of Uses of Gross National Product,
1963–1964 (in percentages of total GNP)

Country	Private Consump- tion	Public Welfare	Defense	Gross Fixed Invest- ment	Inventory Invest- ment	Foreign Balance	Total
Soviet Union	46.5	11.7	11.3	28.9	1.6	no data	100.0
United States	58.9	10.6	10.8	17.9	.8	1.0	100.0

Source: Joint Economic Committee of the U.S. Congress, *New Directions In the Soviet Economy* (Washington, D.C.: U.S. Government Printing Office, 1966), Part II–A, p. 106.

complicated, so crude planning and bureaucratic organizational systems may have been running into more and more trouble — hence the current reforms (discussed in Chapter 13). Sixth and last, it may be that the investment proportion was also reduced in the latter period because of the competing pressure for more military goods (and it may be, as in the United States, that defense is getting much of the best scientific talent).[3]

Some quantitative data may help to illustrate the pressures for different uses of the Soviet GNP. Table 5–2 compares allocations of GNP in the United States and the Soviet Union. Notice especially that the Soviet Union (with much lower per capita product) allocated about the same or higher percentages as the United States to both welfare and defense in addition to the much higher percentage spent on investment. One result was that the Soviet percentage of product going to consumption was much smaller than the United States percentage (and far, far smaller absolutely), but the high investment percentage also caused the much faster growth rate of the whole Soviet product. This combination means that although *present* consumption is a smaller percentage of GNP in the U.S.S.R. than in the United States, the *growth rate* of consumption is higher in the U.S.S.R. than in the United States because it does share in the rapid overall growth.

Note that the earlier period (1950–1958) of rapid growth of Soviet gross national product coincided with a period of slow growth in the U.S. gross national product. In that period the Soviet growth rate was more than twice that of the United States according to official U.S. estimates, and more than three times the U.S. rate according to Soviet estimates. In the second period (1958–1963) the Soviet growth rate declined while

[3] For a more detailed discussion of both periods, see Harry Schwartz, *The Soviet Economy Since Stalin* (New York: J. P. Lippincott and Co., 1965).

the U.S. rate rose. In this period, the official U.S. estimates show the Soviet rate only slightly above the U.S. rate; even the Soviet estimates show their growth rate as less than twice the U.S. rate.

Which period is "normal" or typical of the long run for Soviet growth (or U.S. growth for that matter)? That is impossible to say because neither period is very long nor very "normal." The poor Soviet performance in 1962–63, for example, is caused primarily by the very adverse crop conditions in those years. Official Soviet data disclose a 10 percent *decline* in agricultural output from 1962 to 1963. Agriculture has shown a much better performance in later years. Moreover, tentative data for 1964, 1965, and 1966 indicate that the aggregate Soviet growth rate has picked up again in recent years. The very conservative, semi-official U.S. estimate places the growth of Soviet GNP at only 2.6 percent for 1962–63, but rising dramatically to 7.9 percent for 1963–64.[4] Perhaps the best description of the whole post-war period is obtained by a simple averaging of the rates of the two sub-periods. For the whole period 1950–1963, the averages show a 3.5 percent growth rate of gross national product for the United States according to U.S. official data, about 6 percent for the Soviet Union by U.S. estimates, and about 9 percent for the Soviet Union by official Soviet data.

We may note that the estimates of Soviet growth by the U.S. Joint Economic Committee (quoted above) are among the lowest estimates by Western economists, and that most other estimates are considerably higher. It is, therefore, probably safe to say that the average of the "good" and "bad" periods of Soviet growth in the whole post-war period indicates a growth rate considerably higher than that of the United States. The rapid Soviet growth is even more remarkable when we remember that the share of defense in their national product is estimated to be about the same as the U.S. proportion, or twice that of most of Western Europe.[5] Naturally, none of this tells us what will be "normal" for the future.

Since its rate of growth was more rapid than the U.S. rate in this whole period, the economy of the Soviet Union gained in the "great race" to overtake the U.S. economy. Some very careful estimates by Bornstein[6] show that the Soviet gross national product was about 33 percent of the United States GNP in 1950, 38 percent in 1955, and slightly less than 50 percent in 1958 (a very good year for the Soviet economy and a very bad year for the U.S. economy). Of course, these estimates

---

[4] Estimate by Stanley H. Cohn, in "Soviet Growth Retardation," written for the Joint Economic Committee of the U.S. Congress, *New Directions in the Soviet Economy* (Washington, D.C.: U.S. Government Printing Office, 1966), Part II–A, p. 104. The lowness of the 1962–63 estimates is attacked by Alec Nove, "Two and One-Half Percent and All That," *Soviet Studies* (October, 1964).

[5] See Table 5–2 above; also see Cohn, *op. cit.*, p. 101.

[6] Morris Bornstein, "A Comparison of Soviet and United States National Product," from United States Congress, Joint Economic Committee, *Comparisons of the United States and Soviet Economies* (Washington, D.C.: U.S. Government Printing Office, 1959), Part II, pp. 385 and 392.

reflect Bornstein's particular statistical methods, including his own price-weighting systems, so they should be taken as only a rough indication of direction. The Central Intelligence Agency of the United States, in its famous press conference of January, 1964, declared that the Soviet national product had reached 47 percent of the U.S. level in 1962. At the other extreme, the official Soviet estimate is that the Soviet national product reached 60 percent of the U.S. level as early as 1960.[7]

Suppose we assume that the U.S. national product continues to grow at the 3.5 percent average it has maintained in the post-war period, and that the Soviet economy maintains its 6 percent rate as estimated by the U.S. Joint Economic Committee. Suppose also that the Soviet national product is now 50 percent of the U.S. national product (which is also far below the Soviet claim). In that case, the Soviet gross national product would surpass the U.S. level in 29 years. Of course, *if* the Soviet claim is correct that their product is now more than 60 percent of the U.S. level and that their growth rate continues at about 9 percent, while the U.S. stays at 3.5 percent, then they will catch up much sooner. We must note, however, that these extrapolations are only for total GNP, and the U.S.S.R. is somewhat further behind in per capita GNP (and even further in per capita consumption).

Although this numbers game preoccupies many popular writers, its results are really quite uninteresting. In the first place, our comparative statistics are much too untrustworthy for exact estimates. This question is discussed in the Appendix to this chapter, where we consider the deficiencies of Soviet statistics and the difficulties of comparison. Secondly, we do *not* know that future growth rates will be the same as in the past. The prospects for future Soviet growth are considered in Chapter 9.

Before leaving the question of past growth rates, we can learn some more by examining rates in different sectors of the Soviet economy. For this purpose, we may use official Soviet statistics since we are not interested in the overall growth rate, but only in the relative rates of the different sectors. As long as statistical deficiencies are not too different in different sectors, the official data will give the information we want, regardless of overall under- or overestimation. Table 5–3 shows the two important sectors of agriculture and industry, and divides industrial production into consumer goods and investment goods.

The table indicates that a large part of the growth of Soviet national product is due to rapid industrial growth, while agriculture has been a retarding factor. Thus, the average rate of growth of Soviet industry for the whole period 1950–1964 is claimed to be 11 percent, whereas even the official data claim that agriculture grew at only 4 percent. Industry also grew at a more constant and predictable rate, while agriculture varied greatly from a high of 14 percent to a low of –10 percent. The fact that agriculture is more closely dependent on natural conditions means

[7] Central Statistical Agency of the U.S.S.R., *National Economy of the U.S.S.R. in 1960, Statistical Yearbook*, translated by U.S. Joint Publications Research Service (Washington, D.C.: the U.S. Government Printing Office, 1962), p. 174.

Table 5–3

U.S.S.R. Rates of Growth in Selected Sectors,
1950–1964 (from official Soviet economic statistics)

Year	Gross National Product	Agriculture	Industry	Industry: Investment Goods (Group A)	Industry: Consumer Goods (Group B)
1950–1951	11%	—7%	16%	17%	16%
1951–1952	11	9	12	12	11
1952–1953	10	3	12	12	12
1953–1954	12	6	13	14	13
1954–1955	11	12	12	15	8
1955–1956	12	13	11	11	9
1956–1957	8	4	10	11	8
1957–1958	10	11	10	11	8
1958–1959	8	0	11	12	10
1959–1960	8	2	10	11	7
1960–1961	7	3	9	10	7
1961–1962	6	2	10	11	7
1962–1963	5	—10	8	9	5
1963–1964	8	14	7	9	4
Average 1950–1964	9	4	11	12	9

Notes: The Soviet "GNP" is called Combined Social Product, and is defined somewhat differently from U.S. "GNP". The growth rate for each year was found by
taking the change from the previous year and dividing by the level of the previous
year.

Source: Central Statistical Agency of the U.S.S.R., *National Economy of the U.S.S.R.
in 1960, Statistical Yearbook*, translated by U.S. Joint Publications Research Service (Washington, D.C.: U.S. Government Printing Office, 1962), pp. 105 and 235;
also *Narodnoe Khozaistvo S,S.S.R. v 1962 godu* (published in Russian by Central
Statistical Agency of the U.S.S.R., Moscow, 1965), p. 66.

that it more often causes disruptions in planning. Of course, the generally more rapid rate of growth in industry than in agriculture reflects
the policy of investing far more capital in industry than in agriculture
(as well as the particular organizational and incentive problems of agriculture — as we shall see later).

Within industry in almost every year the production of investment
goods for expansion of capacity grew much faster than the production
of final consumer goods. This reflects the consistent Soviet policy of
having investment goods (averaging a claimed 12 percent growth) *always* grow faster than consumer goods (averaging only 9 percent
claimed growth). This is naturally the key to much of Soviet industrial
growth. A more rapid growth of consumption could only be at the expense of investment and of lowering of the whole rate of industrial
growth (ignoring military and welfare spending, or including these in
"consumption").

In addition to the problems of agriculture and the competing claims of consumer versus producer goods, the Soviet economy faced some problems of low productivity growth in industry in the early 1960's. The situation is apparent from Table 5–4.

Table 5–4

Average Annual Growth Rates of Soviet Industrial Output and Productivity, 1951–1964

| | Output | | Productivity of Inputs | |
Industry	1951–64	1962–64	1951–64	1962–64
All Industry	9.4	7.3	4.4	1.7
Ferrous Metals	9.3	7.4	3.6	1.2
Coal	5.7	3.0	3.1	1.6
Petroleum	13.2	11.4	2.7	4.0
Machinery	11.9	10.1	6.5	3.3
Construction Materials	14.5	7.1	5.8	3.6
Light	7.0	3.5	4.2	.7
Food	7.1	3.5	3.1	−1.4
Chemicals	11.5	10.5	3.3	−3.5
Forest Products	6.2	4.9	5.9	2.6

Source: Joint Economic Committee of U.S. Congress, *New Directions in the Soviet Economy* (Washington, D.C.: U.S. Government Printing Office, 1966), Part II-A, p. 289.
Note: the procedures used in the source to compute productivity growth were both complex and controversial.

This table reveals that Soviet output growth rates fell in the early 1960's, not only because industry was obtaining less growth in the volume of its inputs, but also because the *productivity* of each unit of input was growing more slowly in most areas. The same analyst who prepared the table notes that the decline in Soviet productivity growth was probably due to temporary causes and may experience an upswing in the coming years.[8] A further discussion and comparison of Soviet productivity with U.S. productivity may be found in the next section.

Obviously, considering the average rates of growth, Soviet industrial production might overtake U.S. industrial production long before that point could be reached for the whole gross national product. Indeed, one Western estimate for 1963 puts the *industrial* product of the U.S.S.R. at about 68 percent of the U.S. level.[9] This is the geometrical average of the estimate of 77.2 percent in dollar values and 60.4 percent in ruble values (see explanation in Appendix to this chapter). Several other Western economists have attacked the methodology of these estimates,

[8] James H. Noren, "Soviet Industry Trends in Outputs, Inputs, and Productivity," Joint Economic Committee of U.S. Congress, *op. cit.*, Part II-A, p. 302.

[9] Alexander Tarn, "A Comparison of Dollar and Ruble Values of the Industrial Output of the U.S.A. and the U.S.S.R.," *Soviet Studies*, Vol. 19 (April, 1968), pp. 482–500; also see Robert Campbell and Alexander Tarn, "Soviet Industrial Output," *American Economic Review*, Vol. 52 (Sept., 1962), p. 719.

and even the Soviets have commented that this estimate is too "optimistic." It represents the top of the range of estimates of Soviet industrial production; several current estimates are as low as 25 percent, and the majority of estimates probably range from 40 to 60 percent.

The United States industrial growth rate from 1950 through 1964 averaged about 4 percent. The Soviets claimed their industrial growth rate as 11 percent, but even semi-official U.S. estimates indicate a rate of Soviet industrial growth of over 8 percent for the 1950–1965 period.[10] Thus, even on the basis of U.S. estimates of comparative industrial levels and industrial growth, it is possible to extrapolate a very early surpassing of U.S. levels by the U.S.S.R., *assuming* that past rates continue on both sides. On the other hand, it was noted above that Soviet growth rates have not been as high in 1964–1967 as their 1950–1963 average, and that U.S. growth rates for 1964–1967 have been above our 1950–1963 average. How temporary these recent deviations are from the long-run average remains a controversial issue.

It is also worth noticing that the U.S. and Soviet estimates of Soviet industrial growth are less divergent than the estimates for the growth of Gross National Product. One reason is that the GNP includes more heterogeneous items, involves more difficult definitional decisions, and is more difficult to calculate. Nevertheless, the difficulties with Soviet statistics on industry are also analyzed in the Appendix to this chapter. The reader may also recall the wide range of estimates for Soviet industrial production in the 1930's, and observe how much closer are the estimates for the 1950's and 1960's. This is in part due to improved Soviet statistical practices. It mostly results, however, from the fact that even rapid Soviet growth no longer requires the vast structural change, and the attendant index number problems, which were registered in the 1930's in the switch from a rural, agricultural, and handicraft economy to a mainly urban, industrial, and factory economy.

Notice further that even if total Soviet industrial production should reach the U.S. level, it would still be a long time after that before the levels of production of consumer goods were equal. And since the Soviet population is larger than the U.S. population, it would be even longer before consumption per person would become equal. Finally, at the present rates of growth, Soviet agriculture would never reach the U.S. level.

Soviet Performance Compared With U.S. Performance

Here we consider economic performance in terms of the amount of output produced per unit of input. This is not the same as a measure of economic "efficiency" (which depends on marginal conditions), but it is an interesting comparison that can be made with the available aggregate statistics. It is possible to get excellent comparable

[10] U.S. Congress, Staff Report of Joint Economic Committee, *Current Economic Indicators for the U.S.S.R.* (Washington, D.C.: U.S. Government Printing Office, 1967), p. 20.

defensive

statistics for particular Soviet and U.S. industries, but much harder to make good overall comparisons. We shall first examine labor productivity, then capital productivity, and finally the product per unit of capital and labor.

Output Per Worker. Several good studies of particular industries show a wide range of relative outputs per worker — many of the Soviet industries produce in the area of 40 to 60 percent of the U.S. output per worker, but some are a bit higher and some considerably lower. Thus, Soviet steel production per worker was estimated in 1963 at 47 percent of the U.S. level; but Soviet coal miners in the same year were found to be producing only 15 percent as much as U.S. miners. There was also clearly a vast difference in that year between relative Soviet farm and non-farm labor productivity. Soviet non-farm employees were slightly fewer in number than those of the United States (62 million against U.S. 64 million) and produced probably one-half to three-fourths of the U.S. product. On the other hand, Soviet agriculture employed more than six times as many people (30 million against 4.9 million in the United States) to produce a smaller product.

Fortunately, there is one excellent study by Bergson comparing overall productivity in 1960.[11] He found that the Soviet net national product of goods and services (including education, health, housing, government administration, and defense) was only 34 percent of the U.S. level when both were evaluated in ruble prices, but was 68 percent of the U.S. level when both were evaluated in dollar prices. As we shall see in the Appendix to this chapter, this is because the goods which the Soviet Union produces relatively most abundantly, such as machinery, are *relatively* scarce in the United States, so their prices are relatively high in dollars.

At the same time Bergson found total Soviet employment (adjusted so that all workers in both countries would be the equivalent of male, eighth grade graduates) to be 117 percent of U.S. employment. Dividing the figures in the previous paragraph by 1.17 leads to the conclusion that, with the national products evaluated in ruble prices, Soviet output per employed worker was only 29 percent of the U.S. level. It also follows, however, that with the national products evaluated in dollar prices, Soviet output per employed worker was 58 percent of the U.S. level. Both estimates of the comparison are equally "true"; we can only think of the comparison as a range and we can only say that these are probably the outside limits of the range.

Output Per Unit of Capital. Once again, it is possible to begin with some carefully documented comparisons of particular industries. Thus, it has been found that in 1963 Soviet railways carried 21 to 24 thousand ton-miles of freight per ton of railway capacity, while U.S. railways carried only about 7.2 thousand ton-miles per ton of railway capacity. Similarly, in the iron and steel industry the Soviets pro-

---

[11] Summarized in Abram Bergson, *The Economics of Soviet Planning* (New Haven: Yale University Press, 1964), p. 342.

duce 1.4 tons of pig iron for each cubic meter of blast furnace capacity they possess, whereas the U.S. turns out only one ton per cubic meter of blast furnace. In fact, in most industries the Soviet Union turns out a higher output per unit of capital than the United States — though there are a few, such as cotton textiles, in which the U.S. turns out more product per unit of equipment than the U.S.S.R.

In the aggregate for the whole economy we may recall that in 1960 Bergson[12] estimated that the Soviet net national product of goods and services was 34 percent of the U.S. level when both are calculated in ruble prices or 68 percent of the U.S. level when both are calculated in dollar prices. At the same time he determined that Soviet reproducible capital (including all buildings, all equipment, and non-farm inventories) was 35 percent of the U.S. level in ruble prices or 46 percent in dollar prices. It follows that the Soviet net national product *per* unit of reproducible capital was 98 percent of the U.S. level calculated in ruble prices or 149 percent in dollar prices. Hence Soviet output per unit of capital is equal to or much higher than U.S. output per unit of capital in most areas of the economy.

Why is it that Soviet output per worker is generally much lower than the U.S. level, while Soviet output per unit of capital is typically higher than the U.S. level? One could try to explain the lower Soviet output per worker in terms of less skill, less incentive, or planning mistakes. But the higher Soviet output per unit of capital makes us believe a more basic question is involved. Thus Campbell writes, "At a somewhat deeper level of analysis, however, the most important reason for low labor productivity is that the Russians are using lavishly the resource that they have in greatest abundance."[13]

The Soviet Union has relatively more labor and relatively less capital in its economy than does the United States. It is obviously rational for them to use a higher proportion of labor (their cheaper factor) and a lower proportion of capital (their more expensive factor) than does the United States in most lines of production. For example, Soviet output of iron per blast furnace is higher than that of the United States partly *because* they use a much larger number of workers per ton of iron to speed the process. Conversely, their iron output per worker is lower partly *because* they use less capital. They especially do without automated machinery for transporting iron ore or finished iron from boat or railway to factory or within the factory or back to the boat or railway, the machinery being replaced by large numbers of unskilled auxiliary workers. In this way, the Soviets often have higher production per unit of capital along with a lower production per worker.

Output Per Unit of Capital Plus Labor. Finally, Bergson attempts[14] to estimate the relative Soviet and U.S. outputs per combined "units of capital plus labor." Once again, output is represented by net

[12] *Ibid.*
[13] R. W. Campbell, *Soviet Economic Power*, 2nd ed. (Boston: Houghton Mifflin Co., 1966), p. 149.
[14] Bergson, *op. cit.*

national product, and the Soviet output is said to be 34 percent of the U.S. in ruble prices or 68 percent of the U.S. in dollar prices. To compare the amounts of "capital plus labor," the crucial point is the weight assigned to each factor in each economy. We cannot simply add man-hours to units of capital, but must assign a value to each in each economy. Thus Bergson estimates "labor" according to the total wages of employed workers, and "capital" according to the total price of all reproducible capital (times an interest rate assumed to be 20 percent in the Soviet Union). He then finds that Soviet "labor plus capital" is 59 percent of the U.S. level in ruble prices or 102 percent of the U.S. level in dollar prices. This result occurs mostly because the Soviet Union has relatively less capital (which is therefore scarcer and paid higher prices than in the United States) and a relatively large labor force (which is therefore more abundant and paid lower wages than in the United States). Bergson's final result — which follows from the data just cited — is that Soviet output per unit of capital and labor is 58 percent of the U.S. level in ruble prices or 67 percent of the U.S. level in dollar prices.

Summary of Performance Comparisons. To summarize, Bergson finds (1) that Soviet labor productivity is much lower than U.S. labor productivity, but (2) that their capital productivity is equal to or higher than ours. These two findings are supported by much other evidence and are accepted by most U.S. (and Soviet) economists. His last finding is (3) that Soviet capital-plus-labor productivity is considerably lower than the U.S. level. This third conclusion is highly controversial both as a factual finding and in meaning or interpretation.

The statistical problems in making such comparative estimates are formidable, and it required some heroic assumptions to reach any conclusions. Some of the problems in estimating levels of national product have been noted; more complicated is the calculation of product per worker or product per unit of capital; most difficult and uncertain of all is the measure of product per "unit" of labor plus capital. Bergson admits not only that the quality of the basic data is quite poor, but also that his method is biased against the Soviet economy because it ignores the unemployment that exists in the U.S. economy.[15] Nevertheless, Bergson's data and methods are probably the best that have been used so far in studying this problem. Therefore, we may very tentatively conclude that to the best of present knowledge Soviet product per unit of labor-plus-capital was somewhat below the U.S. level in 1960.

What do these conclusions mean? In spite of his acknowledgement that the relevant quantitative data are "not very incisive," Bergson contends that his study and other sources furnish enough evidence to conclude that the Soviet economy is less efficient than the U.S. economy.[16] Bergson lists as some of the sources of Soviet inefficiency: an incorrect, Marxist value theory; the central planners' lack of information and lack

[15] *Ibid.,* p. 349.
[16] *Ibid.,* p. 341.

of sufficient time or capacity to use all the available information; an irrational price structure; poorly chosen success criteria for managers; and a poor incentive arrangement on the collective farms. But he does point out that the Soviet Union is subject to neither business cycles nor general unemployment.

Some restrictive comments, however, must be made concerning Bergson's interpretation (some of which he might approve). First, production is determined not only by labor and capital, but also by natural resources and technology. Bergson does partly include resources under "capital," and anyway Soviet resources are probably roughly equivalent to U.S. resources, except for the lower proportion of good agricultural areas. But the omission of technology may be serious because its level depends not only on current organization and efficiency, but also on a great many factors in the historical (Tsarist) past. Second, productivity is *not* the same as what economists mean by "efficiency", though it is certainly affected by efficiency. To measure efficiency requires the use of marginal evaluations, whereas Bergson's productivity comparisons use only averages.

Third, other evidence may show that the Soviet economy is less efficient than the U.S. economy. But even "efficiency" is not inclusive enough to have the same meaning as "performance." Bergson's data on efficiency refer only to the *static* (present, timeless) best allocation of *employed* resources. Performance is defined to include also (1) dynamic growth efficiency and ability, and (2) full employment of resources. In both of these other areas, there is some evidence (see Chapters 9 and 10) that the Soviet economy compares much more favorably than when measured by the more restricted static efficiency criterion.

Finally, many of Bergson's list of sources of Soviet inefficiency were certainly true in 1960, and would now be acknowledged by many of the younger Soviet economists. In later chapters, however, it will be observed that a very strong Soviet reform movement has already corrected some of these deficiencies and is working hard to correct the others.

Standards of Living

The Soviet emphasis on investment in basic producer goods industries has been frequently mentioned in this book. This policy has meant a high rate of growth for total output, but a much lower rate of growth for consumer goods than for producer goods. More precisely, conservative U.S. estimates indicate that Soviet consumption per person grew at over 5 percent a year from 1950 to 1958, and then declined to a growth rate of about 2.5 to 3 percent a year from 1958 to 1964.[17]

This U.S. estimate also mentions that the *quality* of Soviet goods and services has improved more rapidly in recent years (the 1958–1963 period), so this factor may offset some of the recorded decline in the

---

[17] D. S. Bronson and B. S. Severin, "Recent Trends in Consumption and Disposable Money Income in the U.S.S.R.," in U.S. Congress Joint Economic Committee, *New Directions in the Soviet Economy* (Washington, D.C.: U.S. Government Printing Office, 1966), p. 499.

growth rate of the *quantity* of output. The study also points out that even the lower Soviet growth rate in consumption was still higher than the U.S. rate, as seen in the related estimate that Soviet consumption per person continued to rise from 27 percent of the U.S. level in 1955 to 31 percent in 1964.[18] If the Soviet consumption per person is 31 percent of the U.S. level (and their official claims are much higher), then it is quite affluent by the standards of the underdeveloped world, though uncomfortable and inadequate in the eyes of U.S. observers.

Furthermore, the relief from very low levels of consumption has come mostly since 1950 following decades of severe austerity. Thus, one of the most thorough U.S. estimates over the long run finds that Soviet real consumption per person rose only 85 percent from 1928 to 1958.[19] This relatively small rise was due to a sharp *decline* in the early 1930's during the collectivization drive and a very large *decline* (of at least 34 percent) during the Second World War. Therefore, in most of this period the level of consumption of the bulk of consumer goods — from shoes to autos — was miserably low.

The situation is a bit more optimistic when we discover that the very slow growth of production of most consumer goods (even slower than the averages reported above) was partially offset by the very rapid growth of free communal goods and services. The same careful researcher who was cited above on the 85 percent growth of average consumption from 1928 to 1958 reported in the same investigation that free communal goods and services rose by 431 percent in that period! In fact, the official Soviet claim is that 35 percent of Soviet consumption is in communal goods and services provided free to the public.[20] U.S. estimates place the percentage much lower, but still far above the U.S. percentage of free communal goods. For this reason, incidentally, simple comparisons of Soviet prices and wages with U.S. prices and wages must understate Soviet consumption levels.

What are these communal services? First and foremost are the services of health and education, areas in which the Soviets show up strongest in comparisons with the United States. Comparative figures in Table 5–5 show both the Soviet data over time and the comparable U.S. figures.

We should note first the very rapid rate of Soviet progress from 1950 to 1964, both in health and education services. There is now complete free health coverage for all Soviet citizens. In the second place these quantitative comparisons indicate that by 1964 the U.S.S.R. had clearly passed the U.S. in these fields. We find that by 1964 the Soviet Union had almost a third more doctors and about 5 percent more hospital beds per 10,000 persons; about 10 percent more students and a third more

[18] *Ibid.*

[19] J. G. Chapman, "Consumption in the Soviet Union," in M. Bornstein and D. R. Fusfeld, *The Soviet Economy — A Book of Readings* (Homewood, Ill.: Richard D. Irwin, 1966), p. 218.

[20] In 1967, the average monthly pay was 103 rubles, but there was an additional 36 rubles of free public consumption per person according to Premier Aleksei Kosygin, interview with *Life Magazine* (February 2, 1968), p. 32A.

Table 5–5

Health and Education in the U.S.
and U.S.S.R., 1950–1964

| | Soviet Union | | United States |
	1950	1964	1964
Doctors (per 10,000 persons)	13.2	20.5	14.7
Hospital beds (per 10,000 persons)	56	94	88
Number of students	34,752,000	46,664,000	41,417,000
Number of teachers	1,475,000	2,435,000	1,651,000
Number of students per teacher	23.6	19.2	25.1

Source: U.S. Congress, Joint Economic Committee, *New Directions in the Soviet Economy* (Washington, D.C.: U.S. Government Printing Office, 1966), p. 503.

teachers, or about six less students per teacher than in the United States. Education is further discussed in detail as an influence on growth in Chapter 9.

It must be reiterated that the bright picture in Soviet medicine and education does not change the gloomy fact that aggregate consumer goods per person (including these communal services) are still less than a third the U.S. level. The gloomiest and most negative feature of Soviet consumption is the housing situation. Its urban housing conditions are apparently the worst of any major industrialized country. Housing did not increase as fast as urban population from 1928 to the 1950's. Thus, in 1958 urban housing space per person was only 5.5 square meters, which was less than in 1928. In 1965 it was still only about 6.5 square meters per person, which was less than half the available space per person in Austria or West Germany; and was even much less than the official Soviet minimum housing norm of nine square meters.[21] It must be admitted, however, that the Soviet government has now — for the first time — committed major resources to housing construction, and is now probably in first place in the world in the rate of growth of housing.[22] Yet even with their rapid growth rate, the Soviet housing situation (legacy of two world wars, a civil war, and industrialization priorities) will continue to be painful for a long time.

Location of Industry

In the years since World War II, the Soviet Union has further dispersed its industry, and has further emphasized the development of the East. The main recipient of the eastern movement has been the new emerging industrial and farming complex which stretches from the Volga to Lake Baikal (as far as from New York to Seattle) but within

[21] Bronson and Sevarin, *op. cit.*, p. 503.
[22] Timothy Sosnovy, "Housing Conditions and Urban Development in the U.S.S.R.," in U.S. Congress Joint Economic Committee, *New Directions in the Soviet Economy* (Washington, D.C.: U.S. Government Printing Office, 1966), p. 553.

relatively narrow (500 mile wide) north-south limits. Furthermore, in spite of recent scientific-sounding talk about location theory and regional self-sufficiency, the eastern movement retains its exciting pioneering flavor.

A Soviet statement says:

> At present (1960), the eastern regions are still considerably far behind the western regions in absolute scale of production. Occupying 4/5 of the territory and having 3/4 of the fuel, power, and raw materials resources in the country, the East contains only about 1/3 of the population and 1/4 of the industrial production.[23]

This means, however, that the Soviet East did rise from a tenth of Soviet production in 1917 to a quarter in 1960. Considering the high rate of growth of all Soviet industry, this is an amazing proportionate rise of the East. This rise was accelerated during the Second World War, but it has certainly continued ever since.

It was mentioned that the most rapid growth of all was in the strip from the Volga to Lake Baikal. The cities of this area grew by over 80 percent between 1939 and 1960, the fastest rate in the Soviet Union, and much faster than the rate of growth of cities even in California in those years. For example, the city of Novosibirsk grew from 400,000 in 1939 to over a million in 1964. Although this region is only 1/8 of the land area of the U.S.S.R., it contains (if we ignore the permanently frozen far North) over 2/3 of its coal reserves, over 4/5 of its oil reserves, and very rich fields of iron ore and other minerals. Whereas 90 percent of Soviet oil came from the Caucasus before the German invasion, the Volga-Ural region already produces about 2/3 of all Soviet oil.

The "third iron and steel center" of the Soviet Union is being built in this area, especially around the south end of Lake Baikal. It will use local coal and iron ore deposits, and will eventually make use of two of the "world's biggest" hydroelectric stations at nearby Bratsk and Krasnoyarsk. The cheap power is expected to lay the basis for non-ferrous metallurgy — in spite of the still relatively expensive and scarce labor supply in the area. In addition, in the virgin lands campaign begun in 1954, over 80 million new acres have been ploughed and cultivated in this region (though the long-run farming prospects are poor in the new areas because of climatic conditions). The foundation thus exists for a whole new economy to flourish in the Volga-Baikal area from farming to fuel and power to basic and finished industry.

SELECTED REFERENCES

1. Thorough U.S. studies of Soviet growth and performance may be found in Abram Bergson, *The Real National Income of Soviet Russia Since 1928* (Cambridge, Mass.: Harvard University Press, 1961); and Abram

---

[23] V. V. Kistanov, "Aspects of the Formation of Economic Regions in the Eastern U.S.S.R.," *Soviet Geography*, Vol. I (April, 1960), p. 53.

Bergson and Simon Kuznets (eds.), *Economic Trends in the Soviet Union* (Cambridge, Mass.: Harvard University Press, 1963).

2. Growth rates and performance for the period since 1950 are discussed most recently by several authors in U.S. Congress Joint Economic Committee, *New Directions in the Soviet Economy* (Washington, D.C.: U.S. Government Printing Office, 1966), Part II.

3. The U.S. and Soviet standards of living have been discussed and compared by Lynn Turgeon; see especially his *The Contrasting Economies* (Boston: Allyn and Bacon, Inc., 1963), Chapter 6.

4. Two brief and valuable pieces on location are D. J. M. Hooson, "A New Soviet Heartland?", *Geographical Journal*, Vol. 128 (March, 1962); and Holland Hunter, "Costs, Freight Rates, and Location Decisions in the U.S.S.R.," in *Value and Plan*, ed. by Gregory Grossman (Berkeley: University of California Press, 1960). Also see S. S. Balzak, V. F. Vasytin, and Y. G. Feigin, *Economic Geography of the U.S.S.R.* (New York: The Macmillan Co., translated from Russian in 1961).

5. Further systematic discussions of the problems of Soviet planning for growth and the perspectives for future growth are to be found in Chapter 9 of this book.

Appendix to Chapter 5
Problems with Soviet Statistics

Does the Soviet Union keep two sets of statistical books, a true one for themselves and a false one for foreign propaganda? Most experts answer clearly in the negative, reasoning that accurate figures are so important in a planned economy that the propaganda value of false official figures would be far outweighed by the internal confusion which might result. Of course, there may be and is some cheating and falsification by managers trying to fool superior agencies. There may also be (and probably is) some additional falsification by intermediate agencies trying to mislead the central planners, since promotions as well as the salaries of officials at every level depend on the statistics of their performance.

We should note, however, the famous "law of equal cheating." Suppose that U.S.S.R. statistics exaggerate in every year from 1928 through 1966. If the percentage of exaggeration remains the same, then the *rate* of growth is unaffected. A constant level of cheating could only raise the whole level of apparent production, but could not raise the rate of growth. Note also that a law of equal mistakes would say that a constant degree of mistaken estimation would similarly have no effect on the rate of growth.

Although it is generally believed that aggregate Soviet statistics are not intentionally falsified, it is true that they have simply not released many statistics which would show poor performance. Before Stalin's death, very few Soviet statistics were made publicly available. Since about 1957 their availability has greatly increased, and a flood of data has been released, though a few key series are still missing.

Suppose we have Soviet data that are not falsified and are published and available. There may still be very difficult questions of interpretation. In the first place, even a particular physical item of production may be differently defined in the two countries. For example, the Soviets under Stalin measured grain in terms of "biological yield" that is, the amount in the field regardless of how much is lost in gathering, storing, and transport. U.S. grain measures are quite different, taking account of all these losses. The revised Soviet measures are now much closer to the U.S. measures, using the so-called "barn-yield."

A second area of difference in interpretation arises from the use of different categories and definitions of the aggregates in the national product accounts. For example, there are differences over how to calculate depreciation, though both the United States and the U.S.S.R. include the result in their concept of gross national product (or its Soviet equivalent). Most important are the differences over what is to be included in what the Americans call "Gross National Product" and the Soviets call "Combined Social Product." The Soviet's "Product" includes purchases of intermediate goods, for example, the steel that is bought by auto producers. The U.S. "Product," on the other hand, excludes such intermediate purchases as double accounting; that is, American economists consider that the Soviet method counts steel twice, once when it is bought as a raw material and once more as part of the price of the auto or other finished good. There would be no problem if there were only one integrated industrial enterprise, or if the degree of vertical integration never changed. In reality, however, increasing specialization tends to increase the number of levels of firms as suppliers, so the statistical count of production changes. For instance, if a Soviet firm producing primary steel and also fabricating the steel split into two firms for the primary production and the fabrication, this would appear to increase their steel production (because the steel would be counted once by itself and once as part of the fabricated product). Clearly, the Soviet measure of economic output is less satisfactory than the Western measure, since it is affected by changes in the structure of industrial organization. Naturally, this does not say that intermediate goods should not be considered in the planning process.

A contrary bias arises from the fact that the U.S. includes and the U.S.S.R. excludes from its "Product" what the Soviet Marxists call "nonproductive" labor. This is mostly services, such as domestic help, advertising, education, and military services. Some Soviet economists wish to reform their accounting to include all services in the GNP. (Incidentally, there *is* some domestic help in the U.S.S.R.) Since some of these services (such as education or the military in most periods) are the most rapidly growing sectors in both economies, this exclusion may lower the comparative Soviet growth rate.

Even if we agree on accuracy, availability, and interpretation of statistics, there is still a fourth problem that drastically increases the difficulties of comparing growth rates. This is the fact that different areas  of each economy grow at different rates, and that different inputs are greatly different in their degree of scarcity and in their relative prices in the two economies. For one thing, this means that it may be misleading to compare any particular isolated industry or indicator. For example, the U.S.S.R. produces more butter than the U.S., but this may only reflect different preferences and the availability of different substitutes (such as margarine). Or, product per unit of labor is much higher in the U.S. than in the U.S.S.R., but this partly reflects the fact that the Soviets tend to use more labor and less capital in production — so that the Soviet product per unit of capital is actually higher than it is in the U.S. in many industries. Of course, these differences result in part from the relatively greater scarcity of labor in the U.S. and scarcity of capital in the U.S.S.R.

If we wish an overall comparison, it is obviously necessary to aggregate all the different industries into one index of output, like the U.S. Gross National Product or the Soviet Combined Social Product. But it is not so simple to add up different products, let alone the services that go into GNP. Suppose the two economies produce only bread and machinery. If we wish to add up one mixture of bread and machinery to compare it with another, this can only be done with a given price for each loaf of bread and each machine. It would be easy if the ratio of prices of bread and machinery were the same in rubles and in dollars, for example $1 per loaf of bread and $2 per machine in the U.S. and 10 rubles per loaf of bread and 20 rubles per machine in the U.S.S.R. In that case the total sales value of bread plus machinery can be expressed either in rubles for both countries or in dollars for both countries, because the ratio of total sales of U.S. to U.S.S.R. will be the same in either price system.

The problem arises because different items have a different scarcity value (or are more difficult or expensive to produce) in the two countries, so there is a different product mix *and a different price structure*. Suppose, for example, that the national product of the U.S.S.R. is 2 loaves of bread and 4 machines, while the national product of the U.S. is 4 loaves of bread and 2 machines. Suppose also that in the U.S.S.R. a loaf of bread costs two rubles and a machine one ruble, while in the United States a loaf of bread costs $1 and a machine is $2. Then, if both products are calculated in dollars, we find that the United States produced only $8 total and the U.S.S.R. produced $10 total. But, if both products are calculated in rubles, we find that the U.S. produced 10 rubles worth and the U.S.S.R. produced only 8 rubles worth.

Which comparison is correct? We can only say that each valuation is "correct" (represents the objective situation) in one country but not the other. So you may take your choice.[24] Notice that the things most val-

---

[24] But see the further discussion of the choice between the two estimates in Abram Bergson, *The Real National Income of Soviet Russia Since 1928* (Cambridge, Mass.: Harvard University Press, 1961), Chapter 3.

uable in one's own country are always most scarce also, so one's comparison is always more favorable in terms of the other country's price structure. Bornstein's study found, for example, that the Soviet gross national product in 1955 was only about one-fourth of the U.S. national product when both were calculated in ruble price-weights. When both national products were weighted according to dollar valuations, however, the Soviet national product was about one-half the U.S. national product.[25] Notice that this great difference in estimates arises from only one statistical problem; consider, therefore, the different possible estimates arising from all the varied statistical problems confronting the investigator at once.

We have explored the problem of adding up (or "aggregating") the product mixes of different countries for comparison. An identical problem arises if we wish to observe changes in one country over time, which is the famous so-called "index number" problem. Thus, the apparent rate of growth of the Soviet economy from 1928 to 1968 is greatly affected by the fact that it now produces a drastically altered product mix with drastically altered relative prices. In fact, the Soviet output mix in 1968 is far more different from the Soviet output mix of 1928 than it is from the U.S. output mix of 1968. Yet if all Soviet goods are valued in 1928 prices (or the 1926–27 prices actually used for a long time), the result is very different than if each good in each year is valued at 1968 prices. Again, there is no one correct way to compare a different mixture of bread and machinery in the different periods.

In practice, it was those products which expanded most rapidly that also experienced the greatest gains in efficiency of production, for example, Soviet steel. Items such as shoes expanded more slowly and gained less in efficiency. But efficiency means lower costs, so items like steel have the greatest long-run declines in relative prices. Therefore, valued in 1968 prices, steel would contribute much less to overall rapid growth than it would in 1928 prices; whereas the slow expanders and slow efficiency gainers, like shoes, would contribute much more to the overall growth rate if we were using 1968 prices. Since the greatest price reductions happen to be in the most rapidly expanding products, the total difference in growth estimates is considerable. This is also true for the United States. For example, in 1899 prices our production of machinery rose by 15 times from 1899 to 1939. But valued in 1939 prices, our production of machinery from 1899 to 1939 rose less than 2 times!

Finally, as a fifth type of problem, all of this assumes that each product remains physically the same over time and in different countries. Actually, it may be difficult to say whether the quality stays the same, or worsens, or is improving. Furthermore, what is the quality and what should be the price of new products, which did not even exist in 1926 or 1928? In many areas, such as the chemical industry, new products rep-

[25] Morris Bornstein, "A Comparison of Soviet and United States National Product," from U.S. Congress Joint Economic Committee, *Comparisons of the U.S. and Soviet Economies*, Part II (Washington, D.C.: U.S. Government Printing Office, 1959), p. 385.

resent the majority of the industry's output in each decade. This problem is, of course, even more difficult in the Soviet Union where initial prices of new products are rather arbitrarily set by officials, rather than by the market.

SELECTED REFERENCES
TO APPENDIX

1. Gregory Grossman, *Soviet Statistics of Physical Output of Industrial Commodities, Their Compilation and Quality* (Princeton, N.J.: Princeton University Press, 1960).

2. Also see the extensive discussion of methodology in Abram Bergson, *The Real National Income of Soviet Russia Since 1928* (Cambridge, Mass.: Harvard University Press, 1961).

PART THREE

INSTITUTIONS OF CENTRAL PLANNING

6

ORGANIZATION FOR
CENTRAL PLANNING

The Soviet Union has at least three different organizational structures at local and regional levels, which converge only at the top national level. It has, like all countries, a governmental structure; but it also has an economic hierarchy because it is centrally planned; and it has an all-important political party structure, representing a one-party control of society. The basic structure of Party, government, and economy is indicated in Figure 6–1. It is the same figure that was presented and discussed in detail in Chapter 1; it is repeated here for the reader's convenience, with a very brief summary discussion.

In Figure 6–1 we show by dark arrows the legal lines of election and appointment in the various sectors. We see in the Party that the local cells (including over eight million members) elect delegates to the Congress, which elects the Central Committee, which elects the Politbureau, which elects the General Secretary. We see in the government that the whole Soviet electorate (numbering over one hundred million people) elects delegates to the Supreme Soviet, which elects its Executive Committee, which elects the Council of Ministers, which elects the Premier.

The dashed arrows indicate the extralegal power of the General Secretary to control Party elections. It also indicates his ultimate power to control the Premier and Council of Ministers. Since this power is not formalized in the Soviet Constitution, however, it is subject to variation in intensity at different times. At present (1968), it would appear that Premier Kosygin shares almost equal power with Party Secretary Brezhnev. In turn, the Premier and Council of Ministers exercise control over the top economic bodies. They appoint both the State Planning Commis-

Figure 6–1
Organization of the Soviet Union

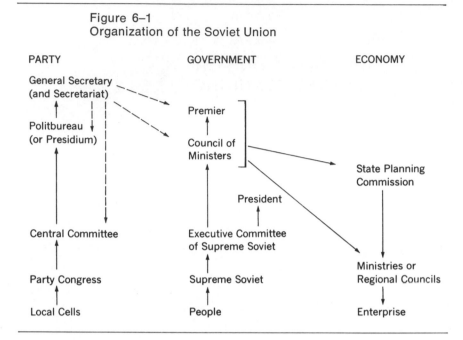

sion and the heads of Regional Councils. The ministries are each headed by a Minister who is a member of the Council of Ministers.

The economic plan, which is a legal document in the Soviet Union, is designed by the State Planning Commission and enacted into law by the appropriate government bodies (and often jointly promulgated by the Party). The Plan is carried into operation at the top level by either Ministries (one minister for each industrial sector) or by Regional Councils (one council for each main territorial division). There are usually several, often complex, intermediate bodies below the top level, all of which give orders to the basic economic unit, *the enterprise*. The nature of Soviet enterprises will be considered before returning to the different structural alternatives of industrial or territorial divisions.

Forms of Enterprise

The Soviet Union still has a small privately owned sector, and a much larger cooperative area, but most production is carried on in government-owned enterprises. In industry, the official data for some important years are shown in Table 6–1.

On the eve of the planning period in 1928 the private sector was still quite significant, and still produced more than the cooperatives. By 1937, however, the private sector was negligible, producing only two-tenths of one percent of industrial production, and declining still further since then. The cooperative sector was sizeable in 1928, but shows a slow but steady decline in percent of total production ever since.

Table 6-1

Soviet Industrial Production by Type of Ownership
(in percentages, rounded to nearest percent)

	1928	1937	1950	1960
Public Organizations	69	90	92	97
Cooperatives	13	10	8	3
Private Producers	18	0	0	0
Total	100	100	100	100

Source: Central Statistical Agency of U.S.S.R., *Narodnoe Khozaistvo S.S.S.R. v 1964 godu* (Moscow, 1960).

The Private Sector. It is illegal in the Soviet Union for a citizen to employ privately another citizen (or even intricate or electrically driven machinery) to produce a commodity for sale, or to sell privately anything he has not himself produced. The only exceptions are the used goods which private citizens may sell through the Commission Stores. In the non-agricultural sector, therefore, only the artisans and craftsmen (such as shoemakers and tailors) who produce consumer goods and services by their own labor, and those who sell their own services (such as domestic servants, chauffeurs, secretaries, some doctors, lawyers, and priests) fit into the category of legal private economic activity. But heavy income taxes and other discriminatory measures have succeeded in forcing many of this group to join either producers' cooperatives or to become employed by the government. The private non-agricultural sector is certainly diminishing and now represents only a negligible share of the total output of consumer goods and services.

On the other hand, the private sector in agriculture represents a very significant (although decreasing) share of total agricultural output. It consists of every household plot allotted to the state and collective farm workers for cultivation (about ½ acre per worker), as well as the small private holdings of industrial workers in the suburban or provincial areas of the Soviet Union. In 1961 Bergson reports that the private holdings of collective farm households constituted 2.1 percent of the whole cultivated area of the U.S.S.R.[1] In the same year, Bergson finds that the private holdings of wage and salary workers (including state farm workers) amounted to only 1.2 percent of the cultivated area. Peasant farms held negligible land by 1961, so the total private land holding totaled only 3.3. percent.

Two things should be noted about these private holdings. First, they have shrunk very little since the 1930's. Thus, Bergson[2] estimates private landholding in 1937 as only 5.3 percent of total cultivated land — including 3.7 percent held by collective farmers, 0.8 percent held by

[1] Abram Bergson, *The Economics of Soviet Planning* (New Haven: Yale University Press, 1964), p. 18.
[2] *Ibid.*

wage and salary workers, and 0.8 percent held by peasant farms (though peasant farms alone had held 96.2 percent of the cultivated land up to 1928). Second, these private plots are worked very intensively. As late as 1959, in spite of their relatively small area, the private land holdings produced over one half of the whole Soviet output of meat, potatoes, eggs, and vegetables. In recent years, they still produced 30 to 40 percent of these commodities.

Until 1958, output of this sector was subject to heavy taxation in the form of compulsory delivery quotas at low government-set prices. Before 1953, these commodity quotas were assigned in terms of given amounts per household on each farm for all commodities produced by the farm, whether or not the household even produced the commodity in question. The aim of the central authorities was simply to requisition as much of the produce as it possibly could. Also in mind was the ideological bias against private production; heavy taxes would make such production relatively less profitable, so that the peasant would turn his efforts to the collective farm. But the constant failures of the collective to earn profits rendered it unable to pay subsistence wages to its members on a regular basis. The burden on the peasant household became intolerable. It was unable to live on what it received from the collective farm, unable to pay the tax on its cow or pig, and yet still liable to compulsory deliveries of milk and meat if it disposed of the cow or pig to avoid the tax.

The government was finally forced to recognize officially this desperate situation and abolished all quotas in 1958. The collective farmer now works his private plot for family consumption and sells the surplus on the free market. Since prices on the free market are higher than those set by the government, the farmer stands to gain from his sales. It is often the case that these earnings are greater than what he receives for his work on the collective farm. He is willing, then, to travel long distances to carry his small amount of produce to market. These long and expensive hauls (in terms of time and energy) are abetted by the transport regulations which forbid private transport of another's products. Transportation is available by government or cooperative agencies, but the farmer prefers to carry the haul himself, and to bargain with his customers over prices. These activities certainly run counter to the collective farm effort. However, the conflict of interests will only be resolved when the collective farm is able to provide a gain for the individual which is greater than the reward he receives from private endeavor (though some farmers may even then prefer their own land in spite of the lower return).

The Cooperative Sector. As noted above, a large percentage of private artisans were encouraged to join producers' cooperatives. These cooperatives were almost entirely nationalized in 1960 and do not exist to any appreciable extent anymore. This form of organization, however, had more genuine features of cooperation and autonomy than the collective farm (its agricultural counterpart), and it is worthwhile to review briefly its major characteristics. The cooperatives' capital assets are provided free of charge by the State. Raw materials, however, must be procured locally because producers' cooperatives do not receive centrally allocated goods. Output plans and prices are set by the local council of cooperatives. Costs are subtracted from revenue and the remaining profit after taxes is either shared or reinvested. The main element in the cost account is the minimum wage. Thus the wage is the first charge of the enterprise. This practice differs from the collective farm which treats wages as a residual (that is, as profits), not as a cost.

As we shall see, private, cooperative and public enterprises all exist in the agricultural sector of the Soviet Union. The cooperative or collective farm (called the *kolkhoz*) can be seen in historical perspective as a compromise between the private and state type of organization. Several years after the revolution the bulk of land remained in fact in the hands of the individual farmers. The government needed to assure the movement of food and raw materials to the cities for industrialization; but the farmers strongly resisted any attempts at control over the land, as evidenced by the widespread slaughter of their own livestock during the collectivization drive of the early 1930's. A "species of compromise" was reached in the Collective Farm Statute of 1935. The collective farm was to be a cooperative of all the farmers of a given village or villages, which occupied nationalized land rent-free in perpetuity.

Remember that the basic aims of the collective farm system were (1) to gain efficiency by large-scale farming, (2) to get a larger proportion of grain to market, and (3) to eliminate an anti-Communist political base. The latter aims of economic and political control were secured by the fact that the management committee and the chairman were "suggested" by the Communist Party and "elected" at a meeting of the farm members. Government or party intervention has left little room for genuine cooperative management. The output plan, sowing plan, livestock plan, and other details were decided by the government or party authority and handed down to the farm. The aim of achieving more efficiency through large-scale farms using the latest technology was achieved only to a very small extent in the 1930's and 1940's, and only began to show some results in the 1950's. One problem at first was the lack of equipment to use on the farms (as well as a lack of skilled personnel and of fertilizer).

Another means for centralizing economic and political control, as well as for using the existing farm machinery and trained personnel as fully as possible, were the Machine Tractor Stations, each of which serviced several farms. In fact, until 1958 these Machine Tractor Stations were the sole source of farm equipment, and exercised operational control over farm activities.

These Stations provided the collective farms with all the machinery needed for cultivation. Production then involved the joint effort of the farm and the Station. The inefficiencies of this arrangement, however, eventually outweighed the control function it performed. The material interests of the two collaborators, the Station and the farm, were in conflict. The latter was interested in maximizing revenues, the former interested in fulfilling its ploughing or harvesting plan in terms of work units and in terms of payment for its services. There were no plans for coordination. Furthermore, as government and party control of farms became stronger, the control functions of the Stations became less important. Finally, another purpose of the Stations was to keep the few tractors working at full capacity shared by all the surrounding farms, but by 1958 there were enough tractors for each farm to have one or more. Hence, in 1958 the Machine Tractor Stations were abolished and the machinery sold to the collective farms.

The basic charge the collective had to meet until recently was the government's compulsory delivery quota (and, before 1958, the payments in foodstuffs to the Machine Tractor Stations for their services). These deliveries were "sold" to the government at very low prices. After these quotas were filled (requiring about three-fourths of total output) surpluses could be sold either to the government at a higher price, or on the free market at even higher prices, or used for reinvestment or for distribution in kind to the members of the farm. Thus, the revenue of the collective farm can be seen as the proceeds of sales at various prices and as produce kept on the farm. Expenditures include taxes, capital investment fund, and production expenses. The remainder is paid out as earnings to the farmers. The individual farmer's income is calculated in terms of the number of days worked and the kind of work done.

It must be emphasized that, unlike the government enterprises or producers' cooperative, there was no fixed minimum wage on the collective farm until 1966. The amount distributed was a residual. Payments were often low and irregular. This poor system of remuneration and incentives made it necessary for the authorities to impose upon the worker a minimum number of workdays, according to the farm's requirements. The authorities at the same time, however, permitted the farmer a private plot and livestock in order to eke out his subsistence. We have already noted that incomes gained from private activities were often greater than those gained from the collective. These problems, reflected in the failure of agriculture over the past years, are at last receiving attention, and changes are slowly being achieved. The recent problems of developing incentives in Soviet agriculture will be examined in more detail in Chapter 7.

Government Agricultural Enterprise. Besides the collective farm, the state farm (or *Sovkhoz*) exists in agriculture. The state farm is run as a government enterprise on budget allocations and centrally allocated material supplies. The most important difference between this and the collective farm is that the farm worker is a rural wage earner. He receives a guaranteed minimum wage and, even if the enterprise suffers a loss, these wages must be paid by the State. Previously, the state farms often operated with continuous losses. This was primarily due to the lack of needed mechanical equipment and chemical fertilizer. Since there is now more investment in supplies for agriculture, we can expect this "higher form of socialist agricultural organization" to be preferred by the Soviet leaders.

In the 1930's the collective farm predominated because (1) farm income was too low to guarantee a wage, (2) there were not enough trained personnel and machinery to run efficient large-scale state farms, and (3) politically, it took wide-spread civil war to get the peasants into collective farms, but peasant resistance to state farms was even stronger. Thus, by 1937 collective farms reached 86 percent of the sown area, while state farms were only 9 percent of the sown area.[3] There was little improvement in the farm situation for a long time; so by 1950 state farms still cultivated only 11 percent of the area, while collectives still had 83 percent of the cultivated or sown area. Conditions in the 1950's began to change, including more farm income and more farm specialists and more machinery, so Khrushchev launched a drive to combine collectives into much larger state farms. The main impact came in the late 1950's. The state farms' sown area rose from 16 percent in 1955 to 43 percent in 1961, while in the same period collective farms' sown area fell from 80 to 54 percent of the whole area. Since then, further changes in this direction have been very slow. Agricultural developments are discussed more extensively in the next chapter.

Government Industrial Enterprise. The largest part of the Soviet national product is produced by public enterprises in industry. The publicly-owned industrial enterprise is the creation of the government, and in the past the government has provided its property, assets, and material resources free of charge. The government expects in return that the enterprise will do what it is told, fulfill its plan, and return its profits (or a certain proportion of them) to the government budget. A director is appointed to be in full charge of the enterprise, although he is checked by various other organizations. He has full responsibility to his superiors for the performance of the firm. The primary task of the director is "to fulfill and if possible overfulfill the output plans" and to utilize the resources placed at his disposal with due regard to the national economy. The manager receives a bonus for fulfilling the plan, and overplan profits can be used for reinvestment or for workers' welfare or may be shared among workers and manager. Although the basic output plan of the enterprise may be in physical terms, firms are expected to keep profit and loss accounts, and to be financially independent. When and if profit becomes more important both as an indicator of performance and an incentive to work, then will the financial operations and calculations take precedence in planned instructions.

The firm faces a strict set of limitations. Prices of inputs and outputs are fixed. The supplies of materials are often subject to control and some materials can only be obtained by means of an allocation certificate. This planning of supplies to each industry or firm is a central focus of Soviet planning. It is a very complicated and difficult business, and the rigidity of material allocations results in some major bottlenecks. It has been one main point of attack in recent Soviet discussions of reform (see Chapter 13).

What the firm faces then is a set of not necessarily consistent plans:

[3] Bergson, *op. cit.*, p. 18.

plans for gross output (the most important), profit, cost reduction, wages bill, materials allocation, and orders received from customers. The manager must maneuver within the boundaries of these material supplies, wage funds, and selling prices in order to achieve his production target. Fortunately for him, there are loopholes. Illegal hoarding of materials, the firm's use of its own workshops to make supplies not included in the Plan, and informal contracts between firms, all contribute to flexibility. The problems of the firm manager and workers will be explored in detail in Chapter 7.

The Ministry System versus the Territory System

From 1932 to 1957 the organization of the planning administration below the Center was by Commissariats or Ministries. Each Ministry was in charge of a certain sector of industry, and their powers were ranked on a priority basis. At first there were just three Ministries: light, heavy, and the timber industry. These expanded to 30 or 40 Ministries, mostly to separate certain priority industries in the heavy industry sector. Each All-Union Ministry was at that time based in Moscow and had charge of all the enterprises in its sector all over the nation. It had departmental divisions for planning, supplies, disposals, deliveries, and other operations. It also had the function of drafting the output and supply plans for the enterprises to submit to the State Planning Commission. This State Planning Commission then had the job of coordinating the plans of the Ministries to arrive at balances between the industries, and a supply and delivery plan for the thousands of centrally allocated goods.

Coordination was extremely difficult partly because each Ministry developed its own self-sufficient empire. (Originally, however, they each had set up such empires partly because coordination was too poor to rely on products from other Ministries.) A Ministry would tend to set up its own vertically-organized national supply system, because of the uncertainty of supplies from other Ministries. Thus a factory producing nails for Ministry A would send its nails to another firm under the same Ministry 3,000 miles away, even though a factory under Ministry B was situated right next door and required the nails. Transportation costs could be greatly reduced by using supplies from the other Ministry, but until recently most prices did not include transportation costs. Thus, coordinated planning, or the utilization of local resources on a regional basis, was impossible. Furthermore, coordination concerning by-products between industries was lacking, since it did not correspond to the self-interest of the individual Ministries.

We should also mention here — as will be shown in later chapters — that coordinated planning also faces more fundamental problems than the Ministry system. By the crude methods used to date, there are problems in arriving at proper balances between products. There are problems of obtaining sufficient, accurate information and enough time to use it. There is the problem that overambitious growth plans led to over-full employment and overcommitment of resources in all areas. All of these and other problems have led each Ministry or enterprise (a) to develop its own auxiliary supplies, (b) to haul supplies enormous distances, and (c) to use large numbers of special men called "pushers" (corresponding to the "expediters" in the U.S. during the Second World War) and other semi-legal devices to obtain necessary supplies.

At any rate, since planning under the Ministry system was very crude, whenever bottlenecks or shortages occurred, deliveries under the formal Plan were superseded by the deliveries according to the importance of the Ministry, that is, its political and economic priority. Both current resources and new capital would then be directed to the Ministry enjoying the higher priority ranking. Each Minister argued for the importance of his industry to the nation's welfare, regardless of what products it produced.

In 1957 direction of industry was shifted from the 40-odd Ministries in Moscow to about 100 Regional Councils (called Sovnarkhozy), with the express purpose of coordinating industries in a given region or territorial unit. It must be understood, however, that the two systems were *not* mutually exclusive. Thus, territorial divisions and regional departments always existed within the industrial Ministries, while some central planning by industrial sectors was retained under the system of Regional Councils. In fact, throughout its history, Soviet planning has oscillated between industrial and regional planning principles, though it has usually and mainly been organized along industrial lines. The two different schemes of organization are illustrated in Figure 6–2.

In summary, under the Ministry system, we see that — on the basis of the Plan designed by the State Planning Commission — each Ministry in Moscow issued orders through its Chief Departments directly or indirectly (through intermediate bodies where necessary) to the enterprises in its industrial sector. Under the territorial system, the central government still issued general orders based on the Plan drawn up by the State Planning Commission; but now each Republic (aided by its own Planning Commission) had one or more Economic Councils issuing orders through *its* departments directly (or through intermediate bodies) to the enterprises in its region. Yet these charts only hint at the complex chains of command involved. Under the Ministry system, the importance of regionalization was recognized, not only in the existence of chief departments for different territories in most of the U.S.S.R. Ministries, but also in the creation of Ministries at the republican level to handle local and light industries in their republic. Under the territorial system, the need for central coordination was expressed not only in the continued power of the U.S.S.R. State Planning Commission to control as well as to plan in certain ways, but also in the rapid creation of certain functional committees at the center (for example, State Committees on Scientific Research, Labor and Wages, Trade) and some continued Ministries (for example, Agriculture, Communications, Civil Aviation).

Of course, as soon as the Regional Councils were established, they began to build local empires and to avoid cooperation with other regions (for reasons discussed below). Thus, a factory in industry A would now

Figure 6–2
Ministerial System and Territorial System

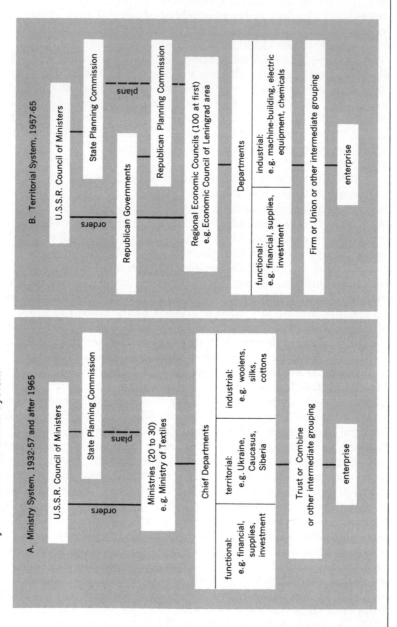

coordinate plans with a factory in industry B in the same region, but it would lose the advantages of contact with factories in its own industry (A) in other regions. Perhaps, the relatively frequent shifts back and forth from regional to industrial planning in the Soviet Union have at least served the useful purpose of breaking up rigid and isolated organizations, whether regional or ministerial. Of course, each major shift would also have the disadvantage of dislocating established information and communication channels.

Some of the disadvantages of the system of industrial Ministries may be noted. First, there was a paper barrier between industries, with each trying for priority in the Plan and self-sufficiency. The reason why Soviet economic units (whether Ministries or Regional Councils) try for self-sufficiency rather than cooperation is that the plan is very taut, so most commodities are in perennial short supply. The plan is taut and there is overfull employment because the frantic rush for industrial growth has in the past led to very ambitious high-pressure plans, which have forced enterprises to operate under great tension and have led to severe shortages and imbalances (as we shall see in Chapters 9 and 10). Where the U.S. problem is usually to find a market in which to sell one's goods, the Soviet enterprise has a virtually guaranteed market but has the opposite problem of finding the necessary supplies for production to meet demand. An order from another Ministry may not be fulfilled, but the Ministry knows it can often better ensure fulfillment of supply orders from one plant to another plant within its own jurisdiction.

Secondly, since the Ministries were all located in Moscow, the central bureaucrats knew little of the local situations. On the other side, it was hard for local plant managers to communicate all the way up the chain of command to Moscow (especially for minor but key needs, such as the right nuts and bolts).

It was claimed that the switch to Regional Councils in 1957 would solve all of these problems. It was further claimed that the new system would inspire more regional planning, more local coordination of plans and operations, and even mergers of nearby duplicate factories run previously by different Ministries. It was also thought that each region would concentrate on those things which it could produce at lower cost. In reality, however, each region tended toward self-sufficiency and production of all kinds of goods. This lowered transport costs, but resulted in the establishment of many small and inefficient enterprises in each line. In other words the 1957 reform did eliminate a great deal of cross-hauling, *but* it then led to regional autarky (or "going-it-alone") as a replacement for Ministerial autarky.

This was because the basic cause of autarky — taut and over-complicated planning — was not eliminated. Like the Ministries, the regions felt they must be fairly self-sufficient because of the poor and unreliable supply system. They believed they had much better control of supplies if the supplier was also in their regional jurisdiction. In addition to producing all kinds of items, each region (like the Ministries before them) also adopted the wasteful practice of keeping huge inventories of all conceivable items, just in case of future need.

In general, the change from Ministries in branches of industry to Regional Councils in territories brought out the vested local interests of each region, great difficulties of communication and coordination between them, and resultant inefficiencies in many nation-wide industrial branches. In the course of returning to the Ministry (branch of industry) system in 1965, Premier Kosygin argued: "The divergence from the branch principle has led to poorer efficiency in the management of the branches, to violations of the uniformity of technical policy, to scattering of competent personnel, and given rise to a multi-stage system of management."[4] Here, he emphasizes the additional problems of the lack of sufficient qualified personnel for each of the hundred-odd Regional Councils, and also the "multi-stage system of management." This multi-stage management refers to the fact that above the enterprise were an industrial department of the region, the Regional Council, and then the national coordinating body of the Regional Councils. Unfortunately, each of these bodies (but especially the Regional Councils) felt it its duty to give large volumes of direct and sometimes conflicting orders to the enterprise manager. In addition, the Central and Republic planning commissions issued their own orders and regulations, so the chain of command was both lengthy and not unified.

It is now quite easy for us to answer the question: was the system of Regional Councils more "decentralized" than the Ministry system of branches of industry? It is true that a few bureaucrats moved out of Moscow to distant localities, but the Regional Councils were merely a different channel for central direction of the firm. In fact, the Regional Councils probably exercised more power of interference over the enterprise than the far-away Ministries ever did. The firm manager still had little or no say in planning, and even more detailed supervision. The plan was still drawn up mostly in Moscow, and the Central Planning Commission took on ever more administrative functions of the old Ministries (especially as the Regional Councils showed tendencies to act for local vested interests). Thus, the regional system may have involved some small measure of administrative decentralization, but none in either the top decision-making of planning or in the freedom of the plant managers.

The Organization of the Planning Mechanism

As we have seen, enterprise managers receive their production directives from a yearly plan. Plans are elaborated in industry for output, inputs, costs, credits, wages, and other indexes. The crucial plan, however, is the plan for materials supply. Once a set of output targets is settled upon, the supply plan must assure the availability and distri-

---

[4] Kosygin at Central Committee meeting, "New Methods of Economic Management in the U.S.S.R." (Moscow: Novosti Press Agency Publishing House, 1965), pp. 51–52.

bution of material supplies required to fulfill all output targets. This is done by the central allocation of the means of production, including basic raw materials as well as machinery.

The central planning organ of the U.S.S.R. is the State Planning Commission. It puts into detailed form both the output and the supply plan, and bears the responsibility for consistency and balance of the two. The State Planning Commission, of course, deals with only the most important commodities, those that must be centrally allocated. This is no small matter, however, involving in most years of the 1950's and 1960's from 1,000 to 2,000 commodities. Other commodities are left to the responsibility of the subordinate planning organs. How is the planning of the main outputs and supplies carried out? The State Planning Commission works very closely with other levels of the hierarchy to formulate a feasible plan. Below the State Planning Commission are the intermediary planning bodies which can be organized along either ministerial (industrial) or regional (territorial) lines. These organs have corresponding subordinate units called chief administrative agen-

Figure 6–3
The Planning Process

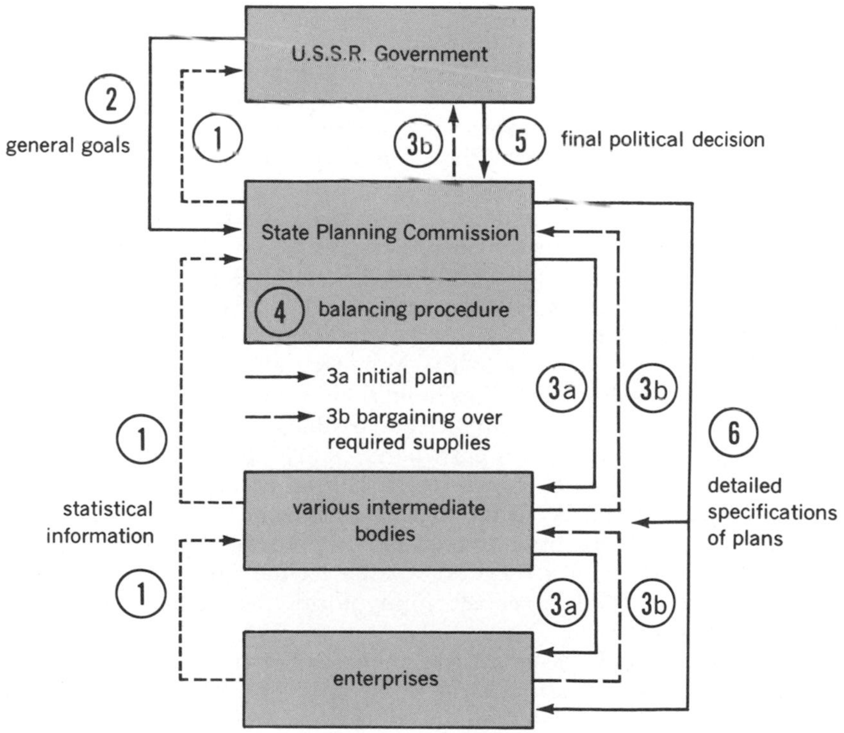

cies. These agencies deal directly with the enterprises which constitute the lowest level. The planning mechanism occurs in six overlapping stages (Figure 6–3). The six planning stages usually distinguished (the number is arbitrary, depending on where we make the separations) are illustrated in Figure 6–3 above; they are discussed in detail in the following paragraphs.

First, both the State Planning Commission and the planning departments of the lower units begin to draw up tentative plans for the next year's (the planned year) production. The State Planning Commission starts first with a statistical analysis of the base year performance in order to uncover failures, bottlenecks, and other causes of supply deficiencies as well as new sources or increases in other material supplies. This process of gathering statistics on past performance from the enterprises requires most of the period from January to June of each year.

In the second stage (June and July) the political leaders set general goals to be specified by the planners. Thus, the Council of Ministers decides upon a set of aggregate output targets. These reflect political and economic policy decisions regarding the growth rate of certain priority industries, and the division of national income between consumption and investment. Using the data collected on the base year (the previous year), the State Planning Commission then calculates a set of "control figures." This is a first estimate of consistent output and supply requirements of each industry, dependent on the overall capacity of the economy.

Meanwhile, the lower organs and enterprises are estimating their input and output requirements based on their performance in the previous year. However, they must await the issuance of the control figures before they can complete even their tentative plans. The control figures serve as guideposts to the industry as to what kind of performance and targets are expected by the central authority (and the industry then devises more detailed targets for the enterprises).

The third stage then follows (from August to October) with a series of bargaining processes between the various levels of the planning mechanism: the firm versus its chief administrative agency, the agency versus Ministry or region, and the Ministry or region versus the State Planning Commission. Each lower level wants as low an output target and as great an amount of supplies as possible, so it can be sure to overfulfill its planned target and earn bonuses. The firm completes its first draft of supply estimates based on the notion of input norms, or technological coefficients. A technological coefficient describes as a ratio how much of a given input is required to produce one unit of a given output. It is essentially a reflection of the technological development of a given industry. The lower the input norm, the higher the advancement of technology.

The written supply requests are then sent by the enterprise up the hierarchy to its chief administrative agency. The agency's plan is just a collation of those of the firms it supervises. The agency, however, is well aware of the pressures from above stressing maximum output and economy in supplies. It is also aware of the tendency for the firm to "pad" its supply requests in order to have a slack or reserve in case of supply failures — or, if possible, in order to use these extra supplies to overfulfill the output plan and thus receive a bonus. The chief administrative agency, however, must also propose a plan for itself that it will have to fulfill; so it will simply add padding at this point. Only much later, *after* the Plan is made into law, will its interests diverge somewhat from its enterprises. *Then,* if it can cut down the supplies going to any one of its enterprises, it can save these extra supplies for emergencies that might occur in one of its enterprises elsewhere. After the Plan is approved by higher authorities, the agency may try to reduce the input norm of the enterprise by claiming that the enterprise can produce at a more efficient level, that is, that it can produce the same amount of goods with fewer material inputs.

When the chief agencies have finished their plan statements, these proposed plans are sent up again to either the Ministry or the regional planning body. Bargaining again occurs, as it is obvious that too low an output plan or too large a request for supplies will be rejected by the State Planning Commission (though again, a Ministry might acquiesce to padded plans until *after* the Plan has been legally approved). Finally, the aggregated output plans and the supply requirements arrive at the State Planning Commission from the Ministry or republic.

The fourth stage of Soviet planning (in October and November) is the attempt of the State Planning Commission to balance nearly all of the conflicting estimates of possible outputs and required inputs. It may be recalled here that each enterprise, agency, and Ministry has now submitted its output plan and the amounts of various inputs it will need to achieve the plan. It would be a coincidence, indeed, if there were an exact correspondence between the total proposed output of any product and the total proposed requests for the product by enterprises using it as an input. If the total demand for some input goes beyond its planned output, something must be changed. Theoretically, the whole plan should be recalculated. In practice, an attempt is made to see if more of that one product could be somehow produced with the existing capacity in that industry. Or else, an attempt is made to lower the "required" supplies of that product (1) by lowering the "needs" of supplies to other industries by making them more efficient, that is, by producing with less of that input per unit of production; or (2) even by finding hidden reserves of that input in the industries using it; or (3) by using the centrally kept reserves of some important inputs; or (4) by importing the product. Furthermore, the fact that each lower level has asked for more than the necessary supplies (and keeps emergency inventories) builds a certain amount of flexibility into the planned balance. As a more unwelcome (but often used) alternative, the planners may reduce the output targets of the lowest priority industries, so the scarce inputs can go to the high priority industries.

If, on the other hand, the planners attempt to increase the output of the scarce input, this has many repercussions which must be taken into consideration. For example, more steel requires more coal, which in turn requires more steel and more machinery and more labor, and so forth, reverberating back and forth in many, many sectors of the economy. As mentioned above, another resort might be an increase of imports, if there is enough credit or enough exports to pay for the additional imports. In Chapter 10, where we examine such balance problems systematically, we shall see that it makes a great difference to the planners whether they must choose an alternative with many repercussions throughout the plan or whether they are able to use a means — like imports on credit — that has no effect on other current plans.

Stage five of Soviet planning occurs in about November and December. The complete plan is submitted to the political leaders in the Council of Ministers and the Politbureau, who view it from a national perspective. Undoubtedly, some jockeying occurs at this top level as individuals attempt to secure more resources for their own pet projects.

Finally, in stage six (in December and January) the aggregate goals of each industry or region, which have now been adopted at the highest levels, are further specified down to lower levels. Eventually, as a rule after the year begins, the individual enterprises receive their individual plans.

Obviously, there are problems with this system, even assuming fairly perfect theoretical planning techniques. First, if the planners are too optimistic about what can be produced with given inputs, the balances achieved will be quite unreal. Whenever an enterprise is given — by mistake — an increase in output with no additional inputs or with insufficient additional inputs, it has an impossible task to perform. Second, if the annual plan comes to the enterprise any time after the beginning of the year, this lateness will obviously cause a certain amount of misguided work. Third, even the finished plan is much too aggregative to specify most of the particular tasks of the enterprise.

In the agricultural sector planning is somewhat different, less precise, and less direct. It is less precise because nature is so unpredictable and because so many individual units are involved. It is less direct and more incomplete because most farming units are not government enterprises, but are private or cooperative. Private farming cannot be directed at all (except by taxation to some degree). Until the recent reforms, the cooperative or collective farms were given compulsory minimum delivery quotas to sell to the government, but were never assigned fixed total targets. Thus, between the fickleness of nature and the lower degree of central control, it is not surprising that the aggregate agricultural plan is seldom close to the actual agricultural output.

In addition to the plan for current production, there is a plan for investment or expansion of production. Once the State Planning Commission has decided to expand production in a certain industry, a Project Committee is formed of engineers and experts in the area in order to make the technical specifications. They must decide the location and scale of new factories, the exact kind of new machinery, and in general the whole range of technology. These issues are discussed in detail in Chapter 12.

The Price System

We may classify the roles which Soviet prices play into three categories: (1) control and evaluation, (2) allocation, and (3) income distribution.[5] First, to the degree that central planners cannot specify all inputs and outputs in complete detail, the decisions of managers are influenced by the prices set on their inputs and outputs. The manager's performance is evaluated basically in physical terms, but prices are needed to supply a common denominator for the different outputs produced as well as the different inputs utilized. Furthermore, any kind of economic or cost accounting (or *khozraschet*) is impossible without prices. Even with distorted prices, cost accounting serves several important functions. One of these functions is to make possible "economizing" of scarce resources by the firm. Another is that it provides a means of checking or evaluating the firm's performance by higher authorities — by stating profits or losses, at least relative to planned profit or losses.

Second, the central planners themselves are influenced by the prices of different substitutes in choosing among technological variants, and in allocating investment among different possible investment projects. Prices are used as the common denominator among different products in calculating various aggregate balances, such as the balance between the supply and demand for consumer goods. Central planners also use differential wage levels to allocate labor to different areas, industries, and skills. Finally, central planners may use prices to influence farmers, both in the collectives and on the private plots, to allocate their resources to certain agricultural outputs rather than to others.

The third function of prices is to play a role in the distribution of income among workers, which distribution still follows the socialist principle of payment according to work accomplished. This implies unequal payments, which provides an incentive for improved and more intensive work or for changing jobs. A man's place in the income distribution is determined, then, by the structure of prices of the goods which he buys, his money wage, his income tax, and transfer payments made to him by the government.

We may distinguish four important classes of prices which carry out the functions of the price system discussed above. These are: (1) retail prices to consumers, (2) prices of labor services (wage rates), (3) wholesale prices to industrial enterprises, and (4) prices of agricultural goods. Here, we only wish to introduce and describe the institutional arrangements in each area. The planning problems connected with prices will be discussed in detail in later chapters.

Retail Prices of Consumer Goods. From the viewpoint of the Soviet consumer, the Soviet economy appears to be quite similar to other

[5] In this classification and in the rest of the discussion, we are following Morris Bornstein, "Soviet Price Theory and Policy," in U.S. Congress Joint Economic Committee, *New Directions in the Soviet Economy* (Washington, D.C.: United States Government Printing Office, 1966), Part I, pp. 63–94.

modern economies. First, he receives a money income. Second, he may spend that income in any proportions he likes on whatever goods he desires to buy. A wide variety of goods is available — though the government does not allow the production or sale of goods like narcotics, sex magazines, or war "comic books" (so they are not among consumer alternatives).

One obvious difference from the U.S. economy is the much larger proportion of goods available at zero price, for example, public health and all education. A second obvious difference from any private enterprise economy is the lack of any possibility of private investment; the individual may not buy a share in a factory or any other enterprise. He may save his money by buying government bonds, by depositing it at interest in the State Bank, by hoarding cash, or by buying life insurance, but he may not invest for profit in a private enterprise. Furthermore, most national Soviet saving is "forced" in the sense that a part of the national income is taken by taxation into the government budget and is used for government investment. Thus, unlike a private enterprise economy, the government — not the private investor — makes all investments and decides the ratio between consumption and investment.

A very profound difference lies in the fact that Soviet consumers have freedom of choice among goods, but no choice among sellers because most goods are sold only by the government monopoly. Consumers do not have "consumer sovereignty" if that is defined as the determination of the output mixture by consumer preferences. If Soviet consumers change their preferences and want other goods not currently being produced, the government monopoly can decide not to change outputs correspondingly. Instead, the government may simply adjust the *prices* of these goods so that consumer demand is brought back into balance with supply at the new prices (this question is considered further in Chapter 10).

Prices of Labor Services (Wage Rates). Workers for the most part are also free to choose among jobs at prevailing wage rates. They face the same government monopoly, though, in the industrial labor market. They must take some job offered at the going wage level if they wish to work. Now suppose too few workers wish to take a particular job (in a geographical area, an industry, or a skill) compared with the labor needed to fill the output target of that industry. In such a case, the output target is not likely to be changed; more probably, the *relative* wage for the job is raised.

The relative structure of wages will thus reflect — along with other determining factors — workers' preferences in the sense that higher wages must be offered to attract workers to more difficult or more skilled jobs. The main factors in Soviet wage determination — each of which is given a certain weight in each industry — include: skill required, disutility or unpleasantness of job, priority of the industry, and locational advantages or disadvantages. The wage rates or bonuses are often used to adjust the supply of workers to the planned demand for labor. The physical plan for output and labor in each area, however, remains as unaffected by changes in rates as it is by changes in retail prices. A detailed discussion of wage determination and of labor's incentives to work in the Soviet Union, as well as the role of Soviet trade unions, will be undertaken in Chapter 7.

Industrial Wholesale Prices. The prices of industrial goods, whether consumer goods passing through wholesalers to retail trade or producer goods for industry itself, are fixed by administrative decree. They are supposed to include the planned average cost of production plus a margin of profit. These prices are vital guideposts to two sorts of people: planners and managers.

Most Soviet planning is done in physical terms. Yet prices certainly play an important role, or should play such a role if the intention is to plan in an optimal manner. Indeed, the Soviet planners do practice financial planning as well as physical — this is to insure that money flows will be in balance and consistent with the physical flows. For example, an enterprise is allotted a certain amount of funds to buy supplies, even though it may also have to present a direct allocation order to the supplier. More important, in the aggregate the total amount of monetary capital must be allocated to various new investments, and it would be very difficult to handle these amounts (and other aggregations of things) without using some kind of money prices.

There are also some kinds of physical decision-making that cannot be done at all meaningfully without the kind of knowledge reflected in prices and costs. For example, is it cheaper to use coal or oil for railroad engine fuel? To make this evaluation one should know the relative prices (or costs to society) of coal and oil and of the kinds of engines that use them. It should be noted, however, that Soviet prices till now have been such poor measures of the real costs of most commodities that many efficient allocational decisions have been impossible to make. This problem is discussed in detail in Chapter 12.

Soviet industrial price policy, however, is important not only to planners but to managers. Even in a highly centralized economy, many technological decisions must be left to each enterprise manager. For example, if he is able to obtain either steel or aluminum for his production, and if one of them is cheaper (but perhaps less useful), should he substitute that one throughout? Or, to the extent that he is judged by the profits he makes, obviously all his prices and costs must enter into his calculations. These problems of managerial performance are further considered in Chapter 7.

Agricultural Prices. Prices in Soviet agriculture are handled quite differently than in industry. Most similar to the industrial sector are the state farms, which are supposed to be run as factories in the fields. Their prices and outputs are set by the central planners. Even the state farms cannot be so closely planned, however, as is industry. The most important additional problems are: (1) too many extremely different conditions, and (2) unpredictably changeable weather conditions.

The collective farms are still less directly controlled. True, until recently they had to contribute to the government a given quota of produce at low, fixed prices. In fact, we have noted that these procurement prices were set so low that the procurements constituted a tax on the collectives. Beyond these quotas, however, the collectives are free to sell their produce at any price they can get either to the government or to any individual who wishes to buy.

During the Stalin era the procurement prices were so low and the quotas so large that these compulsory deliveries constituted a heavy burden on the farm population. In fact, the terms of trade between the procurement prices that farmers were paid and the prices that farmers had to pay for machinery and consumer goods steadily worsened. From 1929 to 1953 the procurement prices of grain did not change; livestock prices did not rise at all from 1929 to 1940, and only doubled from 1940 to 1953. At the same time, from 1940 to 1953 retail prices of basic industrial goods doubled, and retail prices of consumer goods in government stores rose by 74 percent. There was naturally little incentive for producing collective farm goods when farmers reaped such small gains. Khrushchev began to change the situation. He not only continued to lower retail industrial prices, but also raised farm procurement prices in 1953, 1958, 1962, 1963, and 1965.[6] Khrushchev's successors took the more radical step of lowering or abolishing most procurement quotas.

There is another, higher set of prices for the goods that individuals produce by their own labor on small, private farm plots (which explains their tendency to work harder on these plots than on the collectives). The vegetables and livestock from these plots are sold in the cities at any price the seller can get and the buyer will give. Thus, some part of collective farm produce, and all of the surplus private produce of individual farmers, are sold at freely fluctuating prices set solely by supply and demand. These markets have usually soaked up, at very high prices, a large proportion of the excess demand for food.

We have also mentioned before that agricultural labor is paid by an elaborate system of "workdays." These "workdays" count not only the number of days worked but also the skill required in the task. Thus, for the same eight-hour day, a skilled agronomist might be credited with three workdays while a milkmaid might only be credited with half a workday. These and other problems of agricultural wages, prices, and incentives are discussed in detail in Chapter 7.

SELECTED REFERENCES

1. Nove, Alec, *The Soviet Economy* (New York: Frederick A. Praeger, 1961). The first four chapters of Nove's book all discuss the "Structure" of the Soviet economy.

2. Levine, Herbert S., "The Centralized Planning of Supply in Soviet Industry," in U.S. Congress Joint Economic Committee, *Comparisons of the United States and Soviet Economies*, Part I (Washington, D.C.: U.S.

[6] Bornstein, *op. cit.*, pp. 77–78.

Government Printing Office, 1959), pp. 151–176. Contains the best description of the Soviet planning of the allocation of material inputs.

3. Bornstein, Morris, "The Soviet Price System," *American Economic Review*, Vol. 52 (March, 1962), pp. 64–103. Also Morris Bornstein, "Soviet Price Theory and Policy," in U.S. Congress Joint Economic Committee, *New Directions in the Soviet Economy*, Part I (Washington: U.S. Government Printing Office, 1966), pp. 63–98. Gives the most complete description of the Soviet price structure.

4. Hoeffding, Oleg, "The Soviet Industrial Reorganization of 1957," *American Economic Review*, Vol. 49 (May, 1959), pp. 65–77. A good description of the switch from Ministry to Regional Council.

7

ECONOMIC BEHAVIOR UNDER CENTRAL PLANNING

If a technically perfect plan were devised for the Soviet economy, it would certainly not end all of the real problems. Since people are not robots, the performance or execution of the plan depends on the economic conduct of individuals. In order to provide a more realistic background to planning problems, the behavior of managers, of industrial workers, and of farm workers is discussed on the following pages.

A. Managerial Motivations[1]

Soviet managers face somewhat different problems than U.S. managers. Their training and background, therefore, are ordinarily somewhat different from that of their U.S. counterparts. First, a much higher percentage of Soviet managers have college degrees. One reason for this is the traditional prestige accorded all "intellectuals" by European culture. More important is the fact that the Soviet manager, as we shall see, is far more likely to be directly involved with technological problems than is the U.S. manager. From the individual's viewpoint, it is still possible in the United States to achieve a high income position, especially in a family business, without much formal education. In the Soviet Union, on the contrary, a college education is the decisive and almost sole key to high income opportunities, a fact which leads to an

[1] Much of the fact and discussion in this whole section is most conveniently found in David Granick, *The Red Executive* (New York: Doubleday and Co., 1961).

148

even fiercer competition for that education in the U.S.S.R. than in the United States.

Second, the typical Soviet manager has been educated in engineering, and has risen to the top through the production departments of his enterprise. The typical U.S. manager, on the other hand, has majored in business administration, and has worked his way to the top through personnel work, marketing and distribution, or the financial side of business. The reasons for these differences are not hard to find. In the United States, a major task of enterprise is to increase, by application of marketing techniques, the frequently limited demand for its product in the face of stiff competition. Even enterprise research in the United States is directed especially toward new products designed to create "needs" and stimulate sales. Thus a U.S. manager must above all know marketing techniques, what will sell, how to pick salesmen and advertisers, and how to get financial backing for his endeavors.

The Soviet manager's problem is exactly the opposite. He is ordered (at least until recently) to produce as much as possible above the Plan (and even the planned amount is always based on an extremely high estimate of his supply capabilities). And because of taut planning, everything he produces he can sell. The American businessman operates in a "buyers' market"; his Soviet counterpart in a "sellers' market." But supplies are restricted and difficult for the Soviet manager to obtain. Since his primary concern is to produce the most output from limited supplies, an engineering background is vital.

We may also mention one closely related group of differences in the manager's background and motivation, springing in part from these different needs of the two economies. The highest money and prestige in the United States go to the occupations of "business," law, or medicine. Engineering is not as high, and until recently science and higher education have been much further down the scale. In the Soviet Union, on the contrary, with the exception of the artists, the highest rewards go to scientists in research institutes or universities. The next highest rewards go to engineers in heavy industry. All other Soviet occupations, including positions in light industry or distribution and in law or medicine, lag far behind in either money or prestige (medicine commands high prestige but little money).

Finally, we may note that Soviet managers tend to be younger than U.S. managers, a characteristic necessarily shared with all very rapidly developing economies. We may also note that the Soviet pool of managerial talent is restricted (relative to the United States) by the much larger percentage of the population still in the culturally and educationally more backward rural areas. On the other hand, the Soviet pool of managerial talent is enlarged (relative to the United States) by the comparative lack of discrimination against national or racial minorities or against women.

Rewards and Punishments. It pays to be a successful Soviet manager. The manager's salary averages at least five to six times that of the average worker. In addition, he has certain otherwise unobtainable privileges. He may be assigned a private chauffered auto in a society which in the past has produced almost no autos for private use. He may also rate a larger apartment or house in a society that is desperately short of housing space, although this is by no means universally true. Promotion may open up very inviting political heights; Premier Kosygin, for example, worked his way up partly on the economic ladder.

If he fulfills or overfulfills his plan each month, he receives an additional large bonus. These bonuses generally run from 25 percent to 50 percent of the manager's salary. (One detailed study showed managers' bonuses in the high-priority iron and steel industry averaging 51.4 percent of their basic income, although bonuses in the low-priority food industry were only 21 percent.)[2] It also appears that the successful managers can pass on many educational advantages to their children. These advantages are *not* financial for the most part, since Soviet schooling is free and universally open to the talented. In fact only about 20 percent of Soviet students need any parental assistance to stay in school. But the fact that the family has the resources to maintain a high cultural level will be very important in supplying the initial background and motivation to get through school.

If some of these rewards to the successful manager are speculative and hard to measure, it is clear that the unsuccessful manager will lose bonuses and ultimately lose his job or be demoted to a less important operation. At an earlier period, a failure was also liable to be interpreted as criminal negligence or even sabotage to the government. Today, the Soviets generally consider the purely social and economic rewards and punishments to be sufficient and do not resort to criminal penalties.

Evasions of the Plan. Since the manager is under great pressure to produce, he resorts to many evasions. We may note that his performance is judged by several criteria, including wage and raw material costs per unit and other indicators of productivity and efficiency. The main success indicator until the recent reforms (see Chapter 13), however, and the one he strives above all to achieve, is simply the value of the gross output produced. If he does not achieve the planned value of output, he receives no bonus at all. If, however, he exactly meets the planned target, he may receive as much as a full 40 percent bonus, though the average bonus is somewhat less. For each 1 percent overfulfillment of the Plan, managers in high-priority industries receive an additional 4 to 6 percent bonus.

The Soviet manager brushes aside bureaucratic regulations and controls when they conflict with the achievement of output goals. To a great extent, the manager evades specific regulations only in order to meet his Plan. This may or may not be to the national benefit. For example, the manager sometimes merely gets around red tape in order to obtain ma-

---

[2] See J. Berliner, "Managerial Incentives and Decision-making," in M. Bornstein and D. Fusfeld, *The Soviet Economy* (Homewood, Ill.: Richard Irwin, Inc., 1966 ed.), p. 116.

terials that should have been his anyway. On other occasions, however, he may obtain materials illegally that could be better used by a higher-priority enterprise. Unfortunately, some of the manager's devices, like lowering quality in order to produce greater output, yield a bonus for an *apparent* Plan fulfillment which constitutes, in fact, an antisocial act. This type of antisocial behavior is not dissimilar to the well-known evasions of the corporate income tax or anti-trust laws by managers of U.S. corporations. The specific practices of Soviet managers[3] are as follows:

(1) FALSE REPORTS. Obviously, if his production for the month would just miss 100 percent of the planned target by a hair's breadth, the manager may report achievement of his planned target by inclusion of waste or unfinished goods in order to get his bonus. Or, rather than complete falsification, he may simply shift his report of some production from a very high month to a low one. Beyond very, very minor juggling of figures, however, apparently few managers actually do much outright falsification. For one thing, the manager turns in a very large volume of related reports, which are examined for internal consistency by the bank auditors or by his superiors.

More important, there are many different channels of control over the manager; and these channels are independent enough so that collusion by all agents is very difficult. There is first of all the superior agency that controls the enterprise, whether it is under an industrial Ministry or a Regional Council. But these superior organs also may have a material interest in exaggerating the production reports from "their" enterprises, so other lines of control must also exist.

The Communist Party has cells in each enterprise, and these have certain rights to inspect and suggest improvements on enterprise projects. A third line of control is through the trade unions, one of whose functions is the stimulation of production. In fact, during the early 1920's when many managers were still hostile to the regime, the local Communist Party secretary and the local trade union secretary were often given equal powers in the enterprise with the manager. Today, when most managers are themselves Party members, the manager has sole power and responsibility for his enterprise, but the Party and unions do have the right and duty to check on his production reports.

A fourth line of control is through the State Bank, in which every enterprise keeps accounts, and which examines all enterprise transactions to ensure their conformity with the Plan. At times, there have also been special Ministries of State Control, whose sole function was to check on the legality of enterprise actions. In addition, a sixth line of control reaches down from the Central Statistical Agency. Closely related are the activities of the Soviet accountant, who is responsible for the accuracy of his figures *not* to the manager, but to higher authorities.

We should, however, mention that most of these different people —

[3] One especially good article on these practices is: Harry G. Schaffer, "Ills and Remedies," *Problems of Communism* (May–June, 1963), pp. 27–32. Some other articles are in the Selected References to this chapter and Chapter 13.

such as the factory manager, the local Communist Party secretary, the local trade union head, and even the branch Bank manager — are often very good friends, who try not to "disturb" each other. The Soviet press often mentions examples of this phenomenon, called "familyness" or, less politely, collusion. Infractions are usually punished only when they are really gross, or when they specifically run against someone else (or some other "family") and are brought to the attention of authorities who are above all the local checkers.

(2) EASIER PLANS. Let us suppose that the controllers have done their work, and their reports are accurate. The manager still has important devices for improving his apparent performance. For one thing, the central planners cannot have perfect knowledge of plant capacities. Therefore, the manager himself must play an important role in formulating the Plan. He naturally bargains for a lower output target and a higher amount of required supplies. In this way, output targets are more easily overfulfilled.

(3) POORER QUALITY. If a plan cannot be met in the necessary quantities by producing what is supposed to be produced, it can often be fulfilled by producing a poorer quality of good. Some Soviet consumer goods have been of notoriously poor quality.

(4) FEWER STYLES. It is much easier to produce a large amount of one homogeneous good than it is to produce small quantities of many different goods. Managers therefore have an incentive to produce all of one type or style of good, rather than a variety, although the latter might lead to more consumer satisfaction.

(5) EASIEST MIXTURE. In fact, the type or style on which production is concentrated may be chosen, not on the basis of usefulness to the economy, but because it is the cheapest method of achieving the output goal. As a result, if his performance is to be judged by the *weight* or number of tons he produces of a good, the Soviet manager may produce only very heavy goods — for example, very large nails of the heaviest possible metal. Thus, a famous Soviet cartoon shows a single large nail hanging the length of a factory, and a happy manager saying, "We met our monthly quota." If he is judged simply by the *number* of units, then the tendency is to produce millions of very tiny nails. If, however, the criterion of performance is *volume* of goods produced (in so many cubic feet), then the temptation is to produce very large and light products, for example, girders for bridges that are mostly hollow inside — or large nails of the lightest, cheapest metals.

(6) EXTRA SUPPLIES. It is a well-known fact that managers keep on their payroll men whose only function is to expedite the flow of supplies, or to find new sources of supply outside of the planned sources. These men are known as "pushers," though they have some other title on the official payroll. They often enjoy pleasant lives on expense accounts, wining and dining officials of other firms and of various higher organizations who may be able to furnish scarce supplies (by barter or bribery). They are the counterpart of the American "expe-

diters" of World War II, who hung around Washington trying to get a ration of scarce materials for their firms.

(7) HIDDEN RESERVES. A wise Soviet manager piles up inventories of any goods he can get his hands on, regardless of whether he happens to need them or not at the moment. When his output target is raised, he can use these extra reserves — when he is unable to procure more supplies legally. In this way a large amount of resources may be wasted, frozen in an unproductive storage stage of the productive process.

(8) EXTRA LABOR. The manager has a plan for labor and for the total amount of wages he can spend. Overspending on wages, however, is usually very lightly punished if at all, whereas meeting the output target washes him clean of all crimes. Therefore, there has been a strong tendency for Soviet managers to use labor extravagantly, and to spend more than their allotted wage funds — when they can get the funds. Present regulations make it difficult to convert enterprise deposits to cash for overspending on payroll unless this involves overfulfilling the output plan (in which case it is relatively easy).

(9) HIGH-PRICED RAW MATERIALS. A U.S. manager will try to use the cheapest possible raw materials to keep down costs. A Soviet manager, however, is penalized very little for high costs, and given a great reward for overfulfilling his output target; thus, he has no reason not to use high-priced raw materials. Moreover, he is judged not by the value added in the enterprise, but by the gross value of the product *including* the value of the raw materials which were merely bought from other firms. Therefore, the higher the price of the raw materials he buys, the higher the value of his gross output, and the greater his own reward. Naturally, Soviet managers have an incentive to buy the more expensive raw materials for their enterprise to use.

(10) INTENSE DRIVES. Since bonuses for managers (and often for workers) are usually on a monthly basis, the end of each month is a time of feverish activity (called "storming") around the enterprise. Of course, the result is that people tend to relax again at the beginning of each month. This off-and-on pressure does not fit the needs of the modern, complex, and interrelated production process.

(11) RESISTANCE TO INNOVATIONS. The Soviet manager frequently does not react with enthusiasm to innovations that *may* increase his productive capacity or lower costs. In the first place, innovations are risky because they may actually lower output for some months while the transition is being made to new machinery. Managers seldom take the long-run view because they are often switched to other jobs on fairly short notice. The idea of these frequent changes in positions is to prevent corruption and collusion (or "familyness") from developing, but it also means that managers focus their attention on immediate production gains and are not willing to gamble on higher bonuses from greatly increased production at some future date.

In the second place, the manager knows that if the innovation does succeed in greatly increasing his capacity to produce, his production targets will also be increased, so he himself may gain nothing. If the plan is overfulfilled by a large margin, targets are apt to be raised in the same proportion. So a manager is likely to try for a steady 103 percent or 105 percent overfulfillment, but not more.

A Tentative Conclusion. The tendencies described do exist, but they should certainly not be taken to mean that Soviet managers are completely inefficient. The Soviet economy *has* produced higher peacetime growth than the U.S. economy despite these inefficiencies. This dysfunctional behavior does imply that the growth achieved was at greater cost and sacrifice than necessary, or that growth could have been faster with the same amount of effort. The fact that some degree of inefficiency does exist in the old system of central planning is the driving force behind the recent decentralization reforms and the continued fight for more reforms (see Chapter 13).

Many of these evasions of the Plan result in a more flexible functioning of the economy than the official Plan would allow. Planners cannot specify correctly all details because they do not have (1) enough information, (2) enough computer time, or (3) enough planners. Moreover, the planners have conflicting targets and some very distorted prices. Therefore, the managers do somehow carry through the job by various semilegal means, disregarding impossible tasks, and performing others through an informal exchange among enterprises — an exchange not included in the planned allocation of supplies. Still, some managerial infractions, such as using poor quality or improper assortment to achieve most cheaply a large quantity of output, are certainly self-seeking and antisocial in effect. On the whole, however, managers have made the system "work," and work better under imperfect planning than if managers mechanically carried out the plans.

B. Workers' Incentives

Devising an effective incentive system for labor has been part of the central government's responsibilities. Economic and political planners together shaped and changed incentive systems of the past and framed the present one. The result remains an interesting utilization of material rewards (differential wages), non-material rewards (such as social prestige), and penalties. Although basic principles of the wage system emanate from the highest level of Soviet political leadership, actual specification and control of wage rates are assigned to several planning agencies, the most directly concerned being the Ministry of Finance and the State Committee on Labor and Wages (along with the trade unions, as we shall see).

Western writers observe that the wage rates are set in practice to serve two functions. The first is to satisfy the accepted socialist principle of pay according to the quantity and quality of work. The second, a more pragmatic task, is to direct manpower to industries and geographic areas of highest national importance, that is, to distribute labor according to the demand for it. Of course, these two principles need not conflict since a high demand for labor means a high valuation of work done in that area.

Planning and controlling wage levels has been a complex task. Pay for some occupations, such as those for administrative, managerial, and professional personnel, can be prescribed in detailed regulations and can easily be enforced. The earnings of the majority of factory workers, state-farmers, and shop assistants, however, had been formulated on a piecework basis before the recent wage reforms, and thus were more complicated to calculate. The government provides for the categorization of all jobs, and about 2,000 were distinguished in 1965. Furthermore, each job is divided into a variety of grades, with a basic wage rate set for grade one, and coefficients based on this wage determining the pay of each higher grade. Each industry is then given its particular qualifications per grade in an authorized manual.

Planning the Allocation of Labor. Labor has been allocated to different jobs in the Soviet Union by a combination of legal force, social pressure, and market influences. We shall see that, although force played a role during much of the Stalinist period, today the predominant role is played by the market. In theory, the Soviets still attack capitalism for buying the worker's time as a "commodity." By contrast, they claim that the Soviet labor supply is "planned," and not affected by market forces. Yet they also speak of the wage differential as a basic tool to achieve the planned allocation — which in effect lets in the labor market by the back door.

In reality, the central planners can only plan the *demand* for labor needed for the planned output. This they do by setting the maximum number of workers each enterprise may employ and also the top limit on how much each enterprise may spend for wages. On the *supply* side, however, the planners cannot simply allocate labor as they can allocate supplies of raw materials. The Soviet citizen has the right to choose freely any field and any place in which to obtain training and in which to work. Only by determining how many people can get trained in different fields and occupations do the Soviet planners attempt to control aggregate supply. Aside from wartime, the exceptions to this freedom of movement have been minimal. Even in Stalin's day they consisted mainly of (1) the requirement for students to work during the first three years after college at an assigned job, (2) the draft of large numbers of rural youth for industrial training followed by a compulsory assigned job for a few years, and (3) penalties for excessive absenteeism or excessive tardiness. Of course, this does not include Stalin's treatment of political prisoners in forced labor camps under terrible conditions.

At present, planners can influence the existing labor supply only by changes in wage differentials (or in the long run by changes in training and education). In 1959 the levels of average wages in industries ranged from 182.7 percent of the all-industry average in the coal industry to only 65.8 percent in the sewing industry, though there has been in recent years a trend toward equalization of industrial differentials. The full range of wages is far greater than these average industrial figures show, however, because there are additional wage differentials according to location, according to danger or unpleasantness, and certainly according to skill or occupation within the industry. Bonuses also tend to widen the range of wage distribution. Finally, the planners can and do influence the potential labor supply by paying higher subsidies to students in certain fields.

To make matters more difficult for the planners, their market power is lessened by over-full employment or shortage of labor. Workers can usually find jobs of some sort where they please, even though planners would like to entice them to higher-priority areas. In fact, there have always been desperate needs — chronically unfilled — for some kinds of workers in some places, even though there were also unneeded surpluses of other kinds of workers in less important places.

The wage differentials not only attempt to influence the supply of labor (1) by industry or occupation, they are also differentiated (2) by the living conditions of different regions, (3) by the necessary training or skill, and (4) by the danger or unpleasantness involved in the job grade. In each industry a wage rate is set for the lowest grade worker, with higher rates for each higher grade, and with additional higher rates for particular regions. The most important wage decisions are made at the very highest levels, in the Council of Ministers. Most ordinary wage rates are set — as we have noted — by the State Committee on Labor and Wages, in consultation with the Ministry of Finance on the aggregate amount, and in consultation with the Central Council of Trade Unions on the differential rates.

Education provides the main production line for the training of workers at all levels of skills, and the Soviets try to plan their educational system so that it will produce the needed workers. Eight years of elementary school are now required, and the majority of students now continue with two more years of high school. Tuition fees for higher education were abolished in 1956; but in 1958 Khrushchev initiated a system whereby all potential students had to work part-time during their elementary and high school years, and then full time for two years before they could attempt to enter college or an institute. It may be noted that the funneling of many students into industry helped alleviate a severe labor shortage in the late 1950's and early 1960's. Although these young workers were supposed to continue part-time study, it was found that the time lost from studies — especially the two-year lapse — seriously hindered their preparation for advanced study. In 1964, consequently, hours of work were lessened during the first ten years of school, and a large number of the best students were allowed to go directly to the University.

The more general aspects of education as an aid to growth are discussed in Chapter 9 — including the attempt to attract students to various fields in the proportions needed by the society. Here it is only necessary to comment on the direct labor control of graduating students. Each graduate presumably must spend three years at the first job to which he or she is assigned. However, there are qualifications to this rule. First, it is now legal to search out employment mutually agreeable for the student and an employer before the official decision date. Second, top students are always offered several possibilities. Third, with the existing labor shortage, if one finds a preferable job while already at work, it is easy to get the manager of the preferred enterprise to request a transfer of the assignment. Finally, even under Stalin it was a seldom-punished crime to quit the assigned job, and it is no longer a crime at all. The only penalties are possible moral condemnation and a black mark against the student in his workbook by the enterprise he deserts.

Aside from the assignment of college graduates, there is remarkably little organized placement of ordinary workers in the Soviet Union. A 1962 study[4] of industrial recruiting by regions revealed that only 15 percent of new workers were expected to come from vocational or technical schools, over 30 percent were to be trained on the job, and over 50 percent were expected to transfer from other enterprises. Since the Soviet Union officially declared unemployment ended in the early 1930's, labor employment agencies were abolished. Generally, the individual enterprises advertise by conducting tours for and having discussions with those leaving school or the army, by posting notices at factory gates, in newspapers, radio, TV, and on street bulletin boards. Aided by advice from friends and other workers, people may choose among these jobs since the jobs are normally more plentiful than applicants. The only official placement agency, the Administration for Organized Recruitment of Workers, deals only with recruiting for distant areas like Eastern Siberia. Even in the performance of this job, it has been far outstripped since 1954 by the popular appeals of the Party and Young Communist League.

Once workers are placed, there can still be a serious control problem in the form of tardiness, absenteeism, and rapid turnover. In the 1930's the industrial labor force tripled in a short period and consisted of large numbers of peasants just off the farms living in miserable housing conditions. Since there was a terrible shortage of labor, managers not only tolerated the casual working hours and habits, but were quick to grab workers from other enterprises with the promise of better conditions.

Stalin tried many control measures to curb the situation. Workers had to carry workbooks (since 1938) stamped with "valid" or "not valid" reasons for leaving by every manager — in addition to carrying internal passports. Penalties for tardiness and absenteeism became heavier and heavier. Then, in the Second World War all workers were frozen in their jobs. Many countries followed this practice in the war period, but after the war Stalin continued to some extent the freeze on changing jobs (without permission), and retained on the books criminal penalties for excessive lateness or excessive absences from work.

Relaxation of Controls.[5] In practice, these and other Stalinist repressive measures were allowed to lapse quietly soon after Stalin's

[4] See discussion in Emily Brown, "The Soviet Labor Market" reprinted in M. Bornstein and D. Fusfeld, *The Soviet Economy* (Homewood, Ill.: R. D. Irwin, 1966), p. 151.

[5] The following section is based largely on the thorough discussion in Edmund Nash, "Recent Changes in Labor Controls in the Soviet Union," in U.S. Congress, Joint Economic Committee, *New Directions in the Soviet Economy* (Washington, D.C.: U.S. Government Printing Office, 1966), pp. 849–871.

death in 1953. The new leadership clearly felt that a free and well-rewarded worker was more efficient than one compelled by penalty and terror to work. Yet it was only after the liberal decisions of the anti-Stalin Twentieth Party Congress in 1956 that most controls were officially discarded. Not only the political situation but the economic conditions had sufficiently changed by that time to allow relaxation of controls. There was a much larger well-trained labor force; and the Soviet economy had recovered and expanded so as to provide shorter hours, higher real wages, and improving housing and living conditions.

The better conditions were reflected in lower labor turnover. Whereas the percentage changing jobs in 1932 had reached a peak of 15 percent a month, the figure had dropped to a fourth of that by 1957, and by half again by 1960. In 1961 Soviet labor turnover was estimated at only 3 or 4 percent a month, which is very similar to U.S. rates.

The first official relaxation of controls came in 1955 when the draft of rural youth into trade and railway schools, which had been in effect since the 1930's, was completely abolished. Then in 1956 the criminal penalties for quitting without permission, excessive tardiness, and excessive absences were all abolished. Under the 1957 code, if a worker is excessively late or absent, management can only warn or reprimand him, shift him to a lower paid job for three months, or — if the trade union committee approves — dismiss the worker. Since there is still a labor shortage, these non-criminal penalties cannot be very effective. More important today are the rewards for good behavior that management can give, including certificates, notices, titles, and medals of honorable or best worker, as well as valuable gifts, money bonuses, and promotions.

In 1956, in the same wave of reform and relaxation, it was forbidden to hire workers under 16 years of age, excepting 15-year-olds, who could be hired for four hours a day for training purposes only. Also in 1956, it was ruled that 16- and 17-year-olds could only work six or seven hours a day. In 1957, it was decreed that administrative agencies could no longer convict and send persons to "corrective labor colonies," but that only regular courts of law could pass this sentence. Moreover, in 1957 the population of such labor colonies was greatly reduced by a general amnesty to all prisoners "who do not constitute a great danger to the State." Also in 1957 women were prohibited from almost all underground work. Furthermore, the year 1957 saw the first significant reduction in the number of hours worked per week since the Second World War.

More broadly, it was in 1957, 1958, and 1959 — as we shall see — that Soviet trade unions were allowed and encouraged to a great expansion in their role of protector of the rights of individual workers. In 1960 all the minor documents necessary for obtaining a new job were abolished, leaving only the workbook and passport. In 1958 the compulsory education system was extended by a year — and we saw that the two year work requirement for entering higher education was removed for better students in 1964. Workers are guaranteed, as before the war, at least two weeks of leave with pay a year; and a significant percentage (4 to 5 percent) receive considerably more. In 1965 the number of paid holidays was increased from six to eight. Minimum wages were raised in 1956 and again in 1965. Compulsory bond purchases were ended in 1957. Minimum old-age pensions were increased by 50 percent in 1956. Full earnings were granted as disability benefits to those hurt or ill from work beginning in 1957. Maternity leave with pay was extended in 1956 from 77 to 112 days.

We should distinguish in the above list between those general measures that affect everyone relatively equally, like ending compulsory bond purchases, and those that change the distribution of income, like a higher minimum wage. The distinction is especially important in the Soviet case because what the government gives in higher money wages to all it may also take away, for example, by higher sales taxes. Only the real increases in production of consumer goods (described in Chapter 5) are *necessarily* reflections of increases in real rather than money income — though this was a period in which real income was rising. Finally, unpopular piecework was gradually reduced. The percentage of workers paid on a piece-rate basis, which was over 75 percent at its peak, declined from 63 percent in 1961 to 57.6 percent in 1965, and has since fallen still lower. No wonder Khrushchev was quite popular for a time!

Wage and Income Differentials. In addition to their function of allocating labor to different areas and industries, wage differentials are used in the Soviet Union as a major incentive to acquire new skills and to use old skills as fully as possible. In order to provide the incentive for labor in a rapidly expanding economy, the Soviet economy has generally had even wider wage differentials than the U.S. economy. Thus, in 1956 it is reported[6] that the ratio of wages among the third quartile (relatively skilled) of Soviet workers to the first quartile (relatively unskilled) was 1.85 to 1.00. In the same year the corresponding U.S. ratio is reported as only 1.37 to 1.00. There are some very difficult statistical problems with the comparison, so the exact figures should not be taken too seriously, but the fact does remain that Soviet wage differences are as great or greater than U.S. wage differences.

The conclusion is quite different when a comparison is made of the distribution of total income in the two countries. The official Soviet distribution shows that in 1960 the top 10 percent of families had a total of only 4.75 times as much income as the total of the bottom 10 percent, and the Soviets claim that this ratio will move down to about 3.00 to 1.00 by 1970. U.S. experts place the present Soviet ratio at 6.00 or 7.00 to 1.00 in terms comparable to U.S. ratios. But even these adjustments would put the Soviet differential far below the U.S. ratio, which in 1960 revealed the top 10 percent as having 30 times the total income of the lowest 10 percent.[7] The reason for the much higher income inequality

[6] See Murray Yanowitch, "The Soviet Income Revolution," reprinted in *The Soviet Economy,* ed. by M. Bornstein and D. R. Fusfeld (Homewood, Ill.: R. D. Irwin, 1966), p. 237 ftnt.

[7] See: Yanowitch, *op. cit.,* p. 237.

in the United States lies in the fact that the Soviet Union has only wage or salary income, whereas in the United States we also find the categories of rent, interest, and profit income. These latter categories, in which a few U.S. citizens have the very highest incomes, therefore create the overall greater inequality of United States incomes (in spite of the equal or wider spread of Soviet wage incomes).

In order to place present Soviet wage differentials in their proper perspective, we must consider briefly the historical evolution of Soviet wage policy. Immediately after the 1917 revolution, wages were very much equalized in accordance with old socialist ideals. During War Communism, of course, wages were initially equal for all but the most difficult and exhausting jobs, in which cases the ratio was increased as a result of absolute necessity. During the New Economic Policy, wages were again very much differentiated. As will be shown in a later section, however, the trade unions often fought for more wage equality — and obtained considerable equality from 1926 to 1931.

In the 1930's, in order to push rapid industrialization, Stalin kept the average unskilled wage very low to avoid pressure for more consumer goods and to free resources for investment. At the same time, the industrialization drive made it all the more important to foster workers' incentives to obtain better skills and to work hard. Therefore, while the real wages of the millions of unskilled workers were kept very low, the real wage rates of the most skilled workers were being raised. Under Stalin's direction in the 1930's the ratio of most skilled wage rates to unskilled wage rates stood at 3.5 to 1.0 in the officially prescribed wage scales; and piece-rate bonuses undoubtedly increased this ratio in practice. This is a *much* higher wage differential than prevails currently in the United States. Of course, the United States also had much higher wage differentials during its own period of rapid industrialization. Thus, many economists (for example, A. Bergson) argue that U.S. wage differentials for skills were approximately comparable with Soviet differentials when we were at comparable levels of development.

To allow Soviet workers in the 1930's to achieve their desires to increase skill and earnings, the government provided a multiple-level educational system for adults as well as young students. Included within it were on-the-job individual and group training, full time factory schools in methods of mass production, secondary and advanced technical training schools, and the higher institutes and universities. When the supply of unskilled workers from the farms into industry was tripling in the 1930's, the worker training program was very active, and millions of adult workers participated in it.

In any event, from 1931, during Stalin's drive for industrialization, until 1956, when Stalinism was attacked at the Twentieth Party Congress, Soviet slogans continuously denounced "wage equalization." It was maintained that socialism means payment according to the work done by the individual, whereas wage-leveling is only a utopian, unrealistic, and petty bourgeois policy. Since 1956 the more liberal influence has prevailed, and Soviet wage policy has emphasized more equality of high and low wages as a step toward communism. By 1958 the official differential in the wages of the most skilled and the unskilled had already fallen to 2.8 to 1.0, a considerable decline from the 3.5 to 1.0 of the 1930's. Party programs and economic plans now envisage a more rapidly rising minimum wage that will reduce the official wage differential to 2.0 to 1.0 by about 1970.

The changes may be traced more precisely in the ratio of the wages of the highly skilled workers in the ninth decile (80th to 90th percentile of earnings) to the wages of the unskilled workers in the first decile (the lowest-paid 10 percent). In 1929 this ratio of the wages of the highly skilled to the wages of the unskilled workers was 3.15 to 1.00. This ratio had risen to 3.38 by 1956 at the time of the Twentieth Party Congress, but declined to 3.28 by 1959.[8] Since 1959 we have further evidence of reduced wage inequality in that: (1) as noted above, new wage scales already show a lower ratio of skilled to unskilled wages, (2) minimum wages have risen considerably, (3) there is a continuing switch from piece-rate wages to the more equalizing time-rate wages, and (4) there is an increasing area of free goods for public consumption (such as more health and education services). Further, the Party and government promise continuance of these trends to 1970 with "low paid" workers tripling their wages over the 1959 levels by that time, while all workers only double their wages.

What are the economic reasons (partly reflected in the political changes) for this important switch in Soviet policy? In the 1930's, most workers were unskilled and there was a tremendous relative shortage of skilled workers. Managers bid up wages of skilled workers simply to get them, and Soviet leaders felt that high payment for skilled work was a necessary prod to further acquisition and use of skills. By the early 1960's, there was already a very large reservoir of highly trained and self-disciplined workers, and there were even shortages of unskilled workers in some areas. Thus, the extreme differentials had become unnecessary to attract skilled workers; and Soviet leaders preferred to cultivate a more popular, equalitarian image.

In addition to wage workers, the Soviet income distribution includes salaried white-collar employees and salaried engineering-technical personnel. Table 7-1 gives some indication of a narrowing of the gap between the wage and salary levels.

It appears from this table that salaries of Soviet white-collar workers have declined (relatively) below the wage level of blue-collar workers, while the salaries of engineering-technical personnel have also fallen (relatively) toward the average wage level. These smaller differentials certainly give additional evidence of lessening income inequality in the Soviet Union. This reflects a conscious wage-equalizing policy since Stalin's death. Most of the changes in these ratios before Stalin's death merely reflect changes *within* the various categories. Thus, within the category of wage workers in this whole period there was a shift in pro-

[8] See Yanowitch, *op. cit.*, p. 231.

Table 7–1

Soviet Wage and Salary Income Differentials

Year	Average salaries of engineering-technical personnel in percent of average earnings of wage workers	Average salaries of white-collar employees in percent of average earnings of wage workers
1932	263	150
1935	236	120
1940	210	109
1950	175	93
1955	165	88
1960	150	no data

Source: Murray Yanowitch, "The Soviet Income Revolution," reprinted in M. Bornstein and D. Eusfeld, *The Soviet Economy* (Homewood, Ill.: R. D. Irwin, Inc., 1966), p. 233.

portions to the more skilled grades, at the same time that these more skilled grades were relatively increasing their wage rates up to 1956. Moreover, among engineering-technical personnel, the lower-paid occupation groups were increasing most rapidly. Nevertheless, the end result has undoubtedly been a considerable narrowing of overall Soviet income differentials in recent years.

Non-material Incentives. Although less important than they used to be, non-material incentives are still integral to the Soviet system. Compulsory elements of the work structure, which proliferated in quantity and intensity during Stalin's regime (especially during the rapid industrialization and the war), have practically been eliminated. Stalin had frozen workers to their jobs during World War II, brought criminal penalties for job changes in the late 1930's and after, and ordered compulsory recruitment of youth to Labor Reserve schools from 1940 to 1951. Today, what job compulsion remains mainly concerns school graduates, who are required by law to work at their specialties for a specific period. It also affects members of the Communist Party and Young Communist League, who must pledge to accept any job changes before being accepted for membership. Graduates of factory and Labor Reserve schools currently must work four years at an assigned job; middle and higher education, three years at such jobs. Graduates of agricultural mechanization schools are obligated to work where directed for two years.

Mass appeals for recruitment and social emulation in production, however, are two important forms of non-material incentives still utilized. A national campaign for the voluntary recruitment of agricultural, construction, and industrial workers to work and develop the "new lands" of the North and East met with considerable success in the late 1950's. Being a "pioneer" during this campaign merited both self-respect and social approbation, as evidenced by the 350,000 youth who responded to the Party's appeal of 1956. The special role provided by the Young Communist League both in spearheading national propaganda efforts to attract volunteers and in supplying recruits from the ranks of its own 18.5 million members was crucial in 1956, and would undoubtedly be so in future appeals.

Analogously, social emulation in production has traditionally stemmed from the activism of another species of social organization: the work shop and enterprise activities of trade unions. That workers' trade unions have set out to further a type of competition among their members may seem rather peculiar to Western-oriented labor economists. Explanation of this and other "peculiar" functions of Soviet unions is necessarily linked to an understanding of the historical development of unionism within the unique political and economic setting of Soviet society. This subject must now be explored in full.

Soviet Trade Unions. Not only is the environment within which unions operate in the U.S.S.R. determined by the government, but specific functions of trade unions are also affected by decisions of the Communist Party. This governmental and Party influence, usually justified by the "common interests of socialist society" and by the necessities of central planning, creates a sharp contradiction within the goals of Soviet unions. Should the unions serve the government by striving for increases in production and enforcing labor discipline, or should they serve their members by seeking to increase the workers' share of the current social product and to eliminate inequities that develop in the incentive system?

Many functions which are integral to the serving of members' individual interests in private enterprise countries have been absent from Soviet unions. With wages and fringe benefits being bureaucratically determined, the practice of collective bargaining over wages has not existed. Furthermore, with the volume of consumer goods determined, unions could not get more for all workers. Higher wages would simply mean higher sales taxes. Neither have unions regularly employed the strike mechanism. Instead of local struggles, the general wage policy for the whole country is annually dictated in an agreement between the Central Council of the Trade Unions and the appropriate government Ministries and State Committees. This practice became the rule in the 1930's and has remained ever since. The Soviets argue that a definite and firm central wage policy is a necessary basis for planning.

In fact, they claim that a planned economy could never allow separate unions to argue over the total wage bill, because it would then be impossible to make a central plan for output or to determine the level of investment. Local unions do, however, bargain over conditions of labor. Furthermore, some degree of local union service to workers and protection of workers has always existed. Unions do administer a vast social insurance system, make available grievance machinery in case of managerial abuses, and provide recreational facilities for their members. Worker benefits from unionism have shown significant signs of increasing over recent years. Finally, however, managers are also in the unions and also receive their benefits, and this fact highlights the difference between Soviet and Western unions.

Specific functions of unions have varied greatly during their long history in the Soviet Union, and the patterns set provide a vivid reflection of the course of political change the country has followed. Yet one rule has consistently prevailed: unions have remained primarily instruments of the government, and only secondarily representatives of their members' interests. Most of their history manifests a centralized economy's solution to the question of these dual goals.

Union Struggle for Independence, 1917–1928. In the early period of Bolshevik power, there was much controversy over the place of trade unions in the developing Soviet Socialist society. Party policy first expressed by Lenin during 1917, and reiterated at the First Congress of Trade Unions in 1918, held that unions could both remain autonomous and perform vital functions for the government. But alteration of this position was already underway by 1919; a new stance was exhibited at the Second Union Congress of that year. The "government function" of unions was given more emphasis, and Lenin forecast the necessity for unions eventually to "merge with the organs of state power." At the same time Lenin predicted a "withering away" of any government which is elevated and separate from the people, and the emergence of a society where everyone was to learn the business of government. It would be the function of unions to educate the people for this undertaking.

Discussion over the independence of unions continued through 1919 and erupted into heated debate at the Tenth Communist Party Congress held in 1920. Opposition to the increasingly centralist tendencies of the new government came from the so-called Worker's Opposition (led by Shliapnikov and Kollontai), which called for a change to an equalitarian regime run directly by workers as represented by their trade unions. At the other extreme were the centralists (led by Trotsky and Bukharin), who urged immediate absorption of the trade unions by the government, since there could be no conflict between a government of workers and the workers themselves. The clash of these political forces and personalities prompted Lenin's famous oration on the "transmission belt" theory of unionism — a "compromise" stand which actually sounded the death knell for the aspirations of the Worker's Opposition. The Party accepted Lenin's proposition: unions were to be conceived of as intermediaries working for the realization of centrally defined goals.

Although the conception of unions which were independent of governmental control was officially discarded at the 1920 Congress, it is important and interesting that unions did manage in practice to remain active on behalf of the working masses during the period of the New Economic Policy. During that period, a compromise with union activity on behalf of workers remained a necessary, if temporary, reality of governmental policy.

Unions under Stalin's Thumb, 1928–1953. Soon after Stalin's consolidation of power in 1928, the last vestige of actual independence was extirpated. In the 1929 purge, he eliminated Tomsky, the head of the whole Soviet trade union apparatus, and all other union leaders

who showed resistance to Party enthusiasm for a plan of rapid industrialization, low real wages, and high differentials for skills. The policy
of highly differentiated wages was especially emphasized after Stalin's
speech of June, 1931. Under this strict rule, the trade unions were ad-
juncts of the government, which arbitrarily assigned and altered union
functions.

Among the first tasks of the unions in the 1930's was a major role in
the recruitment and settlement of very large numbers of rural laborers
into industrial firms and society. In this regard unions took responsibility for the newcomers' habits, rudimentary skills, housing, and social
insurance. They also served in encouraging the new workers to adjust to
labor discipline, and had a hand in enforcement procedures. This category of functions was removed in 1947 when organized recruitment was
turned over primarily to a specialized central agency.

During the 1930's, unions also became active in government training
activities. They joined with the Supreme Council of National Economy
and the Commissariat of Education to form factory schools for technical
skills; and they organized general education courses, financed from their
own membership dues. Unions also assisted the Commissariat of Labor
in redirecting skilled laborers out of unessential industries and into
high-priority work.

Third, trade unions were given responsibility for increasing labor
productivity while sustaining or improving worker morale. Propaganda
campaigns for promoting labor competition and "socialist" emulation
among workers were the result. The search was for "shock workers" in
the early 1930's, and "Stakhanovites" after 1935 (when the worker,
Stakhanov, chalked up some records in production). The name was
given to all record-producing workers, who were publicly given awards
and recognition, and received better living quarters and rare consumer
goods. They were thus rewarded for exceptional labor by a standard of
living that was clearly differentiated from their fellow workers. Although lower and middle union officials often argued that this system
was antagonistic to Marxist principles, and much resentment was
aroused among ordinary workers, the campaigns prevailed, serving to
spread and intensify the wage differentiation which was an integral
part of Stalinist economics. "Stakhanovism" was finally abandoned because the organization of an enterprise to increase the productivity of a
few selected workers proved to be disruptive to the overall productivity
of the plant.

Finally, in 1933 unions were made administrators of social insurance
for workers. In that year they were first given direct responsibility for
both the regulation and administration of temporary social insurance
benefits and adjudication of pensions. By 1948, over one million unionists were participating as voluntary insurance delegates. Control over
social insurance benefits has given unions a function which uniquely
allows for both labor protection and labor discipline.

Unions in the Present Period. Since the Twentieth Party
Congress in 1956, official attitudes toward trade unions have undergone
a basic alteration. More attention is given to worker rights and to work-

ing conditions. There are also many reports of increased democracy and "answerability" at the local level, as well as more effective grievance machinery. Soviet journalists and politicians now speak of unions as service organizations for "improving the condition of work and life of workers."

Specifically, we find the greatest expansion of the service and protection role of Soviet trade unions in the liberal 1957–1959 period.[9] In 1957 a new law allowed workers to present more easily their grievances to a labor disputes board, composed half of management and half of union representatives. Grievances were to include questions of job and wage grades, payment for overtime or sick leave, and unfair dismissals or transfers. In 1958 trade unions were given powers (1) to help plan workers' housing and work quotas, (2) to check on management compliance with collective agreements and labor laws, (3) to hold and control general workers' meetings, and (4) to pass on dismissals. In 1959 the trade union constitution was revised so that it not only mentions the primary duty to encourage production, but also emphasizes the duty to protect workers from any management violations of laws or agreements.

For the future, the trend away from the "bureaucratic centralism" of Stalin's day offers increased possibilities for union participation in local decision-making, both with regard to production and work environment. The possibility of decentralization and the institution of workers' councils, already present in Yugoslavia and to a very limited extent in Poland, provides further encouragement to those who desire a more independent status for trade unions in relation to the state. Even the prospect of more union independence from the government bureaucracy within socialism has been recently justified in Marxist theory as a "nonantagonistic contradiction of socialism."

C. Incentives in Agriculture

The performance of Soviet agriculture has been much weaker than its showing in industry. To be sure, some of the problems are the same, but agriculture has some additional problems of its own. Its problems have not been neglected. Indeed, the last decade has seen nothing but continuous attempts to remedy the situation. Before turning to the policies applied in recent years, however, we shall first try to clarify the situation in agriculture and define more clearly its problems.

Structure. As background for our discussion of its performance and behavioral problems, the formal structural characteristics of Soviet agriculture must be recalled. The three quite different sectors of Soviet agriculture are: (1) private, (2) cooperative or collective, and (3) state or government; the performance of these three sectors is quite different. According to official Soviet data[10] as late as 1928 the private sector used 97.2 percent of the sown land, leaving only 1.2 percent

[9] See discussion and sources in Nash, *op. cit.*, pp. 857–858.
[10] Summarized in Abram Bergson, *The Economics of Soviet Planning* (New Haven: Yale University Press, 1964), p. 18.

for the collective farms and 1.5 percent for the state farms. Then came the vast collectivization drive under Stalin's harsh leadership. By 1937, the private sector was reduced to 5.3 percent, the state farms had risen to 9.0 percent, and fully 85.7 percent of the sown land was used by the collective farms.

The situation remained unchanged for many years. As late as 1950, the private sector was still 6.4 percent, the state farms 10.9 percent, and the collective farms 82.7 percent of the sown land. Then after Stalin's death, for reasons discussed below, his heirs decided to switch many areas from collective to state farms. In addition, most of the "Virgin Lands" were initially organized as state farms. By 1964, the private sector was reduced to 2.9 percent, the collective farms fell to 52.1 percent, and the state farms rose to 45.0 percent of the total sown land. Most of this change occurred in the late 1950's, however, and the rate of change has fallen off since then.

It must also be explained that the private sector in these figures includes three separate segments. All but 1 percent of the private sector in 1928 was composed of independent peasant farms. By 1964, the independent peasant farm had disappeared completely, and the private sector was divided into half-acre farms run as private plots by collective farmers and similar farms run as private plots by workers on state farms.

Performance. The overall performance of Soviet agriculture is worse by far than that of Soviet industry in the eyes of all observers, even if they agree on nothing else. In the period 1950 to 1958 Soviet industry claimed a 12.4 percent rate of growth, and official U.S. sources admitted that it had a 9.0 percent rate of growth.[11] In the same period, Soviet agriculture claimed only a 5.6 percent growth rate, and U.S. estimates admitted (amazingly) that it had a 5.7 percent growth rate. For the later period, 1958 through 1963, Soviet industry claimed an annual 9.7 percent rate and U.S. estimates gave it a 7.5 percent rate; but Soviet agriculture claimed only a 1.1 percent growth rate, while U.S. estimates found a −0.4 percent rate! Either estimate for the latter period is quite dismal.

A recent Soviet writer[12] confirms with aggregate data this difference in performance between agriculture and other sectors. He finds that in 1959 labor employed in Soviet agriculture was still a startling 38.8 percent of all labor employed in the Soviet economy. Yet, also in 1959, agriculture produced only 17.6 percent of the total Soviet Combined Social Product.

As an initial guide to understanding, we may separate the effects of

[11] The official Soviet data quoted here and below are from *Narodnoe Khozyaistvo SSSR v 1963 godu* (the annual Yearbook published by the Central Statistical Agency, Moscow); while the American estimates are all in U.S. Congress, Joint Economic Committee Staff Report, *Current Economic Indicators for the USSR* (Washington, D.C.: U.S. Government Printing Office, 1965).

[12] A. Granberg, "Agriculture in the System of Interbranch Balances," translated in *Problems of Economics*, Vol. 10, No. 6 (October, 1967).

increased inputs (land, labor, and capital) from increased productivity (improved technology or organization). One recent U.S. study[13] finds a total increase in Soviet agricultural output of 70 percent from 1950 to 1965 — though two-thirds of that increase was concentrated in the five years after Stalin's death, 1954–1958.

The study also reveals that this 70 percent output growth was achieved by an increase of inputs of only about 33 percent. The whole difference is identified as an increase of productivity, though almost all of the productivity increase was also limited to the years 1954–1958. More precisely, the study finds for the whole period 1951–1964 that output increased 3.5 percent a year, inputs by 2.0 percent a year, and productivity by 1.5 percent a year. Yet in the later 1961–1964 period taken alone, he finds output rising only 1.7 percent a year, inputs rising 1.8 percent a year, and productivity therefore *declining* at .1 or .2 percent a year. Our explanation for the poor performance of these years will thus have to explain not only the lesser additions to inputs, but also the reasons for declining productivity of inputs.

General Problems. Before turning to the differences in policies and other factors resulting in the very different performance before and after 1958, it will help to look at the general problems persisting in Soviet agriculture. Clearly, the basic problem of Soviet agriculture is low farm productivity both per acre and per man hour. And, of course, a major reason for the low productivity is that investment has gone primarily into producer goods, with very little spared for consumer goods. Agriculture, in particular, was starved of capital for many years. A man can produce very little from an acre of land if he can only work with his bare hands, and lacks tractors or other advanced machinery as well as fertilizer, insecticides, and other chemical aids — though we shall see that Soviet agriculture has many other severe problems, especially a terrible lack of incentives in some sectors.

We have touched before on the question of the slow rise in Soviet agricultural productivity (especially in the early 1960's), but let us now compare the Soviet and U.S. situations. In the first place, U.S. estimates show a much lower Soviet product per acre than that of the United States (Table 7–2). Even if we assume that U.S.S.R. yields are a bit higher than these U.S. estimates admit, they certainly indicate the direction of the comparison. They show a very real and drastic Soviet problem, especially since U.S. yields are lower than those of several other countries.

In the aggregate, it is possible to compare not only U.S. and Soviet use of land, but also respective agricultural use of labor and material inputs (Table 7–3). These are mostly official U.S. estimates, and official Soviet estimates might put the U.S.S.R. in a better light. It is at least clear, however, that the Soviet Union uses far more land and labor than the United States in agricultural production. Since the Soviet agricultural

[13] D. B. Diamond, "Trends in Outputs, Inputs, and Factor Productivity in Soviet Agriculture," in U.S. Congress, Joint Economic Committee, *New Directions in the Soviet Economy* (Washington, D.C.: U.S. Government Printing Office, 1966), pp. 339–382.

Table 7–2

U.S. and U.S.S.R. Yield Per Acre of Major Crops, 1964

Crop	U.S.S.R. yield per acre as percentage of U.S. yield per acre
Corn, Grain	44%
Wheat	48
Rye	62
Oats	44
Barley	54
Rice (rough)	42
Cotton, Lint	125
Sugarbeets	52
Tobacco	48
Potatoes	59
Hay, all kinds	35

Source: H. E. Walters, "Agriculture in the United States and the U.S.S.R.," in U.S. Congress, Joint Economic Committee, *New Directions in the Soviet Economy* (Washington, D.C.: U.S. Government Printing Office, 1966), p. 478.

product is certainly not much, if any, larger than the U.S. product, it follows that both their product per acre and their product per worker are much lower than in U.S. agriculture. This has the additional consequence that they have proportionately less labor available for industry. Thus, the farm share of total employment in the United States is only 7 percent, but it is 38 percent in the Soviet Union.

The *reason* for this greater use and lower productivity of labor in Soviet agriculture is also revealed for the most part in Table 7–3. That table shows the much lesser use in Soviet than in U.S. agriculture of all kinds of material inputs of capital goods. Thus, Soviet agriculture uses far fewer tractors, trucks, and combines, and less electricity and fertilizer. Naturally, one could "explain" its relatively low productivity of

Table 7–3

U.S. and U.S.S.R. Inputs into Agriculture, 1964

Input	U.S.S.R. Input as Percentage of U.S. Input
Agricultural labor force	655%
Acres of sown cropland	172
Tractors on farms per acre	19
Motor trucks on farms per acre	19
Grain combines on farms per acre	30
Agricultural consumption of electricity per acre	36
Commercial fertilizer used per acre	36

Source: Same as Table 7–2, at p. 476.

labor by its very limited use of capital, or its relatively high productivity of capital by its very great use of labor. We shall see, however, that Soviet farm labor productivity is also low for organizational and incentive reasons — and capital productivity may be higher in part because of more intensive, full-capacity use of farm machinery.

Other particular problems of Soviet agriculture are:

(1) There certainly is a problem of incentives on the farm and a vast migration to the city. Part of the problem is simply that wages are much higher in the city, and are even much higher on the state farms than on most collectives. This is primarily because prices paid for farm goods by the government are kept artificially low in order to provide another source of industrial capital accumulation. In 1966, the average money income of the collective farmer was still only two-thirds of the wage of the state farm worker and only one-half of the wage of the industrial worker. Services are also much worse in the countryside, with little government-built housing, few doctors, little indoor plumbing in many areas, not enough electricity, and terrible roads. Soviet statistics indicate that free goods and services constitute 30 percent of the real wage of the average Soviet worker, but only 16 percent of the collective farm real income.

(2) Another problem arises from the fact that an hour spent in a private plot seems to be more profitable for a farmer than an hour spent on a state farm, and far more profitable than an hour spent on a collective farm. It is officially admitted that, "As a rule, income from a day's work on the plot exceeds that from a comparable effort in the socialized sector."[14] Therefore, the private plot exercises a strong pull on the labor supply, and it is difficult to get even the minimum quota of labor on the state and collective farms. In 1966, collective farmers earned 28 percent of their cash income from their private plots.

In fact, in 1966 the tiny private sector with less than 3 percent of the land, nevertheless produced 17 percent of the total agricultural product (even according to official Soviet figures).[15] This included 60 percent of the potatoes, 40 percent of green vegetables, 40 percent of dressed meat, 39 percent of milk, 68 percent of eggs. These data certainly mean that the absolute production of the private sector was a vital contribution to total output. According to a U.S. study of 1963 statistics,[16] these data also mean that private plots produced much more per acre, *but* that the product per man hour was only 71 percent of the product per man hour in the combined state and collective farm sectors. From fragmentary data, it would also seem that the collectives produced a larger absolute

[14] Communist Party Central Committee Plenum of March, 1965, quoted in J. F. Karcz, "Seven Years on the Farm," in U.S. Congress, Joint Economic Committee, *New Directions in Soviet Agriculture* (Washington, D.C.: U.S. Government Printing Office, 1966), p. 397.

[15] See M. Makeyenko, *Voprosy Ekonomiki* (Nov. 10, 1966).

[16] These data are from an excellent unpublished study by Nancy Nimitz, *Farm Employment in the Soviet Union, 1928–1963* (Santa Monica: The Rand Corporation, 1965).

amount, but that the state farms are more productive per man hour. Some strong reasons for these tendencies in production will be advanced in later sections.

(3) The Soviet climate generally allows a very short time for seeding, plowing, and harvesting operations. The weather in many areas is very extreme, and also quite variable. A recent study for the U.S. Congress states, "Generally speaking, climatic conditions in the U.S.S.R. are much less favorable for agriculture than in the United States, and many portions suffer from recurring droughts."[17]

(4) Agriculture is generally less amenable to central planning than is industry. The reason lies in the very large number of different units, the vast distances between planner and farm, the very great differences in conditions in each area, and the important impact of the very changeable weather conditions. As a result of these conditions, and the additional burden of rigidity imposed by the Stalinist dictatorial thinking and administration, the planners have often made major mistakes in the plans for state farms and in their very considerable influence on the collective farms.

(5) The Machine Tractor Stations were a great drag on agriculture until their abolition in 1958 because their goals differed from the farms they were supposed to help. The goal of the tractor driver was usually to plow as many acres as possible, not to plow deeply or specifically in the areas or at times desired by the farms. The Stations could not be abolished before that time because they were an important instrument of central control when farmers were mostly anti-Communist, ignorant of modern technology, and not always desirous of carrying out State Plans. They also were necessary so long as there was not enough farm machinery to go around. By 1958 the number of state and collective farms was greatly reduced by amalgamation into larger units. The number of collective farms declined, through amalgamation, from 235,000 in 1950 to less than 100,000 in 1954 and to less than 50,000 by 1967. At any rate, by 1958 there were enough loyal agronomists and enough machines for each farm to have at least one well-trained, Communist manager and an adequate supply of farm machinery.

Although the amalgamation of the Machine Tractor Stations with the state and collective farms removed a source of conflict over the use of farm machinery, it produced other problems after 1958. On the technical side, the Stations had been responsible for the maintenance and repair of machinery. This function could *not* be equally well filled by the farms, few of which had sufficient trained mechanics; while very few new repair stations were established by the Soviet government. On the financial side, the total cost of the machinery and buildings to the farms came to 2.4 billion rubles, which constituted a very heavy burden of payment, especially for the weaker farms.

(6) No rent is collected from either state or collective farms, and this

[17] H. E. Walters, "Agriculture in the United States and U.S.S.R.," in U.S. Congress, Joint Economic Committee, *New Directions in the Soviet Economy* (Washington, D.C.: U.S. Government Printing Office, 1966), p. 475.

has two adverse effects. First, those farms with better land or location tend to have much higher incomes than others, with no relation to effort put forth. In addition, this lack makes it very difficult to calculate correctly prices and costs in agriculture so as to know what to plant and what methods to use. To a very slight extent there is some element of rent in the differential farm prices by regions, but these are very crude differences. The Soviets are now beginning to edge toward the introduction of a more precise form of rent, since this would improve both the allocation of resources and the equity of farm income distribution.

(7) Not only is there too much central planners' direction of Soviet farming units, but the units themselves are probably too large for efficient management. By 1950 Soviet collective farms averaged about 1,470 acres and about 100 able-bodied workers.[18] By 1964, following a drive for mergers by Khrushchev, the average Soviet collective farm had increased to 7,350 acres and 418 workers. The average state farm — and state farms now constitute almost half of Soviet farm land — is even larger, averaging 21,405 sown acres and 721 workers. By contrast, the average U.S. farm had only 88 sown acres and 1.4 workers, though many U.S. corporate farms are much larger and employ many more workers. U.S. studies indicate that the minimum cost per unit is achieved between 300 and 400 acres; while one U.S. study even found that output per acre declines above 880 acres.

Yet U.S. conditions are quite different from Soviet conditions, so U.S. results do not necessarily apply to Soviet farms. For comparison, note the very large acreage and large number of workers on the more similar Israeli collective or *kibbutz* (which is said to operate at a high level of efficiency according to some U.S. studies).[19] Note also that in practice much operational control of the Soviet farm is lodged in distinct, decentralized units within the farm. The farm labor force is broken into "brigades," and the brigades are further divided into "teams." In order to improve responsible and knowledgeable decision-making on the farm, there is currently a strong trend toward making these so-called teams (or *zveno*), composed of a few families, the main operative units.

(8) There is an amazing lack of technical information on the average Soviet farm. This might perhaps be corrected by something like the U.S. agricultural extension service, which teaches by example and uses neither command nor centralized "advice," since "advice" by central authorities often sounds like a command.

(9) There is still a deficiency of part-time work available for the winter season when less labor is needed on the farm. The Soviets have

[18] The figures in this paragraph all come from official Soviet and U.S. data, mostly reported and discussed by Roy Laird, "Khrushchev's Administrative Reforms in Agriculture: An Appraisal," in J. F. Karcz, ed., *Soviet and East European Agriculture* (Berkeley: University of California Press, 1966), p. 47.

[19] See M. E. Spiro, *Kibbutz* (Cambridge: Harvard University Press, 1956), pp. 71–90; also see I. Vallier, "Social Change in the Kibbutz Economy," *Economic Development and Change*, Vol. 10 (June, 1962), pp. 337–352.

long been aware of this, and may soon locate more light industry projects in farm areas.

Reform Trends. Khrushchev proposed as early as 1950 under Stalin that the 235,000 small collective farms of that day be amalgamated into larger, more modern, and more easily controllable units. As shown above, by 1954 there were already less than 100,000 collectives; while at the same time the Party brought from the cities about 20,000 Party members to be managerial personnel on the farm. This process has continued, and by 1963[20] managers of collectives were characterized by the facts that: (1) more than 95 percent were members of the Communist Party; (2) a good 66 percent had finished secondary or higher education, and the number with University education was increasing rapidly; and (3) their tenure was becoming more stable (by 1960 some 56.6 percent of them had held their positions more than three years).

Furthermore, in 1953 Khrushchev eliminated local governmental control of farms. In 1955 he decentralized planning to some extent by replacing direct planning with a minimum sales quota. Then, in 1958 he turned over the control of machinery from the Machine Tractor Stations to the farms. Only in 1962 did he reverse the trend to farm autonomy when he returned the farms to a regional control by the Territorial Production Administrations, which brought the collectives completely under the planning structure. Yet the decentralization tendency was continued by his successors, who quickly abolished the Territorial Production Administrations.

Of course, the decentralizing of many decisions to the farm level quite naturally goes along with the strengthening of the individual collective farm units. In this respect, not only did Khrushchev urge the amalgamation of collective farms into larger units, but he also enforced the rapid switch from collective farms to state farms. The collective farm tends to combine the worst features of bureaucracy and private enterprise. In form (and to some slight extent in practice) it is owned by all the farmers who work on it. Therefore, the profit does not all automatically go to the government to be available for investment, but may remain with the individual farmers. As general conditions and productivity have improved, some farms have become very rich and the problem of control over the income has become more urgent. Of course, state farms *could not* be introduced at an earlier period because of political opposition by the farmers, because of the low level of technology and productivity, and because the agricultural losses of those days had to be absorbed by the collective farmers. The collectives ensured the government a minimum amount of surplus or "forced saving" for use in industry, regardless of farm conditions. The original purpose of the col-

[20] According to official Soviet data reported in Roy D. Laird, "Khrushchev's Administrative Reforms in Agriculture: An Appraisal," in *Soviet and East European Agriculture*, edited by Jerzy F. Karcz (Berkeley: University of California Press, 1966).

lective farm, to place the burden of industrialization on the peasant, is no longer necessary because (1) agriculture is now a much smaller part of the Soviet economy, and (2) the whole Soviet economy is much richer so that industry can generate enough surplus to maintain its own rapid expansion.

The government must pay a minimum wage to each worker on a state farm, whereas the collective farmers used to suffer the losses of bad years directly from their own pockets. After 1958, when farm income had improved considerably, the collectives were encouraged to make regular wage-like payments. It is now planned that all collective farms will soon pay a minimum monthly wage; and it is *promised* that the wage level on both collective and state farms will "gradually" be made equal to the industrial wage. Only recently has it become possible to raise the technological level (and the investment in farm machinery) enough so that the majority of farms *could* pay a minimum wage and still be profitable. Furthermore, increased mechanization has, for the first time, been making the gigantic state farm a more efficient unit, which was not possible until Soviet industry could produce enough farm machinery. On the other hand, it must be noted that many of the rapid conversions from collectives to state farms represented only the financial relief of weak and bankrupt collective farms, for whom the change meant mainly a shift to a guaranteed wage and a burden on the government budget. Therefore, these conversions meant rather a necessary improvement in farm income than the "further enserfment" viewed with pity by some Western observers at the time.

In this period, moreover, the Soviet government began to provide more incentive to decentralized initiatives on the farm. By 1953 Khrushchev and Malenkov reduced some of the harsh burden of farm taxes, especially the taxes on private plots. In 1953 and several times later the government also raised the fixed purchase prices that it would pay to collective farms. In 1955 and 1956 price changes also seemed to take more account of rental payments. This was the same period, March 1955, when central production plans for the collective farms were eliminated, though fixed procurement quotas of a certain amount persisted; the collectives could at least plan their own production above the procurement quota. There have continued to be retail price increases in some farm goods (for example, in 1962) in order to provide still more material incentive for farmers.

As a result of increased agricultural investment, better incentives, and more rational decision-making (as well as good harvest years and more acreage), a fairly good rate of growth of agriculture was achieved in the years 1951–1957. Soviet agricultural performance in the years 1958–1963, however, was miserable on the whole. What accounts for the difference? In general, it seems that organization and incentives did a little backsliding, and certainly did not make much improvement in these years. Agricultural investment, moreover, definitely did not maintain its previous rapid growth, perhaps because the government expected the organizational measures previously taken to do the trick alone.[21]

Two U.S. economists[22] report that the share of agricultural investment in total Soviet investment fell continuously from 1957 through 1960, and the absolute amount of government investment in agriculture actually fell in 1958 and again in 1959. This was reflected in actual declines or decreases in the rate of growth of almost every kind of agricultural machinery and fertilizer; and represented a reversion to a very strict policy of starving agriculture to build industry — of doubtful wisdom at this late date.

In addition to the decline in investment, it is worthwhile to review briefly at this point the main differences in inputs and other policies between the 1953–1958 and the 1958–1965 period. During the period 1953 or 1954 to 1958 there were indeed very considerable increases, not only in the investment of capital, but in all types of inputs into the farming sector. These included large increases in the number of specialists and the number of mechanics, a better quality and a more stable managerial force, and, of course, a very large amount of power machinery. This period also included a fairly high proportion of favorable climatic conditions. Most important for the short run, perhaps, even the input of land was greatly increased in the period by the famous "new lands" policy of Khrushchev, under which large amounts of previously virgin territory mostly in central Asia were plowed and planted. The project to open up 80 to 100 million acres of land in a two-year period was quite a breathtaking adventure. The undertaking was absolutely stupendous in concept, even if it was overdone by including too much dry and marginal land. Finally, this period also witnessed an improvement in efficiency due to the Khrushchev-directed switch from wheat to corn in many areas. This change was eminently reasonable, although also overdone in practice.

We have also emphasized the increased decentralization of decision-making after 1953, which undoubtedly had positive effects. Moreover, the significant rise in the real income of Soviet farmers from 1954 through 1958 was actually larger than the rise in urban real income. The measures to raise farm income included both higher payments for farm goods and lower taxes on collective farms. These measures helped to keep more skilled young workers on the farm and provided them a greater motivation for work in the socialist sector.

In the period from 1958 to 1965, however, as we have already noted, there was a considerable decline in the proportion of central investment funds going into the agricultural sector. There was also less credit given to collective farms. In real terms, this meant less machinery, fewer tractors and trucks, and less fertilizer. In addition, the increase in the num-

---

[21] According to Karcz, *op. cit.*, p. 408.

[22] Jerzy F. Karcz and V. P. Timoshenko, "Soviet Agricultural Policy, 1953–1963," Food Research Institute Studies (1964), pp. 142–144.

ber of mechanics and machine operators in the farming area was notably smaller.

We have also noted the reversal in policy which increased the amount of central planning in agriculture at the expense of local decision-making for a number of years. One careful observer states, "As a matter of fact, the 1958 reforms amounted to a reversal of the slow shift of agriculture toward the market sector of the economy."[23] Along with the increased central direction went less material incentive to the farming sector, both on the collective farms and in the private plots. Thus, while urban real wages were rising, there appears to have been an actual decline in the income of the socialized sector of collective farms during 1957 to 1960 ranging from 11 percent to 29 percent in various regions. By 1961, the situation was critical enough that this particular policy was reversed and the collective farm taxes were lowered, while the costs of machinery to the farms were also lowered. Yet also related to the worsened financial situation was the transfer of machinery in 1958 from the Machine Tractor Stations to the farms, which entailed initial payment of high prices, as well as much higher costs for repair and maintenance, while also increasing the tax base of the farms. The tax base rose because the M.T.S. had been paid in kind, and these same goods were now sold for money income.

At the same time, beginning in 1958, there were great pressures exerted to reduce the size of private plots and to reduce the amount of livestock allowed on private plots. Although Khrushchev ended compulsory private deliveries of agricultural goods, this was only to open the door to a complete abolition of the private plots. This was especially evident in the 1958 decision to refuse any further sale by the government of the crucial feed grains or concentrated feed to the private plots.

The restrictions on private production immediately had drastic effects on this crucial sector. Thus, the sown areas of private plots declined 7 percent just from 1959 to 1960. Moreover, according to official Soviet data, between 1958 and 1964 privately held numbers of cattle fell by 4,100,000, hogs by 670,000, sheep and goats by 5,800,000. In the same period, sales in collective farm markets (which come mostly from the produce of private plots) fell by a third, with potatoes and poultry sales falling 50 percent, and beef and milk sales falling 40 percent — at the same time that prices of the goods in these markets rose by 27 percent.

Finally, in addition to all of these dis-incentive policies, and the lowering of capital investment, the negative side of the "new lands" policy now became evident. In the earlier period it had meant a vast increase in the sown areas, especially since only a very small percentage of the new lands was left uncultivated. In the latter period, however, these new lands tended to become dust bowls, partly because they had always been areas of low precipitation, and partly because of an unwise policy of not leaving enough uncultivated areas. The productivity of the new lands plummeted drastically in the period after 1958, though this decline was partly due to bad weather.

[23] Karcz, "Seven Years on the Farm," op. cit., p. 407.

After Khrushchev was ousted, his successors immediately took several steps to improve the farm situation. Apparently, the post-Khrushchev leadership is strongly pursuing the policy — begun by Khrushchev in his last year in power — of large new investments in agriculture. In the Five Year Plan for 1966–1970 all investments in the economy are scheduled to rise by 50 percent, but investments in agriculture alone will rise by 100 percent. Specifically, the new Plan will increase the stocks of tractors on the farm by 50 percent, trucks by 37 percent, and grain combines by 51 percent. Fertilizer is planned to increase to 64 million tons a year by 1970, though this is not so high as the fantastic level set by Khrushchev of 70 to 80 million tons by 1970. In addition, the Five Year Plan provides for more irrigation than was undertaken in the last 20 years. Finally, more credits are to be provided to all of the farming sector. We may be justifiably skeptical that all of these improvement plans will be implemented. In the past, a great many excellent-sounding agricultural plans were not fulfilled because industry has taken priority whenever there was a pinch for scarce resources — as there usually has been.

In addition to these planned increases in inputs, the new leadership immediately undertook some popular moves to increase incentives on the farm. Almost their first action was to lift all of the restrictions on private plots and private ownership of livestock. In the socialized sector, they have lowered collective farm taxes, and have changed the tax base to net income rather than gross income. They have raised livestock prices, which had been among the lowest of farm prices, from 30 to 36 percent in 1965. They have also raised grain prices, including large increases for wheat, rye, barley, and oats. Furthermore, the procurements (or sales quotas to the government) from collective farms were greatly reduced in 1965, and were *fixed* at these lower levels for the next five years. Whereas procurement quotas used to be changed frequently, even during the course of one year, Brezhnev has now stated that "no one has the right to change them." He is especially referring to the fact that the local procurement agencies often increased procurements on successful collectives above the legally required amounts in order to make up for deficiencies on other collectives. This practice has had a terrible effect on incentives; its abolition has been promised many times before, but the promise has always been broken.

In general, the agricultural sector has moved toward the use of the market as a replacement for detailed central planning. For example, state farms were given higher pricing for their products, but must now make a profit to qualify for bonuses, and must accomplish their own reinvestment out of their profits. The post-Khrushchev leadership has also emphasized even more strongly the policy — also begun under Khrushchev — of emphasizing reliance on the "production-principle" rather than central planning. This principle in essence calls for close attention to costs and prices and an attempt to maximize profitability of agricultural output. It assumes more autonomy for farm managers. This attempt to decentralize and rely on profitability is closely related to the re-emergence of the importance of the small production team (the group of families known as the *zveno*) as the operational unit within the farm. The reform package includes more decentralized decision-making at the farm and even at team levels along with more attention to market signals, as a replacement for detailed central planning.

As a further incentive to remain on the farm, retail prices of consumer goods in rural areas, which had been higher than urban prices because of higher "administrative" expenses, are now to be brought down to equality with urban prices. Furthermore, the minimum pensions of all farmers have been raised considerably. Most important, though, has been the strongly emphasized promise to guarantee minimum wages to collective farmers, and to raise the wages of both collective and state farmers to the average industrial level. It appears that this policy is being seriously pursued, since collective farm earnings rose by 16 percent in 1965, although gross agricultural output rose by only 1 percent. If this policy is successfully carried out, then it may serve to remove some of the attraction of working on private plots.

All of these new measures may be expected to yield much larger agricultural output in the near future. In fact, recent years have already shown some improvement. For example, according to official Soviet claims, in 1966 the Soviet grain harvest was the largest in history, and its total agricultural output rose 10 percent over 1965.

At least a few Soviet economists envision further reforms along the lines already manifested in some Eastern European countries. Whether the farm is called a collective or a state farm, it would be free to make its own decentralized output decisions, thus taking full advantage of market signals. There would be no central plan for current outputs and no procurement quotas, though there would continue to be much centrally planned investment. Yet central control of the direction of farm output would exist not only through control over much of the investment, but also through continued setting of the price guidelines for both farm inputs and outputs. It is likely that when it is possible for all farm workers to be given adequate wages, all farms will become state farms. In that way, income distribution will depend only on wages (with some considerable shift to piecework already in evidence), and on bonuses for high rates of profitability. If the state farms became productive and profitable enough for their members, then private plots could be allowed to die from economic competition, rather than by administrative fiat.

SELECTED REFERENCES

A. Concerning Management:

1. An excellent, somewhat popularized, account of Soviet managers may be found in David Granick, *The Red Executive* (New York: Doubleday and Co., 1961).

2. A more scholarly work is David Granick, *Management of the Industrial Firm in the U.S.S.R.* (New York: Columbia University Press, 1954).

3. Joseph S. Berliner, "Managerial Incentives and Decisionmaking: A Comparison of the U.S. and the Soviet Union," reprinted in *The Soviet Economy*, edited by M. Bornstein and D. R. Fusfeld (Homewood, Ill.: R. D. Irwin, 1966), pp. 109–140.

4. J. S. Berliner, *Factory and Manager in the U.S.S.R.* (Cambridge, Mass.: Harvard University Press, 1957).

5. Interesting contrasts to Soviet experience are presented in Barry M. Richman, "Capitalists and Managers in Communist China," *Harvard Business Review* (Jan., Feb., 1967), pp. 57–78.

B. *Concerning Labor:*

6. Emily Clark Brown, *Soviet Trade Unions and Labor Relations* (Cambridge, Mass.: Harvard University Press, 1966).

7. Isaac Deutscher, *Soviet Trade Unions: Their Place in Soviet Labor Policy* (New York: Oxford University Press, 1950).

8. Edward Nash, "Recent Changes in Labor Controls in the Soviet Union," in U.S. Congress, Joint Economic Committee, *New Directions in the Soviet Economy* (Washington, D.C.: U.S. Government Printing Office, 1966), pp. 849–870.

9. An interesting book on a similar planned economy is Janos Timar, *Planning the Labor Force in Hungary* (translated by Lynn Turgeon; White Plains, New York: International Arts and Sciences Press, 1966).

10. Gertrude Schroeder, "Industrial Wage Differentials in the U.S.S.R.," *Soviet Studies*, Vol. 17 (January, 1966), pp. 303–317.

C. *Concerning Agriculture:*

11. Jerzy F. Karcz, editor, *Soviet and East European Agriculture* (Berkeley: University of California Press, 1966).

12. Several useful articles on Soviet agriculture are in U.S. Congress, Joint Economic Committee, *New Directions in the Soviet Economy* (Washington, D.C.: U.S. Government Printing Office, 1966); especially Jerzy F. Karcz, "Seven Years on the Farm: Retrospect and Prospects," pp. 383–450; D. B. Diamond, "Trends in Outputs, Inputs, and Factor Productivity in Soviet Agriculture," pp. 339–382; Keith Bush, "Agriculture Reforms Since Khrushchev," pp. 451–472; H. E. Walters, "Agriculture in the United States and U.S.S.R.," pp. 473–482; R. E. Neetz, "Inside the Agricultural Index of the U.S.S.R.," pp. 483–494.

13. Roger A. Clarke, "Soviet Agricultural Reforms since Khrushchev," *Soviet Studies*, Vol. 20 (Oct., 1968), pp. 159–178.

8

INTERNATIONAL
ECONOMIC RELATIONS

Organization of the Soviet Trade System

All trade in the U.S.S.R. is conducted by state trading corporations, specializing in the export and import of centrally assigned commodities. Some two dozen of these enterprises are under the jurisdiction of the Ministry of Foreign Trade; another four engage only in the administration of foreign aid exports to developing nations and are part of the U.S.S.R. State Commission for Foreign Economic Relations. For a particular product one corporation is always in a monopoly position, contracting as the exclusive buyer or seller intermediary between domestic and foreign enterprises producing or purchasing the product. For example, in a transaction between the U.S.S.R. and Poland, a Soviet export firm buys from a Soviet factory, it pays the retail price minus the turnover tax, and it then ships these goods to a Polish import company. On receipt of acceptance documents, the Soviet central bank will pay the Soviet export company from the Polish importer's account at the Polish central bank, and the Polish central bank then collects from the import enterprise.

The Ministry of Foreign Trade maintains fairly tight control over these state and trade monopolies by detailed plans for volume, assortment, prices, and transport of trade commodities. The central bank organization (Gosbank) provides further close control for planned trade goals, allocating foreign exchange for purchases only on the basis of approved contracts by trading companies or other authorized purchases.[1]

[1] U.S. Senate Committee on Foreign Relations, *op. cit.*, p. 244.

In countries with which it deals, the Soviet government establishes trade delegations with diplomatic accreditation. Such a delegation is charged with promoting commercial relations between the U.S.S.R. and the country to which it is assigned, studying the economic situation of that country, issuing permits with regard to imports and goods passing through the U.S.S.R., and supplying information to the Ministry of Foreign Trade and other interested bureaus. The United States is the only major trading country in the world in which there is not a trade delegation attached to the Soviet diplomatic mission. Oddly enough, the trade monopoly of the U.S.S.R. is represented in the United States by the Amtorg Trading Corporation of New York, incorporated in 1924. Amtorg operates as a private commercial company, but is staffed solely by personnel of the Soviet Ministry of Foreign Trade.[2]

For various reasons (which are examined below), the Soviets most often conclude bilateral trade agreements. Bilateralism has been viewed as most capable of preserving consistency between the foreign trade program and the domestic plan, thus preventing unexpected demands for resources already earmarked for other uses. In more recent years, agreements of from three to five years have replaced some of the more usual one-year contracts. Long-term agreements with capitalist countries have given added stability to forecasts of trade effects.

Method of Planning International Trade

The annual planning of international trade is largely based on the requirements of the domestic production Plan. Of course, before annual adjustments are considered, the Soviets begin with a core of more or less regular imports and regular exports. Thus, they usually export large amounts of grain, iron ore, coal, and oil. They usually import tin, cotton, and sugar, among others. The annual juggling consists of (1) changes in the amounts of these regularly traded goods, (2) new imports to fill new domestic bottlenecks, and (3) new exports from newly discovered unwanted surpluses. Since there is constant pressure to increase imports to ease bottlenecks, there is also constant pressure to find more goods to export and more markets for them.

The sequence of planning the annual adjustments may be visualized as follows. First, and most important, the planners examine the domestic Plan to find those areas in which there is a deficit, that is, those areas in which domestic production cannot meet the planned demand, or in which it would be very costly to produce that much. Some of these deficits are "chronic," as for example those in tin, natural rubber, and tropical fruits. These products and many others are imported at roughly constant levels year after year. Other deficits develop as a result of sudden changes in the Plan or through miscalculations in the planning process. On the basis of both the usual and unusual needs for this year, an import plan is drawn up that will just fill the key domestic deficits.

[2] U.S. Senate Committee on Foreign Relations, *op. cit.*, p. 247.

Second, the planners add up the now-determined imports to see how much total export will be needed to pay for these planned imports. Then they examine the planned domestic production to find which particular goods will be in surplus over domestic needs, or which products can most easily and cheaply be increased in production; and those products are designated for export. It has already been noted that there are many traditional exports, such as lumber and petroleum. The Soviets simply plan every year to produce "surpluses" of these commodities for sale abroad. Finally, the export and import plans are supported by detailed plans for geographical distribution and for financing.

If at first the import and export plans are out of balance — because not enough exports can readily be found to pay for imports — the planners attempt to scrape together more "non-essential" goods for export. These extra exports are usually taken from the low-priority consumer goods industries. The planners are seldom driven to the extreme of cutting down imports which are essential for domestic production — the loss of which would mean lowering the domestic plan. In theory, they might also make some adjustments in the domestic plan, and then recalculate the trade plan. In practice Soviet planners have so far found such secondary and further adjustments too time-consuming, and too disruptive of domestic planning. Therefore, they have usually stopped with a foreign trade plan influenced by the domestic production plan, but with little or no reciprocal influence.

It is impossible here to go further into the general theory of foreign trade planning in a centrally planned economy. It is a complex subject depending on the entire difficult, mainly mathematical, Western literature on trade as well as the entire literature on central planning. The argument must rest with the above brief discussion, while the remainder of this chapter looks further at more concrete and particular problems that foreign trade has displayed under Soviet central planning.

The Volume of Trade

In general, the foreign trade of the Soviet Union and the Eastern European planned economies has been much smaller relative to their national income than the trade of comparable Western economies. For example, as late as 1964 the Soviet ratio of exports plus imports to national income was only 5.3 percent, whereas the U.S. ratio was 7.9 percent. Furthermore, in almost every case the trade of the Soviet Union and the Eastern European countries has been less than what it was when they were private enterprise economies; though recently their trade ratios have been rising rapidly, so that they are now approaching the earlier figure.

Immediately after the Revolution, Soviet trade ceased for a few years. Then, there was a gradual recovery, and a rapid increase during the First Five Year Plan. In 1930–1932 exports plus imports rose to about 7 or 8 percent of national product — because imports of machinery were crucial to the industrialization drive. By 1936–1938, however, exports plus imports had fallen to only 1 percent of national product. This decline, as will be seen later, was partly due to the elimination of the worst bottlenecks for which machine imports were needed, and partly due to drastic declines in prices for items which the Soviets could export.

During World War II Soviet trade figures began climbing to a rather different order of magnitude. During the war, the government readily accepted economic cooperation and aid from its allies. The higher levels of trade were maintained to some extent after peace settlements. However, as the East and West blocs emerged as separate political-economic areas of influence and competition, inter-bloc trade stagnated or declined. Foreign trade remained a small percentage of national income, but that percentage began increasing very rapidly again in the 1950's. In fact, trade of the planned economies in that period expanded more rapidly than trade of the private enterprise economies. By 1960, though, the planned economies still had only about half the trade volume of comparable private enterprise economies. Only a few, such as Hungary, have now reached a volume of trade apparently as high as similar private enterprise economies.

Soviet trade has continued to expand rapidly in the 1960's, though a little less in 1963–1965 than in 1960–1963, as shown in Table 8–1. The jump in imports was due partly to grain purchases from the West, rather than long-term trade expansion.

Table 8–1

Annual Growth Rates of Soviet Exports and Imports
(percentages, values in current prices)

	1960–61	1961–62	1962–63	1963–64	1964–65
Exports	7.9	17.2	3.4	5.6	6.3
Imports	3.5	10.8	9.3	9.6	4.1

Source: H. W. Heiss, "Soviet Union in the World Market," U.S. Congress, Joint Economic Committee, *New Directions in the Soviet Economy* (Washington, D.C.: U.S. Government Printing Office, 1966), p. 921.

What is the *explanation* for the generally lower trade ratios of the Soviet and Eastern European economies? The older, pat answer was that the Communists followed a policy of self-sufficiency and low levels of foreign trade, a policy called "autarky."

The traditional Western view could be represented as follows: In the Soviet experience, political-military desires for self-sufficiency coupled with an extensive, varied resource base have resulted in a relatively small amount of foreign trade and further insulation from the impact of foreign economic relations. Although specialization in products for which they have a comparative advantage can equally benefit planned and capitalist economies, the Soviet Union until quite recently followed autarkic (or go-it-alone) principles as its primary foreign trade guideline. Beginning in the late 1920's, the Soviet policy was to buy abroad only those goods that could not be produced domestically, or could only be produced domestically at excessive costs in terms of time or resources. Exports were not encouraged as an end in themselves, since they were generally limited to the amount necessary to pay for imports specified in the plan.[3]

This over-simplified view has now been challenged,[4] especially in light of the rapid trade increases of the Communist countries in the 1950's and 1960's. The fact that their trade ratios still remain lower than non-Communist ratios must be explained by many factors, of which alleged Soviet desire for political and military self-sufficiency can only be one. This must be so since the final result has been increasing interdependence with the West in some vital respects.

First, remember the Western obstacles to Soviet trade. There was the *cordon sanitaire* or economic blockade against the Soviet Union by the private enterprise economies immediately after the Soviet Revolution. The United States did not even recognize the Soviet Union until 1933. Then the world-wide depression in the 1930's ruined the trade of all primary-producing countries, since their exports — for example, Soviet grain — suffered complete demand and price collapses. Later, the cold war led to an attempt at economic warfare by the United States in its embargo of "strategic goods" — though some of these were "strategic" only by the wildest stretch of the imagination. Our allies at first cooperated with our embargo and with the related prohibition of all long-term credit. Soviet trade with the West began to rise only when Western Europe began to ignore most of these U.S. obstacles to East-West trade.

The Soviets also created some obstacles to trade. Ideologically, there certainly was some desire for self-sufficiency in the face of a hostile world. Furthermore, there never was a Marxist theory of international trade by or between planned economies. Good Marxists assumed that the whole world would be socialist together, and all socialist countries would unite to put their economies directly under one world plan. Even in the postwar world Soviet economists were hesitant to deal with the fact of trade between many planned and unplanned economies, much less to accept the Western theories explaining the advantages of a large volume of trade. Thus, Soviet economists labeled the theory of comparative cost or comparative advantage as "a pseudo-scientific, reactionary . . . theory."[5] In recent years, Marxist economists, especially in Eastern

---

[3] This view is presented to some degree in U.S. Senate Committee on Foreign Relations, "Soviet Foreign Trade," in M. Bornstein and D. Fusfeld, *The Soviet Economy* (Homewood, Ill.: Richard Irwin, revised edition, 1965), p. 243.

[4] See for detail the excellent collection of articles edited by Alan A. Brown and Egon Neuberger, *Trade and Planning: Interactions Between International Trade and Central Planning* (Berkeley: University of California Press, 1968).

[5] Quoted in J. Wilczynski, "The Theory of Comparative Costs and Centrally Planned Economies," *Economic Journal* (March, 1965), p. 66.

Europe, have been working on methods for optimum foreign trade planning.[6]

A more serious difficulty for the Soviet planner than the lack of a theory of foreign trade is the arbitrary and irrational Soviet price system. Soviet prices reflect accurately neither preferences nor scarcities. The foreign trade planner thus finds it hard to calculate either the costs of exports or the benefits of imports; yet this is exactly what any attempt to achieve optimal efficiency requires. This problem is compounded by the fact that foreign trade offers a vast array of substitutes for domestic products in many uses. To consider properly these possibilities, and to modify the domestic Plan accordingly, would put an added burden on the Soviet planners, and would require better coordination among a vast number of departments and enterprises. In general, Soviet trade has always been reduced below its potential because of all the theoretical as well as bureaucratic difficulties of integrating it into the planning matrix. Nevertheless, the Soviet government has recently ordered a "profound study" of both import and export possibilities to take full advantage of the international division of labor.[7]

Some international transactions, of course, bring obvious gains to the economy; it takes neither sophisticated theory nor fancy pricing to recognize this fact. Planners view trade as a welcome way of filling temporary deficits, as in grain procurements. They also recognize that acquiring modern foreign machinery in key areas and obtaining the best of foreign technology are important aids to rapid growth. Moreover, total Soviet trade has recently increased greatly over prewar times simply because the U.S.S.R. is no longer alone, but now has a group of allied countries in Eastern Europe. As a result of these factors, a (hopefully) more peaceful international atmosphere in the future, a growing realization of the advantages of increased trade, and the habitual use of imports in key industries, a further rapid expansion of Soviet and Eastern European trade in the future can be expected.

Geographical Distribution of Trade

The geographical-political distribution of Soviet trade in recent years may be seen in Table 8–2.

Note, first, the predominance of Soviet trade with Eastern European Communist countries. Within that group, the Soviet Union traded most heavily with the two most industrialized countries; in 1964, of all Soviet trade, 17.6 percent was with East Germany and 12.1 percent with Czechoslovakia. Among the Communist countries outside of Eastern Europe, Soviet trade with China was in first place in 1956, but descended to last place by 1967.

In total amount, trade with Communist countries was still 69.7 per-

[6] See discussion by Alan A. Brown, "Centrally-Planned Foreign Trade and Economic Efficiency," *The American Economist*, Vol. 5 (Nov., 1961), pp. 11–28; also Wilczynski, *loc. cit.*
[7] *Pravda* (Feb. 20, 1966).

Table 8–2

Distribution of Soviet Trade by Areas, 1964
(as percentages of total)

Area	1964
Eastern European Communist Countries	58.0
Other Communist countries	11.7
(including China, Cuba, and Yugoslavia)	
Industrial West	20.0
Less developed countries	10.3
Total	100.0

Source: Heiss, *op. cit.* in Table 8–1 above, p. 922.

cent of total Soviet trade in 1964. Nevertheless, there has been a moderate trend toward increased trade with non-Communist countries. Earlier data show that exports to all non-Communist nations rose from 17 percent of the total in 1950 to more than 30 percent by 1964; and that for imports, the corresponding change was from 20 to 31 percent. Finally, notice that two-thirds of Soviet trade with non-Communist nations was still with the "developed" economies in 1964. Yet earlier data reveal that there has been a quite rapid drift toward a higher volume and proportion of Soviet trade with the less-developed countries.

The Soviet Union has conflicting goals with respect to the direction of its trade. For political-military reasons, and because institutionally it is easier to plan and conduct trade with other planned economies, she seeks to avoid extensive trade with private enterprise economies. The Western private enterprise economies are, however, reliable sources of certain modern technologies and equipment, and the world market does provide a vast array of very profitable trade opportunities. It would appear that the Soviet Union will continue a high proportion of its trade with the other planned economies, but will continue to rely on the West for breaking internal planning bottlenecks and for much machinery and equipment for growth. Incidentally, even the very slow shift of the U.S.S.R. away from certain types of heavy industrial machinery imports from Eastern Europe has caused some painful readjustments in the rigid plans of those countries.

Commodity Structure of Soviet Trade

The categorization of total trade levels into individual commodity figures shows considerable variation in the importance of trade items. An analysis of trends is shown in Table 8–3.

Some interesting history is portrayed in this table. In 1913, before the Revolution, grain had been a third of all exports. In fact, exports were 60 percent agricultural and another 34.4 percent raw materials! This is understandable when it is recalled that Russia in 1913 had 82 percent of its population in rural areas, and that at least 48 percent of

Table 8–3

Structure of Soviet Exports and Imports,
1913–1964 (percentages)

Item	1913	1928	1938	1964
Exports: Total	100.0	100.0	100.0	100.0
Machinery & equipment	0.3	0.1	5.0	21.0
Fuel and raw materials	42.8	63.1	57.7	65.0
Grain	33.3	3.3	21.3	3.5
Consumer goods	23.6	33.5	16.0	10.5
Imports: Total	100.0	100.0	100.0	100.0
Machinery & equipment	15.9	23.9	34.5	34.4
Fuel and raw materials	63.4	67.8	60.7	31.5
Consumer goods (including grain)	20.7	8.3	4.8	34.1

Sources: Heiss, *op. cit.,* p. 927; Lynn Turgeon, *The Contrasting Economies* (Boston: Allyn and Bacon, Inc., 1963), p. 287; and Franklyn Holzman, "Foreign Trade" in A. Bergson and S. Kuznets, *Economic Trends in the Soviet Union* (Cambridge: Harvard University Press, 1963), p. 293.

its national income originated in agriculture. The fuel and raw materials total was impressive because Russia was the world's largest exporter of petroleum. The low level of industrialization was reflected by the great need for imports of fuel and raw materials — in spite of the growth of Russian production of these necessities.

During the 1920's, especially during the NEP period of very small, more commercial peasant farms, the former export surplus of grain nearly disappeared, as the peasants both produced less and consumed more of it themselves. Exports of lumber and petroleum rose more quickly toward prewar levels, but still left total exports in 1927 at only 34.7 percent of the 1913 level. Exports thus did not recover rapidly enough to finance desired imports, while long-term credit was almost impossible for the U.S.S.R. to obtain. Therefore, the vitally needed industrial imports were also restricted. Even by 1927 imports had risen to only 38.9 percent of their 1913 volume.[8]

During the 1930's, collectivization gave the Soviet government more control over agricultural production and marketing, so grain again became a major export. Thus, in spite of the low standard of living, large amounts of food were exported while only a negligible amount of consumer goods were imported. At the same time, most imports consisted of machinery and raw materials for industry, especially producer goods for heavy industry.

During the first Five Year Plan grain exports and machine imports climbed very rapidly. Once the worst bottlenecks were broken and Soviet industry had built a firm base, however, imports could be reduced,

[8] See Franklyn Holzman, "Foreign Trade," in A. Bergson and S. Kuznets, *Economic Trends in the Soviet Union* (Harvard University Press, 1963), p. 286.

allowing the very painful exports also to be reduced. Trade was further reduced because world terms of trade had turned against the Soviet Union; that is, from 1929 to 1932 prices of Soviet exports (mainly agricultural and raw materials) declined by 51.3 percent, while prices of Soviet imports (mainly equipment) fell only 32.0 percent. By 1937 Soviet exports had fallen to one-half of one percent of national income — though the pattern of grain export and machinery import persisted.[9]

In the period since the Second World War, grain exports continued to rise slowly in total amount, but declined rapidly as a proportion of all exports. The year 1964 was an exceptionally bad one for agriculture; so grain exports slipped to about half of the usual amount, and were less than grain imports for the first time. In fact, in that year 3.1 percent of all *imports* were in grain, an act necessitated by the desire of the Soviet authorities to both maintain consumption levels at home and meet their export commitments. The rest of the rise in consumer imports is simply a result of rising consumption, and rising consumer demands for a share in national product.

The industrial progress of the Soviet Union is strongly reflected in the steadily growing share of machinery and equipment in Soviet exports, much of it to the less developed countries. Before the Revolution almost none of these heavy industrial goods had been exported by Russia to the world market. On the other hand, the Soviet Union's own continued need for certain foreign equipment in its program of rapid industrial development is evident in its even higher percentage of *imports* in the form of machinery and equipment — from Eastern Europe as well as from the industrialized Western economies.

Balance of Trade and Adjustment Mechanisms

If exports suddenly decline below imports in a private enterprise economy, every Western text explains, in theory, "price" and "income" effects will automatically tend to restore balance. The price effect comes about when export demand falls, thus putting surpluses on the domestic market, lowering prices and thereby causing foreign purchases to rise again. The income effect refers to the decline in income and employment which results from a decline in exports, and subsequently causes a reduction in imports (the size of which depends on the marginal propensity to import and the "multiplier").

Neo-Keynesian economists point out that the automatic mechanisms may not be sufficient to restore equilibrium in the balance of payments; or that governments with higher-priority, conflicting goals may not allow them to work. The conflicting goals arise because the "adjustments" to unemployment and reduced imports are painful, and most governments today take steps to prevent them from developing.

What has been said of income adjustment mechanisms in the neo-Keynesian model of private enterprise economy is even more true of centrally planned economy. The nations of Eastern Europe and the

[9] Data from *ibid.*, p. 290.

U.S.S.R. plan for full employment of resources. Should unemployment begin to develop as a result of a decline in exports or for any other reason, they would immediately take steps to utilize the newly unemployed labor. The implementation of this policy is certainly much more rapid than of Western fiscal and monetary policies, and this serves to all but eliminate downward income and price effects and their subsequent downward impact on imports.

Soviet foreign trade prices do adjust to changing external economic conditions, particularly in trade with the West, but the nature of the adjustment is quite different from that of a private enterprise economy and requires a few words of explanation. As already noted, the domestic prices of the Communist countries are chaotic and irrational and are not, in any sense, consistent with each other. As a result, it has been impossible for these countries to find a set of prices within the bloc which would provide them with a satisfactory and consistent basis for trade. The only alternative which is available, one which they have seized, is to conduct intrabloc trade on the basis of world prices (with some modifications). It goes without saying, of course, that East-West trade is also conducted at roughly world prices. Since they contribute so little to world trade, the centrally planned economies could only enter the world market on existing price terms.

What about the relationship between the world prices at which they trade, and the domestic internal prices of the same products? There has been no discernible relationship between the two sets of prices. Sometimes world price is far below domestic price, sometimes far above. Since foreign trade is nationalized, the financial aspects of this anomalous situation (large accounting profits on some goods, large accounting losses on others) are not disastrous. It is only necessary to grant foreign trade corporations large subsidies where a transaction involves them in a loss, and to levy heavy taxes where the result is an abnormal profit.

To return now to the adjustment mechanism. The basic goal of the foreign trade planner is to preserve the trade plan so as not to disrupt the domestic economic plan. This is accomplished in East-West trade by altering foreign trade prices whenever necessary. Generally, this means that Soviet foreign trade prices change with world prices. That is to say, if prices of planned imports rise, the Soviets *will* pay more for them, unless they can immediately replace them by domestic production or from alternative markets. If prices of planned exports fall, they will generally accept lower prices — and export even more at these lower prices — in order to preserve to the extent possible their foreign exchange earnings. In the way just described, the pricing mechanism assists the Soviet economy in adjusting to balance of payments problems and in fulfilling its internal plans.

It is important to note, however, that because of the complete divorce of internal and external prices, the adjustment mechanism differs in a substantial respect from that in a market economy. In a market economy, a change in foreign trade prices will have an impact on domestic prices and this, in turn, will affect the structure of output in the economy. Thus, a rise in world price of some commodity will lead to an increase in output of that commodity and thereby increase exports or decrease imports, and will have a longer-run impact on the balance of payments. This is not true, or at least much less true, in the Soviet case. The Soviet producing enterprises have absolutely no connection with foreign trade and no knowledge of the price at which foreign trade is conducted. Furthermore, even if their selling price fluctuated with foreign trade prices, this would not have any impact on their output plans, which are largely determined for them by the requirements of the overall economic plan.

In intrabloc trade, price changes are much less useful in the adjustment process. As we noted, intrabloc trade is conducted at some approximation to world prices. Once having settled on a structure of world prices, however, these tend to remain relatively fixed for long periods of time. Thus, world prices of 1957 were used relatively unchanged for the 1957–1963 period. To the extent that prices do not change, changes in trade balances have to be met by increasing or decreasing quantities exported and imported. This is often very difficult to do because of the requirements of the overall economic plan. As a result, bilateral negotiations between bloc nations are often long and involved. Sometimes, undoubtedly, prices are changed in order to attain balance when it seems impossible to do so by further exchanges of goods. At other times, this end is achieved by the acceptance of goods which are really not wanted and which may be resold elsewhere if the opportunity presents itself. The absence of flexible foreign trade adjustment mechanisms in a framework of very rigid internal national economic plans makes life hard for those who are responsible for intrabloc foreign trade.[10]

Trade Agreements, Bilateralism, and Inconvertibility

We saw that Soviet trade is based on a "foreign trade monopoly," that is, it is tightly controlled by the Ministry of Foreign Trade and a small number of its subsidiary enterprises and agencies. This is inevitable in any centrally planned economy, since the foreign trade plan must be an integral part of the whole economic Plan. Furthermore, planning necessitates that most trade be governed by long-term, fixed and certain "trade agreements" made by the Soviet government with others (though this prevents a certain degree of flexibility in taking advantage of changing conditions). Of course, the situation in trade may

[10] Many of the background facts for this section are in Franklyn D. Holzman, "Some Financial Aspects of Soviet Foreign Trade," in F. D. Holzman, *Readings on the Soviet Economy* (Chicago: Rand McNally and Company, 1962), pp. 729–745. The issues discussed here are more completely examined in Franklyn D. Holzman, "Soviet Central Planning and the Foreign Trade Institutions and Adjustment Mechanisms," in Alan A. Brown and Egon Neuberger, *Trade and Planning, Interactions Between International Trade and Central Planning* (Berkeley: University of California Press, 1967).

change drastically after the present decentralization reforms are completed (see Chapters 13 and 14). It may lead, for example, to allowing domestic enterprises to enter into direct foreign trade negotiations. Here, however, we confine ourselves to central planning.

Because of reliance on central planning and planned trade agreements, as well as the fact that their own price systems are somewhat arbitrary, the Soviet Union as well as the Eastern European planned economies generally prefer to make simple *bilateral* (or two-party) agreements for *exchange of goods*. This is quite different from the traditional practice of Western private enterprise of buying imports for money in many markets and selling exports for money in many — often quite different — markets. Of course, the Western multilateralism sometimes leads to balance of payments difficulties, but usually it allows buyers and sellers to take much fuller advantage of all possible places to buy and sell. On the other hand, the bilateral trade agreements of the centrally planned economies do not have to exclude multilateral trade. A bilateral agreement may provide for bilateral imbalance, to be corrected by other bilateral imbalances.

Thus bilateralism by itself does *not* mean that all of the trade agreements of the centrally planned economies must provide for trade balance; balance rather results from the policy of "inconvertibility." "Currency inconvertibility" means not allowing the citizens and enterprises of a country to convert their own currency into any foreign currrency without government authorization. This means that they cannot buy goods in other countries unless explicitly authorized to do so, which makes it possible to prevent all non-essential imports. Western countries sometimes do this when they are importing more (and spending more abroad) than they are earning from their exports — that is to say, when they have severe balance of payments problems.

All the planned economies have currency inconvertibility, but also something which may be called "commodity inconvertibility." This has been defined as follows: "Commodity inconvertibility means not allowing foreigners who hold your currency to spend it on imports (from you)."[11] Commodity inconvertibility thus prevents any unplanned or unauthorized *export* of goods. This is a practical necessity for any planned economy, which cannot allow sudden depletion of supplies of any good, since this would upset the Plan. Furthermore, the arbitrary prices of the planned economies make it necessary to negotiate separately each exchange, because otherwise foreigners could make enormous profits by buying some items at domestic prices. It is the exact opposite of the Western reaction to imbalance with regards to export. There is seldom, if ever, a problem of limited supply in peacetime in the West, but rather an attempt to stimulate the deficient foreign demand for exports.

It is thus the system of central planning by direct controls which involves currency and commodity inconvertibility in the Soviet Union —

---

[11] Franklyn Holzman, "Soviet Central Planning and the Foreign Trade Institutions and Adjustment Mechanisms," in Brown and Neuberger, *op. cit.*

and which makes them impossible to remove as long as this mode of planning continues. Further, central planning and consequent inconvertibility together make necessary the systems of bilateral exchanges by fixed trade agreements and bilateral balances, which are negotiated by the government trade monopoly. The usual way to avoid a strictly equal and bilateral exchange of goods is to pay for any imbalance by giving your currency or other IOU's, which could then be used to buy your goods or the goods of any other nation. That, however, is impossible in this situation for the reasons explained above.

The main point is that, even if the Soviets were willing to make their currency "convertible" into their exports, foreigners still would not take their currency. No one wants to hold a currency whose prices are not unambiguously defined, and most of whose vast array of goods cannot be purchased by foreign importers. This restriction on convertibility holds necessarily within the bloc of planned economies. Since the Soviets deal with Western nations solely in Western currencies or gold, Soviet-Western trade is quite multilateral.

Bilateral balancing has thus been the rule within the Eastern European bloc, and this prevents them from taking advantage of many potential multilateral exchanges, except by very complex multiple — balanced — treaties. In an effort to eliminate bilateral balancing of trade, the International Bank for Economic Cooperation was established in 1964 in Moscow. It encourages imbalances in particular bilateral exchanges by allowing the build-up of credits which presumably can be used to pay for opposite imbalances in other exchanges, thereby attempting to provide a kind of limited convertibility. Yet this Bank has not generated widespread multilateral trade in Eastern Europe because of the other continuing obstacles. Especially, there is the problem that goods of some Eastern European countries (and therefore currencies to buy them) are less desirable (more inconvertible) to their trading partners than goods of other countries. Also, there is no penalty for keeping a deficit forever on the books, so little trust is put in the future balancing process by the potential surplus nations, who are in the position of granting involuntary credit.

Coordination Among Planned Economies

Within the socialist community, we have mentioned, the Soviet Union participates in intergovernmental commercial treaties or "trade agreements." The treaties include "most favored nation" treatment with regard to export-import operations, transportation of freight or passengers, the exchange of technicians, students, and specialists, and the organization of trade fairs. The "most favored nation" clause means that each socialist country must automatically receive as good a treatment from the Soviet Union in these respects as is granted to any other country. We must note, however, that the "most favored nation" clause has always before been most important with regard to tariffs and price discrimination. Since all of the socialist bloc countries trade with each other at world prices (in theory), and since most of them have no tariffs, the "most favored nation" clause is of little practical importance within the bloc. The main purpose of these treaties and long-term agreements within the socialist bloc has been to insure the availability of basic supplies needed to meet yearly output targets.

Effective coordination of trade policies or output plans (or both) for planned economies could not be efficiently carried out with just bilateral agreements. Inconsistencies and contradictions would probably result even if only a half dozen countries attempted coordination by a mass of individual contracts. Thus, where coordination of trade and output has been proposed in the socialist bloc, there has been a concomitant push toward multilateral agreements. In January, 1949 a communiqué from Moscow announced the formation of the *Council for Mutual Economic Assistance* (Comecon) to pursue "broader economic cooperation among the countries of the People's Democracies and the U.S.S.R."[12] By the end of that year, member nations were the U.S.S.R., Czechoslovakia, Hungary, Poland, Bulgaria, Rumania, East Germany, and Albania. Thus far, the withdrawal of Albania has been the only change in membership.

A basic principle of the new organization was the sovereign equality of all member countries, and to this end it was resolved that all recommendations or decisions of the council must be adopted by the unanimous vote of members interested in questions being examined.[13] Furthermore, decisions reached were to be advisory; the organization possessed no enforcement powers. From 1949 to 1953 Comecon more or less confined its role to registration of bilateral commercial agreements among its members.[14] Nevertheless, new long-term contracts for material supplies were worked out, expert study commissions were established, and the exchange of technicians was arranged.

It was not until 1953–1955, after the death of Stalin, that a "new course" toward coordination of output and a pattern of specialization was begun. By early 1956 skeletal balances of the total supply and demand of key materials were being drawn up for the entire bloc. In the making was an attempt to facilitate the second long-term development plans of the Eastern European countries at the same time as the Sixth Five Year Plan of the Soviet Union. The direction this evolving cooperation scheme might have taken, *if* it had been adopted, was predicted by Western experts:

> . . . the Soviet Union was to remain the key trading partner of each country; she was to export capital goods and basic materials, including iron ore, coal and cotton, and agricultural produce; she was to import machinery, some raw materials, including coal and a large variety of consumer goods. East Germany and Czechoslovakia were to supply mostly machinery and manufactured foods, along with a few raw material items, such as potash and coke. Poland was to export coal, coke, railway equipment, chemicals,

[12] Quoted in the U.S. Senate Committee on Foreign Relations, *op. cit.*, p. 253.

[13] See John Pinder, "EEC and Comecon," *Survey* (January 1966) No. 58, p. 102.

[14] See J. M. Montias, "Background and Origins of the Rumanian Dispute with Comecon," *Soviet Studies*, Vol. XVI, No. 2 (October, 1964), p. 130.

and manufactured consumer goods; Hungary was to supply bauxite, diesel engines, agricultural products, and consumer goods; Rumania, Bulgaria, and Albania were to supply oil and ores, as well as agricultural products. At the same time, trade with the primary producing countries in Southeast Asia and the Middle East was scheduled for substantial increases.[15]

But political instability in Hungary and Poland in 1956 and opposition to the suggested specialization format by the less developed countries in Comecon during 1956–1958 prevented a multilateral economic cooperation pact from materializing. The Hungarian and Polish revolts can be regarded in part as protests against the degree of political and economic hegemony the U.S.S.R. held over Eastern Europe, a position which aroused charges of discrimination and inequity in intrabloc treatment.[16] Whether as an admission of "violations and mistakes which debased the principle of equality" — as stated in a Soviet policy statement of October 30, 1956 — or as a straight appeasement offering, the Soviet Union soon negotiated new agreements designed to improve intrabloc economic relations. Abolished were the long-standing practices of unfavorable currency exchange rates for students, technicians, diplomats, and other visitors to the U.S.S.R., and the low prices paid by the U.S.S.R. for uranium, nonferrous metals, coal, petroleum, and other imports. Soviet claims to a share in the capital of former "joint companies" — an organizational device used after World War II to expropriate a share of key resources from bloc countries which had been allied with Hitler's Germany — was renounced, and a substantial amount of Comecon members' debts were cancelled. Perhaps of most importance was the extension of $1.75 billion in credits — equal to one-third of credits extended to these countries during the previous ten years — in the period from January 1956 to June 1957.

To the less developed countries in Comecon, however, although these concessions and loans were certainly welcome, they still missed the crux of a growing antagonism to the specialization proposals. Exchange of commodities between bloc partners officially takes place at "world prices," that is, the price prevailing on the capitalist market in "usual conditions of supply and demand." Using the world price pattern, however, puts any developed country in a position of exploiting a less developed one, according to Marxist theory and even according to most non-Marxist theory. "An advanced country is enabled to sell its goods above their value even when it sells them cheaper than the competing countries," while a less developed country "may offer more materialized labor in goods than it receives, and yet it may receive in turn commodities cheaper than it may produce them."[17] Coordination of output and a di-

---

[15] N. Spulber and F. Gehrels, "The Operation of Trade within the Soviet Bloc," in F. D. Holzman, *Readings on the Soviet Economy*, p. 141.

[16] See U.S. Senate Foreign Relations Committee, *op. cit.*, p. 257.

[17] Soviet statement cited in N. Spulber, "The Soviet Bloc Foreign Trade Systems," in M. Bornstein and D. Fusfeld, *The Soviet Economy* (Homewood, Ill.: Richard Irwin, Inc., 1962), p. 302.

vision of labor based on existing capital-labor structures and product specializations of CMEA countries became regarded, especially by the Rumanian delegation, as capable of keeping an undeveloped country in a vicious circle of continued exploitation and slow development. Thus, the national interests of these countries would need to be sacrificed, or modified considerably, if the socialist bloc was to benefit as a whole.

By 1957 or 1958 the basis of Rumania's intrabloc economic policy had jelled into a remarkably independent position. Industrialization was to adhere to the pattern first set after World War II: the Soviet style of stressing heavy industry, low levels of personal consumption, and the collectivization of agriculture.[18] Any regional specialization plan would have to lay emphasis on future costs and profitability if Rumania was to agree to a participating role. The national interests of Hungary and Poland have been closest to the Rumanian position, but their stance in the CMEA has been considerably less vehement.

From 1957 to 1962 trade and commercial exchanges throughout the bloc grew substantially, but little progress was made toward integrated planning. In Rumania the Communist Party maneuvered along a difficult path toward its industrialization goals, finding credits to build a chemical industry from Western companies after Soviet hesitation, and expanding machinery imports from both the West and some Comecon members (the U.S.S.R., East Germany, and Czechoslovakia). Still, criticism of the Soviets for not making large enough credits for their industrialization program were voiced in 1960, and meaningful compromise within Comecon seemed unlikely.[19]

Some progress toward a socialist "international division of labor" and the utilization of multilateral arrangements had, however, actually occurred. Since June of 1957 the Soviet Gosbank had additionally become a clearing house for any multilateral compensations. In spite of the lack of means to enforce its recommendations, the Comecon by 1962 had been successful in facilitating: the linking of major electric power systems of six countries into an international electric power grid, with headquarters in Prague; creation of the transcontinental "Friendship" oil pipeline carrying Soviet crude oil to Poland, East Germany, Czechoslovakia, and Hungary; agreements between the U.S.S.R. and Czechoslovakia for the extraction of Soviet iron ore and between the U.S.S.R. and Poland for the joint development of potash mining in Byelorussia; the development of Soviet phosphorite deposits by the U.S.S.R., Hungary, Bulgaria, Czechoslovakia, and East Germany.[20]

Specialization has also been achieved to varying extents with regard to ninety types of machines, twenty-seven metallurgical products, five chemical products, and numerous others. In certain cases specified plants within a country were given output goals for the entire bloc. In other instances, cooperation consisted of dividing up the assortment for

[18] See Montias, op. cit., p. 130.
[19] Montias, op. cit., p. 141.
[20] U.S. Senate Committee on Foreign Relations, op. cit., pp. 258–259.

a given product, for example, five-ton trucks to one country and ten-ton trucks to another. But most cooperation efforts were still formulated in bilateral contracts.[21]

Late in 1961 a change was developing in Soviet attitudes toward Comecon integration. Discontent with the extent of Comecon's progress began to show, and a less conciliatory attitude toward the position of the less developed countries was taken. Whereas prior to this time the U.S.S.R. had been apparently sincere in offering, as a compromise, specialization based both on existing and future cost conditions; by the end of 1961 it was "evident . . . that present profitability was meant to be the dominant consideration."[22] At the same time dissatisfaction with the limited degree of bloc integration, frankly admitted during 1962, resulted in a more vigorous push by the Soviet leadership for planned coordination of the entire Comecon region in the 1960's.

In June 1962, the First Secretaries of the seven Eastern European countries and of the U.S.S.R. met in Moscow, deciding to form a permanent Executive Committee for strengthening Comecon's power to implement recommendations and stating in rather general language that long-range intrabloc cooperation should be increased. This June meeting provided an appropriate backdrop to the release in August of a major policy declaration by Soviet Premier Khrushchev. A sober Nikita Khrushchev criticized Comecon's progress relative to the successes of the European Common Market, and called for development of bloc-wide coordination of major investment plans, capital movements across national frontiers, joint investment projects in lines of production of mutual interest, and a mechanism for supranational, regionwide planning and for the direction of trade and capital movements.[23]

Opposition to a supranational planning mechanism surfaced only a few months after it was proposed. Press reports indicated a rather general unreceptiveness to the idea of "common planning organs" to guide industrial expansion of Eastern Europe. The majority implicitly preferred the familiar voluntary system of economic collaboration, under the loose guidance of traditional Comecon organs and the new executive committee.[24]

As a result a conference of the First Secretaries of the Communist Parties held in July, 1963 did not face squarely the joint planning proposals. It became clear from the official conference communiqué and editorials in Communist Party newspapers that economic nationalism was again thwarting a drive toward greater cooperation and specialization. It also became generally known at this time that Rumania was leading the resistance to pressure from Moscow, and that a bitter conflict was materializing.

[21] Spulber, *op. cit.*, p. 305.
[22] Montias, *op. cit.*, p. 143.
[23] See U.S. Senate Committee on Foreign Relations, *op. cit.*, p. 259–260.
[24] See *Ibid.*, p. 260.

The Rumanian reaction crystallized into the famous manifesto of April 24, 1964, stating:

> The idea of a single planning body for all Comecon countries has the most serious economic and political implications. Management of the national economy, on a planned basis, is one of the fundamental, essential, and inalienable attributes of the Socialist state . . . The state plan is one and indivisible.[25]

Less abstractly, the Rumanian Deputy Premier G. Apostol declared on July 7th that in spite of increased pressure from the Soviet Union his country would hold to its present policy:

> We believe that the idea of supranational control is in conflict with the principles of socialist cooperation. We also adhere to the principles of equality of all Communist Parties, of noninterference in the internal affairs of socialist countries, mutual support, and the right of all countries to choose their own social system.[26]

With existing guarantees of the principles of sovereignty within the structure for decision-making in Comecon, it is obvious that the resistance of Rumania (and others to a lesser degree) cannot be peacefully overturned in order to effect multilateral, general coordination for Eastern Europe and the U.S.S.R. There was a very limited advance in financial coordination in 1963 by the adoption of a system of international payments on the basis of "transferable rubles" and by the establishment of the International Bank for Economic Cooperation. Otherwise, regional integration is no further advanced than it was in 1962. Reliance on the traditional forms of bilateral, and perhaps, triangular or quadrangular agreements remains the prospect for the near future.

Let us review the reasons why the Bloc has had so much difficulty multilateralizing its planning and its trade. First, there is the factor behind the Rumanian dissidence: the sharp disagreement — particularly between the advanced and the less developed members of the Bloc — about the nature of long-term specialization and division of labor which should guide their mutual development plans. In effect, each nation sees its own best long-run interests as not being maximized by the plans of the group. Second, it is difficult enough to plan for the future with reliable prices as a guide; the uncertainties become almost insuperable under the chaotic pricing conditions which exist in the Bloc. Third, there is the inconvertibility of Bloc currencies as a result of the factors mentioned earlier. Inconvertibility cannot be removed without a rationalization of Bloc pricing and a substantial relaxation of direct controls and central planning. While inconvertibility remains, trade and payments cannot be multilateralized because no country will want to hold the currency of any other country. The fact that an International Bank has been set up and accounts are kept in transferable rubles does not

[25] Quoted in U.S. Senate Committee, *op. cit.*, p. 261.
[26] *Ibid.*

change this situation: a nation with an unplanned surplus still has to spend that surplus in one particular country. Calling the surplus "Transferable Rubles" rather than levas, zlotys, or ordinary rubles does not make it any easier to spend, given irrational prices and a central planning which provides for no exports above plan.

One major problem which has faced Comecon since the mid-1950's has been a relative shortage of fuels and industrial raw materials. Each nation has been anxious to develop its own fabricating industries and to import from other Comecon nations the fuel and raw materials needed to feed these industries. The reason for this behavior is not hard to find: resources for investment are overburdened and the extractive industries are extremely capital intensive. Soviet economists estimate that it requires 3 to 3½ times more capital to export a ruble's worth of fuel or raw materials than a similar value of machinery. So far, the Soviet Union has grudgingly shouldered part of the raw material burden by expanding its extractive industries to meet Comecon needs. Their reluctance to continue in this role along with (1) the general dissatisfaction within the Bloc with their mutual machinery imports, and (2) the possibilities of getting better "buys" in the West, may eventually lead to a substantial diversion of intrabloc trade to the West.

Intrabloc trade turnover taken from the U.S. Senate Foreign Relations Committee is presented in Table 8–4. This table does reveal some slight decline in the intrabloc trade of most Eastern European countries as a percentage of their total trade in the five years from 1958 to 1963. This slow change is likely to continue, but the pattern of intrabloc trading is so strongly entrenched that there is very little probability of a rapid or radical change.

Soviet Trade and Aid to China

According to one careful Western observer, "Unquestionably, mainland China could not have achieved anywhere near the rates

---

Table 8–4

Intrabloc Trade as Percent of Total Trade Turnover
of the Countries of Eastern Europe, 1958–1963

	1958 (exports plus imports)	1963 (exports only)
Bulgaria	86.0	79.8
Czechoslovakia	70.3	70.4
East Germany	79.5	76.1
Hungary	71.9	no data
Poland	58.4	60.1
Rumania	77.9	67.4
U.S.S.R.	73.8	63.3

Source: U.S. Senate Committee on Foreign Relations, "Soviet Foreign Trade," reprinted in M. Bornstein and D. Fusfeld, The Soviet Economy (Homewood, Ill.: Richard Irwin, Inc., revised edition, 1966), p. 263.

of industrial growth she actually attained without the capital goods, particularly complete plant installations, and technical assistance she received from the Soviet Union."[27] This statement must be amplified by a consideration of the financial forms of the aid and trade, the types of aid and the kinds of goods, and the benefits to China and costs to the Soviet Union. It will be necessary to allude briefly to the tangled web of political relations as well, but there is no space to specify it fully here.

From the very beginning of the Chinese Communist government in 1949 up to the open conflict with it in 1960, the Soviet Union gave generous aid to and was the main trading partner of China. Apparently none of the aid took the form of free grants. Most of it took the form of loans at the relatively low interest rate of 2 percent, but repayable in the relatively short period of 10 years. This may be compared with the usual Western loans to the less developed countries at rates of 5 to 6 percent or higher for 20 to 25 years or longer.

Between 1950 and 1957 alone, Soviet loans amounted to the quite respectable figure of 5,294 million yuan. Under various estimates, this translates to something like $1,370 to $2,240 million U.S. dollars for that eight year period.[28] Yet almost all of this has now been repaid by the Chinese with an equal value of goods and services; and all other Chinese-Soviet trade transactions were roughly equal exchanges. How then can we speak of Soviet "aid" to China, and how can we claim that this aid was of great importance?

The crux of the answer is that these loans allowed China to import massive amounts of Soviet capital goods and technical services at a very decisive stage in her development. In the first six years of Chinese industrialization, from 1950 through 1955, these credits financed more than one-fourth of all Chinese imports from the Soviet Union.[29]

These imports included many whole plants, with agreements for 291 of them concluded by 1959. By 1960, the Soviet Union had completed installation of 130 entire plants, including almost every vital area of the Chinese economy. Other Eastern European Communist countries had completed 27 entire plants, and had another 37 under construction.[30] In addition to whole plants, the Chinese imported much individual machinery, and other equipment from the Soviet Union. Thus, all plants and equipment constituted very high percentages of total Chinese imports from the U.S.S.R. in these crucial years: 31 percent in 1955, 42 percent in 1956, 50 percent in 1957 and 1958, 63 percent in 1959, and 62 percent in 1960.[31]

Services imported from the Soviet Union included large numbers of Soviet technicians in China and large numbers of Chinese students learning in the Soviet Union. Between 1950 and 1960, a total of 12,300 Soviet and Eastern European specialists and technicians worked in

[27] Alexander Eckstein, *Communist China's Economic Growth and Foreign Trade* (New York: McGraw-Hill Book Co., 1966), p. 137.
[28] *Ibid.*, p. 154 and 167.
[29] *Ibid.*, p. 170.
[30] *Ibid.*, p. 143.
[31] *Ibid.*, p. 151

China. At the same time, about 8,000 Chinese engineers and more than 7,000 Chinese students received advanced training and education in the Soviet Union.[32] The abrupt withdrawal of all Soviet technicians (and their blueprints) in 1960 constituted a major blow to the Chinese economy. This withdrawal was certainly caused by previous Chinese conflict with the Soviet Union, but it in turn became an important cause of further conflict.

The Soviet share of total Chinese trade was around 50 percent in the late 1950's. Yet even as late as 1963, long after the Chinese-Soviet conflict was public knowledge, the Soviet Union still had a fifth of all Chinese trade, and was still her most important single trading partner. In the late 1950's Chinese trade was also most important to the Soviet Union, though the Chinese share of Soviet trade was only a little over a fifth at its peak. Communist China held first place in Soviet trade in 1955, 1956, and 1959; and held second place in 1957, 1958, and 1960. After that, however, China's share of Soviet trade dropped precipitously, and by 1964 her share was below that of any of the Eastern European Comecon countries.[33]

Lastly, the China aid program did involve considerable cost to the Soviet Union, even though it was financed by loans almost all fully repaid. In the first place, the largest loans were made in 1950 to 1952; but at that time the Soviet Union was still just finishing its own recovery from the vast Nazi war devastation. It made no loans to any other country in that period, and the loans to China constituted a sizeable burden for an economy the size of the Soviet economy in those years.

Furthermore, it was noted that the largest percentages of Soviet exports to China were in plant and equipment. Yet Chinese exports to the Soviet Union from 1950 to 1963 were 80 percent finished consumer goods or raw materials and semimanufactures for the production of consumer goods. Thus, Soviet trade with China aided Chinese growth, but Chinese trade with the Soviet Union may have been a restraining factor on Soviet growth. On the other hand, these consumer goods from China did at least afford a convenient way of satisfying the immediate demands of Soviet consumers.

Trade with the West

Although the percentage of Soviet trade outside Eastern Europe has increased substantially, and is now around 30 percent of U.S.S.R. total trade turnover, the largest part of this proportional increase has been with the underdeveloped countries. Trade with the industrial West has increased in quantity since the mid-1950's, but has not changed much as a percentage of total Soviet trade.

Table 8–5 indicates the present importance of East-West trade. Notable is the much higher significance that East-West transactions have in the total trade of Eastern Europe and the Soviet Union than in the

[32] *Ibid.*, p. 169.
[33] *Ibid.*, p. 146; and Heiss, *op. cit.*, p. 922.

Table 8–5

Comparative Impact of Two-Way Trade Between
Western and Eastern Europe (1962)

	Percentage of Total Exports	Percentage of Total Imports
Exports of Western Europe to Eastern Europe	4.2	
Exports of Eastern Europe to Western Europe	15.8	
Imports of Western Europe from Eastern Europe		4.0
Imports of Eastern Europe from Western Europe		14.8

Source: U.S. Department of Commerce, *U.N. Monthly Bulletin of Statistics*, (March 1964), pp. 90–91. In these data "Eastern Europe" includes the U.S.S.R.

total trade of Western Europe. These figures follow, of course, from the fact that Western Europe is a much larger trading area.

The U.S.S.R. itself comes into world markets and trades with both industrial and less developed private enterprise economies to the extent annually of about $2 billion of goods.[34] Dominant exports to the West have been petroleum, coal, iron ore, and cotton — with the bulk of machinery and the exports of manufactured goods going to the underdeveloped countries. In turn, the greatest part of Soviet imports from the industrial West has been in machinery and manufactured commodities. The growth of machinery imports in recent years has been substantial, advanced equipment from the West — as in the past — often serving as prototypes for Soviet modernization efforts. Thus, of all imports from the industrialized private enterprise economies of the West, Soviet imports of machinery and equipment grew from a high 31.2 percent in 1958 to an even higher 47.1 percent of the total in 1962.[35]

The countries of Western Europe and Japan have traded relatively much more heavily with the U.S.S.R. than has the United States, Canada, or Australia. Soviet trade plays its most important role for the receiving countries in the less developed private enterprise economies. Soviet trade with the less developed countries is partly a matter of comparative economic advantage, but reflects political factors as well. The importance of Soviet trade for the less developed private enterprise economies is illustrated in Table 8–6.

In 1964 Soviet foreign trade (exports plus imports) with all non-Communist private enterprise countries totalled $4,664.8 million. Of this amount, Soviet trade with the industrial West totalled $2,997.6 million, with the United States only $183.2 million, and with the less developed nations $1,440.5 million.

[34] Leon M. Herman, "Economic Content of Soviet Trade with the West," *Law and Contemporary Problems* (Autumn 1964), Vol. 29, No. 4, p. 972.
[35] See *ibid.*, p. 978.

Table 8–6

Importance of Soviet Trade to Selected Private
Enterprise Economies, 1962

Country	Percentage of Partner's Total Exports Going to U.S.S.R.	Percentage of Partner's Total Imports Coming from U.S.S.R.
A. North American and Australia:		
1. United States	.1	.1
2. Australia	1.3	.1
3. Canada	.1	less than .05
B. Western Europe and Japan:		
4. Austria	4.3	2.8
5. Belgium-Luxembourg	.6	1.0
6. Denmark	1.5	1.1
7. France	1.5	1.5
8. West Germany	1.5	1.5
9. Japan	3.0	2.6
10. United Kingdom	1.8	1.9
11. Greece	7.7	2.9
12. Sweden	2.7	2.0
C. Less Developed Countries:		
13. Brazil	3.2	2.2
14. Ghana	4.6	1.5
15. India	5.3	5.5
16. Indonesia	4.8	1.4 (1961)
17. Iran	14.7	3.1
18. Malaysia	7.7	.2
19. Sudan	4.5	3.3
20. Egypt (U.A.R.)	15.4	7.8

Source: U.S. Congress, Joint Economic Committee; *Annual Economic Indicators for the U.S.S.R.* (Washington, D.C.: U.S. Government Printing Office, 1965), pp. 120–124.

Balance of Payments. The Soviet balance of trade with various areas is shown in Table 8–7. The Soviet balance is favorable with regard to Communist countries and the less developed countries, but very unfavorable in relation with the more developed Western economies. Yet in most years the total has been favorable — as it was again in 1965. The year 1964 was exceptional because of the heavy Soviet net import of Western grain, unlike their usual net export of grain.

Table 8–7 also reflects the fact that over the last decade Soviet imports have exceeded her exports to the West, most of the difference being financed though sale of substantial amounts of gold.[36] The CIA has esti-

---

[36] U.S. Senate Committee on Foreign Relations, *op. cit.*, p. 248.

Table 8–7

Soviet Net Surplus of Exports Over Imports
to Various Areas (in millions of U.S. dollars)

Areas	1962	1963	1964
Communist countries	339.7	113.0	59.5
Industrial West	—164.4	—180.4	—451.6
Less developed countries	400.0	281.2	336.9
Total Soviet Surplus	575.1	213.7	— 55.3

Source: Heiss, *op. cit.,* p. 933. Numbers are rounded so they do not add exactly.

mated that as of January, 1964, U.S.S.R. gold reserves had been reduced to "less than $2 billion,"[37] due to the chronic trade imbalances with the West.

In 1963 Soviet gold sales were $560 million; in 1964 they made further sales of about $500 million. Whether or not these sales are a problem for the U.S.S.R. depends on the availability of domestically produced gold — a datum which has been kept secret since 1935. It also depends on the amount of long-term credit the Soviet Union can obtain and the ability of the Soviets to come up with new products desired in the West. Given the continued Soviet desire to expand imports of Western machinery, further Soviet gold exports may be expected. Presumably under these pressures, the Soviet Union has launched a drive to obtain long-term credits from the Western companies with which it deals. Officials have let it be known that the biggest orders will go to companies with the most generous credit arrangements, if prices and delivery terms are also competitive.[38]

Technical Cooperation. A recent addition to East-West transactions has been in the area of technical cooperation.[39] There has often been implicit cooperation involved in exporting advanced machinery to the Soviets — as in the chemical and automobile industries, where machinery and equipment carried with them blueprints and the technological results of research and development work. More explicit agreements for the export of technical know-how and even for co-production have also been made. For example, there was a trade agreement between France and Rumania for technical aid in agriculture "and other fields," and there have been some cases of industrial collaboration between Western firms and Polish and Hungarian state enterprises. Further developments in this area may be expected *if* there is more of a political thaw and *if* there are continued labor and capital shortages in Eastern

[37] *Ibid.,* p. 249.
[38] *Ibid.,* p. 250.
[39] John Pinder, "EEC and Comecon," *Survey,* No. 58 (January, 1966), pp. 110–111.

Europe. The most striking recent deal has been the Fiat auto plant sale by Italy to the U.S.S.R.[40]

Politics and Future Trade. The volume of trade between the U.S.S.R. and the industrial West has certainly not been based wholly on economic criteria. The usual yardstick proposed by economists, the comparative advantages of one country relative to another, has been kept in the closet as a result of overriding political considerations on both sides. In the Soviet Union the matter of exporting what can be called "strategic goods" is settled internally by planners and politicians for the most part before the state trading enterprises receive their orders. In the United States and Western Europe, however, restrictions on such exports must be made public in the form of legislation and administrative regulations in order to let private enterprise exporters know what can and cannot be sold to Communist countries.

Western Europe and Japan have been more liberal than the United States in the range of goods they allow to be sold to the Soviet Union. Generally, the political and military "hazards" of trading with the Communist bloc have been played down in Europe and played up in the United States. This is partly because Western Europe is far more dependent on external trade than the United States, and therefore less willing to forgo profitable trading opportunities for political reasons. Nevertheless, it is appropriate to recall that exports to the entire socialist bloc were (in 1964) still only 4.2 percent of the global exports of Western Europe.

The conservative argument against expanding trade with the U.S.S.R. may be summarized as follows. First, dependence of a Western country on purchases by the Soviet government's state trading enterprises opens the possibility that trade could be used for purposes that are either strategic (for example, withholding oil at a critical moment) or political (for example, buying elsewhere unless a Western country or firm complies with certain political stipulations). Second, state monopolies can use their bargaining power to exploit economically those with whom they trade by buying cheaper or selling dearer. (The great size of the world market and resultant possibility of substituting other sources for Soviet goods renders this argument very weak.) Third is the fear of economic disruption, that the subsidized Soviet trading companies might sell at losses, or might even shatter world prices by intentionally "dumping" goods onto a market.[41] Fourth, it is argued that trade with the Eastern nations strengthens them economically, hence militarily. Fifth, the conservatives cite the unwillingness of Soviet bloc members to trade more freely with the West.

Other Western experts disagree with these views. For example, the view that Soviet trade with the West is guided primarily by political and

---

[40] See, e.g., Committee on Banking and Currency, U.S. House of Representatives, *The Fiat-Soviet Auto Plant and Communist Economic Reforms* (Washington, D.C.: U.S. Government Printing Office, 1967).

[41] See Pinder, *op. cit.*, p. 106.

strategic motives is looked upon as "oversimplified" and "misleading."[42] It has been said that when the Japanese undersell in the West, it is called "cutthroat competition"; but when the Soviets undersell, it's "dumping." The fact of the matter is that the Soviets sell at below world prices in the West only because they must in order to gain entry. Time and again, when provided with a guaranteed share of the market (as in the case of the diamond market), they have gladly accepted world market prices. "Dumping" means reduced earnings of foreign exchange, and they are in Western markets primarily to maximize their earnings. With regard to alleged dumping of raw materials, it has even been argued that "the growing volume of Russian purchases of many basic materials . . . help to maintain prices."[43] The conclusion is that it is "difficult to impute a consistent political 'line' to Russian traders in the world's commodity markets."[44]

Perhaps most important, the policy of restricting exports to the U.S.S.R., even of so-called "strategic" goods, is remarkably shortsighted. It may, of course, weaken Soviet military capacity in the short run. In the long run, however, it strengthens their strategic potential because they are forced to develop substitutes. The way to weaken a nation is to make it dependent.

At any rate, at present the United States and the N.A.T.O. countries of Western Europe do agree that "strategic goods," especially the military variety, should not be sold to Communist countries. The United States goes further, however, in a rather general embargo of any goods which are "detrimental to the national welfare," according to the Export Control Act of 1949. Interpretation of this law in the past has often meant that U.S. companies were prohibited from selling goods that their European competitors did not deem politically dangerous. For example, deals for large amounts in carburetors and $43 million in automotive machine tools were denied permits.[45] Still, latitude does exist under U.S. legislation. Presently, the trend of case interpretations is toward allowing sale of non-military goods by U.S. companies if the socialist bloc will surely get the same goods from other Western nations, and toward liberalizing the application of the term "detrimental." Under the Johnson Act of 1934, the United States also prohibits the extension of anything but short-term credit to nations which have reneged on past debts to us. The Soviet Union, like most other socialist bloc nations, falls into this class by virtue of World War I and Lend Lease debts. While Western Europe followed our lead in this matter for many years, they now extend credit quite freely to all of the nations of Eastern Europe.

It is significant that the United States has adopted a policy of excepting Yugoslavia and Poland from the rigid strictures applied to the rest

[42] See, e.g., Nove, *op. cit.*, p. 278.
[43] *Ibid.*
[44] *Ibid.*
[45] Stanley Metzger, "Federal Regulation and Prohibition of Trade With Iron Curtain Countries," *Law and Contemporary Problems*, Vol. 29, No. 4 (Autumn 1964), p. 1003.

of the socialist bloc, especially since 1957. Both countries have been allowed sales of surplus agricultural products for local currency under Public Law 480, and were granted "most favored nation" treatment.[46] With regard to future East-West trade, we may be somewhat optimistic. Favorable to growth are (1) the weakening of the socialist bloc political and economic ties and the strong desires of Eastern Europeans to buy more from the West, (2) the rapid economic development of Eastern Europe, with the likelihood of their producing more goods that are saleable in the West, and (3) the expectation that U.S. restrictions on imports from and exports to the East are likely to be relaxed rather than tightened in the near future.[47] There is also the distant possibility that the decentralization of the economies of Eastern Europe now in progress may allow them to be included in some form of Continental European trade association.

Economic Relations with the Underdeveloped Countries

During Stalin's reign, there was little trade between the Soviet Union and underdeveloped countries in Africa, Asia or Latin America. Soviet trade with the non-socialist countries was largely confined to the import of highly fabricated products of advanced economies. Politically speaking, Stalin argued that the bits of decolonization then occurring would result in most cases in "puppet" governments, still under the thumb of the old imperialist rulers. Therefore, he refused these new countries both political and economic assistance.[48] In purely economic terms, he must have recognized the inability of the war-torn Soviet Union in the early postwar years to take on any burden of aid to the less developed countries.

Shortly after Stalin's death, in March, 1953, a credit of thirty million dollars was extended to Argentina for the purchase of oil equipment. In 1954 and 1955 substantial credits were given to Afghanistan, Burma, and India (for construction of the huge Bhilai steel mill). A more active policy of aid and trade in carefully selected countries emerged during the mid-1950's and has been pursued to varying degrees subsequently.

Reasons given by Western observers to explain the change are mainly (a) the growing importance of these nations with regard to the so-called "East-West conflict," (b) the increased rate of decolonization in the 1950's and 1960's, (c) a recognition by the Soviet Union of a degree of reality in Asian and African independence, and (d) development of the fuel and raw material shortages in Comecon.[49] The new attitudes toward the underdeveloped countries were voiced clearly during

[46] *Ibid.*, p. 1010.
[47] Pinder, *op. cit.*, p. 110.
[48] See Branko M. Peselj, "Soviet Foreign Aid — Means and Effects," *Law and Contemporary Problems,* Vol. 29, No. 4 (1964), p. 983.
[49] See Curt Gasteyer, "The Soviet Union and the Tiers Monde," *Survey,* No. 43 (August 1962), pp. 10–22. Also, Milton Kooner, "Trade and Aid," *Survey,* No. 43 (August 1962), pp. 44–54. Also, Alec Nove, *loc. cit.*

the 20th Congress of the CPSU, in February, 1956, in a policy declaration by Party Secretary Khrushchev:

> These countries, although they do not belong to the socialist world system, can draw on its achievements to build up an independent national economy and to raise living standards of their people. Today they need not go begging for modern equipment to their former oppressors. They can get it in the socialist countries without assuming any political or military commitments.

Forms of Soviet Aid. Aid that is offered is usually given according to a bilateral agreement between the U.S.S.R. and another country. It is manifested in four forms: (a) by giving a loan of a specified amount for a specified project or group of projects; (b) by a straight grant for a designated purpose; (c) by direct military assistance; or (d) by an agreement for technical aid or cooperation.[50]

In comparison with the U.S., the Soviet Union and other CMEA countries extend little of their aid in the form of direct grants. Until 1958 virtually all aid consisted of goods and services delivered on credit at low interest rates. Usual charges for credits from the U.S.S.R. have been around 2½ percent, while from Czechoslovakia and others they have averaged only slightly higher. The time interval over which a particular credit can be drawn varies, but frequently it is limited to seven years. Credits are always granted to the public sector of a country, never to private corporations.

Repayment of loans also varies: three-fourths of all credits granted specify payment in 12 annual installments, the first being due the first year after the project is completed. Some loans are given for long terms up to fifty years; while other loans by the socialist bloc countries are shorter, and are payable from five to nine years after completion of the project. Repayment is always specified to be "in kind" so that underdeveloped nations will not have balance of payment problems when they repay the loans. This means, however, that the actual "interest" on the loans will then depend largely on the prices assigned to the goods accepted in repayment.

Levels and Distribution of Aid and Trade Among the Underdeveloped Countries. In addition to the $2.5 billion in military assistance, $6.6 billion was extended by Comecon countries as economic aid from 1954 to mid-1964. Aid to the less developed countries from the Soviet Union alone from 1955 through 1964 amounted to about $4 billion in military aid with over $5 billion in economic aid. Of the total economic aid, $2,125 million went to Asia, $2,061 million to the Middle East, $729 million to Africa and $115 million to Latin America (exclusive of Cuba). The largest recipients were India and Egypt (U.A.R.), who together received about 40 percent of the total.[51]

[50] See Peselj, *op. cit.*, p. 988.
[51] See Lee Tandy, "Soviet Foreign Aid to the Less Developed Countries," in U.S. Congress, Joint Economic Committee, *New Directions in the Soviet Economy* (Washington, D.C., U.S. Government Printing Office, 1966), p. 951.

Most Soviet aid has gone into industrial development. "By the end of 1965, about 55 percent of total Soviet extensions had been allocated for industrial development, 20 percent for agricultural and major multi-purpose projects, and nearly 15 percent for transportation and communications facilities."[52] Very little has actually gone into spectacular, but economically useless projects. It was previously mentioned that *all* Soviet aid has gone into the public sector. India, especially, has received much help in the public sector of her industry, thus helping to develop it at a faster pace than private enterprise in some fields. That most of this aid was industrial is seen in the fact that India alone accounts for 45 percent of total Soviet aid to heavy industry.

In addition to the aid mentioned above, the Soviet Union helped Cuba to the extent of $1.1 billion dollars from 1961 to 1965, mostly to offset the effects of the U.S. economic prohibitions on trade with Cuba. To the aid total, one must also add the export of technicians and education to many countries, paid for at very low rates. From 1955 to 1965, about 13,500 academic students and about 25,000 military and technical students from the less developed countries were trained in the Soviet Union. At the same time, about 65,000 Soviet economic and military specialists were sent to these countries.[53]

The trend which Soviet aid has followed over this short ten-year period is marked by a few key events. It had its well-publicized beginnings in large projects for India and Afghanistan in 1955. Its peak year was 1960, when $1 billion in credit was authorized, making Soviet aid the same proportion of GNP as that of the United States for that year. There was then a lull and retrenchment of aid commitments from 1961 to 1963. Finally, there were substantial resumptions in 1963 and 1964. Total Soviet grants and credits were somewhat less than 10 percent of those given by the United States over the decade.

The turnabouts in the 1960's have been explained by one analyst as follows.[54] The sharp cutbacks that were pronounced after the year of greatest Soviet aid commitment reflected both domestic and external pressures on the Party and Government to reevaluate the policy and precedent they were setting. From within the U.S.S.R. came a skepticism about the economic and political effectiveness of this aid commensurate with alternative domestic uses. From the other socialist-bloc countries came resentment that what was aiding "neutralist" nations was not available to further their own development toward communism. Most vociferous were Albania and China. And concomitant with the timely questions of the efficacy and equity of aid to "neutralist" countries came a general slackening of economic growth rates in the U.S.S.R., providing additional impetus for evaluating foreign aid in relation to national goals.

[52] *Ibid.*, p. 954.
[53] *Ibid.*, p. 950.
[54] M. Goldman, "A Balance Sheet of Soviet Foreign Aid," *Foreign Affairs*, Vol. 43, No. 2 (January 1965), p. 359.

The substantial increase of aid again in 1963–64 is analyzed by Goldman as evoked by political exigencies during those years. Mentioned first is the necessity of some additional grants so that existing debts could be repaid and previous positive political effects would not be jeopardized. The desperate need for funds by the Egyptian government is cited. The second factor bringing Soviet aid back to the level of the late 1950's has allegedly[55] been the spur of competition with China for influence in both the "neutralist" and "socialist" underdeveloped areas (though the still small ability of China to supply aid does not make it much of a competitor).

Trade between the U.S.S.R. and the underdeveloped countries has also undergone a rapid growth since the mid-1950's. From 1955 to 1962 trade turnover (exports plus imports) with the less developed nations rose 266 percent, while total trade turnover of the U.S.S.R. increased by only 100 percent.[56] Table 8–8 shows import and export trends to the underdeveloped areas.

Table 8–8

Soviet Imports and Exports from the Less Developed Areas (millions of current U.S. dollars)

Area	Imports 1955	Imports 1962	Exports 1955	Exports 1962
Latin America	78.0	74.0	24.3	38.4
Middle East	44.9	134.6	53.7	211.2
Africa	16.5	57.9	2.5	58.7
Asia	57.6	334.4	21.5	250.1
Europe (Iceland, Portugal, Spain)	13.4	12.8	10.3	9.2
Total	210.4	614.0	112.3	567.7

Source: Official Soviet trade publications, reported in U.S. Congress, Joint Economic Committee, *Annual Economic Indicators for the U.S.S.R.* (Washington, D.C.: U.S. Government Printing Office, 1965), pp. 116–117.

Note that both Soviet exports to and imports from the less developed areas rose with astounding rapidity in this period. In terms of different areas, trade with Latin America and the less developed areas of Europe mostly declined or remained about the same. But trade with the Middle East, Africa, and Asia shot up at a very rapid pace. Machinery items have been the most important of the Soviet exports to the less developed countries, with other manufactured goods second. Leading import commodities (in 1963) were rubber, raw cotton, cocoa leaves, wool, hides and skins. According to the U.S. Senate Committee on Foreign Relations, the Sino-Soviet bloc's share of the total trade of the less developed countries is around 6 percent, while that of the industrial private enterprise nations is about 75 percent.

[55] *Ibid.*, p. 360.
[56] U.S. Senate Committee on Foreign Relations, *op. cit.*

With regard to trade relations between the U.S.S.R. and the less developed "neutralist nations," Western zealots often argue that all such trade is intended as a vehicle for subversion. They claim that it allows Soviet trade and technical personnel into the imprudent country, where they will conduct propaganda; that the country will become dependent on Soviet spare parts for Soviet equipment; and that — at the very least — Soviet trade will make these other nations dependent on her as a market.[57] There is certainly some merit to these arguments. The Soviets have used economic ties for political purposes. It is probably fair to say that Soviet *aid* is almost exclusively motivated by politics — as is that of the United States. Trade, on the other hand, represents an admixture of politics and economics with the latter factor certainly dominant. The major motivation behind Soviet trade with the less developed nations is simple comparative advantage. These countries want Soviet machinery, equipment, and manufactured products; and the Soviets want their raw materials. As a result of trade, the Soviet Union, like the U.S., certainly has the power to exert political pressures, but this power has so far rarely been used.

Opinions regarding the political effectiveness of the Soviet aid program have been as varied as the actual results. Certainly its political impact has been disproportionate to its size of only 10 percent of U.S. aid. According to one observer, "Soviet successes have overshadowed American ones."[58] Most relevant to this success has been the sense of timing, the dramatic nature, and the excellent publicity Soviet aid projects receive. Examples are the Bhilai steel mill in India, the Aswan dam in Egypt, "attractive and impressive" hospitals, hotels and institutes. Once undertaken, Soviet aid projects get priority treatment — a corps of the best engineers and designers, and the best resources available, are devoted to their completion.[59]

On the negative side, inefficiencies in packing and storage, in coordinating material shipments, and some improvident building in particular climates has resulted in both needless waste and rapid deterioration. The most damaging evidence is the fact that Soviet aid-givers "have not succeeded in utilizing aid to bring Communist rule to underdeveloped areas."[60] Examples of countries which received considerable Soviet assistance, but which later disagreed violently with Soviet policies, include Yugoslavia, Albania, China, Algeria, Iraq, and Indonesia. It appears that the influence of Soviet aid and trade can only be determined in conjunction with political forces that are beyond their control.

What about the future? It seems unlikely that the Soviets are interested in making the internal sacrifices necessary to amass a much larger grant and aid program in light of the very questionable effectiveness of past programs. On the other hand, it is reasonable to expect

[57] See A. Nove, *op. cit.*, p. 290.
[58] Goldman, *op. cit.*, p. 349.
[59] *Ibid.*, p. 350.
[60] *Ibid.*, p. 358.

that one important by-product of the rapidly rising Soviet standard of living will be increased imports from the underdeveloped nations, particularly of coffee, cocoa, tea, vegetable oils, and tropical fruits. An increase in trade along these lines would go a long way toward cementing friendships.

SELECTED REFERENCES

1. The most important reference is the impressive collection of original articles edited by Alan A. Brown and Egon Neuberger, *Trade and Planning, Interactions Between International Trade and Central Planning* (Berkeley: University of California Press, 1967).

2. F. D. Holzman, "Some Financial Aspects of Soviet Foreign Trade," in Holzman, F. D., *Readings on the Soviet Economy* (Chicago: Rand McNally & Co., 1962), pp. 719–735.

3. J. M. Montias, "Background and Origins of the Rumanian Dispute with Comecon," *Soviet Studies*, Vol. XVI, No. 2 (October 1964), pp. 125–151.

4. John Pinder, "EEC and Comecon," *Survey*, No. 58 (January 1966), pp. 101–117.

5. Lynn Turgeon, *The Contrasting Economics*, Ch. XI (Boston: Allyn and Bacon, Inc., 1963 revised edition forthcoming), pp. 281–321.

6. Three articles from the publication of the U.S. Congress, Joint Economic Committee, *New Directions in the Soviet Economy* (Washington, D.C., U.S. Government Printing Office, 1966), are:

> Hertha W. Heiss, "The Soviet Union in the World Market," pp. 917–934.
>
> Leon M. Herman, "Soviet Foreign Trade and the United States Market," pp. 935–947.
>
> Leo Tansky, "Soviet Foreign Aid to the Less Developed Countries," pp. 947–965.

7. Egon Neuberger, "International Division of Labor in CMEA," *American Economic Review* (May 1964).

8. Michael Kaser, *Comecon, Integration Problems of the Planned Economies* (New York: Oxford University Press, 1965).

9. J. Wilczynski, "Strategic Embargo in Perspective," *Soviet Studies*, Vol. 19 (July, 1967), pp. 74–86.

10. P. J. D. Wiles, *Communist International Economics* (Oxford: Basil Blackwell, 1968).

PART FOUR

PROBLEMS OF CENTRAL PLANNING

9

PLANNING FOR GROWTH

How much of national income should go for consumption and how much for investment in expanded facilities? After examining this theoretical question, the discussion turns to actual Soviet prospects and plans for future growth. The emphasis in this and the following chapters is on domestic planning, so international relationships are largely ignored, and the Soviet Union is considered as a closed or isolated economy unless explicitly stated otherwise.

Investment versus Consumption

In the case of a centrally planned economy like the Soviet Union, it may be assumed that *aggregate effective* demand always rises as rapidly as aggregate supply, though *particular* goods may be unsaleable for various reasons. Thus, there are no retardations nor depressions caused by lack of demand. If the problems of demand are thus eliminated, then growth will depend simply on how fast output can be expanded. Before investigating the specific Soviet setting, it may be useful to summarize some of the elementary theorems of growth economics.

Since all problems of demand are assumed away, the remaining supply problem may be resolved into two questions. First, how much of each input (such as land, labor, and capital) can be procured under existing circumstances for use in production? Second, how much output can be obtained from these inputs in the production process?

Production is Determined by Labor, Capital, Natural Resources, and Technology

Many different physical inputs constitute the production base of an economy. For convenience, these may be grouped into three

215

categories of capital, labor, and natural resources. *Capital* includes inventories of raw materials and goods in process as well as all plant and equipment. *Labor* means the number of man-hours available as well as the degree of skill of the available labor force. *Natural resources* is defined as all useful materials, including land, known to be in the territory of the economy. Resources may be depleted by use or by natural erosion, but may be increased by new geological discoveries. *Technology* is the knowledge that determines how much output can be produced by a given combination of inputs. Therefore, the level of potential output is a function of the presently available (1) capital, (2) labor, (3) natural resources, and (4) technology. A thorough analysis of the growth potential of any existing economy should consider each of these inputs in turn as well as the interrelations among them.

The real gross national product of the United States grew by 3 percent a year from 1919 to 1959.[1] It has been shown that part of that growth was due to the growth of the labor force and part to the growth of the capital stock; but more than half the growth was accounted for by technical improvement. No one would deny the importance of improvements in technology or the quality of labor or capital; and therefore no one denies the urgent need for such things as research, education, and public health measures. Recent studies, however, have shown that it is very difficult to get exact quantitative estimates of just how important have been the respective contributions resulting from the growth in the different factors or technology.[2]

For the purposes of this discussion, it is possible to leave aside the intricate factual questions involved in separating out the behavior and influence of each of the components of growth. The level of potential output may always be considered to be determined solely by the amount of supply of any one factor (such as labor) and by the amount of output produced by a given level of that input (such as the output per worker). Of course, the amount produced by any one factor, such as labor, is influenced by the levels of all the others, such as land and capital, and by improvements in technology.

In order that the analysis may consider only the quantitative growth of a factor, changes in its quality — such as improvements in labor skills by education — will be lumped in with technological change. First, economic growth theorems will be solely related to growth of labor, and then solely related to the growth of capital. The other factors, however, and especially technology, will always be brought into the picture through their effects on the amount produced per unit of labor or of capital.

---

[1] United States Congress, Joint Economic Committee, Staff Report, *Employment, Growth, and Price Levels* (Washington, D.C.: U.S. Government Printing Office, 1959), p. xxiii.

[2] See, e.g., E. D. Domar, "On the Measurement of Technological Change," *Economic Journal,* Vol. 71 (December, 1961), pp. 709–729; also R. M. Solow, "Technical Progress, Capital Formation, and Economic Growth," *American Economic Review,* Vol. 52 (May, 1962), pp. 76–86.

Full Employment Growth

After allowing for frictional movements from job to job, it may be assumed that the Soviet labor force is always fully employed. Potential growth of output is then determined by the growth of the labor force and by the amount produced per unit of labor.

The "law" of diminishing returns states that the successive increases in total output, as additional workers are hired, will be less and less. It holds true only *if* capital, natural resources, and technique remain unchanged, and *if* some minimum scale of employment is reached. Given these assumptions, the law of diminishing returns cannot be other than true. All other things remaining the same, it is obvious that if enough workers are crowded onto a single plot of land or even the entire world, the crowding alone will eventually cause the product of an additional worker to decline. But of course, "other things" — especially technology — do not remain the same over time. Furthermore, many of the Classical economists — Malthus for example — went much further than the truism embodied in the law of diminishing returns. They predicted that diminishing returns per worker in the economy as a whole *would* come about in actual fact. The Reverend Malthus reached this dismal conclusion on the grounds that population increase would be very rapid, and would far outweigh the slow increase of capital, technology, and resources.

The Malthusian population controversy has great importance in the Soviet Union (and China) both in theory and practice. Marx called the Malthusian theory of people breeding like rabbits a slander on the human race.[3] Marx wanted to emphasize that the evils of poverty — both in the advanced capitalist countries and in the colonial and semi-colonial countries — are *not* primarily caused by too much population, but are social diseases caused by too much exploitation and profit making. Marxists argue that in the history of capitalism the improvement of technology has greatly surpassed the rise of population, so tremendous further increases in the product per capita could be achieved if they were not held back by the institutional barriers imposed through the capitalist and imperialist systems. The Soviet economists have gone much further than Marx: they declare that more workers simply mean more output, and that socialism solves all economic problems, so no degree of population growth can ever be a problem in any socialist country.

Even if we accept the idea that the Soviet brand of socialism can insure a high rate of growth of output, this does not prove that the rate of growth per person could not be higher if there were less population growth. In other words, additional workers may add to the total product, but surely a point could be reached where the number of workers grows faster than the amount of capital. In that case, each additional

[3] For a full presentation of Marx's views on Malthus, see R. L. Meek, editor, *Malthus: Selections from Marx and Engels* (New York: International Publishers, 1958).

worker has less capital with which to work, so he will produce less than the previous average. Thus, more population may mean greater absolute growth of product (good — perhaps — for military and prestige purposes) *but* a much slower growth of output per worker (and therefore a heavy drag on the improvement of individual welfare). China seems to have recognized this in practice with a belated birth control drive, though with very hesitant theoretical recognition of the problem.

Full Capacity Growth

So far, we have concentrated on the increase of the labor force and its product per worker. It is more interesting and useful for our purposes, however, to estimate the potential growth of output in relation to the increase of capital and the product per unit of capital. Of course, the output per unit of capital will reflect changes in technology, natural resources, and the labor supply.[4]

Before we discuss growth, a very simple relationship may be stated between output and capital at any given moment. The national product or output *must equal the output per unit of capital times the amount* of *capital in use.* Thus we may write the simple formula:

$$\text{Output} = \frac{\text{output}}{\text{capital}} \times \text{capital}$$

This formula, obviously, is true by definition; but it is fruitful to think in these terms.

In the United States there are about three dollars of capital goods in use for every dollar of our annual national product. So our ratio of output to capital is about one-third. Therefore, when the value of our capital stock, including all machines and factories, was about $1,500 billion, we produced annually about $500 billion output.

Now this analysis may be extended to a growing economy. The "rate of growth of output" is defined to be the increase in output as a ratio to present output. For example, if the economy produced $100 last year, and it now produces $103, then the rate of growth is 3/100, or 3 percent a year. The rate of growth of output is determined by the growth of capital and the changes in output per unit of capital. More precisely, the rate of growth of output is equal to the increase in capital (or savings) from output *times* the increased output from the increased capital. Thus we may write the equation of growth:

$$\begin{array}{l} \text{Rate of} \\ \text{growth of} \\ \text{output} \end{array} = \frac{\text{Increase in output}}{\text{output}} = \frac{\text{increase in output}}{\text{increase in capital}} \times \frac{\text{increase in capital}}{\text{output}}$$

This equation is also true by definition.

Notice that an increase in capital is the economist's definition of "investment." Moreover, let us *assume* (because it is generally true in the planned Soviet economy) that the amount of investment is just

[4] This approach is detailed in E. D. Domar, "Expansion and Employment," *American Economic Review*, Vol. 37 (March, 1947), pp. 34–35.

equal to the amount of saving. Therefore, the "increase in capital" not only means the same thing as "investment," but also means the same thing as "saving." If the equation of growth is put into these more relevant terms, it may be written:

$$\text{Rate of growth of output} = \frac{\text{increase in output}}{\text{investment}} \times \frac{\text{saving}}{\text{output}}$$

This merely affirms that how fast the economy grows depends on how much is saved and invested, *and* how much is produced by the new investments.

Let us take an example of the use of this equation of growth. If the ratio of saving to output is 9 percent, and if the ratio of increased output to investment is one-third, then we find:

$$\text{Rate of growth} = \frac{1}{3} \times .09 = .03 \text{ or 3 percent a year.}$$

This has been approximately the performance of the economy of the United States over a long period of time.[5]

Soviet Growth Experience

In the detailed examination in Chapter 5 of Soviet growth in the postwar period, it was found that for the years 1950–1963 conservative U.S. estimates place Soviet GNP growth at 6 percent a year, while official Soviet figures put their growth at 9 percent a year. This compares with the U.S. official figure of 3.5 percent a year for the U.S. growth rate. It has been also emphasized that these averages cover two very different periods in Soviet development. In the 1950–1958 period the U.S. estimate of Soviet GNP growth was 7 percent, while the official Soviet figure was 10.5 percent. In the 1958–1963 period, the U.S. estimate of Soviet growth drops to 4.5 percent, while the official Soviet figure drops to 7 percent. No conclusive evidence was found to show that this was more than a temporary decline.

Assume, therefore, that the 1950–1963 average is the long-run average, and consider merely the U.S. estimate of that average. This conservative estimate of 6 percent is still high enough to call for an explanation in terms of the growth formula. If it is assumed for the moment that the Soviet ratio of increased output to investment is the same as the U.S. ratio, then in this simple analysis the higher rate of growth can only be explained by a higher ratio of saving and investment from current output (or income). Thus, if the Soviet ratio of increased output to investment is also one-third, then a 6 percent growth rate can only be explained by an 18 percent ratio of saving to output. According to the formula:

$$\text{Soviet growth rate} = \frac{1}{3} \times .18 = .06 \text{ or 6 percent.}$$

[5] For empirical data on the ratios and the average growth rate, see, e.g., Simon S. Kuznets, *National Product Since 1869* (New York: National Bureau of Economic Research, Inc., 1946).

Actually, the Soviet saving ratio has usually been even higher than 18 percent a year, often reaching as much as a fourth to a third of national income. To account for the saving to output ratio in the Soviet case — apparently higher in reality over the long run — we may advance two main reasons. First, the Soviet government extracts a very high proportion of saving from its national income, regardless of the wishes of individual Soviet citizens. The individual American businessman voluntarily saves a much lower proportion of his income.

Secondly, all Soviet saving is used for investment because the planners can always find a use for new capital. In fact, Soviet planners usually complain of a "scarcity" of capital. This is because they attempt to invest more than the entire available amount of savings. In the United States, on the other hand, when businessmen cannot find a profitable investment for all of their savings, some planned saving does not become investment in new capital (except statistically as "investment" in unwanted inventories). U.S. economists often complain of "too much" planned saving, while planned investment in additional capital is less than it could be. In some years "too much" supply of all goods (relative to money demand) even causes a decline of U.S. production and a depression situation, rather than any growth of output.

It is also obvious from the formula that the Soviet people have to pay a price for their high rate of investment and growth of output. If the Soviets save 18 percent and the United States saves only 9 percent of national output, and if both begin with the same $100 output, then in the first year the Soviet consumption would be only $82, while U.S. consumption would be $91. It is impossible to have both higher consumption and higher investment out of the same output; the Soviets have sacrificed some present consumption for more investment. Furthermore, in reality total Soviet output is still far below the American level, so the Soviet consumption level is even lower. In purely human terms, moreover, we must stress that when the Soviets began their rapid industrial expansion, their consumption was at a miserably low level. Therefore, each percent of national product taken from consumption in order to make investments meant a very great amount of present human misery in order to grow for the future.

Of course, the simple growth formula also indicates that *if* the Soviet Union continues to grow twice as fast as the United States, then after some years both their total output *and* their consumption would be larger than those of the United States. That is true, however, only *if* they continue to build new capital at the same rate and *if* they keep the same increase of output per unit of new investment. It is necessary to investigate both of these assumptions to assess future Soviet growth.

The Political-Ethical Issues

Up to this point, the issue of economic growth has been examined in the cold economic terms of the basic so-called Harrod-Domar model.[6] Now it is necessary to investigate why the question of

LIE

---

[6] See Domar, *op. cit.*

investment versus consumption is *the* vital political issue around which
Soviet politics must turn and by which Soviet lives are determined.

On the ideological side, it may be noted that the Soviet economists
follow a similar model derived from Marx. Actually, in the 1920's several Soviet economists, notably G. A. Feldman,[7] devised some quite
sophisticated dynamic growth models as tools of long-term planning.
Unfortunately, the Stalinist dictatorship distrusted any innovation in
the social sciences, and attacked these models as "bourgeois formalism"
and "mathematical formalism." As a result, Feldman's pioneering work
was ignored for several decades, while Soviet growth planning was left
to political whim.

At any rate, the Soviet economists now use models derived from the
reproduction schemes in Volume 2 of Marx's *Capital*, which anticipated
the Harrod-Domar model by many decades. Although it was cruder
mathematically, Marx's model showed all the essentials. It states implicitly: (1) what the conditions are for a steady growth at full capacity, and (2) that the growth rate of output will be higher if there is a
higher ratio of producer goods to consumer goods (or of investment to
consumption).

Of course, these Marxist models also show that the economy with the
higher ratio of investment will *eventually* also have a larger amount of
consumption — but the interesting question is how many years the
populace must wait for consumption, that is, at what date is optimum
consumption desired. Of course, this is a political and ethical decision,
not an economic one. It should also be noted that it is possible to go too
far in reducing consumption, even from the cold and calculating viewpoint of economic growth. To reduce consumption opportunities below
some point will lower labor productivity, and — after some time — may
even cause strikes or revolutions. A certain minimum percentage of consumption remains necessary if the gains made by more saving and investing of capital are not to be cancelled out by negative side-effects. To
put it another way, there are definitely both political and economic maximum limits to the possible percentage of saving and investment.

Finally, on the ideological front, one must note a strange and false
notion which Stalin raised to the level of an unassailable dogma. This
is the idea that steady growth cannot be achieved unless the investment
sector always grows faster than the consumption sector.[8] Actually,
Marx merely showed that this is sometimes the case in a "capitalist"
economy, and that in its extreme form it is a disproportion that usually
leads to a depression. The Soviets do not claim to have a capitalist

[7] See the discussion in Evsey D. Domar, "A Soviet Model of Growth," *Essays in the Theory of Economic Growth* (New York: Oxford University Press,
1957). The original Feldman article, "On the Theory of Growth Rates of National Income," is translated in Nicolas Spulber, *Foundations of Soviet
Strategy for Economic Growth: Selected Soviet Essays, 1924–30* (Bloomington:
Indiana University Press, 1964).

[8] An extended critique of this doctrine may be found in P. J. D. Wiles, *The
Political Economy of Communism* (Cambridge, Mass: Harvard University
Press, 1964), pp. 272–300.

economy, and they do not desire a depression, so it is hard to see the relevance of this notion of Marx to their forced conclusion. The real reason for Stalin's doctrine that investment goods *must* grow faster was merely to reinforce the arguments for ever more investment. In reality, steady growth may be achieved with any constant positive rate of net investment; the investment sector must grow more rapidly than the consumption sector only if one wishes not steady, but constantly accelerating growth.

There is no reason to value the consumption by future generations above that by the present population. It would seem therefore that a Marxist, who bases himself on a socialist type of humanist ethics, would decide to maintain an *equal* percentage increase of consumption and investment, once a country has made the initial push for industrial development. At any rate, assuming a constant marginal output-capital ratio, the economist can only calculate the different growth rates to be gained by alternative ratios of investment to consumption. Which alternative ratio of investment to consumption should be selected is a political choice, and — in a democracy — ought to be decided by the collective ethical evaluations of present versus future consumers.[9]

Most political disputes in the Soviet Union have had this issue as one of the underlying bones of contention. In the 1930's it was, of course, vitally necessary to raise the level and percentage of investment by a drastic amount if industrialization was to be seriously begun. Chapter 4 examined the concrete form that this theory took: collectivization of agriculture and the removal of large amounts of agricultural goods to use as exports to buy machinery, as cheap raw materials for industry, or as food for industrial workers.

Now it is seen that the application of growth economics may be quite different in form in the industrially developed Soviet Union of today. There are still violent political disputes over the percentage of investment to consumption, but the debate is over a small percentage either way. Now that industry is established, no one would argue that it is necessary to again double or triple the investment percentage in a few years' time. Moreover, agriculture is relatively much smaller and industry relatively much larger now. The debate no longer centers on shifting a large product from agriculture to industry, but rather on how much of the total product is to go for wages of workers (mostly in industry) and how much should go into the surplus of government profits and taxes for more investment.

Prospects for Future Soviet Growth

The prospects for future Soviet economic growth may be evaluated within the context of the model offered above by asking (1) how much capital can the Soviet Union save and invest each year? and (2) how productive will that new capital actually be?

---

[9] See the similar view by a Soviet economist in V. Volkonskii, "Methods of Mathematical Economics and the Theory of Planning and Administering the Economy," translated in *Problems of Economics* (1967).

Saving of Capital

The Soviet Union, as mentioned above, has saved and invested an enormously high percentage of its national income. The proportion was certainly over a quarter in the early 1930's, was perhaps 35 or even 40 percent in some years,[10] and has remained very high ever since. According to official Soviet data, the share of "means of production" in the output of the industrial sector taken alone was only 39.5 percent in 1928, but rose rapidly to 53.4 percent by 1932, then continued to rise steadily till it was 70.6 percent by 1955, and has continued with small increases since then.[11] The producer goods sector increased its percentage of all goods because of the high levels of investment. The question is whether the Soviet Union can continue to invest such a high percentage — still more than one third — of its national income.

In formal terms, the Soviet government can decide what it wishes. In realistic political terms, however, we have seen that the Soviet politician must consider the increasing pressure of workers for more immediate gains in consumption. Although the Soviet Union is far from a political democracy, each of its leaders recognizes the wisdom of courting the favor of the rank and file of the Communist Party, if not the whole population. In economic terms, it was shown above that the investment percentage of income is held to some maximum by the need to provide sufficient consumer goods to provide incentives for labor to maintain and increase its productivity.

There is some indication that the percentage of investment in the national income will at least stop growing (and may even begin to decline) because past trends and also all future Soviet plans show the growth rate of consumer goods coming ever closer to the growth rate of producer goods. It seems that the two will be allowed to grow at about the same rate in the future, though this is not yet acknowledged to be a good thing in theory. Thus, the supply of capital is likely to continue increasing at about the same percentage, not rising, and perhaps dropping a little.

Product Per Unit of Capital

Many different things affect the product per unit of capital, including the incentives and productivity of both workers and managers, the amounts of labor and raw materials, and the organization and efficiency of allocation and use of all factors. Chapters 10, 11 and 12 will discuss the planned allocation of resources in the Soviet Union; in general, it will be revealed that there has been much inefficiency, but that the allocation procedure is improving. Current trends in the reform of organization, including greater decentralization and improved incentives, will be discussed in Chapter 13. Here it is still necessary to con-

[10] See Franklyn Holzman, "Discussion of Economic Development in Mainland China," *American Economic Review,* Vol. 51 (May, 1961), pp. 518–519.

[11] See Central Statistical Board of the U.S.S.R. Council of Ministers, *National Economy of the U.S.S.R.* (Moscow: Foreign Languages Publishing House, 1957), p. 47.

centrate on a few more factual questions. The analysis begins with the availability of trained manpower and the vital role of Soviet education. Next it considers the level and rate of technological improvement, perhaps the most important single factor in growth. Finally, the investigation turns to the results of all of these factor changes as reflected in the actual trends in the productivity of labor and of capital.

Manpower and Education. Soviet population growth — like U.S. population growth — has been declining in the 1960's. The U.S. population growth rate was down to 1.2 percent in 1965. The Soviet rate was only 1.1 percent in 1965, and is expected to decline further to 1.0 percent or lower in future years, mostly because of declining birth rates.

Furthermore, in the 1950's and early 1960's the Soviet Union still had a great lack of able-bodied men because of past calamities. It must be remembered that Soviet manpower losses were very high in World War I and the following Civil War, were significant during the collectivization drive of the early 1930's, and were fantastically high during the bloody fighting of World War II, in which Hitler threw the bulk of his armies into the U.S.S.R. In fact, as noted earlier, it is estimated that deaths and birth deficits resulting from the war have caused the present population of the Soviet Union to be 40 to 45 million below the level it would have been if there had been no war, a deficit which is larger than the whole population of England or France. Only recently has the lack of babies during the Second World War begun to have less effect on the supply of labor, and the proportion of able-bodied young workers begun to return to normal.

Yet all modern economic studies agree that the rate of economic growth is not so much influenced by the total growth of the labor supply as by the level of *training* of the labor supply. Some of the training and education problems of the Soviet Union may be seen in three goals set by the Soviet government in May, 1963. First, the system was turning out relatively too many top specialists and not enough middle level technicians. The goal was announced that there should be three or four times as many secondary specialized school graduates (trade or technical school at the U.S. high school level) as there are specialists graduated with a higher education in the economy — but this ratio was only 1.42 to 1 as late as 1965–66. Secondly, there are relatively too many specialists in the western regions and not enough in the rapidly developing eastern areas. So it was decreed that educational facilities are to be expanded more rapidly in the East. Thirdly, graduates still do not stay where they are sent for very long, especially in the more rustic eastern regions. So it was decreed that graduates will receive diplomas only after one year at the place to which they were assigned.

It is easily seen that the Soviet leadership does indeed view education primarily as an instrument for training the required labor force, though it is also supposed to provide the citizen with a socialist political outlook. As a means to growth, the general rise in educational level has been of vast importance. The average educational level of industrial wage workers has improved from 3.5 years of schooling in 1929 to 7.5 years in 1965. Similarly, the proportion of highly skilled workers climbed from 19 percent of the total in 1925 to 65 percent in 1961. Over the same years (1925 to 1961), semiskilled workers declined from 41 percent to 35 percent, and unskilled from 40 percent to less than 1 percent. Training in agriculture, however, has progressed far more slowly. As late as 1959, unskilled workers constituted 71 percent of the manual labor force in agriculture.

By 1965 attendance in grades one through eight was 100 percent of the respective age group in Soviet schools. Enrollment in grades nine through eleven was about 50 percent of the respective age group, though all of the rest were enrolled part-time or engaged in on-the-job training or apprenticeship training. Finally, full time enrollments in higher education were only 6 percent and part-time about another 6 percent on the respective age group.

Total Soviet enrollment in all schools in the academic year 1963–64 was 65.1 million, including 3.3 million in higher educational institutions. In comparison, the United States (with a smaller population) had in the same year 53.6 million total enrollments, including 5.0 million in higher educational institutions. The aggregate U.S. lead in higher education also is evident in graduations. In the academic year 1963–64 the total of U.S. graduates in higher education was 614.2 thousand, including 498.7 thousand bachelor's and first professional degrees, 101.0 thousand M.A.'s, and 14.5 thousand Ph.D.'s. In the year 1964 Soviet higher education graduated only 369.6 thousand students in total. This figure includes 354.3 thousand first professional degrees, mostly representing five years' training, and 15.3 thousand advanced degrees, mostly with the "aspirant" degree, equivalent to a U.S. level between the M.A. and Ph.D.[12] It will be shown below, however, that the Soviets have recently greatly increased the number of students enrolled for advanced degrees, and that the situation is reversed in some specialized fields that may be the key to economic growth.

It must be emphasized that all 754 institutions of higher education in the U.S.S.R. in 1965 were operated by the central government as a free public service. Not only is tuition free, but most students are given sizeable stipends or scholarships, amounting for advanced students to more than the average industrial wage. On the other hand, the Soviet government regulates maximum admissions into the different fields (on a competitive basis) according to the expected proportionately required supply in those fields. Furthermore, the programs are mostly far narrower and more specialized than in the United States, with the major exception that all students must take Marxist social science courses. In recent years it appears that Soviet training has become a little less specialized, but it is still far more so than in the United States.

[12] All data from Seymour M. Rosen, "Changing Guideposts in Soviet Education," in U.S. Congress, Joint Economic Committee, *New Directions in the Soviet Economy* (Washington, D.C.: U.S. Government Printing Office, 1966), appendices A and B.

The emphasis among fields in the Soviet Union thus reflects government policy. "During the 1928–64 period, the Soviet Union trained about 5,800,000 professionals in all fields, of whom about one-third were in engineering fields and about one-fifth were educational specialists."[13] By 1965 the dominance of these two fields (and especially engineering) was even stronger, as may be seen in Table 9–1.

Table 9–1

Composition of Soviet Graduates, 1965

Fields	Percent
Engineering-industrial	40
Educational-cultural*	36
Agricultural	9
Socioeconomic	8
Health-medical	7
	100%

* ". . . two-thirds of educational-cultural field graduates are trained as research scientists in universities and as science teachers in pedagogical institutes . . ."
Source: Nicholas DeWitt, "High-Level Manpower in the U.S.S.R.," in U.S. Congress, Joint Economic Committee, *New Directions in the Soviet Economy* (Washington, D.C.: U.S. Government Printing Office, 1966), p. 805.

The engineering-industrial fields not only are large in quantity of students, but demand high quality work. For example, in the years 1950–1964 only 62 percent of the students who entered the engineering-industrial fields graduated, while 80 percent graduated in the educational-cultural fields, and 95 percent in the health-medical fields. Incidentally, it may be noted that the preponderance of engineering in admissions was even higher than in graduations.

Furthermore, the excellence of Soviet training has been admitted by several careful U.S. observers. For example, one says, "The quality of Soviet professional training in scientific, engineering, and applied fields today is, on substantive grounds, comparable to that offered in the West."[14] It has also been observed that the basis of student selection in the U.S.S.R. is still merit rather than money or father's position, a fact which makes for more effective use of human resources.

The Soviet effort in theoretical research also stands out clearly in the statistics. By 1965 there were 2,000 research institutes employing 2,497,000 people, including 765,000 professionals, 418,000 semiprofessionals, and 357,000 research and academic personnel. For some years the demands of research institutes were expanding faster than the supply of advanced degree holders. Therefore, in a crash program

[13] Nicholas DeWitt, "High-Level Manpower in the U.S.S.R.," in U.S. Congress, Joint Economic Committee, *New Directions in the Soviet Economy* (Washington, D.C.: U.S. Government Printing Office, 1966), p. 802.
[14] DeWitt, *op. cit.*, p. 816.

the number of postgraduate students in training for the "aspirant" degree was pushed up from 23,000 in 1959 to 83,000 in 1965.

Finally, comparisons with the United States show definite Soviet leads in the production of most kinds of specialists. By 1964 the U.S.S.R. was annually training four times as many engineers as was the United States, three times as many physicians, and twice as many agricultural specialists. Yet, as previously noted, in the academic year 1963–64 the United States graduated a total of 614,194 of all kinds of higher educational degrees, whereas the Soviet Union produced in 1964 only 369,620 higher educational graduates. It is no surprise, therefore, that the United States was producing three or four times as many graduates in all the less specialized fields.

Technological Progress. A recent U.S. report[15] finds that current Soviet technology still lags behind U.S. technology and that in the period after World War II the rate of Soviet technological improvement was just slightly higher than the U.S. rate. The report bases these findings on a detailed study of 25 technological indicators in the two countries. The author of the report, Boretsky, claims that further fragmentary data put the average technological lag as of 1962 at about 25 years. All of his calculations, however, are *very* rough. One could challenge the selection of the indicators, the data used, and especially the relative importance of the different indicators. It is probably safe to conclude only that (as of 1962) the Soviet economy was still technologically behind the U.S. level in most sectors by some amount.

The selected indicators of this U.S. report also reveal that Soviet technological progress is faster than the U.S. rate in many sectors but certainly not in all sectors. An unweighted average would show the U.S.S.R. progressing at 136 percent of the U.S. rate. But an unweighted average has no economic meaning in this case because we must know the relative importance of the different areas. Boretsky weights them according to the amount of labor saving in each area, and finds on this basis that the Soviet rate of technological progress was just 104 percent of the U.S. rate in the 1950–1962 period. This finding again depends heavily upon the selection of the indicators, the accuracy of the data, and — especially — the weighting or relative importance attached to each indicator. It is probably safe to say only that, according to these data, Soviet technological progress in the postwar period has been equal to or greater than U.S. progress.

Boretsky points out, however, that we would have expected the Soviet rate to be *much* higher. The reasons for this expectation include the facts that (1) the Soviet Union had the opportunity to borrow technology from the United States; (2) higher Soviet investment rate would allow it to put into operation more new capital goods, which would embody more new technology, and — as we shall see in the next section

---

[15] Michael Boretsky, "Comparative Progress in Technology, Productivity, and Economic Efficiency: U.S.S.R. versus U.S.A.", in U.S. Congress, Joint Economic Committee, *New Directions in the Soviet Economy* (Washington, D.C.: U.S. Government Printing Office, 1966), pp. 149–150.

— (3) the Soviet labor-to-capital and capital-to-output ratios appear to be growing closer to the U.S. ratios, implying a closing of the technological gap.

For the future, it may be expected that Soviet technological advance will continue at or above the U.S. rate for some time (still ignoring such intangibles as changes in organization, incentives, and efficiency of allocation). In the first place, if Boretsky's estimates are not incorrect, the Soviet technology still lags in many key areas, so Soviets can continue to borrow more advanced technology. Moreover, it is expected that they will continue to invest a high proportion of product in new fixed capital, so they will still have plenty of opportunity to embody the latest technology. Finally, it was shown in the previous section that the Soviets are committed to the investment of large amounts of resources to education and research, and are very rapidly increasing the numbers of both practical engineering and theoretical scientific personnel. This factor may be expected to result in more rapid technological improvements.

✓ *Rates of Productivity Growth.* In Chapter 5 the report of Bergson's detailed study of Soviet productivity showed that in 1960 Soviet output per employed worker was 29 percent of the U.S. level in ruble prices or 58 percent of the U.S. level in dollar prices. Likewise, Bergson found that Soviet output per unit of reproducible capital was 98 percent of the U.S. level in ruble prices and 149 percent of the U.S. level in dollar prices. Finally, Bergson found that Soviet output per unit of capital-plus-labor was 58 percent of the U.S. level in ruble prices and 67 percent of the U.S. level in dollar prices. It was noted then that these data have severe limitations if the object is to draw conclusions about relative performance.

For the purpose of evaluating growth prospects, it is possible to add certain estimates by Boretsky as to the comparative rates of *improvement* of these productivity ratios.[16] He finds that in the period 1950–1962 Soviet product per worker grew much faster than U.S. labor productivity — 4.3 percent a year in the Soviet Union compared to 2.4 percent a year in the United States. In the same period Soviet product per unit of capital declined while the U.S. ratio rose; it fell 3.8 percent a year in the U.S.S.R. compared to a rise of .2 percent a year in the United States. Finally, Boretsky finds that Soviet output per unit of capital-plus-labor in 1950–1962 grew at about the same pace as the U.S. combined productivity — both grew at about 1.7 percent a year. Since Boretsky's figures cover comparisons over time as well as comparisons between two countries, they are obviously even shakier and more limited than Bergson's.

The fact that the marginal output/capital ratio (the ratio of increased output to new investment) has declined for a number of years is confirmed by official Soviet data shown in Table 9–2. The first line of Table 9–2 shows the declining output growth of the 1958–1963 period, most of

[16] See Boretsky, *op. cit.,* pp. 150–151.

Table 9–2

Output, Capital, and Output-Capital Ratio

Item	1958	1959	1960	1961	1962	1963
1. Rate of Growth of Output (increase of output as % of preceding year's output)						
	10	9	8	7	7	5
2. Growth of Capital (investment or saving as % of this year's output)						
	18	20	20	22	23	19
3. Marginal Output-Capital ratio (1 ÷ 2)						
	0.56	0.45	0.40	0.32	0.31	0.26

Source: A. I. Notkin, "Rates of Development of Socialist Production and the Rise in Public Consumption," *Production, Accumulation, and Consumption* (White Plains, New York: International Arts and Sciences Press, translated from Russian in 1967), p. 38.

the reasons for which we have already enumerated (from increased defense spending to bad weather and poor incentives in agriculture). The second line shows the attempt to increase investment in some years as a partial offset to the other problems. Line 3 shows the reflection of the situation in a declining ratio of increased output to investment (which also reflects the shift to increased production of some heavily capital-using products, such as housing).

At any rate, if Boretsky's estimates are accepted as correct indications of at least the direction of movement, the following picture is revealed. The Soviet Union was raising its much lower labor productivity faster than was the United States, while its relatively high capital productivity was falling toward the U.S. level. In other words, the Soviet Union was beginning to find trained labor relatively more scarce, and was starting to use it more intensively. On the other hand, capital was becoming relatively more abundant in the Soviet Union, and was now being used with less labor. These findings would seem to imply that the Soviet economy is beginning to look much more like the U.S. economy in technological terms (the labor/capital ratio). Finally, in spite of Boretsky's finding that the Soviet output/capital ratio has been falling toward the U.S. ratio at least since 1950, the reader should recall Bergson's finding that in 1960 it was still equal to or above the U.S. ratio.

Predictions of Future Growth Rates. The most conservative U.S. estimates, those by the CIA and by Stanley Cohn,[17] project Soviet GNP growth at a rate of 4.5 to 5.5 percent, while optimistically predicting a U.S. rate of 4.5 percent. Boretsky[18] predicts a Soviet growth rate

[17] See Cohn, in *New Directions in the Soviet Economy, op. cit.,* pp. 124–127.
[18] Boretsky, *op. cit.,* p. 155.

of 5.5 percent. Both of these estimates are based on their authors' projections of expected growth of capital and labor supplies, as well as growth in the productivity of labor and the productivity of capital. In this brief resume it is impossible to improve or even repeat these complex calculations.

As a more tentative conclusion, it has been shown that the Soviet investment ratio is much higher than the U.S. ratio, though pressure for immediate consumption *may* lower it somewhat. In addition, it was seen that the Soviet ratio of increased output per unit of added capital (investment) is still as high or higher than the U.S. ratio, though it may be diminishing toward the U.S. level. At any rate, advances in education, research, and technology should keep it respectably high. Nevertheless, even if both of these crucial Soviet ratios are lowered a bit in the future, and if the United States continues at its long-run average growth rate, it would still seem likely that the Soviet economy will continue over the long run to grow much more rapidly than the United States — assuming no really drastic changes in the situation of either country.

It was found in Chapter 5 that the most conservative U.S. estimates place Soviet growth since 1950 at about 6 percent, though the Soviet official rate stands at 9 percent. If it is assumed that the much higher rates of the 1950–1958 period as well as the much lower rates of the 1958–1965 period were temporary, then the best estimate for the future would be the average since 1950. In terms of the simplest growth formula, it might be assumed that the Soviet added output/investment ratio will decline no further than to the long-run U.S. ratio of one-third. In other words, it could be argued that in the Soviet Union further diminishing returns to capital, which arise because of limited labor and natural resources, will be fully offset by technological improvements based on Soviet advances in education and research. Then if Soviet net additions to capital remain above 18 percent of the national product (as seems likely), the growth rate of the national product would remain above 6 percent (compared with the U.S. long-run rate of about 3.5 percent). The reader, however, should review the detailed material presented here himself and may reach his own speculative conclusions.

SELECTED REFERENCES

1. Campbell, Robert W., *Soviet Economic Power* (Boston: Houghton Mifflin, 1966, second edition), especially Chapter 8.

2. Domar, Evsey D., "A Soviet Model of Growth," *Essays in the Theory of Economic Growth* (New York: Oxford University Press, 1957).

3. The interesting views of one Soviet economist on the proportin of investment to consumption may be found in S. G. Strumilin, "Concerning the Problem of Optimum Proportions," *Problems of Economics*, Vol. 5 (July, 1962), pp. 3–13. Further very interesting Soviet views on the economics of growth are provided in the collection translated as *Production, Accumulation, and Consumption* (White Plains, N.Y.: International Arts and Sciences

Press, 1967), including S. P. Pervukhin, "Production and Consumption at a New Stage," A. I. Notkin, "Rates of Development of Socialist Production and the Rise in Public Consumption," I. B. Kvasha, "Capital Intensity," and V. G. Venzher, "Characteristics of the Collective-Farm Economy and Problems of its Development."

4. A discussion of the important and interesting contribution of women to Soviet growth is in Norton T. Dodge, *Women in the Soviet Economy* (Baltimore: Johns Hopkins Press, 1966).

5. Relevant articles on technology and human resources in U.S. Congress, Joint Economic Committee, *New Directions in the Soviet Economy* (Washington, D.C.: U.S. Government Printing Office, 1966), include: Michael Boretsky, "Comparative Progress in Technology, Productivity, and Economic Efficiency: U.S.S.R. versus U.S.A.," pp. 133–256; J. W. Brackett and J. W. DePauw, "Population Policy and Demographic Trends in the Soviet Union," pp. 593–702; Murray Feshbach, "Manpower in the U.S.S.R.," pp. 703–788; Nicholas DeWitt, "High-Level Manpower in the U.S.S.R.," pp. 789–816; and Seymour M. Rosen, "Changing Guideposts in Soviet Education," pp. 817–848.

6. A survey of several areas from the comparative growth viewpoint is in Abram Bergson and Simon Kuznets, editors; *Economic Trends in the Soviet Union* (Cambridge, Mass.: Harvard University Press, 1963).

7. U.S. Congress, Joint Economic Committee, *Soviet Economic Performance: 1966–67* (Washington, D.C.: U.S. Government Printing Office, 1968).

10

PLANNING FOR BALANCE

The problem of balance or consistency in the economy has two aspects. The macro aspect is the problem of seeing that the aggregates in the economy, such as aggregate demand and aggregate supply for all goods, are equal to each other. The micro aspect lies in the need for supplies of *each* commodity to equal the requirement or demand for it by all other firms and industries. For example, enough rubber tires must be provided to meet the needs of the auto industry. It is best to begin here with the simpler aggregative relationships.

Aggregate Balance versus Inflation

The question of aggregate balance in the Soviet economy is mostly a reflection of the growth problem already discussed. Basically, the resources supplied for investment must just equal the amount required or demanded for investment, while the amount supplied to consumers must just equal the amount they will demand at present incomes and prices. In this chapter it is assumed that the politicians have already told the planners what percentage of national output is to be put into investment. Now the planners must calculate the amounts of consumer goods and the wages and prices that will be consistent with the given investment decision. The analysis presented here first examines the real quantities and problems involved, then some of their reflections in monetary policies.

The Real Problems. The economy of the United States has been plagued frequently by lack of adequate demand for the products of private enterprise. In the planned economy of the U.S.S.R. there has *always* been sufficient aggregate demand since the planning period began in 1928, and there has never been general or aggregate unemployment. The reason is that a lack of aggregate demand can always be corrected without great dislocation in a planned economy through the device of additional government investment. In reality, the problem has usually been that the government has demanded much more for investment than could be supplied, and has failed to provide enough consumer goods to satisfy household demand.

Since aggregate demand has always more than equalled the amount of resources and manpower available, aggregate unemployment has been nonexistent since 1928. Of course, the Soviet Union does have a considerable amount of "frictional" and "structural" unemployment. "Frictional" unemployment may be defined as ordinary labor turnover. "Structural" unemployment occurs when the structure of industry and technology changes, so that millions of workers must change jobs from one place to another, from one industry to another, or from one skill to another. These changes require large amounts of retraining and moving expenses. The number of workers involved and the time necessary for "readjustment" has recently become great enough that numerous observers report significant unemployment from this source. The Soviet Union may also have some "seasonal" unemployment. This occurs because there are times of the year in certain industries, especially agriculture, when much labor is needed and times when very little is needed. It may not be profitable for a society to transfer these workers to another job for only a few months of the year, though the Chinese now use them to build dams and roads.

As implied above, the main problem of aggregate balance in the Soviet economy has been due not to lack of demand creating unemployment, but rather to excessive demand causing inflation. The main reason for the inflation of the 1930's and 1940's was the excessive increase in government demand for investment goods, military supplies, and "free" or non-priced welfare services. This created an excess demand for all inputs, including labor. The excess demand for labor pushed up wage rates much faster than productivity, and so workers' demand for consumer goods rose faster than total production and much faster than output of consumer goods.

The excessive wage payments occurred as a result of decisions both at the national level and at the level of each firm. In the initial industrialization and wartime periods, the planners called for much larger increases in investment and military goods than in consumer goods; and the discrepancy was usually even greater in the fulfillment of plans. Related to the high level of investment and military spending was the practice of overfull employment planning mentioned earlier. At the level of the enterprise, overfull employment planning meant being given output targets which, for most firms, were essentially unachievable with the amount of labor and other inputs legally available to them.

In order to meet their production plans, therefore, Soviet managers found themselves competing strenuously for materials and labor. Material goods prices were effectively controlled at the enterprise level, and most deliveries of goods were ordered by direct central priorities and rationing. Workers, however, respond mainly to the incentive of higher wages, so this was the path followed by managers competing for labor inputs. Managers in the 1930's and 1940's were able to overspend their payrolls with few if any penalties, but were under extreme pressure to meet output targets. In that period, they bid notoriously high to obtain the scarce supply of workers, and even hoarded unneeded workers against future needs.

As a final result of this process, the workers attempted to spend their rapidly increasing wages on the much smaller increase in consumer goods. The consequence was too much money chasing too few goods in the consumer goods market, and steadily rising prices until 1947. This is the basic pattern of prewar and wartime inflation: excess demand for labor as a joint result of the high rate of investment and overfull employment planning; and excess demand for consumer goods as a result of wages rising faster than productivity and faster than the output of consumer goods. Since 1947, the problem has been under control because (1) the State Bank only allows enterprises to overspend their payrolls to the extent that they increase output above plan, and (2) the degree of overfull employment planning appears to have been sharply reduced.

Now the process must be examined more precisely in terms of the required balances. The discussion here is in words, while the same argument is presented in equation form in Appendix A to this chapter. As a first approximation, ignoring all other changes, it might be said that consumer goods prices will rise or be inflated if the amount of wages is greater than the value of consumer goods. Neglecting the fact of some voluntary saving, there will be aggregate balance or equilibrium in the consumption sector only if the value of consumer goods just equals the total wages paid. If the value of consumer goods at present prices is less than the total wages, government will have to inflate consumer prices or tolerate long lines of unsatisfied customers. If the value of consumer goods at present prices is greater than the total wages, government will have to deflate consumer prices or there will be goods gathering dust on the shelves.

To add body to this analysis, some more detail must be inserted into the picture. The main point to be considered is that labor may produce not only consumer goods, but also investment and military goods (or free welfare goods, which similarly do not soak up wages). Suppose, with no increased capacity to produce, that some workers are switched from consumer goods to investment goods or military production. In this case, there would be fewer consumer goods, but the same amount of wages, thus causing inflationary pressure in the consumer goods market.

In the actual Soviet case, productive capacity has been increasing, so proportionate shifts to investment or military goods have only meant a slower growth of consumer goods than wages, rather than an absolute decline. Only in the drastic circumstances of the First Five Year Plan and the Second World War was higher investment or more military production associated with an actual lowering of consumption. Nevertheless, in most years wages climbed much faster than the slow growth of consumer goods, so inflationary pressures did result.

As a further approximation to Soviet reality, one should note some complicating factors. First, in addition to their basic cost-prices, all Soviet consumer goods have a large sales or turnover tax placed upon them. Obviously, an inflationary imbalance might be corrected by raising this turnover tax. Second, wages available for spending may be reduced by many other kinds of personal taxes or licenses, of which the income tax has been the most important to date. Lastly, if workers increase their personal savings, by bank deposits or purchase of government bonds, then they obviously have less money left to spend for consumption. If these complicating factors are considered, then the resulting statement is more complex: there will be balance in the consumer goods sector only if the turnover tax plus the cost price of consumer goods times amount of consumer goods is just equal to the wages paid out in all production, less the amounts of personal saving and personal taxes. Otherwise, there will be imbalance and deflationary or inflationary pressures.

With this analysis, it is possible to examine just what alternatives are open to the planners to correct a financial imbalance. *First*, the amount of labor devoted to consumption versus investment and military goods might be changed, but assume that that is a political decision and cannot be changed. *Second*, technology and the amount of capital might eventually be increased, but assume that this problem is short-run, so consumer goods production cannot be increased in that way.

The *third* alternative, as noted all along, is to raise the price of consumer goods to soak up the wages paid out for additional investment or military spending. How satisfactory a technique is this for meeting the inflation problem? Actually, price inflation does not directly affect physical planning. However, there are adverse side-effects. Inflation (1) does actually disrupt the calculations of planning insofar as all prices and accounts are rapidly changing, (2) changes relative incomes and reduces the equity of income distribution, and (3) allegedly may dampen the worker's incentive to work since he realizes that extra wages will have little buying power. This latter point, (3), is quite debatable. It is often argued that, with just a little inflation, workers may still be under a money illusion, that is, they may be more conscious of their rising money wages than of rising prices, and not be conscious of their declining real wages. It has also been argued that rising prices *force* a worker to work harder in order to maintain income, even though he knows that each hour's wages buy less. This is especially the case when the workers concerned are at a very low income level.

A *fourth* alternative reaction to excessive consumer demand at present prices is to leave the disequilibrium as is, doing nothing, and allowing so-called "repressed inflation." The Soviet Union has often been forced to live with this alternative, but the results are not good. As stocks of goods in stores get very low, people must spend long hours in lines to get anything — and some unlucky consumers will get nothing. This system of distribution is obviously both inefficient and inequitable. Needless to say, the prospect of long hours of queuing and being unable to spend one's money reduces workers' incentives to work and to earn money wages. While repressed inflation has only been serious in the Soviet Union in the years 1929 to 1935 and 1940 to 1947, it has existed chronically ever since central planning began. To sum up: repressed inflation involves inequity and wasted time standing in lines, and is a less desirable alternative than open inflation because of its more adverse impact on incentives to work, since workers accumulate money they cannot spend.

A *fifth* alternative is to leave the imbalance, but add rationing to get equal shares of income. This rationing was in force in the Soviet Union when repressed inflation was severe, in the years 1929 to 1935 and 1940 to 1947. Rationing has many bad effects, including reduced workers' incentives and reduced satisfaction derived by workers from a given amount of consumer goods. Moreover, if the imbalance is significant and lasts a considerable time, rationing leads to black markets. Black markets add illegal activity to other woes, and undermine the objective of rationing by greatly lessening the equality of distribution. Furthermore, rationing is costly to administer and enforce.

A *sixth* alternative in theory is to lower wage rates in all sectors and, thereby, decrease consumer demand. In practice, this would be a foolish, if not politically infeasible, policy. It would certainly adversely affect incentives to work.

Seventh, taxes may be increased, which is a politically feasible way of reducing wages. Taxation may be in the form of higher personal income taxes, which lower disposable wages-after-taxes, or in the form of higher sales and turnover taxes, which raise prices-after-taxes. Either way, taxes lower the volume of goods that workers can actually demand, and reduce inflationary pressure. The kind of tax does make a difference, however. Workers are much more conscious of the loss of real income the taxes represent if higher wages are immediately followed by higher income taxes, which leave take-home pay unchanged, than they are if the higher wages are followed by higher sales taxes and prices.

Finally, *eighth*, the government might offer higher interest rates on bonds or bank deposits in order to encourage voluntary personal saving. From 1927 to 1958, the Soviet government used compulsory bond sales to mop up excess purchasing power. In 1957, all bonds were frozen or declared irredeemable for 20 to 25 years. Compulsory bond sales, of course, really amount to taxation. Such sales were necessary because voluntary savings are fairly insignificant so far in the Soviet Union, and because higher interest rates are not likely to elicit a quantitatively important response. For example, interest rates on bonds were 10 to 13 percent in the 1927 to 1931 period, and yet sales had to be forced. The response is limited or "inelastic" partly because previous experience has made doubtful the safety of such money loaned to the Soviet government. Moreover, most Soviet citizens have too low an income to reduce voluntarily their consumption by significant amounts for a higher rate of interest, particularly if there is expectation of rising prices, which there was before 1948. As Soviet citizens become more affluent, and if prices continue to remain stable, however, this picture could well change.

Facts of Soviet Fiscal Policies. With these problems of balance in mind, it is useful to examine a Soviet national budget. The Soviet budget includes much more than the U.S. budget, since it covers the financing of a large share of industrial investment and a wide variety of free welfare services, such as the complete educational and health needs of the nation. It also includes the equivalent of our state and local budgets. Thus, fully one half of Soviet national income is funnelled through the budget!

A recent summary of the percentage breakdown of available revenues and expenditures of the Soviet government is presented in Table 10–1.

Table 10–1

National Budget of U.S.S.R. for 1964

Revenues

Turnover tax	38.9%
Deductions from profits	30.4
Social insurance markup	5.3
Tax on cooperatives and collective farms	1.4
Government borrowing (bonds and bank deposits)	0.1
Direct (personal income) taxes	7.2
Other revenues	16.7
	100.0%

Expenditures

Investment in the national economy	44.0%
Social-cultural welfare spending	36.1
Defense	14.4
Administration	1.2
Repayments and interest on the national debt	0.1
Other expenditures	4.2
	100.0%

Source: Central Statistical Agency of the U.S.S.R., *National Economy of the U.S.S.R. in 1964* (in Russian only: Moscow, 1965), p. 771.

Notice on the revenue (or income) side that fully 69.3 percent of all Soviet government revenue comes from the turnover tax and from profits, both of which are part of the sales price paid by the purchaser of goods. The same can be said of the social insurance markup, which is a payroll tax. So, unlike the United States practice, most Soviet government revenue is collected by government enterprises. In fact, it is planned that all personal income taxes, taken directly from the individual, will be eliminated in the near future. Since the government determines income distribution in the first place, there is no need to redistribute by income taxes; and sales taxes (or "turnover taxes") affect incentive less adversely than income taxes. This is especially true in the Soviet case where sales taxes are effectively hidden — no one knows the sales tax element in price.

On the spending side, the biggest item is one that also appears in hardly any U.S. government budget: it is the government's investment in the national economy. Until the reforms of 1965 (discussed in Chapter 13), this was done through non-returnable grants to enterprises. The only other sources of Soviet investment are the somewhat smaller retained profits of enterprises, the depreciation funds of enterprises, short-term credits granted by the State Bank for working-capital needs, and reserve funds for investment put aside by the collective farms (so-called "indivisible funds").

During the period 1928 to 1948, the government put much more money into the economy than it took out of circulation. Money taken out is reflected in budget surpluses, while in that period money was put in by excessive issuance of Bank credit. The excessive flow of credit to enterprises — much of it eventually used to pay higher money wages — was the financial reflection of the real problems discussed above, that resulted in inflation or very rapidly rising prices. Since 1948, however, the Soviet Union has achieved stable or even falling prices. This may be observed in Table 10–2, adapted from Holzman.

Notice in Table 10–2 that controlled prices in the government stores only doubled from 1928 to 1932, whereas farm market prices — free to reflect the true scarcity — rose by thirty times. This was the period of a drastic reduction of consumer goods to provide resources for the foundations of industrialization. Of course, everyone wanted to buy goods in the government stores, but very little was available. The Soviet government, therefore, had to enforce rationing to make sure that each worker had at least a minimum of goods. On the other hand, there were freely moving prices in the collective farm markets, which sold goods from private plots or surpluses (over their quota) from collective farms. These collective farm markets were in effect a legalized black market for the remaining goods.

Note also that by the late 1930's prices had stabilized somewhat, and that controlled prices were at about the same level as free prices. This was the result of a rise both in the volume of consumer goods and in the sales taxes levied on these goods. Since the great contrast between free and controlled prices was removed, it was possible to end rationing. Then, in the period of the Second World War and Reconstruction, 1940 to 1950, there was once more extreme inflationary pressure. This was expressed in higher prices, very limited goods in government stores, rationing, and astronomical prices in the farm market. The situation was the result of two conflicting trends. First, there was a concentration of resources on production for the armed forces at the expense of

Table 10–2

Index of Consumer Goods Prices in the Soviet Union
(all available years, 1928 = 100)

Year	Government Stores (controlled prices)	Collective Farm Markets (freely moving prices)
1928	100	100
1932	200	3,000
1933	400	2,000
1936	700	700+
1937	700	700+
1940	1,000	1,780
1945	2,545	13,575
1947	3,895	11,530
1948	3,235	4,175
1949	2,770	2,880
1950	2,215	2,770
1951	2,035	2,810
1952	1,925	3,100
1953	1,740	2,595
1954	1,640	2,855
1955	1,640	2,855
1956	1,640	2,610
1957	1,640	2,412

Source: Franklyn D. Holzman, "Soviet Inflationary Pressures, 1928–1957," *Quarterly Journal of Economics.* Vol. 74 (May, 1960), pp. 167–188. This same article also provides the fullest available explanation of the causes of these price movements, and is the basis for the discussion in the text.

consumer goods. At the same time, however, wages continued to rise and could not all be taxed away if workers' incentives were to be maintained.

Despite the rapid increase in wages, it is incorrect to speak here of "wage-push" inflation since money wages only rose from 1928 to 1940 half as much as government prices of consumer goods; and by 1947 the money wage rise was only a third of the price rise. Furthermore, Soviet unions do not bargain for higher wages; the higher money wages resulted from competitive bidding of Soviet managers to get more labor in order to fulfill impossibly high plans. Thus, prices and money wages were rising, but *real* wages were falling. The fundamental reason was the lack of consumer goods, caused by the shift of labor to producing goods for industry and defense.

After the Currency Reform of December 1947 (see Chapter 4), a new era began, reflecting a close financial control over wage increases as well as prices. From 1948 to 1954, not only did government stores' prices constantly fall, but the free prices on the farm market dropped even faster and approached parity with government prices for a while. During this period, prices could be lowered because wage rates were increasing more slowly than productivity, and consumption was increasing as a share of the national product. In the period since 1954, the gains in productivity have been passed on mostly in equivalent increases in wages, leaving aggregate prices roughly stable, though with some fluctuations in relative prices.

Soviet Price Policies for Balance. The Soviet price for each article is planned so that the price (before taxes) will equal the sum of all the components of operating cost plus a margin of profit. Prices should then be reasonably consistent with one another; and, so long as they are constant over the planning period, they may be used to calculate the aggregate balances necessary in the economy. These prices, moreover, are supposed to be set so that demand just equals supply. This supply-and-demand price has always been higher for all consumer goods than their "cost"-plus-profit price. The difference has been made up by the turnover tax. Of course, the differential varies from product to product, so the rate of turnover tax is also very different among goods. The turnover tax is positive for almost all consumer goods, exceptions obtaining in the case of house rents, bus fares, and a few other goods and services which receive subsidies. Since the huge turnover tax goes almost immediately to the government, individual retail enterprises retain only the usual profit margins.

The vast difference between the turnover tax rates in consumer goods and producer goods have been calculated from actual Soviet figures in one excellent U.S. study.[1] It was found in 1964 that in heavy industry the cost of production and marketing accounted for 82 percent, profit for 11 percent, and turnover taxes for only 7 percent of the value of output. By contrast, in food and other light industries the cost of production and marketing accounted for only 67 percent, profit for only 8 percent, and turnover taxes for a full 25 percent of the value of output.

Despite the levy of turnover taxes, many prices have remained chronically below equilibrium levels. There have been, of course, errors in calculation by planners. In addition, it is expensive and complicated to change prices very often. The result has been prices below the equilibrium and queues of consumers, some of whom are doomed to disappointment. As noted earlier, it also means weakened incentives to work.

The prices of industrial producer goods have remained much more stable. Demand is regulated by the direct rationing of many supplies to the firm. Thus, balance is maintained directly, though the prices may be quite irrational from other points of view, and are far from true equilibrium levels.

Financial Planning and the Banking System. In the maintenance of balance, the Financial Plan is assigned an important role. The Financial Plan includes not only all the transactions going through the State Budget, but also the investment expenditures by industry out of its own reserves, and the credit advanced to industry by the banking system. We have already mentioned in other contexts the two main reasons for such detailed financial planning, even under a system of centrally

[1] Morris Bornstein, "Soviet Price Theory and Policy," U.S. Congress, Joint Economic Committee, *New Directions in the Soviet Economy* (Washington, D.C.: U.S. Government Printing Office, 1966), p. 68.

planned production. One reason is the continued use of money wage differences to guarantee incentives to work, and accompanying need for rational consumer prices to make the system effective.

The other reason for detailed financial planning is the vital role that money-costs and prices play in the relation between the central planning apparatus and the management of each enterprise. The enterprise not only receives output targets, but is given a figure for "planned cost" and an additional small percentage of "planned profit." If the enterprise performs more poorly than expected, it will make less than its planned profit. This was always taken as an indicator of inadequate performance though, until recently, an enterprise would still have been rated largely successful if it met its output targets. It is only after the 1965 reforms, as will be seen in Chapter 13, that a failure to achieve planned profit results in less funds available for reinvestment, less money for bonus payments, and less collective welfare spending.

Many Soviet enterprises are efficient enough to make more than their planned profit. Formerly, almost all profits went right back to the government unless they were assigned to immediate reinvestment. Under recent reforms, however, the excess profit goes partly into the enterprise's own reserve funds account at the Industrial Bank, to be used for reinvestment within the industry. In theory, it should be as easy for an enterprise or an industry to be assigned new investment funds (in the Financial Plan) from central budget grants or loans as from its own reserves. In practice, the enterprise or industry always retains more control over the spending of reserve funds banked under its own name. The other part of the excess over planned profits goes to the "Enterprise Fund" (formerly called the "Director's Fund"). This fund supplies the money for bonuses to workers (at the discretion of the manager), and may also be used for collective spending on employee's housing or recreation. Obviously, the intent of these rules is to make the enterprise cost-conscious and alert for opportunities to economize (and we shall see that all the recent reforms are intended to greatly strengthen this trend).

The banking system plays an important role in the execution of the Financial Plan. The most important banking organization is the State Bank, whose President is a member of the U.S.S.R. Council of Ministers. In addition to its Head Office in Moscow, it has over 8,000 others including regional offices, regional suboffices, and thousands of local agencies. It holds the bank accounts of all Soviet enterprise. The Bank's prime purpose is the provision of working capital for government enterprises through the extension of short-term credit, of which it has a monopoly. Another vital function is the strict control of wage funds: the Bank does not allow an enterprise to draw on its regular account to pay wages unless it is within the wage plan. Finally, it also carefully supervises the payments between enterprises, all of which must be handled through its accounting and clearing system.

The State Bank also holds all money for the Treasury. Thus the State Bank, in addition to being responsible for close financial supervision of the accounts of all enterprises, also receives and disburses the budgetary funds of the government. For reasons of financial discipline, the State Bank allows enterprises to draw only enough money to meet their transaction needs. To prevent unplanned funds from accumulating, enterprises are even forced to pay their profit taxes monthly, though these taxes are then adjusted at the end of the year.

The financial reforms of 1930–1932 also assigned the disbursement of all long-term investment capital to four special banks: for Trade, Agriculture, Communal and housing needs, and Industrial Investment. After two reorganizations, however, by 1959 there was left only one Investment Bank for all Soviet capital needs. The Investment Bank operates through 1,200 suboffices and also utilizes many branches of the State Bank. The "Investment Banks" are not really banks, as noted, but are simply disbursing agents which supervise the spending of those investment funds granted to the enterprises from the government Budget or from retained profits or from depreciation reserves. Most long-term investment in the planning era has come from the central Budget, through the investment banks, in the form of interest-free grants paid into the State Bank account of the investing firm. It will be shown in Chapter 13, however, that since the 1965 reforms, the new direction is to make enterprises pay interest for their long-term capital — so as to make them aware of the need to economize it.

Finally, by far the largest number of banks are the Savings Banks, totalling some 75,000 in 1962. These banks have little to do directly with investment, and are primarily concerned with safeguarding the deposits of tens of millions of individual investors, on which they do pay a steady 2 or 3 percent interest. Of course, all funds of the savings banks, beyond a necessary reserve, are invested in State Bonds for use as revenue by the government Budget. These Savings Banks also issue to individuals against their deposits a check like a traveller's check for use when travelling on vacation or for business. The Savings Banks also function as the salesmen of government bonds to the population. Other minor functions include payments to individuals on the government debt, collection of Party and other dues, collection of fees for public utility services, and the management of a lottery. All depositors may participate in this lottery, but the cost to the losers is the loss of the interest on their savings for a year.

Relations between Industries: Micro Balances

This chapter has examined the aggregate (or macro) balances between the major parts of the economy, such as consumption and investment. Now the analysis must look at the individual (micro) balances required between different industries. In this context, each "industry" is defined as a collection of enterprises producing a single product for which no close substitute exists.

Compared with the latest proposed mathematical models, Soviet planners have in the past used a fairly simple approach called the "method of balances." For example, according to the form they use, one might state the aggregate balances in the following way. The disposable personal income of all Soviet citizens might be shown (omitting some details) as a balanced budget of their income and expenditures:

Workers' Budget

Wages	Consumer spending
Pensions	Personal saving
Source of Disposable Income	Spending Disposable Income

The government revenues and expenditures that must be planned are:

Government Budget

Taxes	Investment
Profits	Welfare
Loans	Military
	Surplus — deposited in State Bank
Total Income	Total Spending

The same method of establishing a balanced intake and outgo is used for each product or industry. Thus, the balance for the iron industry might be portrayed as follows:

Iron Industry

1. Imports	1. Exports
2. Reduction in inventory	2. Increase in inventory
3. Production listed by plants or regions	3. Uses by other industries, usually listed by region
Total Sources	Total Uses

Of course, it is only the totals that must balance.

An important economic question is the units in which commodity balances are stated. For example, the plan for iron industry may be calculated in tons of iron. The requirements would read x tons of iron needed for exports and inventories, y tons of iron needed for the steel industry in the Urals, z tons of iron needed for the railway industry in the Ukraine, and so forth. The Soviet planners also present each balance in rubles. This causes no problem so long as each ton of iron always has exactly the same price in rubles as all the other tons of iron. Of course, in reality the ruble price differs on the many kinds of iron, so some questions of weighting and aggregation are actually involved. This is obviously even more the case with such aggregates as "consumer goods."

Nevertheless, if we ignore the practical need for some aggregation of different things, it is only necessary (and sufficient) that the price be constant per unit during the time covered by the plan. It will cause no problem to the balancers that each particular price may be arbitrary in relation to all other prices, because only one price enters into each balance. For this reason, the question of the "value" of a good (discussed in the next two chapters), or the effects of consumer preference, or the different labor of supplying one good as opposed to others, does not affect the balance problem. Hence, although Marxist and non-Marxist writers disagree on how to "value" or price goods, they agree in practice on how to balance industries and sectors. In fact, the Soviet method of balances is a close relative of the Western "input-output method."

This doctrinal situation helps to explain why Soviet economists have spent so much effort on this particular problem, and have encountered many fewer theoretical difficulties in balancing problems than in optimizing problems.[2] Of course, it is also true that this problem, especially in the macroeconomic area of achieving a *full* employment of workers and resources, is of overwhelming practical importance. Furthermore, this was an area in which Marx did make a contribution.[3] Marx's scheme of balanced economic growth has been translated with some difficulty by several Marxist economists as a simplified type of Keynesian scheme of national income accounting.[4] Marx's scheme has also been translated by the Marxist economist Lange, using a great deal of verbal skill and ingenuity, into a simple input-output model.[5]

It should be noted to their credit that the Soviet economists of the 1920's grappled with most of the problems of balance in a very sophisticated manner. In fact, Wassily Leontief,[6] the creator of the input-output method, was an economics student at Leningrad University during the 1920's, and undoubtedly benefited from the Soviet experience and debates before he emigrated to the United States. Aside from Leontief, several other Soviet economists constructed models that might have led to a full-blown input-output analysis. Unfortunately, most of these economists were on the most conservative side of the debate on development. When Stalin attacked and even imprisoned some of them in the early 1930's, he condemned *all* of their theories and related theories as "bourgeois" or guilty of "mathematical formalism." The condemnation included early growth models as well as balance models. Given the dogmatic and repressive atmosphere, it was unhealthy to pursue such models any further. Even the Marxist writer, Dobb,[7] comments that:

> In the second half of the '30's a half-hearted attempt was, indeed, made (prompted, it has been said, by Stalin) to revive a discussion about a synthetic "balance of the National economy." . . . The

---

[2] For a recent and sophisticated discussion by a Soviet writer see A. A. Konus, "Dynamic Intersector Balances in Perspective Planning," *Economics of Planning*, Vol. 4 (1964), pp. 1–15.

[3] See Marx, "The Reproduction and Circulation of the Aggregate Social Capital," *Capital*, Vol. II, Part III.

[4] See, e.g., the confused discussion by Shigeto Tsuru, "On Reproduction Schemes," in Appendix A of Sweezy, *op. cit.*, pp. 365–374.

[5] See Oskar Lange, *Introduction to Econometrics* (New York: Pergamon Press, 1959), pp. 218–228.

[6] See, e.g., his simplified explanation in W. Leontief, "Input-Output Economics," *Scientific American* (October, 1951), pp. 3–9.

[7] Maurice Dobb, *Soviet Economic Development since 1917* (New York: International Publishers, 1966 edition), p. 361.

discussion scarcely got beyond questions of classification (i.e. a listing of the actual relationships of which account must be taken); it was soon to be dismissed by authority as unsatisfactory and was rather abruptly adjourned. After that for two decades silence reigned.

The intensive analysis of input-output relationships was revived only after the anti-Stalinist Twentieth Congress of the Communist Party in 1956. As mentioned above, Soviet economists are now doing a great deal of advanced work in this field. Yet the planners apparently still use the "method of balances" in all actual planning. So far, the discussion has only produced a few regional experiments with input-output, considerable statistical analysis of the past with this analysis, and much advocacy of use for future planning.

One of the great difficulties with the Soviet method of balances has been that it does not take into account the secondary effects on other industries of a change in the output of any one industry. For example, an increase in Soviet auto production means an immediate need for more rubber tires, but it also implies that the rubber tire industry will need more rubber as well as more tire-making machinery, and so forth, *ad infinitum*. By contrast, the input-output method automatically takes into account all secondary and further removed effects.

More specifically, it was observed in Chapter 6 how each Soviet enterprise supplies the State Planning Commission with estimates of its requirements, based on input norms or technological coefficients. A technological coefficient describes in a ratio how much of a given input, say iron, is required to produce one unit of a given output, say steel. But what happens when all of the enterprise requirements are added together by the Planning Commission, and the Commission finds an imbalance?

For instance, suppose that the planned supply of steel is one million tons short of the total enterprise requirements. If steel production is to be increased, this means additional requirements for iron ore, coal, limestone, and other ingredients. Exactly how much is required of each must be calculated from the respective technological coefficients. For example, if production of one ton of steel requires 1.5 tons of iron ore, then this coefficient or ratio (1.5/1) means that an additional one million tons of steel requires an additional 1.5 million tons of iron ore. In turn, the additional production of iron ore, coal, limestone, and other inputs into steel, must require additional inputs of the commodities used in *their* production. The chain of secondary effects is endless. How this endless chain is solved in one calculation by the input-output method is shown in the next section.

If instead of producing additional steel the planners decide to stick with the original plan of steel output, then balance can be achieved only by cutbacks in the output of all commodities dependent upon steel as an input. Thus, depending on their technological coefficients or needs for steel, there would have to be reductions in the planned production of autos, trucks, rails, and so forth. Each of these in turn would mean reductions in other commodities using them as inputs, another endless chain that could only slowly approach balance as the result of a great number of adjustments.

Thus, by the method of balances, it would be necessary to go through several approximations and changes affecting every balance (because all are interrelated) before getting all the different industries to balance. This takes so long, even with Soviet short cuts, that the balancing process not only takes a great deal of energy, but also a lot of time, and is usually completed late. As a result, the final plan usually arrives at the enterprise *after* the period covered has already begun. Furthermore, this complicated planning process has been absorbing an increasing percentage of the labor force, which might well be used elsewhere.

Theoretically, the input-output method would remedy the main defect of the balance method, since it does take into account all of the indirect adjustments to any change in one item.[8] It is also more suitable for use with electronic computers. It would not only be faster to calculate one balanced plan by the input-output method, but this method would actually make it possible easily to present several alternative balanced plans, from which the politicians could pick the plan they desire, or even change particular output targets, and yet be certain of all the secondary effects. It will be shown that it is theoretically possible to have an almost infinite number of different balanced plans with given resources, as the desired final bill of goods is varied. (The question, examined in Chapter 12, is to know exactly what is desired as well as the cheapest means of getting it.) It should be noted that the problem of speeding up planning and reaching a final desired approximation to a good balance is now becoming more urgent. This is because (1) Soviet industry comprises a growing number of enterprises, whose relationships are more complex and interrelated, so that secondary effects are harder to calculate intuitively; and (2) the increased complexity makes more difficult the problems of gathering and aggregating the necessary information.

In practice, it is important to mention one Soviet short cut in the actual use of the method of balances. If more steel is ordered by the politicians, then — as shown above — the planners should theoretically order more iron and coal and other inputs for the steel industry. But this would upset the balances for iron and coal and everything else that goes into steel. To prevent many of these secondary effects from disrupting planning, the planners first try to get each industry to accept a higher target with *no* additional resources. For example, the steel industry may be told that it is wasting too much coal, so it should find a more efficient way to use the coal it has. The steel industry might also be told it has excessive reserves or inventories of coal, so it can use some of those to make more steel. In this way, the secondary effects of a change in the

---

[8] This is the view of the more liberal Soviet economists, see, e.g., V. S. Nemchinov, "Mathematical Methods in Economics," in V. S. Nemchinov, editor, *The Use of Mathematics in Economics* (London: Oliver and Boyd, 1964, English edition edited by A. Nove), p. 24.

amount of one product are kept to a minimum by removing the assumption that a fixed ratio of each resource is necessary for production of each unit of output. Of course, this short cut can only be used within narrow limits.

Another problem is that Soviet politicians have wanted to fix not only the amounts of final goods (such as autos or tanks), but also the amounts of intermediate goods (such as oil or steel). This is understandable because some of these intermediate goods, steel for instance, give prestige to a developing country. Nevertheless, it is easier and more rational to decide only upon the final bill of goods that is desired, and to leave the planning of intermediate goods to the planners. Then even the method of balances could produce a consistent plan in a direct and limited number of steps.

Let the planners begin with fixed needs or demands for final goods, assuming they are within the limits of what is possible with available labor and resources. Then calculate the necessary inputs to produce each of these final goods. Then use these inputs as the additional (secondary) targets for industries. Then calculate. the inputs necessary to produce the secondary or intermediate targets, and make those the additional third round of output targets. And so forth, with what will turn out to be rapidly diminishing additional amounts for further rounds, till the planners can stop and ignore any further additions.

An interesting variation of this idea, by which the Plan could be calculated with very little centralized computation, has been suggested by several Western economists.[9] The Planning Commission is given a list of final output targets that must be achieved. Then (1) the Commission tells each industrial Ministry what its final output must be; (2) each Ministry reports to the Commission what its input requirements are to produce that final output; (3) the Commission adds together these intermediate input needs; (4) the Commission tells each Ministry to add these additional outputs of each commodity to its total output; (5) the Ministries report back again to the Commission their additional input needs to produce this additional product . . . and so on till the added amounts become negligible. This method would eliminate the need for complex computer calculations, but it would require prompt and trustworthy information from each industry.

The Input-Output Method in the Soviet Context

For those readers who are interested in its details, this section provides a systematic explanation of the input-output method. The input-output table may be used for two very different purposes. First, it may be used as an accounting device to record the last year's national economic results in a very detailed and revealing way. Second, it may be used with estimates of future relationships to plan a balanced national economy for the next year or for any future period.

[9] The version presented here is from Benjamin Ward, *The Socialist Economy* (New York: Random House, 1967), pp. 44–49.

As an accounting record, its unique feature is that it shows transactions between industries as well as aggregate consumption and other aggregates. Let a very simple form of the Soviet economy be assumed for purely illustrative purposes. All enterprises are owned by the government, and wages are the only form of income. There are no personal savings, no government debts, a balanced budget, no exports nor imports, and no depreciation nor replacement. There are only three industries producing three kinds of products, which are the whole output of the economy. These industries might be called *A, B,* and *C;* or, to add a little color to the picture, one might call them the sectors of Agriculture, Manufacturing, and Construction, In reality, there are several other economic sectors, and each of those sectors contains many different industries. Manufacturing alone contains a thousand or so industries, each of which should be analyzed separately, with a separate entry in the table. This simplified input-output table might look something like Table 10–3.

It is necessary first to explain the individual figures in this table and then to give names to some of the totals. Under the column of Manufacturing, for example, there is the figure *10* in the row for Agriculture. This means that *10* billion rubles of the output or product of Agriculture became an input into Manufacturing. Notice that the total gross output of Agriculture was *96* billion rubles. Of this gross output *16* billion went as inputs (for intermediate uses) to various industries, and so was used up within industry. This *16* billion intermediate use of Agricultural goods includes the *10* billion used in Manufacturing, plus 5 billion used in Construction, *plus 1* billion used up by Agriculture itself in its own production process.

Subtracting *16* from *96,* one finds that the final or net output of Agriculture available for final uses was only *80* billion rubles. Of this *80* billion, *20* went for new investment, *10* for articles of military use, and 5 for public welfare goods, which left only *45* billion rubles of Agricultural product for personal or individual consumption. An exactly similar analysis could be made for the rows showing the outputs of the Manufacturing and Construction industries.

If we read down the input column under Agriculture, we find that it used up, out of the intermediate products of industry in this period, *1* billion rubles worth of its own output, *30* billion of Manufacturing, and 5 billion of Construction. In addition, Agriculture had to pay out *40* billion in wages for labor, and *10* billion in profits for the use of capital and *10* billion in its part of the government military and welfare services. In the centrally planned Soviet economy profit and taxes have been mixed together in the federal budget, so in practice one cannot say that profit goes to pay only for capital and that taxes go only for government services. At any rate, the labor expended in this period, the capital goods used in this period, as well as government services provided in this period are the primary inputs needed to keep industry functioning. Welfare, of course, might be considered a part of the payment to all labor. Notice that the input services are valued in the accounts by the payments for them; labor by wages paid, capital by profits paid, and government services by taxes paid.

Table 10-3

Soviet Inputs and Outputs (imaginary figures in billions of rubles)

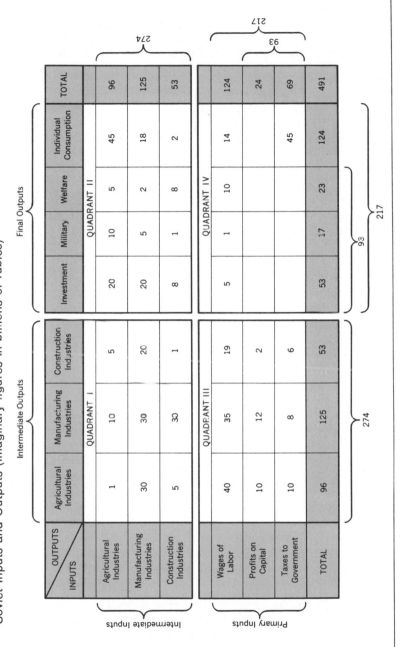

OUTPUTS / INPUTS	Intermediate Outputs			Final Outputs					TOTAL
	Agricultural Industries	Manufacturing Industries	Construction Industries	Investment	Military	Welfare	Individual Consumption		
	QUADRANT I			QUADRANT II					
Agricultural Industries	1	10	5	20	10	5	45		96
Manufacturing Industries	30	30	20	20	5	2	18		125
Construction Industries	5	30	1	8	1	8	2		53
	QUADRANT III			QUADRANT IV					
Wages of Labor	40	35	19	5	1	10	14		124
Profits on Capital	10	12	2						24
Taxes to Government	10	8	6				45		69
TOTAL	96	125	53	53	17	23	124		491

Intermediate Inputs — Primary Inputs

274 — 93 — 217

Discussion has so far centered on the figures in three of the four quadrants into which the input-output table is divided. In Quadrant I are found the intermediate inputs and intermediate outputs, or the relationships between industries; in Quadrant II, the final or net outputs of material goods from each industry for investment, military, welfare, and individual consumption; in Quadrant III, the primary inputs of labor, capital, and government services.

What do the figures in Quadrant IV represent? They show service inputs (rather than material inputs) into final products. For example, the figures in Quadrant III in the row opposite wages show that labor put 40 billion rubles of work into producing material goods in Agriculture, 35 billion into material goods in Manufacturing, and 19 billion into material goods in Construction. But the figures in Quadrant IV in the row opposite wages show that labor *also* put in 5 billion rubles of work into direct services to investment projects, 1 billion into military service (or soldiering), 10 billion into welfare services (such as nursing or teaching), and 14 billion into services direct to the consumer (for example, by barbers or domestic workers). In addition, note that individual consumers paid out 45 billion (in sales or turnover taxes) for the government services to them.

Next, one may note in the table those items which will always be found in an accounting balance for the last year's record; and which the planners must design so as to be in balance for the next year's plan. Obviously, the "value" of what is produced (the intermediate plus the final outputs) by each industry must equal the "value" of what went into each industry (the primary plus the intermediate inputs). This is a necessary accounting and real physical identity, since something cannot come out of nothing, no matter what one's theory of "value" and price is. This necessity of matching the inputs or sources (including initial inventories) with the outputs or uses of each industry's product (including final inventories) is exactly what the Soviets attempt in their physical and ruble balances for each product. In the input-output table for the next year's plan, the total for each industry's input column must equal the total for that industry's output row (for example, Agriculture's total output *or* input is 96 billion rubles).

If all of the industries are summed together, their total inputs (primary plus intermediate) must equal their total outputs (intermediate plus final). In other words, the sum of Quadrants I and II (outputs) must equal the sum of Quadrants I and III (inputs), or identical totals of 274 billion rubles in our example. Of course, the sum of the columns in Quadrant I (intermediate inputs) equals the sum of the rows in Quadrant I (intermediate outputs), since the same numbers are being added together in different directions. By subtraction, the value of Quadrant III, that is, the value of all final material ouputs (net of intermediate outputs) must just equal the vaue of all primary inputs into industry (net of intermediate inputs). Of course, this will not generally be true of any particular industry, because each will have different ratios of its output going to intermediate and final goods.

It was observed that a macrobalance of primary inputs (or incomes) and final outputs (or expenditures) is required, which means that Quadrant III must equal Quadrant II. Therefore, it is no surprise that the value of II plus IV must also equal the value III plus IV, which is 217 billion rubles in the illustrative table. In other words, the total final output (of material goods plus services) must equal the total primary input (into industry and directly as services). As a sub-balance, notice that if wages just equal consumer goods and services (in the example both are 124 billion rubles), then profits plus taxes must just equal investment plus military plus welfare goods (both are 93 billion rubles). Finally, note that the sum of all the rows of all four quadrants equals the sum of all the columns of all four quadrants (either is 491 billion rubles).

Aggregate Definitions. According to the usual U.S. national accounting, the final output of material goods plus services (Quadrant II plus IV) is defined as the "Gross National Product." Notice that from the viewpoint of inputs or income, the Gross National Product will be the same sum as the total wages, profits, and taxes from the production of goods and services (Quadrant III plus IV). The Soviet accounting notion is quite different, and is called the "Combined Social Product." It differs from the Gross National Product because the Combined Social Product includes all the intermediate products of Quadrant I, but excludes all of the final services of Quadrant IV (as the Soviets claim Marx would do in examining the value of all output). Thus, the Soviet Combined Social Product is simply the total of all intermediate *and* final outputs of all material goods (Quadrant I plus II). Once again, from the point of view of inputs or income, this amount is identical with the sum of all primary *plus* all intermediate inputs into industry (Quadrant I plus III).

The most inclusive measure of national value would be the U.S. Gross National Product plus intermediate outputs, *or* the Soviet Combined Social Product plus services. Either of these would be the same as the total value of Quadrants I plus II plus IV from the output view *or* I plus III plus IV from the input view. This sum has no name and is not used by either country, though it might be useful for some problems.

The sum of all four quadrants, 491 billion rubles in the example, is neither named nor used. This latter sum is truly meaningless, however, because it adds both Quadrants II and III into the aggregate. Yet these two quadrants are merely two different ways of looking at the same thing: the total inputs net of intermediate inputs *or* the total outputs net of all intermediate outputs. In accounting or in a balanced economy these two must be identical, so the sum of Quadrants I plus II plus III plus IV includes so much double accounting that it has no meaning.

Industrial Balances. To return to the mainstream of the analysis, once the aggregate balances (such as wages and consumer goods) are secured, the main object of the planners is to obtain balanced relationships among the industries. This means that the main concentration of the planners is on Quadrant I relations, such as the tons of coal necessary for the steel industry, or the tons of steel necessary for the truck-building industry. To increase the total product of a single industry, the planners must know how much to increase the intermediate outputs of other industries to meet its additional requirements.

Suppose, for example, the planners wish to increase the output of Agriculture as shown in Table 10–3 by 1 ruble. How much more intermediate Agricultural goods, Manufactures, and Construction will be required? If the table is changed into percentages or kopecks of input per ruble of output, it will be easy to read off the direct effects. Thus, for a total output of 96 billion rubles, Agriculture required 1 billion rubles of its own Agricultural goods, 30 billion of Manufacturing, and 5 billion of Construction. It must be *assumed* that any increase of Agriculture, say in the next year, will require the same proportions of the intermediate products of Agriculture, Manufacturing, and Construction. Then it may be calculated that 1 is slightly over 1% of 96, 30 is 31% of 96, and 5 is a little over 5% of 96. There are 100 kopecks in 1 ruble. Thus, it may be said that an increase of 1 ruble in Agriculture will require a direct increase in intermediate uses of over 1 kopeck of Agriculture, 31 kopecks of Manufacturing, and over 5 kopecks of Construction.

If the same calculations are made for Manufacturing and Construction, it is possible to make a complete table of requirements per unit of gross or total (intermediate plus final) output.

For example, one can see at a glance that to increase the output of Construction by 100 kopecks (or one ruble) directly requires a 38 kopeck increase in output of Manufacturing. The fraction, 38/100 or the required increase-of-Manufacturing/increase-of-Construction, is called an input-output coefficient. It may also be called a "technical" coefficient, because it reflects a technological relationship. These coefficients each state the ratio of direct input increase required for a given output increase. Thus, any industry could read off all of its additional input requirements for any planned increase in output.

With the knowledge of the last year's accounts obtained from Table 10–4, the planners could also estimate a balanced plan for the next year. Suppose the planners know the input-output coefficients for the last year (such as Table 10–4), and assume that these coefficients remain the same for the next year. Then if the planners are given by the society a desired bill of final outputs, they can set up an equation of demand and supply for each industry, and can solve them simultaneously for consistent total outputs.

Suppose, for example, that final demand rises in the next year to 100 billion rubles for Agriculture, 50 billion rubles for Manufacturing, and 20 billion rubles for Construction products. Suppose, also, that the input-output coefficients for the next year remain the same as those in Table 10–4. Then the planners may estimate the next year's plan so that total supply just balances with intermediate and final demand. The method of calculation is illustrated in Appendix C to this chapter. It turns out that Agriculture would have to be 118.4 billion rubles, Manufacturing 145.1 billion, and Construction 62.0 billion.

The equations are simple to solve for just three sectors or industries.

Table 10–4

Direct Inputs per Ruble of Output (in kopecks calculated from quadrant I and total output column of Table 10–3)

OUTPUTS / INPUTS	Intermediate Outputs			Final Output	Total Output 100 kopecks = 1 ruble
	Agricultural Industries	Manufacturing Industries	Construction Industries		
Intermediate Inputs Agricultural Industries	1	8	9	82	100
Manufacturing Industries	31	24	38	7	100
Construction Industries	5	24	2	69	100
Primary Inputs	63	44	51		
Total Input	100	100	100		

When *1,500* or *2,000* industries are used in a realistic plan, however, the job becomes very difficult. Even high-speed electronic calculators will require significant time to calculate a whole new plan each time the planners wish to change a single final demand. One additional type of information not made explicit in Table 10–4 would enable them to make necessary changes very easily. Table 10–4 only states direct requirements. In planning, however, it is not enough to know that a one-ruble production increase of Construction directly requires 38 kopecks of Manufacturing. The planners would like to know *all* of the secondary effects of the increase. For example, if Manufacturing is required to increase its output by 38 kopecks, then Manufacturing itself requires a further increase in inputs from other industries, specifically 8/100 of 38 kopecks from Agriculture, 24/100 of its own product, and 24/100 from Construction. And these increases require still further increases. For example, Agriculture will also require as an input from Manufacturing 31/100 of 8/100 of 38 kopecks for its own increased output. The interrelations or indirect effects are clearly circular and almost endless, though in all economic cases the indirect effects rapidly diminish with each further round.

Fortunately, the input-output method leads to a simple mathematical way (described in Appendix B to this chapter) of calculating the limits toward which all of the indirect effects will tend. Using this method, which may be conveniently computerized for any number of industries, a final table may be presented showing all of the indirect effects of increases in any output. It is more useful to do this, not for gross or total output, but for the net or final output, as that is what we really wish to determine. This is because only the final output is actually available for use as consumption, investment, military, or welfare goods. The result, computed from the direct input-output coefficients (or "technical" coefficients) shown in Table 10–4, follows in Table 10–5.

Table 10–5

Direct plus Indirect Requirements per Ruble of Final
Output (in kopecks, calculated from Table 10–4
as explained in Appendix B to this chapter).

OUTPUT / INPUT	Intermediate Output			Final Output
	Agricultural Industries	Manufacturing Industries	Construction Industries	
Intermediate Input Agricultural Industries	1.07	.53	.18	100
Manufacturing Industries	.16	1.58	.40	100
Construction Industries	.16	.66	1.19	100

This table shows all of the direct-plus-indirect input-output (or "technical") coefficients for each product. Thus the planners can tell at a glance that, if they wish to increase the final output of Construction by *100* kopecks (or *1* ruble), then they must increase the output of Manufacturing by *66* kopecks to include all additional direct and indirect inputs of Manufacturing. Note that even if the direct input of one industry into another is zero, an increase in the output of the other industry may still require *some* small indirect increase. In fact, it usually does require an indirect increase of the second industry because that industry is likely to supply inputs to some third industry that in turn supplies inputs to the first industry.

Limitations of Input-Output Model

It must be very clear what the input-output model can do and what it cannot do. Given the technical coefficients and the list of desired final outputs, planners can calculate the total output (both intermediate and final) required of each industry. If they are also given technical coefficients showing the amount of labor and capital required per unit of output, they can similarly calculate the required amounts of each of these primary inputs.

Yet the limitations of the input-output method are equally clear, and should always be kept in mind by planners. First, the technological co-efficients are assumed to be fixed for the period of the Plan, say five years. This is clearly an unrealistic assumption, certainly for any economy with rapid technological improvements, such as the Soviet economy. In fact, the coefficients often change in particular industries. Moreover, input-output assumes that the coefficients are identical for each firm in an industry, and that they remain constant regardless of the scale of production. In reality the coefficients are different for each firm, rapidly change with increases in scale, and vary with changes in technology over time. A really complete model would somehow have to allow for dynamic change of the coefficients within the planning period, though Leontief shows that the U.S. coefficients change slowly enough to have little effect for a number of years.

A second limitation of the input-output method is that the planners cannot be certain that the required primary inputs of labor and capital will in fact be available. If, for example, there is less labor available than the plan of desired final output would require, is it not necessary to set lower final outputs and recalculate the entire plan? Naturally, if there is more labor available than is required, it may not be too diffi-cult to increase various final outputs as well as the appropriate inter-mediate outputs. However, a reduction of final outputs due to a shortage of labor would be a much more painful process.

In theory, the input-output method could easily be used to calculate a new plan with smaller proportions of all outputs to correspond with the actual available labor supply. Since it automatically takes into consid-eration the indirect as well as the direct effects of such changes, the in-put-output method would thus appear to be far more efficient than the method of balances. In practice, however, the Soviet planners do not immediately begin to reduce final outputs if they find a shortage of in-puts, whether the shortage is in total labor or in intermediate inputs for some particular industry. Rather they attempt first to reduce the input-output coefficients, which we have so far taken as fixed or constant.

How do the Soviet planners perform this remarkable feat of reduc-tion of technologically based coefficients, without discovery of any new technology? They do it by pressure on the individual enterprises to in-crease their efficiency. Thus, for example, the individual enterprise may be forced to introduce new technology which it had previously known but not used. The enterprise might also use new sources of sup-ply which it had previously kept hidden. For example, Soviet enterprises have been notorious for keeping exceptionally high inventories of goods, which they will utilize for just such occasions. The enterprise may also, within the plan or beyond it, hire extra shifts of labor. If the planners are thus able to reduce the direct input-output coefficients by a sufficient amount, they can stop all significant secondary effects. They can then retain the original planned amounts of final output, essentially by squeezing more out of each unit of input. In this way recalculation of large parts of the Plan can be avoided.

Finally, notice that both the Soviet method of balances and the input-output method provide only balanced or consistent plans between industries. Neither method, however, provides an optimal or most efficient plan in any sense. In other words, neither method helps choose between different methods of technology or between different sets of final outputs, nor do they question the efficiency with which any firm operates, but rather assume each of these as given. The actual process of decision-making on the optimal list of desired final outputs, as well as the choice of technology, will be discussed in the next chapter. It may be noted that balance and efficiency are solved simultaneously by a market economy, but they are quite distinct problems under central planning. A planned economy may be balanced, and still be far from optimal efficiency. Here it need only be added that the input-output problem for the planners remains the same regardless of where planners receive the list of final outputs, whether from the politicians or the individual consumers or some combination of these groups. Nevertheless, although the input-output method does not itself choose an optimal variant, if it actually allows several more variants to be considered than does the method of balances, it may allow the politicians to choose a plan much closer to the optimum.

Appendix A to Chapter 10

Macroeconomic Balances in the Soviet Economy

1. First approximation:
   C　= value of all consumer goods
   W = total amount of wages paid
   Balance requires:
   $$C = W \tag{1}$$

2. Second approximation:
   C　= real amount of consumer goods
   P_c = price of consumer goods
   L　= number of laborers or workers
   W = wage rate per worker
   Balance requires:
   $$C \cdot P_c = L \cdot W \tag{2}$$

3. Third approximation:
   C, P_c, L, and W as in second approximation but also
   $$L = L_c + L_i + L_m + L_w \tag{3}$$
   where:
   L_c = number of workers in consumer goods
   L_i = number of workers in investment goods
   L_m = number of workers in military goods

L_w = number of workers in welfare goods
Therefore balance requires:
$$C \cdot P_c = (W \cdot L_c) + (W \cdot L_i) + (W \cdot L_m) + (W \cdot L_w) \qquad (4)$$

4. Fourth approximation:
   C, P_c, W, L_c, L_i, L_m, and L_w as in third approximation but also
   S = value of personal saving by workers
   T_p = value of personal taxes on workers' income
   T_t = rate of turnover tax or sales tax
   Balance requires:
$$(T_t \cdot C) + (P_c \cdot C) = (W \cdot L_c) + (W \cdot L_i) + (W \cdot L_m) + (W \cdot L_w)$$
$$-S - T_p$$

Appendix B to Chapter 10

Input-Output Model

The text presented a full discussion of the input-output approach with numerical examples. It may further aid some readers, however, to see a generalized algebraic discussion of the problem.

Assume there are n separate industries. The total output of each industry, including intermediate and final outputs, is represented by the letters, $X_1 \ldots X_n$. The final output of each industry is represented by the letters, $x_1 \ldots x_n$, and the intermediate output of each industry is represented by the letters, $x_{11} \ldots x_{1n}$. The meaning of the subscripts in the intermediate outputs is understood as follows: the first number indicates the industry producing the output, while the second number indicates the industry to which the output is supplied as an input. For example, x_{12} means that this is the amount of output from industry 1 required as an input in industry 2. Thus, the picture of required output from each of the industries is as follows:

$$X_1 = x_{11} + x_{12} + \ldots + x_{1n} + x_1 \qquad (1a)$$
$$\vdots$$
$$X_i = x_{i1} + x_{i2} + \ldots + x_{in} + x_i \qquad (1i)$$
$$\vdots$$
$$X_n = x_{n1} + x_{n2} + \ldots + x_{nn} + x_n \qquad (1n)$$

These equations may also be summed together with the following result:

$$X_i = \sum_{j=1}^{n} x_{ij} + x_i \text{ (where } i = 1 \ldots n) \qquad (2)$$

Here i is an individual industry producing output for use as an input into industry j.

At this point, it is necessary to introduce the direct input-output co-efficients (sometimes called "technical coefficients"), which represent technical ratios fixed for the duration of the planning period. The direct input-output coefficients are represented by the letters $a_{11} \ldots a_{nn}$, where the first number of the subscript represents the industry producing an output, and the second number represents the industry using it as an input. For example: if there is an intermediate good, x_{12}, it is equal in amount to the coefficient a_{12} times the industry output X_2, where indus-try 2 demands as an input this part of the output of industry 1, that is: $x_{12} = a_{12} X_2$. To put it another way, the technical coefficient a_{12} repre-sents the ratio between the amount of intermediate goods required by industry 2 from industry 1, or x_{12}, to the total output of industry 2, or X_2, that is:

$$a_{12} = \frac{x_{12}}{X_2}.$$

In general, each input-output coefficient represents the ratio between the goods required by the using (or demanding) industry from the producing (or supplying) industry to the total output of the using industry. Thus where i represents an industry producing an output and j represents an industry using it as an input, the input-output coefficient may be rep-resented as:

$$a_{ij} = \frac{x_{ij}}{X_j} \tag{3a}$$

or

$$x_{ij} = a_{ij} X_j \tag{3b}$$

Utilizing this terminology, plus the assumption that the technical input-output coefficients are fixed and constant during the planning period, it is possible to substitute the coefficients times the total output of the using industries for the demand for intermediate goods in every case. In other words, into each of the equations (1a . . . 1n) may be substituted the amount of coefficient times total output as defined in equation 3b. When this substitution is made, the new picture of re-quired (or demanded) output for all industries is as follows:

$$X_1 = a_{11}X_1 + a_{12}X_2 + \ldots + a_{1n}X_n + x_1 \tag{4a}$$

$$\vdots$$

$$X_i = a_{i1}X_1 + a_{i2}X_2 + \ldots + a_{in}X_n + x_i \tag{4i}$$

$$\vdots$$

$$X_n = a_{n1}X_1 + a_{n2}X_2 + \ldots + a_{nn}X_n + x_n \tag{4n}$$

The input-output method merely requires setting up these equations for every industry, and then solving them. If the technical coefficients are known, and the desired final demands are given, it is simple (but very tedious) algebra to solve for each of the total outputs.

In practice, in order to reduce the enormous number of calculations required for a large number of industries, matrix algebra is always utilized. The entire set of a coefficients may be called the matrix A. The summation of the above equations ($4a \ldots 4n$) may then be written as:

$$X_i = AX_i + x_i \qquad (5)$$

where A is the matrix of a coefficients, X is the vector of all total outputs, and x_i is the vector of all final outputs (where i runs from 1 to n). By rearranging and subtracting, the result is reached that:

$$(I - A)X_i = x_i \qquad (6)$$

where I is an "identity matrix." An identity matrix is simply a matrix consisting of the value 1 along the main diagonal with all other elements equal to zero. It may be assumed that the matrix A is known and constant, and note that the identity matrix I is always known. In this form, therefore, one may assume as given to the planners either the list of desired total outputs (X_i) *or* the list of final outputs (x_i), and the planners will always be able to calculate the other one.

In other words, if the planners are given a list of desired final outputs (x_i), and since they are assumed to know the technical input-output coefficients ($I–A$), it follows that total outputs (X_i) are the only remaining unknowns in the equation, and hence may be calculated. Since final outputs are what the politicians really desire, it makes most sense to give this list to the planners. If, however, as Soviet politicians are prone to do, the politicians themselves wish to specify the total outputs rather than the final outputs, it is also possible for the planners to calculate the final outputs from the given total outputs and the matrix of input-output coefficients.

Note that matrix A, which was called the set of direct input-output coefficients, is derived from the type of data presented in the illustration in Table 10–3, and results in the coefficients presented in Table 10–4. It was shown, however, that the planners clearly require a set of coefficients showing direct-plus-indirect requirements for the production of each unit of final output. Such a set of coefficients was illustrated in Table 10–5. These direct-plus-indirect technical coefficients are, of course, what is required in the solution of equation #6. In other words, the table of direct and indirect requirements of inputs per ruble of final output turns out to be the transposed inverse of the difference between the identity matrix (I) and the matrix (A) of direct input-output coefficients. Thus, Table 10–5 is the matrix $(I–A)_T^{-1}$, where the T shows it is transposed and the −1 shows it is the inverse. It is this table or matrix that is actually combined with final demands to estimate the required total outputs for each industry.

Appendix C to Chapter 10
Example of Input-Output Calculation

Suppose the technological facts remain as in Table 10–4, but the demands for final output have increased to 100 billion rubles in Agriculture, 50 billion in Manufacturing, and 20 billion in Construction. Then the table could be shown this way:

Table 10–6
Direct Inputs per Ruble of Output (in rubles)

OUTPUTS / INPUTS	Intermediate Output			Final Output Demanded	Total Output
	Agricultural Industries	Manufacturing Industries	Construction Industries		
Agricultural Industries	.01	.08	.09	100	?
Manufacturing Industries	.31	.24	.38	50	?
Construction Industries	.05	.24	.02	20	?

Let A be total Agricultural output, let M be total Manufacturing output, and let C be total Construction output. From the information in Table 10–6, we can write an equation for each industry showing the demands for intermediate output plus the demands for final output. The three equations are:

$$A = .01A + .08M + .09C + 100$$
$$M = .31A + .24M + .38C + 50$$
$$C = .05A + .24M + .02C + 20$$

The solutions for the total outputs are:

$$A = 118.4$$
$$M = 145.1$$
$$C = 62.0$$

SELECTED REFERENCES

1. The standard reference to input-output problems is Hollis B. Chenery and Paul G. Clark, *Interindustry Economics* (New York: John Wiley and Sons, Inc., 1959).

2. The best brief and simple discussion is in William M. Miernyk, *The Elements of Input-Output Analysis* (New York: Random House, 1965).

3. Some simpler Soviet articles are in L. Berri, F. Klotsvog and S. Shatalin, "An Experimental Calculation of a Planned Interbranch Balance for 1962," *Problems of Economics* (June, 1963), pp. 3–10. Also A. A. Gatanava, "The Use of the Balance Method in Economic Planning," *Problems of Economics* (June, 1963), pp. 11–17.

4. A more advanced Soviet contribution is A. A. Konus, "Dynamic Intersectoral Balances in Perspective Planning," Economics of Planning, Vol. 4 (1964), pp. 1–15.

5. Two careful non-Soviet approaches to their balancing problems are in J. M. Montias, "Planning with Material Balances in Soviet-type Economies," *American Economic Review*, Vol. 49 (Dec., 1959), pp. 968–985; and H. S. Levine, "Input-Output Analysis and Soviet Planning," *American Economic Review*, Vol. 52 (May, 1962), pp. 127–137. Also see H. S. Levine's classic article, "The Centralized Planning of Supply in Soviet Industry," reprinted in F. D. Holzman, *Readings on the Soviet Economy* (Chicago: Rand McNally and Co., 1962).

6. A U.S. discussion of the actual data in recent Soviet experiments is in Vladimir G. Treml, "The 1959 Soviet Input-Output Table (As Reconstructed)," in U.S. Joint Economic Committee of Congress, *New Directions in the Soviet Economy* (Washington, D.C.: U.S. Government Printing Office, 1966).

7. One good U.S. article on the contribution of banking to balance is G. Garvey, "Role of the State Bank in Soviet Planning," in J. Degra and Alex Nove, eds., *Soviet Planning, Essays in Honor of Naum Jasny* (New York: Oxford University Press, 1964). A comprehensive study of financial balance problems may be found in Franklyn D. Holzman, *Soviet Taxation: The Fiscal and Monetary Problems of a Planned Economy* (Cambridge, Mass.: Harvard University Press, 1955).

11

VALUE AND PLANNING

Marx and his earliest followers assumed without proof that it is possible to plan rationally in a socialist society, "socialism" being defined here simply as public ownership of all means of production. They considered it impractical utopianism to describe in detail the problems of the unborn socialist economy.[1] Since the planned economy of the Soviet Union has survived and has developed for a significant length of time, detailed planning can no longer be called a "utopian" project. Soviet Marxists, indeed, consider that the possibility of rational, efficient planning has now been proven in practice, so need not be proven theoretically. Whatever the merits of this squelching answer, the long theoretical debate about the *possibility* of rational planning in socialism teaches many lessons, and will serve as a very useful background to our study of Soviet optimal planning.

Need for Rational Prices

The most famous denial of the possibility of rational planning came from Ludwig von Mises in the 1920's.[2] Mises argues that the calculation of economic choices requires a knowledge of "rational" prices for both inputs and outputs. For example, if a farmer wishes to know whether to produce oranges or apples, he must know their relative

[1] All of the pre-1917 discussions by socialists and anti-socialists on this problem are discussed in Carl Landauer, *European Socialism* (Berkeley: University of California Press, 1959), Vol. II, pp. 1602–1635.

[2] See Ludwig von Mises, "Economic Calculation in the Socialist Commonwealth," in F. A. Hayek, editor, *Collectivist Economic Planning* (London: Routledge and Kegan Paul, Ltd., 1935).

prices at the time in order to maximize his revenues. Or, if a planner wishes to decide whether railroad locomotives should use coal or oil, he must know the relative prices of coal and oil in order to minimize costs.

In socialism, however, the government owns the coal and oil as well as the locomotives. Therefore, says Mises, since there is no market and no competition between producers, there can be no rational prices. If the coal and oil producers are merely commanded to turn over a certain physical product to the locomotive-makers, no one can know which kind of fuel will cost more. In short, there is no free market in socialism, so there are no rational prices, so there can be no meaningful calculation or rational planning of the allocation of resources.

Optimal Conditions and Planning

An evaluation of Mises' objection requires a brief explanation of how economists define "rational" prices and "rational" planning. Rational prices are defined as those which lead to an "optimal" pattern of outputs and inputs, by the accurate representation of the marginal utility of each output and the marginal cost of each input. As early as 1897 the economist Pareto[3] made explicit the conditions necessary to obtain an optimum welfare situation for all individuals, given the existing technology and the existing distribution of income. He defined what is now called a *Pareto optimum* "as a position from which it is not possible by any reallocation of factors, to make anyone better off without making at least one person worse off."[4]

The Pareto optimum is commonly said to require at least three conditions: First, there is the condition of consumer satisfaction, "*The Exchange optimum*, which requires that for each individual, the rate of substitution [the ratio of preference of one additional unit of one good to another] be the same for all pairs of goods in the economy."[5] Roughly, this means that each consumer should be equally satisfied with the *last* dollar's worth of each good he buys. Second, there is the condition of producer efficiency, "*The Production optimum*, which requires that for each product the rate of substitution between any pair of factors will be the same."[6] Roughly, this means that each producer should get an equal addition to production from the *last* dollar's worth of each producer good he buys.

Third, there is a combination of the production and consumption conditions in the "*Top Level optimum*. It requires that the subjective rate of substitution, common to all individuals, be equal to the . . . rate of objective substitution for all pairs of goods in the economy."[7] Roughly, this means that the mixture of outputs should be the same as the prefer-

---

[3] V. Pareto, *Cours d'economie politique* (Lausanne, 1897).

[4] E. J. Mishan, "A Survey of Welfare Economics, 1939–1959," in American Economic Association and Royal Economic Society, eds., *Surveys of Economic Theory*, Vol. I (New York: St. Martin's Press, 1966), p. 163.

[5] *Ibid.*

[6] *Ibid.*, p. 164.

[7] *Ibid.*

ence for outputs by all consumers, the mixture of inputs should be the same as the preference for inputs by all producers, *and* that the addition of one unit of one commodity requires the sacrifice of an equally desirable amount of some other commodity for both consumers and producers. Fortunately, only a very general concept of these conditions — as an allocation of inputs and outputs that cannot be improved — is necessary to the present argument,[8] especially since their concrete application to the Soviet economy in the form of linear programming is discussed in the next chapter.

It *is* important to note the limitations of a Pareto optimum welfare situation. First, it *assumes* a given distribution of income, so it says nothing about the equity of this distribution of income. Second, it deals only with the most efficient allocation of resources *at a given time* with a given technology, so it says nothing about the dynamics of growth, neither the saving of capital nor the improvement of technology. Third, it simply assumes the possibility of full employment in the aggregate, so it says nothing about the macro balance problems of unemployment or inflation. So if a private enterprise economy with pure and perfect competition does reach the Pareto optimum, it may still have inequitable income distribution, unemployment, inflation, and no growth.

Within these narrowly defined limits of economic efficiency, as early as 1908 the Italian economist Barone[9] applied a Pareto optimum kind of analysis to a pure centrally planned economy. He points out — or implies according to later economists — that economic calculation of the Pareto optimum allocation does not require "prices" in an actual market. We only need three kinds of information. First, we must know what resources are available, including men and machines as well as raw materials. Second, we must know the preference scale of "consumers," whether these are individuals or planners or politicians or some weighted sum of these. Third, we must know the "production function" of each output, that is, what combination of resources is necessary to produce each output at the present level of technology.

In a private enterprise economy — as in socialism — the third kind of information (about production possibilities) is furnished by engineers. In a competitive private enterprise economy, however, market prices *automatically* reflect the first and second types of information, that is, the relative scarcity of different resources as well as the relative preference of consumers for different products. *If* a knowledge of the actual information of resource scarcities and consumer preferences can be obtained, however, then socialist planners will be able theoretically to calculate rational "prices" for all resources and for all products. These "prices" would be merely data for planners to use, and need not ever be paid to anybody.

[8] For details, see the references at the end of this chapter.
[9] Translated from Italian in E. Barone, "The Ministry of Production in the Collectivist State," in F. A. Hayek, ed., *Collectivist Economic Planning* (London: Routledge and Kegan Paul, Ltd., 1935).

If this information were available, the planners of socialist industry would then have the same information as the private enterprise managers. They could then presumably calculate the optimum allocation of resources for the goal of the maximum welfare of all society in much the same ways as private enterprise managers calculate for the maximization of profit.

Information and Computation Problems

In the next stage of debate, Hayek[10] admits that *in theory* the planners might accumulate all the millions of pieces of necessary information and might then solve all of the millions of equations necessary to make an optimal decision. *In practice,* Hayek argues, no conceivable force of planners could actually gather all of the various kinds of information from every factory and farm, and from every private and public consumer. Furthermore, *in practice,* even with all of the information, it would take hundreds of years to solve correctly all of the equations for just one year's plan.

Hayek does not directly refer to Soviet experience, but it is clear that he believes that *any* centrally planned economy must be terribly inefficient. While conceding its theoretical possibility, he argues that any planned economy must base its decisions on only partial bits of information and very rough calculations. The result, he predicts, is far below the optimum efficiency of allocation of resources compared to that of a competitive private enterprise model.

Nor are these purely academic problems to be dismissed by any socialist. The high rate of Soviet growth proves the possibility of planning; however, it *does not* tell us how much is lost by the inefficiency of Soviet planning. Even Soviet economists have admitted that with the continued use of present methods and with increasing economic complexity, the Soviet Union would eventually need more than its total population just for management of the planning process. Many have argued that this problem could be solved by automated information-collecting and the use of computers. Yet others argue that even these improvements will not suffice to maintain, much less raise, the level of efficiency in Soviet planning.

Central and Decentralized Solutions

The most famous answer to Hayek's criticism of the practicability of socialist planning was given by Lange.[11] He replies that a decentralized or market socialism would have no more trouble than competitive private enterprise in reaching rational prices and optimum allocation of resources. He refers to a system in which the public owns all firms, but each firm *acts* as an independent unit. The manager is instructed to set his prices and output so as to maximize firm profit, and

[10] See F. A. Hayek, *Collectivist Economic Planning* (London: Routledge and Kegan Paul, Ltd., 1935).

[11] Oskar Lange, *On the Economic Theory of Socialism* (Minneapolis: University of Minnesota Press, 1938).

may receive a bonus for making more profit, though the profit itself goes to society.

Lange also explored a socialist model of intermediate decentralization in which planners set prices, but managers still control production. Suppose that the planners begin by setting arbitrary prices. He argues that the prices could still be rational guides for managers *if* the central planners react promptly to any shortage of supply by raising prices and react to an excess of supply by lowering prices. These moves will induce the managers to increase or reduce the outputs, respectively. Both this and the preceding model are now being followed to some extent in Eastern Europe. (The present trends are explored here in Chapter 14.)

Central planning has been most fully defended by the British Marxist, Maurice Dobb.[12] Dobb points to the existence and rapid growth of the planned economy of the U.S.S.R. as proof of its practicability. He also considers the three main problems of socialist planning — growth, balance, and efficiency — and concludes that all three could be better solved under central planning than under capitalism, even though he admits that the planners may have far from rational and accurate price data.

We explore each of these questions in separate chapters, so it suffices to give a very brief résumé of Dobb's stand. First, he argues that growth depends primarily on the ratio of new investment to national product. He maintains that the decision on this ratio does not depend on relative prices because it is not economic, but must be primarily political (as we saw in Chapter 9). He believes that the choice will be more conducive to growth when made by a centralized socialist government than by multitudinous private capitalists.

Second, Dobb contends that the problem of a consistent (*not* necessarily optimal) balance of physical goods and actual money flows can be solved with any constant but arbitrary prices. Thus a socialist economy can and docs insure continuous full employment of men and resources, while capitalist economies periodically suffer unemployment. (The theoretical and actual Soviet problems with balance were fully discussed in Chapter 10.)

Third, Dobb admits it is true that rational prices are necessary for static Pareto optimal efficiency, but argues that this criterion is much less important in economic practice than balance and rapid growth. Anyway, he argues, new computing methods and machines now permit fairly good planners' calculations of the equations for prices and outputs. Moreover, he maintains, capitalist prices are also far from perfectly rational, since there is monopoly on the sellers' side and irrational advertising pressure on the consumers. (Soviet theoretical problems of planning for efficient production are discussed in Chapter 12, while problems of efficiently implementing the plan in practice have been considered in Chapter 7.)

[12] See, e.g., Maurice Dobb, *Economic Theory and Socialism* (New York: International Publishers, 1955), pp. 55–93. But also see the Marxist analysis by Paul M. Sweezy, *Socialism* (New York: McGraw-Hill Book Co., Inc., 1949).

A Tentative Summary of Conclusions on Efficiency

How do different economic systems measure up to the criteria of Pareto optimum efficiency? Pure and perfect competition under private enterprise does seem obviously to meet these conditions. The rational consumer will buy each good until his ratios of marginal utilities equal the ratios of prices; and prices are the same for all consumers. The profit-maximizing producer will buy inputs to the point where the ratios of their marginal products equal their price ratios, and prices are the same for all producers. These facts also mean that for all outputs and inputs the ratios of marginal utilities will equal the ratios of marginal products, which is one way of stating Pareto optimum efficiency. On the other hand, it may be shown that to the degree that competition is imperfect or monopolistic, private enterprise will not reach the optimum allocation of resources. Further, it has already been noted that this optimum allocation does *not* mean that there is equitable distribution of income, full employment, stable prices, or rapid growth.

What about a competitive or market socialism, in which the government owns all resources but each firm acts independently to maximize its profit by its own price and output decision? If there is pure and perfect competition under market socialism, it turns out that the resulting allocation of resources is exactly as efficient as under pure and perfect competition in private enterprise. The two may differ only with respect to "equity" or distribution of income and budgets among consumers and among producers (and possibly with respect to growth and aggregate balance). Market socialism will distribute as *private* income only wages, not profits, nor rent, nor interest. The profit, rent, and interest receipts will be used either to add to wage income or to expand production. On the other hand, to the degree that competition is imperfect or monopolistic in this system, market socialism will also not achieve an optimum allocation of resources. Moreover, it may still be subject to unemployment, inflation, or a low rate of growth.

Finally, how do the optimum efficiency conditions apply to a centrally planned socialist economy? Recall that the informational ingredients of these conditions are: (1) consumer preferences, (2) availability of resources, and (3) technological possibilities of production. It is not theoretically necessary that these be discovered automatically through the market mechanism. *If* central planners have the complete detailed information on these three items throughout the economy, and *if* they are able to perfectly calculate all of the equations involved, then (as Hayek admits) they can reach the same optimum mix of inputs and outputs as would exist under pure and perfect competition. The same rational prices will also emerge as a by-product of the planners' calculations, though they are not further needed in a fully planned system.

In reality, however, central planners will have imperfect information about the millions of preferences, resources, and production processes. They also cannot possibly solve the millions and millions of equations involved for want of time and calculators, even with the use of the most modern electronic machinery. They must, moreover, take more *time* to make readjustments to new situations than the market does in certain respects. Thus, the market allegedly reacts more quickly to maladjustments of supply and demand for products, though the market may take far longer to react to aggregate imbalances such as unemployment or inflation. Furthermore, planning in practice costs a considerable amount in terms of the time and effort of men and machines, while the market mechanism is allegedly "free," though there is much duplication of competitive effort in the market. Thus, imperfect planning must involve some considerable departure from optimum efficiency. As with imperfect competition, the difficult question is the quantitative degree of inefficiency under imperfect planning.

One point about propaganda should be firmly kept in mind both here and in the concluding chapter of this book. A debater always considers the theoretical ideal behavior of his favorite economic system, but stresses the actual imperfect behavior of his opponent's economic system. We should be aware that Mises and Hayek attack the actual or realized operation of an imperfect planned socialist system from the viewpoint of a pure and perfect competitive private enterprise system. Lange stresses the theoretical possibilities of a pure and perfect market socialist system in contrast to the actual operation of imperfect private enterprise economies. Dobb and Sweezy emphasize the theoretical potential of pure and perfect planned economies by contrasting them to the monopolistic and imperfect actual operation of private enterprise economies. When we examine the pure and perfect form of each of these, we find that *in theory* they are equally capable of reaching a Pareto optimum condition. The real questions are, in practice, how close each system approaches static efficiency, how their equity of income distribution, growth rates, and aggregate balance compare, and how related political and social behavior compare (all of which are reconsidered in the last chapter of this book).

The "Law of Value" in Socialism

Soviet economists have not discussed efficiency planning in terms of welfare economics until recently, but have often discussed many of the same issues in the dogmatic form of a debate about the applicability of Marx's "Law of Value" to a socialist economy. The debate over the "Law of Value" has a long history in the Soviet Union and it may help to give that setting before we examine the issues as they actually affect present day planning. The Marxist "Law of Value" states, as shown in Chapter 2, that the value of any commodity is equal to the amount of average socially-necessary labor embodied in it, that is, the amount of labor necessary under present technological conditions.

History of the Debate. During the period of War Communism, from 1917 to 1921, the Soviet Union did not in practice make much use of prices or of money. This lack of prices and money was idealized in theory as a true state of communism. Therefore, during this period it was held very dogmatically that the "Law of Value" has no application under socialism, but is only a description of the situation under competitive capitalism. Then, in the period of the New Economic Policy of the 1920's, trade and exchange became general and the use of money permeated the economy. In this period there ensued a great deal of debate over the uses of prices in socialism and over the methodology of planning, but without much clarification of the use of the Marxist "Law of Value." It was in this environment of intense discussion in the mid-1920's that Leontief studied at Leningrad University and first considered the problems that later led to the input-output method of planning.

Unfortunately, Stalin killed off this promising discussion (and some of the discussants as well), and attacked all model-building as "bourgeois, mathematical formalism." As a result, the years of Stalin's dictatorship from 1928 to 1953 were uncreative and terribly dull in economics.[13] The tasks of Soviet economists in these years were characterized by one harsh critic as "perpetual propagation of Marxism, peremptory assessment of the processes of disintegration in capitalism, and exorbitant praise for the success of Soviet industrialization."[14] At any rate, it is a fact that in all those years there were no translations and few discussions of Western economics. It is a more damning fact that in all those years there was published *no* new textbook of economics and planning; the first weak effort toward a new Soviet textbook was published in 1954. Available statistical data were greatly reduced in the late 1930's, and their publication almost ceased after 1937; Soviet statistical yearbooks began to appear again only in 1957.

During the five year plans of the 1930's Stalin stressed that there were no limits to what could be done — there was neither need nor possibility for the operation of an authentic "Law of Value," but room only for the law of the "plan." Soviet economics in this period reverted to a loose Marxist formulation that "value" would disappear in socialism, which was taken to mean that the planners could do anything that Stalin desired. In fact, the official Soviet view urged planners "not to study, but to change economics, to disregard economic laws."[15] Stalinist planning was mostly empirical, using little theory and no attempt at optimal efficiency, but simply pushing as much investment as possible. At that period, Soviet planners merely used the rule of thumb in basic industry that it is wisest to follow the technology and output mix of the United States.

[13] For a feeling of the enormous difference that the change in political atmosphere made, read the drivel written on planning in the Soviet textbook of *Political Economy* (U.S.S.R. Academy of Sciences, 1954; English edition published by Lawrence and Wishart, 1957) produced collectively under Stalin's direction. Then compare the brilliant collection of articles issued just five years later in the Khrushchev era by the more progressive Soviet economists, called *The Uses of Mathematics in Economics* (edited by Nemchinov, Moscow, 1959, English edition published by Oliver and Boyd, 1964).

[14] Vladimir Treml, "Revival of Soviet Economics and the New Generation of Soviet Economists," *Studies on the Soviet Union*, Vol. 5, No. 2 (1965), p. 4.

[15] S. Strumilin, quoted in *ibid.*, p. 3.

It might also be noted that while Stalin was rejecting any but purely empirical methods of planning, various important theoretical advances were beginning to poke their heads up from the practical operational fields of Soviet engineering and project making. For example, it was in 1939 that the Soviet mathematician, Kantorovich, was employed by an engineering firm to advise on the optimal use of their machinery. As a result, he published the first paper on what has become the most famous of all planning methods, the method of linear programming. Yet this discovery, too, was buried under the heap of ideological trash produced under the Stalinist dictatorship. It is true that U.S. economists took several years to recognize the importance of linear programming after its first appearance here, but in the Stalinist atmosphere any general utilization of such a radically new economic concept was simply inconceivable. Not only was an official dogma promulgated in scholastic detail, but Stalin executed or imprisoned several of the most brilliant and daring economists of the 1930's.

In 1943 came the first official breakthrough and recognition of value problems in the Soviet Union. At that time, in a famous article first appearing in a Soviet journal,[16] there appeared a vague but definite statement that the "Law of Value" does apply under socialism. Nothing more concrete, however, evolved in the Soviet discussions until Stalin himself took a hand in the discussion. Stalin in 1952 made his last authoritative pronouncement on the subject,[17] leading to a major debate throughout the socialist countries and the ranks of Western Marxists.

Stalin argues that "wherever commodities and commodity production exist, there the law of value must also exist."[18] By commodity production he means production for sale in the competitive market place, just as Marx described competition in the market place of capitalism. Stalin saw commodity production in the Soviet Union existing almost exclusively in the collective farm markets and in the exchange of goods between the collective farm and the government-owned factories. Thus, one sympathetic Western Marxist writes, in agreement with Stalin, that:

> Under socialism in a country like the U.S.S.R. where a semi-private agricultural sector continues to exist alongside the state sector, commodity production (and therefore the law of value) will also continue to exist, although in a relatively restricted sphere.[19]

The crux of the question, however, is that under pure centrally planned socialism there is no free competitive market exchange of goods between state-owned firms; and, therefore, there is no "commodity production" in the sphere of producer goods in the peculiar sense used by Stalin.

---

[16] "Some Problems in the Teaching of Political Economy," translated in the *American Economic Review* (September 1944).

[17] Joseph Stalin, *Economic Problem of Socialism in the U.S.S.R.* (New York: International Publishers, 1952).

[18] *Ibid.*, p. 18.

[19] Ronald Meek, *Studies in the Labour Theory of Value* (New York: International Publishers, 1956), p. 293.

Thus, the same Western Marxist writer continues, again in agreement with Stalin, that:

> So far as manufactured goods are concerned, their situation is somewhat anomalous, since although they are technically "commodities" the concept of a supply price is not really applicable to them, and I can not see that there is much point in attempting to analyse their prices in terms of our conceptual apparatus.[20]

In other words, Stalinist economic theory (really a theology) could admit only that *some* manufactured goods are "commodities" because they exchange on the market with some agricultural goods, though this is a very small peg upon which to hang a value theory. It was still argued that there is no possibility — or perhaps no need — to plan prices within the manufacturing sector in accordance with value. This very limited recognition of the importance of economic value did very little to improve the quality of the Soviet debate.

It was not until Stalin's death, and especially after the severe and public criticism of Stalin in 1956, that Soviet economists once again felt really free to discuss the importance of money and prices. After 1956, almost all Soviet economists did come to agree that the "Law of Value" has great importance in socialism, that is, that planning must be based on the objective facts of social needs and costs. And it was only at this time that official Soviet recognition was given to Leontief's input-output discovery and Kantorovich's linear programming discovery — indeed, claiming both as purely Soviet achievements. This claim was made in spite of the fact that the work of both had returned to the Soviet Union only *via* the extensive research and writings of Western economists.

After it was admitted that the "Law of Value" does apply to a socialist economy, there arose in the Soviet Union three different views[21] of the value of manufactured means of production. The most restrictive view[22] argues, as Stalin did, that the "Law of Value" operates only in "market exchange," so values may be calculated only for consumer goods and for the few producer goods exchanged between manufacturing enterprises and collective farms. The second view[23] maintains that the "Law of Value" operates under any kind of exchange, so values may be calculated for all exchanges between government enterprises. The third and most radical view[24] argues pragmatically that the need for valuation under socialism arises from the necessity in the planning process

[20] *Ibid.*

[21] These three views are discussed in detail in Gregory Grossman, "Gold and the Sword: Money in the Soviet Command Economy," in H. Rosovsky, ed., *Industrialization in Two Systems* (N.Y.: John Wiley, 1966).

[22] See, e.g., Ostrovitianov, *Stroitclstvo kommunizma i tovarnodenezhnye otnosheniia* (Moscow: 1962).

[23] See, e.g., I. A. Kronrod, *Dengi v sotsialisticheskom obshchestve* (Moscow: 1960).

[24] See, e.g., I. S. Malyshev, *Obshchestvennyi uchet truda i tsena pri sotsializme* (Moscow: 1960).

of measuring the amount of labor expended on each product; so all products must be valued.

These more progressive or radical Soviet writers stress, as seen in detail below, that the current Soviet price structure is highly irrational and misleading. Soviet prices omit rent, interest, and any meaningful category of profits, though they include a fixed and arbitrary profit rate. Moreover, prices remain set for many years, but since supply and demand conditions are constantly changing in any dynamic economy, this implies that prices are far out of line during much of this time. One reflection of this distortion is that many commodities must be subsidized for long periods, while others carry heavy sales or turnover taxes. Most chaotic of all are agricultural prices. Even Stalin once cited a case in which the price of bread was lower than the price of the flour it contained.

It may be asked why in more recent years not only the progressives, but even Stalin and his followers, began to talk about the need for rational valuation and calculation in the Soviet economy. The increased need seems to grow out of the increased complexity of the Soviet economy. For one thing, it has many more enterprise units and more varied products than it did in earlier days — at the present time over 200,000 separate enterprises and over 2,000,000 different products. Second, there are many more technological possibilities and variants open to the Soviet planners in each industry. Third, there is a much wider variety of consumer goods to choose among, and the average income now puts the Soviet consumer far above the absolute biological need level. After 1956, the new political atmosphere emphasized prompt satisfaction of the wide variety of consumer needs. Fourth, although there had been plenty of reserve labor in the rural areas in the 1930's, the terrible losses of the Second World War made it urgently necessary to use labor most efficiently. Fifth, the problems of an increased international trade began to call most urgently for more rational calculation.

The more progressive Soviet writers emphasize the enormous losses in each of these areas caused by an irrational price structure. The seriousness of the problem not only has been stressed by U.S. critics,[25] but was recognized in print by Soviet critics at least as early as 1957.[26] All of the defects in the price system add up to the net result that relative prices do not correctly reflect "value," scarcity, or consumer demand. Since society is very complex, planners have to make many decisions in ignorance of the information which a rational price system would provide them. One famous progressive Soviet writer says that more efficient planning could increase output by 40 to 50 percent.[27] This is no small matter.

[25] See, e.g., Jere L. Felker, *Soviet Economic Controversies, the Emerging Marketing Concept and Changes in Planning, 1960–1965* (Cambridge, Mass.: MIT Press, 1966), *passim.*

[26] See, e.g., I. Malyshev, *Voprosy ekonomiki* (1957), No. 3, p. 32.

[27] See L. V. Kantorovich, *The Best Use of Economic Resources* (Cambridge, Mass: Harvard University Press, translated in 1965).

NNP per worker   23.6   46.4

NNP per unit of K   98.3   108.5

NNP per adjusted worker   29.2   58.0

NNP per W + K   54.5 – 40.0   54.9

NNP per adj: W + K   57.8 – 44.4   66.7

Source: A. Bergson – Econ of Sov. Planning, p 342

Correction of class lecture on Static efficiency

Static Comparative Efficiency, 1960

USSR as % of U.S.

	rubles/rubles	$/rubles
Net Natl Product (NNP)	34.1	67.7
Employment — W	144.5	
Employment adjusted for educational differential	116.7	
Capital (K)	34.7	45.6
W + K (20%r, 8% i)	62.6, 85.3	123.4

Further reasons for increased Soviet interest in optimal efficiency may be found in the relationship with the Western economies. On the one hand, there is the race to grow more rapidly than the United States, for which maximum efficiency is extremely helpful. On the other hand, there is the fact that great advances in practical methods of planning have been made in the Western countries, and these are available for imitation. Of course, the new planning methods have been used in the United States only for planning at the micro or enterprise level, since the United States has no national economic planning. In the U.S.S.R., however, the new planning methods have been applied not only at the enterprise level, but also have been applied — or at least the attempt is being made to apply them — at the macroeconomic level of national economic planning.

   Marxist Economic Laws and Planning Models. Is there a conflict between the Marxist economic "Law of Value" and the modern theories and methods of rational economic planning? Specifically, can the Soviet Union continue to promote Marxist economics while using the latest planning devices? There are three opposing views. First, most Anglo-American experts, such as Campbell,[28] believe that there is indeed a conflict between Marxism and modern planning theory. An extreme view is expressed by Zauberman, who claims:

> that the price arrived at in the calculus [of the new Soviet mathematical models] . . . turns out to be in unmistakable conflict with that derived from Marx. Marx's price is a cost price, while the conservative Soviet critics of the . . . mathematical scheme . . . correctly identified . . . [its] value-weights as scarcity prices, typically marginalist in their nature. Many of these critics . . . have rightly pointed to the deep roots of the mathematicians' price in the subjective value concept, and to its incompatibility with Marx's objective value, reducible to 'congealed' socially necessary labor.[29]

It follows, according to this argument, that Marxist value economics must be eliminated if the Soviet Union is to plan rationally.

   Strangely enough, the major premise of this argument is accepted among the second group, the more dogmatic (orthodox?) Soviet Marxist economists, such as Boiarskii.[30] Boiarskii agrees that there *is* a con-

[28] See, e.g., Robert W. Campbell, "Marx, Kantorovich, and Novozhilov," *Slavic Review*, Vol. 20 (October, 1961), pp. 402–418. A discussion of more general conflicts is given by Joseph Berliner, "Marxism and the Soviet Economy," *Problems of Communism*, Vol. 13 (Sept.–Oct., 1964), pp. 1–10.

[29] Alfred Zauberman, "Revisionism in Soviet Economics," in Leopold Labedz, ed., *Revisionism* (New York: Frederick A. Praeger, 1962), p. 276.

[30] See, e.g., A. Y. Boiarskii, "On the Proper Relationship Between Mathematics and Economics in a Socialist Society," translated in *Problems of Economics* (Jan., 1962), pp. 12–24. Also see the similar views in A. I. Kats, "Concerning a Fallacious Concept of Economic Calculations," translated in *Problems of Economics* (Nov., 1960), pp. 42–52. A history of the various viewpoints in the Stalin era is available in Gregory Grossman, "Scarce Capital and Soviet Doctrine," *Quarterly Journal of Economics*, Vol. 67 (August, 1963), pp. 311–343.

flict between Marxist economics and certain modern theories of planning. Since he believes in the absolute truth of Marxism, however, his conclusion is directly opposite to that reached by Campbell. He concludes that these planning theories must not be followed in the Soviet Union. Particular devices, such as input-output or linear programming, may be used if they are first completely purged of their marginal utility taint.

A third position is that of the less dogmatic (progressive? creative? revisionist?) Marxists in the Soviet Union, such as Novozhilov or Kantorovich.[31] They hold that modern theories of economic planning are quite compatible with Marxism, and that the modern instruments of rational planning should be used to the fullest extent. For these views, Novozhilov and others have been labeled as revisionists of Marx both by their own dogmatic Soviet colleagues and by most Anglo-American experts. Nove,[32] a more perceptive critic, writes however that:

> One should not assume, as some Western critics do, that Marxian economics is inherently inconsistent with reality, that the 'vulgar Marxist' simplifications of the late-Stalin period are the essence of the theory. Novozhilov, for instance, would certainly argue that his theories are consistent with Marxism; are indeed the correct application of Marxist theory to the circumstances of the Soviet Union.[33]

In fact, Novozhilov[34] himself admits that some of his categories of calculation under socialism, such as profits, are semantically similar to those used under capitalism, but argues strongly that this is due only to the mathematical similarities in all optimization problems.

A great many of the Soviet writers now argue that there is no conflict between Marxism and the modern neo-classical theories of rational allocation of resources.[35] Specifically, the more progressive Soviet writers point out that to advocate a mathematical device (like a rate of interest) for rationally allocating capital in a planned economy is quite different

[31] See, e.g., L. V. Kantorovich, "On the Calculation of Production Inputs," translated in *Problems of Economics* (May, 1960), pp. 3–10. Also see Benjamin Ward, "Kantorovich on Economic Calculation," *Journal of Political Economy*, Vol. 68 (Dec., 1960), pp. 545–556. Further see V. V. Novozhilov, "On Choosing between Investment Projects," translated in *International Economic Papers*, Number 6 (1956), pp. 67–87. Also see V. V. Novozhilov, "Calculation of Outlays in a Socialist Economy," translated in *Problems of Economics* (Dec., 1961), pp. 18–28. Finally, his fullest presentation is in V. V. Novozhilov, "Cost-Benefit Comparisons in a Socialist Economy" in V. S. Nemchinov, editor, *The Use of Mathematics in Economics* (London: Oliver and Boyd, Ltd., translated under the editorship of A. Nove in 1964, Russian edition 1959).

[32] Alec Nove, "Introduction" to V. S. Nemchinov, editor, *The Use of Mathematics in Economics* (London: Oliver and Boyd Ltd., 1964 edition in English, first Russian edition in 1959), p. x.

[33] *Ibid.*

[34] *Ibid.*, p. 189.

[35] See, e.g., A. Postyshev, "The Labor Theory of Value and Optimal Planning," translated in *Problems of Economics* (1967). He identifies the famous "shadow prices" of linear programming with Marx's value in terms of labor.

from advocating that any profit (or interest) be given as individual income. If the neo-classical theory of allocation, which has largely been concerned with the allocation of scarce resources in capitalist firms, also happens to meet the similar problems of socialist firms, there is no reason not to use it.

The progressive Marxists of the West, like the early Lange, argue that there is a qualitative difference between the technical problems of planned allocation of resources and the political-ethical problems of class ownership and distribution. They agree that the technical problems of socialist planning may be best discussed in terms of "bourgeois" neo-classical economics. Yet they still believe that the political-ethical questions of income distribution by classes, as well as the macroeconomic problems of capitalism, are to be understood in terms of Marxist political-economy.[36]

If the more progressive Soviet attitude were accepted, then there would be no conflict between Marxism and any prospective tool of Soviet economic planning. Since it is far from fully accepted, each action of Soviet planners is still gauged by the politicians in terms of a very dogmatic interpretation of Marxism.

Prices and Efficiency

A careful examination of recent Soviet debates on specific price policy raises two questions: Why are prices essential in Soviet optimal planning? What is the relation of the Soviet theory of value to its practical application in pricing policies?

The Importance of Prices in Soviet Planning. Previous chapters have mentioned some of the uses of prices in the planned Soviet economy. First, wages (with given retail prices) provide the stimulus or incentive for workers and managers to do their best work. Moreover, since not every detail is centrally planned, the structure of prices will influence many managerial decisions about technology as well as output mixtures. This will happen whenever managers' bonuses are based on the *value* of the total product or on monetary profits.[37]

Second, it was observed that many planning decisions about balance involve prices. For example, consumer prices must be set so that demand for goods equals supply at the given prices. Similarly, wages must be set so that the demand equals the supply of workers at the given wages. All of the prices mentioned so far are concerned with the execution of the plan or the influencing of the behavior of workers and managers and

---

[36] This view of the distinction between Marxist political economy and technical bourgeois economics is presented by the Marxist writers, Paul Baran and Paul Sweezy in "Economics of Two Worlds," in *On Political Economy and Econometrics: Essays in Honour of Oskar Lange* (New York: Perganon Press, 1965), pp. 15–29.

[37] An excellent Soviet statement of the importance of rational prices for managers appears in N. Fedorenko, "Price and Optimal Planning," translated in *Problems of Economics* (1967).

consumers in accordance with the plan. But what about prices in the calculation of the plan itself?

Prices enter the problems of balanced growth in a relatively simple way, not involving a theory of value. In theory, balances among industries could be analyzed in wholly physical terms. This is the case to some degree in Soviet practice in the application of their "method of balances"; it can also be achieved in the Leontief input-output method. Where prices are used, they may be any arbitrary or randomly chosen prices, *provided* that (1) they remain constant during the planning period, and (2) they are consistent among themselves, so that the price of a commodity is not less than the total of the costs of the goods going into it. This is because prices are used in the balancing procedure only for purposes of aggregating different things. This is true, for example, of the sources and the uses side of the balance of a single industry; or, for example, of the total of all wages balanced against the total price of all consumer goods.

The situation is quite different in the other problem of planning, the optimization of economic efficiency. Though there are many consistent balances, there is only one *optimal* input and output mix. The choice of that optimal mix depends on what value or price is chosen for each of the inputs and outputs. The optimization problem has two aspects: (1) the choice of a maximum or most preferred output mix, and (2) the choice of a minimum cost or most efficient technology. A solution may be reached *either* by minimizing costs or by maximizing the value of output; it is not necessary to do both. In order properly either to calculate costs or evaluate output, however, it is necessary to have prices that rationally reflect social costs and social needs.

As a concrete example, suppose the Soviet economy produces only two kinds of outputs: apples and oranges. With the given amount of labor and capital inputs available, assume the economy can produce either (a) five apples and ten oranges *or* (b) ten apples and five oranges. Which output mixture should be produced to maximize output? That obviously depends on the value or price of each output, relative to the price of the other output. If the relative prices (values) are two rubles an apple and one ruble an orange, then output is maximized by choosing mixture (b), ten apples and five oranges. But if the prices were one ruble an apple and two rubles an orange, then it would be maximized by choosing mixture (a), five apples and ten oranges.

The case is exactly analogous if planners wish to minimize the cost of inputs. Suppose the only inputs available are capital and labor. To produce a certain required amount of output (for example, a given number of apples and oranges), there are two technological processes available: involving either (a) the use of five units of labor and ten units of capital *or* (b) the use of ten units of labor and five units of capital. Each "unit" is a physical measure such as hours of labor expended or numbers of machines used. Which process will minimize the cost of inputs? Again, this depends on the relative prices of the inputs. The planners choose (a) if a unit of labor costs two rubles and a unit of capital one ruble, but choose (b) if a unit of labor costs one ruble and a unit of capital two rubles.

In both cases, it is impossible to optimize, or to make a rational economic choice, without the use of some standard of valuation or price system. In the second example, an engineer could only say that in physical terms either technological process or combination of inputs will produce the same output. But the social welfare cannot be maximized unless the planners know the true value of the inputs, so they can say which combination produces the output at the least cost to society. In the next chapter, it will be shown how these kinds of calculations may be made for an input-output table of the whole society, provided that the planners know the prices of each input or output.

Price Policies. The Soviet views on price policy follow fairly clearly from their different views on value. One view, which has been labeled "voluntarist," is simply to have the planners set prices as they desire. This view derives from the notion that the "Law of Value" has no application to the socialist economy, and that prices need have no effect on planning. Needless to say, this view no longer has any explicit defenders in the Soviet Union.

On the other hand, the Soviet price structure still bears an unfortunate resemblance to what might be expected of it under such a view. That is to say, in practice Soviet prices do not seem clearly correlated with any particular value theory, though a major reform is now under way. Before the reform, at least, there were many gross and obvious examples of price distortion. Some of these were mentioned earlier. Another, which clearly affects some important decisions, is the fact that consumer goods prices included an enormous turnover tax, while most producer goods were free of any turnover tax. Finding alternative methods of setting taxes or determining the return to society from each commodity was a major aim of the debate on prices.

Several groups of Soviet economists do agree that the Marxist "Law of Value" does apply to a socialist economy, but offer differing legalistic interpretations of it. All agree that price must equal the total of (1) current labor expenditure, (2) past labor reflected in the cost of materials and capital depreciation, and (3) some profit (called "surplus for society"). Expenditures on current labor, materials, and depreciation are presently included in price. The problem is how to calculate the surplus or profit. The most dogmatic group would calculate the surplus strictly as a given, constant ratio to (1) current labor expenditure. The second would calculate the surplus as a given ratio to (1) current labor expenditure *plus* (2) past labor reflected in the cost of materials and capital depreciation. The most progressive group would calculate the profit as a given ratio to the stock of capital, the same formula on which Marx's "price of production" is based. Finally, the small group advocating "price of production" shades over into an even smaller group of so-called "imputationists." They would set prices, not on the basis of any authoritative theological dogma, but by imputing prices from the objective facts either of social costs or of social needs.

One widely known approach, which falls within the imputationist group, is that of the Soviet economist Novozhilov.[38] In Western economic terms, he calculates the "opportunity costs" of using scarce resources. Opportunity costs are the measure of the sacrifice made in other projects by using a limited resource in the project under consideration. Novozhilov always calculates these costs in terms of labor so as to maintain Marxist orthodoxy. He calculates not only the usual labor costs, but also so-called "indirect" labor costs. What are these indirect labor costs? If capital and natural resources are used in certain projects in large amounts, then there may not be sufficient capital and natural resources remaining to use them as desired in all other projects. In that case, the other projects will have to switch to the use of more labor and less capital, thus "indirectly" causing an increase of labor costs.

Since these goods are limited or "scarce," they must be rationed; that is the function of the calculation of the "indirect labor costs." In choosing the alternative with the minimum cost, the planner compares not only current labor costs and the using up of capital and materials, but also the indirect labor costs or opportunity costs of directing scarce resources here rather than elsewhere. In this sense the so-called "indirect labor costs" play a role similar to the rate of profit (and rent) in private enterprise, which rations capital (and natural resources) to different industries so that the marginal return is uniform for all industries. If Soviet enterprises borrow all capital from the government, then this calculation acts like a rate of interest, insuring that (1) investment funds are used where most profitable to the society, and (2) investment goes to just that point where aggregate supply and demand are equal.

Summary

What may be learned from this discussion? Mises argued the impossibility of socialist planning because lack of a market would mean lack of knowledge of rational prices. Socialists have answered that optimal planning *could* be achieved if planners have a knowledge of preferences, scarcities, and production possibilities. Dobb even argues that planners could do better than the market if not only optimum allocation is desired, but also full employment and rapid growth. Hayek objects that in practice the central planners could never get and digest all the necessary information. Lange rejoins that socialism could be decentralized so that a competitive market could provide rational prices for socialist managers.

The Soviet approaches to allocation theory and modern methods of planning have also been examined. The older, more dogmatic Marxist economists believed Marxist economics is absolutely opposed to modern Western allocation and optimal planning theories. The younger Soviet re-

[38] See, e.g., V. V. Novozhilov, "Cost-Benefit Comparisons in a Socialist Economy," in Nemchinov, *op. cit.* A similar approach to prices, deriving them strictly according to the needs of optimal planning is clearly stated by V. S. Dadaian and others in "A Symposium on Problems of Political-Economy," *Problems of Economics,* Vol. 10 (July, 1967), pp. 3–19.

formers, however, have reinterpreted Marxism to show that there is no conflict, and have derived very similar theories and methods in a Marxist form. They are now trying to formulate and apply these methods to actual price and output calculations for optimum production (investigated further in the next chapter).

SELECTED REFERENCES

1. The impossibility of efficient planning in socialism is argued in F. A. Hayek, *Collectivist Economic Planning* (London: Routledge and Kegan Paul, Ltd., 1935).

2. The defense of socialism, especially its decentralized form, is presented in Oskar Lange and F. M. Taylor, *On the Economic Theory of Socialism* (Minneapolis: University of Minnesota Press, 1938).

3. The case for centrally planned socialism may be found in Maurice Dobb, *Economic Theory and Socialism* (New York: International Publishers, 1955), pp. 33–92 and 239–246.

4. The best history of the debate on socialism is presented in Abram Bergson, "Socialist Economics," in Howard Ellis, ed., *A Survey of Contemporary Economics*, Vol. I (Philadelphia: Blakiston, 1948), pp. 412–448.

5. A more advanced text gives a list of at least ten questions still unanswered in the theoretical debate on the possibility of socialist planning, Benjamin Ward, *The Socialist Economy* (New York: Random House, 1967).

6. A good introduction to welfare conditions is in Kenneth Boudling, "Welfare Economics," in B. Haley, ed., *A Survey of Contemporary Economics*, Vol. II (Homewood, Ill.: Irwin, 1952), pp. 1–38. A more recent and thorough discussion is E. J. Mishan, "A Survey of Welfare Economics, 1939–1951," in American Economic Association and Royal Economic Society, eds., *Surveys of Economic Theory* (New York: St. Martin's Press, 1966).

7. A simple technical exposition of the optimum conditions may be found in F. Bator, "The Simple Analytics of Welfare Maximization," *American Economic Review*, Vol. 47, (1957), pp. 22–59.

8. A general review of the Soviet debate on value theory from an anti-Marxist viewpoint may be found in Alfred Zauberman, "The Present State of Soviet 'Planometrics,'" *Soviet Studies*, Vol. 14 (July, 1962), pp. 62–74. The progressive Marxist side of the debate is presented briefly in V. Nemchinov, "Mathematics and Electronics in the Service of Planning," *Problems of Economics*, Vol. IV, No. 7 (Nov., 1961), pp. 3–9. A more conservative Soviet view is manifested in P. Matislavskii, "Quantitative Expression of Economic Relationships and Processes," *Problems of Economics* (Jan., 1962), Vol. 4, No. 9, pp. 3–11.

12

PLANNING FOR OPTIMUM EFFICIENCY

This chapter considers the actual methods of calculating optimum efficiency. First, the analysis explores the choice of the optimal output mix. This choice should reflect demand, that is, consumer preferences. Second, the chapter analyzes the choice of technologies from among the available processes of production, within existing limitations of resources. After this brief discussion of the theory of optimal planning, the analysis turns to the history of Soviet practices and Soviet debates on the problem. Finally, a few of the limitations of any optimal planning scheme are mentioned.

Choice of Output Mix

In Chapter 10, concerning the balance or equilibrium of output, discussion centered on the question of how it is possible to guarantee just sufficient inputs to produce a given output. In this section, it is shown how to solve the far more difficult problem of finding not only a balance of given output demands with the available inputs, but also of *choosing* that mixture of outputs which will furnish the maximum possible total "value" or social satisfaction.

To make the problem more concrete, and easily comparable with the illustration of the balance problem shown in Chapter 10, the discussion begins by repeating Table 10–4 from that chapter with a few modifications. Two output sectors are used, Agriculture and Manufacturing; while the primary inputs are divided into Labor, Capital, and Natural Resources.

As usual, within the heavily outlined box are shown the technical in-

Table 12-1

Facts for Output Maximization

INPUTS / OUTPUTS	Direct Inputs per Unit of Total Output		Price of a Unit of Output (in rubles)	Limits on Total Number of Outputs and Inputs
	Agriculture	Manufacturing		
Agriculture	.01	.08	3.0	greater than zero units
Manufacturing	.31	.24	1.5	greater than zero units
Labor (in hours of labor time)	2	1	not applicable	equal to or less than 100 billion hours
Capital (in numbers of machines)	2	3	not applicable	equal to or less than 210 billion machines
Natural resources (in tons)	1	0	not applicable	equal to or less than 30 billion tons

put-output coefficients relating the sectors of the economy. For example, the box shows that .08 units of Agricultural product are used ·directly in producing each unit of Manufacturing. Below that box are the technical coefficients showing the use of each of the primary inputs in the output sectors. For example, we can see that two hours of labor time are required in the production of a unit of Agricultural goods. In the next column the price of each output is stated; for example, a unit of Agricultural output is worth three rubles. Finally, in the last column, some limits are imposed on the answer. Thus, the output of each product must be positive or greater than zero. Furthermore, there are available only 100 billion labor hours, 210 billion machines, and 30 billion tons of natural resources.

Since the technical coefficients are known, if the planners are given a set of final outputs, they can calculate exactly what intermediate inputs and primary inputs are required for a balanced plan (as shown in Chapter 10). *The new problem introduced here is* that the planners are not to be given the total or final outputs by an outside authority, but are *to choose those final outputs that will maximize their total value.* The table says only that both final outputs must be positive. Here it must be emphasized once more that it is impossible to maximize different outputs merely in physical terms, since there is no standard for comparing the mixture: one apple plus two oranges, versus the mixture: two apples plus one orange. It is necessary to have some set of prices showing the relative worth or value of the different outputs. The question of exactly how these prices are derived is left to a later section. Here it is merely assumed that these prices are given to the planners.

In other words, it is impossible to maximize the number of units of Agricultural goods plus the number of units of Manufacturing goods, because each of these will be given in non-comparable units. The essence of the problem is to maximize the *value*:

Price of Agricultural goods times Number of units of Agricultural goods
plus

Price of Manufacturing goods times Number of units of Manufacturing goods.

Given the technical coefficients and the prices of the outputs, this maximization problem can be solved within the limits of the available primary inputs. The actual performance of these calculations could be performed by the method of linear programming. The general method is discussed in Appendix A to this chapter. The solution to the specific problem shown in Table 12–1 is presented in Appendix B to this chapter.

The optimum solution turns out to be 26.5 billion units of final Agricultural output and 21.1 billion units of final Manufacturing output. What is important at this point, however, is neither the exact solution nor the mechanics of getting it, but the facts that must be known to set up the problem as well as what the solution tells the planners. The solution gives those particular outputs which constitute the maximum possible under the given circumstances when valued at the given prices.

The planners must know, in order to set up and solve the problem, only the three kinds of facts illustrated in Table 12–1. First, they must know the total amounts of each available input, such as the number of workers in the labor force. These amounts of resources available constitute the constraints or limitations to the possible amounts of production. Second, they must know the prices of each output, since these prices constitute the valuation of the outputs based upon social demand preferences (discussed in a later section of this chapter). Third, they must know the technical coefficient relating each output to its inputs. Given these ingredients, they may calculate that combination of final outputs that gives the maximum value of output — or maximum economic welfare — with these inputs. Notice that it is also a balanced output mix because the analysis began with an input-output table.

The case taken here is one where it is assumed that the technical coefficients are fixed and unique for each output, that is, there is only one way to produce each output. Notice that this assumes constant or proportionate returns to each increase in the scale of production during the planning period, so that each doubling of input leads to a doubling of output. This case of fixed technical coefficients and constant returns leads, of course, to a very special and very simple case of optimization. The reality may force the planners to deal with the much more complicated case where there are several different ways to produce a single output, so that they must choose which variant or set of technical coefficients will be the optimal one. The next section examines the choice of technical variants with fixed output. This is followed by a brief investigation of the interrelation of the two problems, that is, the choice of output mix and the choice of technology.

Choice of Technology

From where do the technical coefficients come, or by whom and how are they derived? In theory, the central planners must determine these coefficients on the basis of their knowledge of all the engineering data on methods of production as well as all of the costs and prices for each output produced by each plant. In practice, many technological decisions are made at a lower echelon than that of the central planners, though this only transfers the problem to local enterprise economists or engineers. Furthermore, as far as the central planners are concerned, most of the means of production now being used were already produced last year; so current technological choices may actually be very limited, and the problem arises for the most part only when future investments are planned.

It might also be argued that this particular simplification, the use of fixed technical coefficients, may actually represent more of reality than one would expect. For example, price studies in the United States have shown that there is a constant return of output per unit of cost over a wide range of the production possibilities of a firm.[1] Furthermore, the famous studies of Leontief himself[2] indicate that the assumption of fixed coefficients leads to only negligible distortions in the study and prediction of input-output relationships. Thus, the simple case of fixed coefficients, discussed in the previous section, may not misrepresent the problem too much.

There are, nevertheless, many cases in which important technological choices must be made, while the output targets are fixed for the purpose of planning. In fact, Soviet planners are ordinarily presented with a fixed set of output goals, which have already been chosen by the political leadership. Their task has not been to choose output ratios so as to maximize the value of output, but rather to choose the most efficient technology in producing the given outputs, so as to minimize the cost of production. The ingredients of the Soviet planning problem for a given year are, therefore, (1) the total required outputs, (2) the available technological variants, and (3) the prices of each input.

[1] See, e.g., Joe S. Bain, "Price and Production Policies," *A Survey of Contemporary Economics*, edited by Howard Ellis (New York: McGraw-Hill Book Co., 1948), p. 140.
[2] See, e.g., W. Leontief, *The Structure of the American Economy, 1919–1929* (Cambridge, Mass.: Harvard University Press, 1941).

Since the total output of each industry is given, the planners may conveniently examine the technological problem for each industry taken alone. Here the coat-manufacturing industry is analyzed by itself, taking the problem to be typical of the other sectors as well. The following table shows the facts that must be known to choose the most efficient technology for this industry.

Table 12–2

Facts for Choice of Technology

OUTPUT / INPUTS	Direct Input per Unit of Total Output			Prices (in rubles per unit)	Limits on Total Number of units of Outputs or Inputs
	Coat Manufacturing Process 1	Coat Manufacturing Process 2	Coat Manufacturing Process 3		
Labor (hours)	.53	.48	.67	10 rubles	No upper limit, but assume greater than zero
Capital (machines)	.06	.15	.03	4 rubles	Less than or equal to 10 million machines
Other* (tons)	.15	.08	.11	2 rubles	Less than or equal to 11 million tons
*"Other" includes natural resources and all intermediate inputs					Total output of manufacturing must be equal to or greater than 100 million units

This table shows three different processes for producing a fixed amount of an identical commodity, coats in this case. Each process utilizes different amounts of the inputs, according to the coefficients shown in the first three columns. Each input has a different price, stated in the fourth column. And each input is available in different amounts, as shown in the last column. From the facts listed in this table, it is possible to calculate which process — or combination of processes — produces the planned output with the least cost of input. Suppose the linear programming method explained in Appendix A to this chapter is used. It turns out that the optimal or least-cost solution is to produce 37.5 million coats by process *1*, *48.9* million by process 2, and *13.6* million by process 3. The calculations leading to this solution are presented in Appendix C to this chapter.

So far, the analysis has considered the simple cases of (1) the maximization of the value of output with given inputs, and (2) the minimization of the cost of inputs with a given set of outputs. The first method chooses among different output mixtures, while the second chooses among technological variants of production processes. The additional theory of the combined problem is how to maximize output by choosing the best mixture of outputs *and* the best technological processes to produce that mixture. In *theory*, it is possible to combine all of the data into one mathematical problem, feed it to a computer, and have the computer choose both output mix and technology at the same time. This would require, however, (1) very many and very complex calculations overloading present computer capacity, and (2) enormous amounts of accurate micro information relayed from enterprises to central planners.

In practice, therefore, it may be better for the planners to calculate an optimal output mix on the basis of the last year's coefficients, then for each industry to be given an output target and calculate its best technological processes by itself. The input requirements would then usually conflict with those originally estimated. Then, however, the central planners could use the technology chosen by each industry as the given basis (along with output prices and input or resource limitations) for an ordinary problem of choice of output mix. The new output targets — which would be optimal and consistent — would then be given to the industries to use with the technology already determined by the industries. Of course, perfect optimization would require a further modification of the technology for the new output levels, but further rounds of this planning process would probably be prohibitively expensive.

Soviet Practice and Views on Plan Choices

To date, linear programming and other modern methods have only been used in the Soviet Union within single enterprises or to calculate least-cost methods for a single project or problem. The central planners are given long-run output targets by higher authorities. For many industries, the targets for a year are based on "known capacity," which is often nothing but the previous year's performance plus 10 percent. For the most important industries, the technical coefficients are calculated as carefully as possible. Then input requirements and "balances" are set up for each industry. Any inconsistencies are ironed out mainly by pressuring industries to produce more with no increase in input, as explained in Chapter 10. Some kind of balance is usually achieved, but it is optimal only to the degree that the politicians chose an optimal output mix and the industries or project-makers chose optimal technology.

One Soviet modification of central planning should be emphasized.

Especially in the early years of the planning era, the "priority principle" overrode all established plans. The priority principle meant that if the plans were in error, particularly if there were not enough supplies to go around, an unwritten code said that those sectors the planners considered most important had an absolute priority in obtaining inputs. This meant that the planners could engage in overfull employment planning and could make errors without worrying that the things in which they were really interested would suffer. Specifically, it formerly meant that the steel, coal, and oil industries received the inputs they needed, while the low-priority consumer goods sectors could never obtain enough inputs to fulfill their plans. One reason that accurate planning is so much more important today is that new technology and new demands are changing the planners' priorities so rapidly that the old unwritten principle is no longer dependable.

It has been stressed that Soviet planners have usually assumed the final output plan as given by political decision and so have primarily concentrated on the choice of technology. But the choice of technology is mainly the choice among investment projects. New investment, after all, is the area in which most technological choices are made, because established facilities are using certain fixed kinds of capital goods and technological procedures, which may be varied only within narrow limits in current production. Only with new investment — the addition of new capital goods — does the choice between old and new types of technology arise. In the Soviet Union the problem of cost minimization in the choice of new technology has been much debated under the title of the "choice of the best investment project."

One ideological obstacle in the past was the very dogmatic Soviet interpretation of Marx, which held that "capital is not productive," or that "capital produces no value." Somehow, this led Soviets in practice to charge no interest on fixed capital given to enterprises (until the reforms of 1965). It also led them in official planning theory — at least till 1958 — to treat capital as a valueless or free good. Assuming capital to be free means that planners would always choose as the least-cost variant that investment project which requires the least labor, *regardless* of how much capital is needed. This would be a mistake anywhere, but was an especially unfortunate tendency in the Soviet Union where capital was so scarce relative to the demand for it.

For Marxist or any economics and for a socialist or any economy, capital is productive or valuable in one sense: if capital is added, either output is increased or costs are reduced. This is very different from an ethical judgment that the *owners* of capital should or should not be rewarded for its use. When Marx argued that only labor produces "value," although with the help of physical capital goods, he was emphasizing that only workers put human effort into the product. Since, according to Marx, only human effort should be rewarded, the owners of capital should not be rewarded for the use of capital goods. The dogmatic Marxists seem to have confused Marx's ethical conclusion against distributing income to capitalists with the question of whether capital goods could increase labor productivity (which Marx never denied).

In the Soviet debate over the best investment technique for reducing costs, the dogmatists did not want to admit the valuable role of more capital in reducing costs. The practical problem, however, remains: there are an infinite number of possible investment projects in which the added capital could reduce labor and other current operating costs; the planners *must* choose among these projects because there is only a limited amount of capital at any one time. To repeat endlessly that capital produces no value is no help to the planner.

The general way to make the choice of where to invest more capital is to compare the amount of capital needed with the reduction of cost achieved in each project. Interestingly, without a whisper about theory, Soviet engineers have been doing just this by a crude rule of thumb ever since the 1930's. Their rule is called the Coefficient of Relative Effectiveness (or CRE). The CRE was officially adopted as a useful device for Soviet planning in 1958.[3]

For any new projects, the Soviet CRE directly compares the additional capital needed with the saving in labor and in other current costs. Suppose two new projects are proposed, and Project 2 will use more capital investment but will have lower current costs than Project 1. The CRE of Project 2 compared with Project 1 is then *defined* by the simple formula:

$$CRE = \frac{\text{Cost in } 1 - \text{Cost in } 2}{\text{Capital in } 2 - \text{Capital in } 1}$$

As an example of these calculations, suppose that the planners wish to produce 100 million rubles worth of shoes per year, and that there are two possible technological ways of doing it. One variant requires an investment of 55 million rubles, and an annual cost of production of another 50 million rubles. The second variant needs an investment of 75 million rubles, but has an annual cost of production of 49 million rubles. Then the Coefficient of Relative Effectiveness of Project 2 as compared with Project 1 can be calculated as:

$$CRE = \frac{50 - 49}{75 - 55} = .05$$

In other words, the second variant requires an investment of an additional 20 million rubles for a saving in annual operating costs of only 1 million rubles. The return on this extra investment then is 5 percent. This return must be compared with returns to other uses of the 20 mil-

---

[3] See "Recommendations of the All-Union Scientific-Technical Conference on Problems of Determining the Economic Effectiveness of Capital Investments and New Techniques in the U.S.S.R. National Economy," translated in *Problems of Economics*, Vol. 1 (January, 1958), pp. 86–90, reprinted in F. D. Holzman, *Readings on the Soviet Economy* (Chicago: Rand McNally, 1962).

lion rubles of capital which may have higher or lower CRE's. If the average return to most investments in the economy is 6 percent, then Project 2 would have to be rejected because the additional capital would have below-average returns. If there were no other way to accomplish the planned increase in output, then the optimal decision would be to invest in the project requiring less capital in spite of its higher current operating costs.

The Soviet CRE is thus a rationing device to distribute the limited supply of capital, and is quite similar to some of the rules of thumb used by many U.S. managers and managerial economists. One very general textbook rule in the U.S. economy is to continue to invest till additional investment would bring the enterprise's profit rate (or "internal rate of return") down to the level of the going rate of interest on borrowed capital. In Soviet planning, the project CRE plays the role of the profit rate while the social average CRE (or minimum CRE required of new investments) acts as interest rate. In another similar U.S. approach, a minimum CRE of 5 percent might be translated as a 20 year "payoff period," that is, a requirement that any added investment must pay off in that much added returns in not more than 20 years.

There are, however, some important differences between the Soviet CRE and the profit or interest rate in the United States. Obviously, no private individual receives the return on capital in the Soviet Union; it is purely a planning device for the optimal distribution of investments. Also, the CRE is a somewhat cruder device than the profit and interest rate comparison. The CRE does not use present discounted values, and it does not take account of the different number of years of savings in costs. Furthermore, the minimum required CRE is set at different rates in each industry. Because of this, capital is misallocated inasmuch as it is used for investment opportunities with lower returns in some industries than those available in others. Perhaps most important, one must always keep in mind that the distorted price structure makes any such calculations unreliable and misleading.

The CRE approach might also be considered a very, very backward relative of optimal programming. The CRE method requires approximately the same information required for the cost minimization programming problem that was described above. In the Soviet use of the CRE method, the output plan, or rather the plan for the *increase* in capacity to produce, is fixed for each good. The prices of inputs are known, and so are the input-output coefficients for each possible technological method of production. With these facts, the planners can calculate the cheapest ways to achieve the required increases in output capacity. In addition, since capital is limited and to be rationed, the planners have to know in advance the total available investment funds. The Soviet method thus restricts itself to finding the cheapest methods of production *within the limits of the available capital*. The planners must switch to more labor-using methods to achieve the plan when all the capital would be exhausted too soon by the very cheapest methods. The planners assume that there is always enough labor to achieve the plan. If this assumption should turn out to be wrong, a recalculation of the whole plan would be necessary.

It would be much more direct and useful to Soviet planning — at least in theory — if the political leadership no longer established fixed output plans. They could limit themselves to stating their preferences for final public and investment goods, while leaving the output mix of consumer goods to consumer preferences. Then the problem could be set up to do what is really desired: to maximize output on the basis of (1) the given demand preferences (of the government and the consumer), (2) the range of technical possibilities, and (3) the limited amounts of each resource. With limits given on the amounts of labor and raw materials as well as capital, the resulting plan would be feasible the first time it is calculated — and there would be no need to squeeze out a balance in a rough way or to recalculate the whole plan.

One major stumbling block to maximum output calculation has been the political leadership's reluctance to give up control over the exact amounts of each product. They apparently do not believe that their preferences could be or would be followed, especially concerning the aggregate ratio of consumption versus investment and military and welfare goods.

Ideology and Criticism

It was noted above that Soviet engineers and project-designers have used the CRE criteria since the 1930's, yet without theoretical justification. After economic debate became free again in 1956, a considerable discussion of investment criteria led to the official approval of the CRE as one of several criteria in 1958 — but still with little or no theoretical explanation.[4] Since then, Soviet planners have used linear programming in several specific problems, and have edged toward the vision of some form of optimal programming for the national plan. All of these methods are ways of allocating scarce capital based upon the relative returns to different capital projects, but the more dogmatic Soviet economists still deny that capital is productive in any sense.

As mentioned in Chapter 11, a new wave of reformers has now appeared, of whom the economist Novozhilov is perhaps typical.[5] He puts forth an elaborate version of the CRE method, and justifies the use of a return on capital, all in terms of the Marxist labor theory of value. He emphasizes the facts that were mentioned above: (1) that capital goods, including plant, equipment, and raw materials, are available in only a limited supply at a given time, and 2) that capital goods do serve a useful function by reducing costs. He provides a Marxist rationale for using an interest rate by saying that more capital goods merely make

[4] See a discussion of the earlier Soviet debates on investment criteria in Gregory Grossman, "Scarce Capital and Soviet Doctrine," *Quarterly Journal of Economics*, Vol. 67 (August, 1953), pp. 311–343.

[5] See, e.g., V. V. Novozhilov, "Cost-Benefit Comparisons in a Socialist Economy," in V. S. Nemchinov, editor, *The Use of Mathematics in Economics* (London: Oliver and Boyd, translation 1964).

labor more productive or that they "save labor." At the same time, he adds that private owners of capital (as distinct from capital goods) are not productive and do not deserve any return.

Novozhilov's basic concept[6] is that an increased use of capital in one project will save labor in that project, but will mean less capital available for other projects, so there will be higher labor costs in those other projects than if the capital were used there. These higher costs in other projects he calls "indirect labor costs." Thus he justifies the CRE method by making it a measure of the labor saving in one project against the increased ("indirect") labor costs elsewhere, rather than by calling it by the ideologically repugnant names of "return on capital" or "interest rate." As noted above, his concept of indirect costs is quite similar to the Western idea of "opportunity costs," the opportunities given up elsewhere in order to invest here.

Novozhilov emphasizes that, in order to compare all projects in the economy that might have made use of the same capital to save labor, it is necessary to use the same minimum acceptable CRE rate as a requirement for approval *in all projects* of the economy. This would represent a considerable improvement on present Soviet practice, which uses different CRE's for different sectors of the economy, and therefore misallocates capital as explained earlier.

In fact, when Soviet conservatives argue against Novozhilov that "profitability" should not rule over the planned development of heavy industry, this can only mean that the conservatives feel that their preferences for heavy industry are not fully reflected in the relative prices of the goods produced by heavy industry. It sometimes appears that the conservative critics actually intend to approve even more capital-using projects in the heavy industries and to increase the output of these industries beyond their original targets. If this is the case, it should be admitted, and they should argue openly, not against the rules of optimization, but for still more national preference (and higher prices) for investment goods than for consumer goods.

Western Criticism

Western economists, on the other hand, attack Novozhilov and his comrade-in-arms, Kantorovich, on the basis that:

> . . . Kantorovich's and Novozhilov's theories are cost theories of value. In terms of Alfred Marshall's famous metaphor, they still imply that since one blade of the scissors is stationary (that is, that demand is given), it is the action of the other blade (cost or supply) that cuts the paper. They represent an advance over the more primitive labor-cost theory of value that Marx employed, but still fall short of complete generality.[7]

Campbell's critical statement needs some qualifications or clarifications. First, Novozhilov's theory would seem to accord with Marx's special case of the Marshallian model (as presented here in Chapter 2), so that

[6] *Ibid.*, pp. 77–84.
[7] Robert W. Campbell, *op. cit.*, pp. 415–416.

Novozhilov could certainly maintain that he is exactly within the Marxist tradition when it is properly interpreted. Second, it was shown that Novozhilov's theory is sufficient to cover the choice of most effective investment when outputs are given, so that he does present a sufficient theory to cover the particular circumstances actually met by Soviet planners under the present institutional setup.

A more vital objection to the method so far proposed by Novozhilov is the one mentioned in the last section — his assumption that the total output of each commodity is fixed in the plan independently of any value calculation. This has to be the case when the problem is approached in terms of minimizing costs. But the problem was set in this fashion only for ideological convenience, so as to sound genuinely Marxist by reducing everything to labor costs, and so as to leave output decisions to the political leadership. In Soviet reality the problem faced by the planners is most usefully approached as the maximization of the value of all outputs with given amounts of land, labor, and capital.

This means, however, that one would have to attach a price tag reflecting the value to society (or the demand of society) for each output. Putting output values in terms of demand rather than labor time would indeed sound heretical to Soviet Marxists. It has already been observed, however, that there is a minority Western opinion which argues there is no real analytic conflict, but rather an ethical difference between the Western demand-based theory and the Marxist theory of value.[8] Whether the planners sound most Marxist by minimizing labor cost, or sound neo-classical by maximizing the utility of outputs, they will arrive at the same mathematical results if they begin with the same technical coefficients and constraints. Moreover, many of the more progressive Marxists see no substantive conflict with Marx's "political-economy" in any technical-economic scheme, even those recognizing the importance of utility or demand in the allocation of resources.[9] They argue that just as Western physical and biological sciences are compatible with Marxism, so also is technical economics — in spite of the vast differences on the broader political and ethical issues.

Practical Decision-Making. Once it is accepted in theory that planners should maximize the value of output according to prices determined by the preferences of "society," the practical problem arises as to *who* represents society. This has led to a sharp debate among Eastern European economists and to a few muted rumblings even among Soviet economists. The issue is very sensitive politically, because all of the choices of both prices and outputs must be consciously planned under Soviet centrally planned socialism. Decisions are not made automatically by the market, because there is no market for producer goods, no market for collective consumption goods (public welfare and warfare expenditures), and a restricted market for consumer goods.

---

[8] See Howard J. Sherman, "Marxist Economics and Soviet Planning," *Soviet Studies*, Vol. 18 (October, 1966), pp. 169–188.

[9] Kantorovich has actually formulated a full solution for output maximization based on final demands; see Ward, *op. cit.*, pp. 553–554.

Individual consumers can choose whether or not to buy available goods, but which ones are to be expanded is a planning decision, which may or may not be made according to consumer preferences. At present, Soviet political leaders still set down most of the preferences that planners are ordered to follow. Let us examine the present situation and the ideal situation in each of the sectors: collective consumption goods, personal consumption goods, and producer goods.

In any modern economy, the political leaders must make decisions in a large sphere of collective spending or "collective consumption" — road-building or defense, for example. These collective or public goods are defined as goods in which all people must share, or in which the benefits cannot be divided; thus, individuals cannot choose to buy these goods or not to buy them. One Communist goal is, in fact, to enlarge the sphere of collective consumption. Thus, in the Soviet Union the political leaders *must* decide between the competing needs for military defense, for medical care, for education, and for all other welfare spending. The Soviet planners attempt to follow the political preferences for these collective goods. *If* Soviet leaders were democratically elected, then it would be socially optimal for the planners to set the prices of these collective consumption goods exactly in accord with the preferences revealed to them by the political leaders.

On the other hand, there is quite clearly no need for the political leaders to interfere in the consumer choice between the amount of clothing to be produced versus the amount of food to be produced. As pointed out below, it is in the interests of the political leadership to provide an output mix of consumer goods as close as possible to what the people desire. Therefore, it is optimal from any point of view for the prices and outputs of most individual consumer goods to be set by the planners exactly in accord with the preferences expressed by the individual consumers. These are the basic principles of price-setting for consumer goods.

At least two deviations from the socialist ideal of "maximum satisfaction" may be noted in the Soviet case. First, Soviet top political leaders are still appointed by a dictator or a small group of self-appointed and self-perpetuated leaders. This means that Soviet political decisions in the area of collective consumption do *not* necessarily reflect the people's desires. Second, the Soviet political leaders still determine much of the product-mix in the area of individual consumption. These consumer goods choices should be left to individual desires both from the viewpoint of maximum social welfare and from the leaders' own view, though the leaders do not seem to understand this fact at present. It would be to the politicians' own advantage (for economic growth, not to speak of political popularity) to give the consumer as close to what he wants as possible. The point is that the further the Plan strays from consumers' desires, the more resources must be allocated to consumption to achieve a given level of consumer satisfaction, and the less are available for other objectives. Or if a given level of resources is allocated to consumption, then an output mix different from that which would be dictated by consumers' preferences means that the household sector receives a lower level of satisfaction, resulting in less incentive to work and in political discontent. Only in special cases, such as extra encouragement to book buying or extra discouragement of harmful drugs, would the public interest call for planners to lower or raise prices to different levels than would result from individual consumer demand.

Measurement of Preferences. Assuming the political leaders have made their own decisions in the area of collective consumption goods, how should the planners be instructed so that they will most accurately translate the leaders' preferences into an optimal plan? Certainly, if they are to produce an optimal plan reflecting the leaders' preferences for final goods, they should *not* be given lists of intermediate outputs, such as targets for steel, though the Soviet leaders are fond of this practice. In fact, they should not even be given lists of exact amounts of final outputs. Rather, the political leaders must give the planners their relative preferences for final goods only in the form of ratios between different collective goods, which would state their relative desires for one additional unit of each good. These marginal preferences may not be easy for Soviet political leaders to state clearly, but neither are such ratios or prices easy to specify for any political leaders. For example, how does the U.S. Department of Defense decide its relative desire for one long-range bomber versus one short-range bomber?

In the area of personal consumption, planners can certainly attempt to follow the sum of individual desires. To measure household demand for goods presently on the market, they must determine how much money consumers are willing to spend on each commodity. Specifically, Soviet planners must first attempt to discover those prices which will just clear the market, given the present level of production. These short-run prices only reflect consumer preferences at present levels of supply. Planners must also discover by the use of questionnaires the relative consumer preferences for all products at higher income levels, as well as for new articles before production. This kind of sampling of consumer preferences (and the calculation of so-called "elasticities of demand") is now being undertaken extensively in the Soviet Union. Interestingly, the Soviets check their questionnaire results against data concerning consumer behavior in other countries with higher consumption per person.

The problem of price-setting is even more complex with respect to producer goods. The planners should ideally follow their own "preferences" (without interference by political leaders), deriving their preferences or valuations from the planned output of other goods to be produced and the technology to be used. They can only estimate relative social gains from the production of different producer goods according to their guesses as to the future course of technological development, for example, the future need for steel versus the need for aluminum.

Assuming present technology remains unchanged in the future (though this is patently untrue) then the relative need or preference for each producer good can be calculated. On that basis, relative prices can then be assigned to each of them for planning purposes. Since the price of producer goods is only one element in the planning problem, this rough approximation may not lead the planners too far astray. Of course, it would be better to base producer goods prices on a perfect knowledge of future technological developments, but present technology should be a fair approximation for some years — provided that present prices are corrected for a few of the most obvious temporary deviations from the long-run price trend.

Economists and engineers can tell how to produce a maximum of whatever output is desired, but they cannot say what output is to be desired. After the society (through its political leaders, through the consumer goods market, through questionnaires, a referendum, or any other means) has stated its preferences, economists can calculate prices and optimal outputs. Once relative preferences or demands for an additional unit of each output are known, these data form (in a rational planning system) the basis for the "prices" used by planners to compute the optimal output mixture.

Limitations of Soviet Optimal Planning

Present Soviet planning is a much cruder affair than this sophisticated analysis would indicate. The answers to growth, balance, and optimization problems are determined in a much simpler fashion. The rate of growth, as was noted, is ultimately a political decision. Then, to achieve that rate of growth, the Soviet planners ask each plant or enterprise what it needs in the way of inputs, though from the previous year's results they know something of the "capacity" of the plant. The technical or input-output coefficients are based on technological data, but are modified by the bargaining that goes on between the plant and higher echelons of planners. On this basis the planners try to put together a balanced plan for each industry taken by itself. When it is impossible to get a balance on the basis of the planned goals provided by the political leaders, in the light of the "fixed" technical coefficients, changes in output goals are avoided if possible. Instead pressure is put on plant managers to reduce the "fixed" technical coefficients. With these and other adjustments noted above, a single plan is produced, approximately balanced at least on paper. This procedure, clearly, does not yield an optimal plan.

In theory, optimal methods of programming, such as linear programming, can solve any planning problem. In practice, however, these methods provide no panacea for Soviet planning. A huge amount of accurate information is necessary.[10] Soviet central planners would not only need more information, but would also need it in different forms and categories than those presently available. Moreover, they would somehow have to prevent the systematic distortion of information now practiced by many self-seeking individuals at various levels of reporting from factory directors right up to Ministers.

Second, once the millions of pieces of information are gathered, it is still an enormous job in terms of time and labor to actually perform

[10] See, e.g., the Soviet recognition of this problem in A. Postyshev, "The Labor Theory of Value and Optimal Planning," translated in *Problems of Economics,* Volume 10 (December, 1967), pp. 3–15.

the necessary calculations. If every detail of the economy's technology and output mixture is to be planned, the problem would even tax the capacity of the total number of available modern electronic computers. Finally, even if the information is obtained and all the equations calculated, it is no simple task to get managers and workers to execute the plan exactly as directed.

When looking at Soviet reality, one finds some careful macro planning for growth, some crude planning for balance among industries, but very little consideration of optimum technology and output mixes. With improved methods of optimal planning, Soviet GNP might grow considerably more rapidly. This shortcoming in optimization is reflected — and made inevitable — by the helterskelter and irrational structure of Soviet prices. Irrational prices have made optimization impossible, but the new price reforms (see Chapter 13) may produce somewhat more rational prices.

In defense of actual Soviet practices, it has been argued[11] that optimal planning is not so difficult as it seems in the abstract, because planning is not done from scratch, but always starts with an existent technology and output mix. Moreover, in many industries there are only a few processes or even just one technology available, so physical planning of technology without rational prices is not so difficult as it might seem in theory.

The view defending Soviet performance is that centrally planned socialism successfully provides rapid economic growth, even though it is at the expense of a certain degree of economic efficiency at any given time. This view has also been expressed pointedly by Wiles, who writes:

> There is substance in the charge that "scarcity" economics is finicky and academic. . . . The loss of 'welfare' or 'efficiency' through an incorrect micro-economic allocation of resources is surely less than that brought about by unemployment, restrictive labor practices, the refusal to share trade secrets or the suppression of workable patents, could any of these losses ever be measured? Thus in the Soviet economy [suppose] there are always too few hairbrushes and too many nailbrushes in view of the resources available, while in a 'capitalist' economy this proportion is always more nearly right. But the production of both these articles is growing at about 10 percent per annum in U.S.S.R. and at about 2 percent per annum in 'capitalist' countries. In the end the Soviet citizen will be better supplied even with hairbrushes.[12]

There can be no denial of the rapidity of Soviet economic growth in most of the past periods. Nevertheless, it must be said that this growth was achieved through expenditure of enormous effort put into expansion and new investment. Moreover, it is legitimate to emphasize that the effort or sacrifice was *much* greater than would have been necessary with perfectly optimal planning. One may be allowed some cynicism,

[11] See, e.g., the British Marxist Maurice Dobb, *Economic Theory and Socialism* (New York: International Publishers, 1955).

[12] P. J. D. Wiles, "Scarcity, Marxism and Gosplan," *Oxford Economic Papers* (October, 1953), pp. 315–316.

however, as to how perfect a calculation could have been achieved in the early period of initial industrialization regardless of the methods used. The main thing was the ability of centrally planned socialism to extract and utilize very large amounts of saving for investment purposes. Perhaps now that the tasks of the Soviet economy are no longer so few in number nor so heroic in size, but are rather many, complex, and marginal, more perfect calculations are both more possible and more useful.

Appendix A to Chapter 12

Linear Programming in the Soviet Context

"Optimal programming" may be defined as any technique for reaching an optimal set of inputs and/or outputs in any economic situation. In fact, the techniques of optimal programming are used for even wider applications than economic problems. "Linear programming" is one particular form of optimal programming in which certain artificial restrictions are imposed in order to simplify the problem and the calculations. In linear programming it is assumed that each technological process or activity used in production is linear, in the sense that a doubling of the inputs in constant proportions will lead to a doubling of the output. This situation is linear in that such equations will be straight lines on a graph — at least in the case of two inputs and one output.

Linear programming is nevertheless much less restrictive than the input-output method in two important respects. First, input-output allows for only one technological method of production of each output, whereas linear programming allows for several. Second, the input-output method does not put a valuation on the resulting outputs, whereas linear programming does use and require relative prices for each output. Thus, input-output can at the most provide consistent or balanced plans for total outputs and primary inputs *with given* final outputs (and given methods of technology). Linear programming on the other hand allows a choice among several techniques of production and also allows planners to choose that mixture of outputs whose total value will be the maximum possible.

The problem of optimization under linear programming may therefore be set up as follows: first, the object is to maximize the value of final output, where value (V) equals prices (p) times final outputs (x) that is:

$$\text{Maximize} \quad v = p_1x_1 + p_2x_2 + \ldots + p_nx_n \quad (1)$$

The maximization procedure is subject to certain restrictions, reflecting the objective conditions of production. These are (a) the fact that there must be sufficient production of each total output to cover its intermediate uses, and (b) the fact that there is a limited amount. The technical coefficients showing the input required for each output are represented as $a_{11} \ldots a_{mn}$, where the first subscript to the coefficient shows the commodity which is an input into the output given by the second number. Total outputs are represented as $x_1 \ldots x_n$.

Thus, for total outputs the result is the familiar set of equations, showing the uses of each total output as an intermediate input into other outputs:

$$a_{11}x_1 + a_{12}x_2 + \ldots + a_{1n}x_n \leqq x_1 \qquad (2a)$$
$$a_{21}x_1 + a_{22}x_2 + \ldots + a_{2n}x_n \leqq x_2 \qquad (2b)$$
$$\cdot \quad \cdot \quad \cdot \quad \cdot \quad \cdot \quad \cdot \quad \cdot \quad \cdot \quad \cdot \quad \cdot \quad \cdot$$
$$a_{n1}x_1 + a_{n2}x_2 + \ldots + a_{nn}x_n \leqq x_n \qquad (2n)$$

This set of equations differs from the input-output equations only in that in each case the left side of the equation (the total intermediate uses) may be less than the right side of the equation (the total output of each commodity) because final demand or final output is omitted from the left side of the equation. In this way, the model allows for the determination of maximum final outputs as the difference between the total outputs and the intermediate uses — unlike the input-output model where the final outputs or demands were specified exactly.

A second set of restrictions represents the limited amounts of primary inputs ($L_1 \ldots L_m$), which inputs might be considered as various specialized types of labor, as well as various specialized types of capital and raw materials (these latter being regarded as embodied labor from the Marxist view). This set of equations will show the requirements for primary inputs (the technical coefficients for each primary input multiplied by the respective outputs) added together to give a sum that must be less than or equal to the amount of the primary inputs that is available. In this case, to avoid more confusing subscripts, let the technical coefficients be represented as $b_{11} \ldots b_{mn}$, where the first number of the subscript indicates the primary input and the second number indicates the output for which it is used. Thus, the equations are:

$$b_{11}x_1 + b_{12}x_2 + \ldots + b_{1n}x_n \leqq L_1 \qquad (3a)$$
$$b_{21}x_1 + b_{22}x_2 + \ldots + b_{2n}x_n \leqq L_2 \qquad (3b)$$
$$\cdot \quad \cdot \quad \cdot \quad \cdot \quad \cdot \quad \cdot \quad \cdot \quad \cdot \quad \cdot$$
$$b_{m1}x_1 + b_{m2}x_2 + \ldots + b_{mn}x_n \leqq L_m \qquad (3m)$$

The final set of restrictions is the usual economic one that all of the final output must be positive. These restrictions may be stated thus:

$$x_i > 0 \ (i = 1 \ldots m) \qquad (4)$$

This insures that some amount of each product will be produced for the market, as obviously must be the case in an optimal economic system.

In this system the technical coefficients for intermediate inputs (the a_{ij}), the technical coefficients for primary inputs (the b_{ij}), the available amounts of primary inputs (the L_i), and the prices of outputs (p_i) are all known and presumed constant. The outputs (x) are the unknowns, and the function composed of prices times outputs is to be maximized. The actual calculation procedure for the maximization is usually done by converting the inequalities into equalities. Thus, "dummy" variables are inserted into each of the inequalities, using a "slack" variable where the restriction is "less than," and a "surplus" variable where the restriction is "greater than." In fact, the dummy variables inserted into equations 2a . . . 2n are none other than the final demand, x_1 . . . x_n, which thus enter into this set of equations. In this way, although more variables have been created, it turns out that the restrictions have been transformed into an equally large number of equations, each of which represents an equality.

The other problems involved in actually calculating the maximum set of outputs are purely mechanical, so need not be detailed here (see selected references at end of chapter for methods of calculation). Nevertheless, it must be mentioned that very great advances have been made in simplifying the calculating methods. For example, it is known that the maximum set will be found at an extreme point in a graphical sense. The famous "simplex method" of George Dantzig then explains the efficient procedure for checking which extreme point is the maximum. There is a very practical importance for Soviet planning in these continual advances in the simplification of calculations. These advances make it far more feasible for modern electronic computers to actually do the job of calculation for a very large number of inputs and outputs.

Finally, the typical problem of choice of output mix shown above requires output prices, but it is of interest to note that the solution of this problem can also produce the "prices" of the inputs as a by-product. These "prices" are not set by the planners for use in any actual transaction, nor are they produced by any actual market exchange, but are purely an intermediate product of the mathematical calculation of maximum outputs. Hence, they are called "shadow prices."[13] These shadow prices reflect the scarcities of the inputs. Using them, it would be possible to compute the minimum cost technology. Of course, the central planners would have already decided upon the same technology in determining the way to produce a maximum output, so they would have no reason to repeat the problem. Nevertheless, when decentralization is discussed in the next three chapters, it will be seen that managers may then make very good use of such input shadow prices as are given them by the central planners.

Appendix B to Chapter 12

Optimal Choice of Output Mix

The facts presented in Table 12–1 may be stated in equations as follows:

DEFINITIONS OF SYMBOLS: M is total output of Manufacturing, A is

[13] See the simplified explanation of shadow prices in Heinz Kohler, *Welfare and Planning* (New York: John Wiley and Sons, 1966), pp. 121–122; or the thorough mathematical explanation of shadow prices in R. Dorfman, P. Samuelson, and R. Solow, *Linear Programming and Economic Analysis* (New York: McGraw-Hill, 1958), pp. 339–340.

total output of Agriculture, X_m is final output of M, X_a is final output of A, P_m is price of M, and P_a is price of A.

The problem is to maximize the so-called "objective function":

$$f(X_m, X_a) = P_m X_m + P_a X_a$$

subject to the following constraints:

(1) $2A + M \leq 100$ billion hours of labor
(2) $2A + 3M \leq 210$ billion units of capital
(3) $A \leq 30$ billion tons of natural resources
(4) $-.99A + .08M < 0$ (because $X_a > 0$)
(5) $.31A - .76M < 0$ (because $X_m > 0$)

In order to get the function $P_m X_m + P_a X_a$ into terms of A and M, note that $P_m = 1.5$ rubles, $P_a = 3$ rubles, $X_m = .76M - .31A$, and $X_a = .99A - .08M$. By substitution, the function to be maximized is:

$$f(A, M) = 1.5(.76M - .31A) + 3(.99A - .08M)$$
$$\text{or } f(A, M) = .9M + 2.51A$$

The solution is shown graphically in Figure 12–1. In this graph, the five constraints are shown by five solid lines, each of which is numbered according to the number of the constraint equation which it represents. These five lines set the bounds of feasible production of various combinations of A and M. A heavier line goes through the extreme points C, D, E, and F, each representing a basic optimal solution, one of which must be the maximum value-of-output solution. To find which point is the maximum, the slope of the objective function $.9M + 2.51A$ is calculated. The two dotted lines indicate the slope of the objective function (which derives mainly from the relative prices of X_m and X_a). Then the maximum solution is selected by that dotted line farthest from the origin which still passes through one of the extreme points.

The point so selected is point E. At that point, $A = 30$ billion units and $M = 40$ billion units. Since $X_a = .99A - .08M$ and $X_m = .76M - .31A$, the maximum output mix is $X_a = 26.5$ billion units of Agriculture and $X_m = 21.1$ billion units of Manufacturing. It follows also that the maximum value of final output is:

$$P_m X_m + P_a X_a = 1.5(21.1) + 3(26.5) = 111.2 \text{ billion rubles}$$

Appendix C to Chapter 12

Optimal Choice of Technology

The facts presented in Table 12–2 may be stated in equations as follows:

DEFINITIONS OF SYMBOLS: X_1 is output of coats by process 1, X_2 is output of coats by process 2, X_3 is output of coats by process 3, L is hours

Figure 12–1

Optimal Choice of Output Mix by Linear Programming

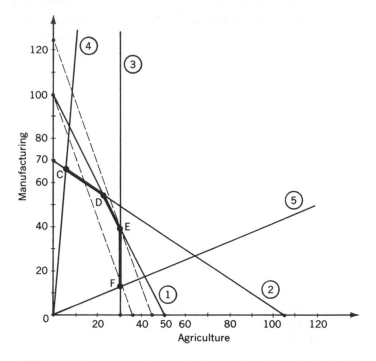

NOTE: Solid lines numbered according to equations of constraints in text.
C,D,E, and F are extreme points, representing basic optimal solutions.
Dotted lines show the slope of the objective function: $P_m X_m + P_a X_a$.

of labor, K is units of capital, R is tons of all other resources or inputs, P_1 is price of labor, P_k is price of capital, and P_r is price of all other inputs.

The problem is to minimize the so-called "objective function":

$$f(L, K, R) = P_1 L + P_k K + P_r R$$

subject to the following constraints:

(1) $.15X_1 + .08X_2 + .11X_3 \leq$ 11 million tons of R
(2) $.53X_1 + .48X_2 + .67X_3 >$ 0 hours of L
(3) $.06X_1 + .15X_2 + .03X_3 \leq$ 10 million units of K
(4) $X_1 +\ \ \ X_2 +\ \ \ \ X_3 \geq 100$ million coats

Unfortunately, since there are three inputs and three production processes, it is impossible to show the solution on a two-dimensional diagram. On a three-dimensional diagram the constraints will set up boundaries of a space concave to the origin. In order to choose the minimum cost point from among those extreme points close to the origin, the "objective function" is plotted as a series of planes: that plane is selected which is closest to the origin and still passes through one of the extreme points. That optimal solution point shows the values of labor (L), capital (K), and all other resources or inputs (R) which — given their prices — add up to the minimum cost necessary to produce 100 million coats.

The optimal solution point also indicates the combination of processes to be used.[14] In this case, at the optimal point the minimum cost solution is that process 1 produces 37.5 million coats, process 2 produces 48.9 million coats, and process 3 produces 13.6 million coats — for a total of 100 million coats.

For that amount of production, the table shows that these processes require all of the capital (10 million units), all of the other resources available to the industry (11 million tons), plus 52.8 million hours of labor. Recall that P_1 is 10 rubles an hour, P_k is 4 rubles a unit, and P_r is 2 rubles a ton. It follows that the minimum cost of the required output is:

$$P_1L + P_kK + P_rR = 10(52.8) + 4(10) + 2(11) = 590 \text{ million rubles.}$$

SELECTED REFERENCES

1. Three journals published in English with frequent articles on optimization problems are *Problems of Economics* (translations of Soviet articles), *Economics of Planning* (published in Scandinavia with international contributors), and *Mathematical Studies in Economics and Statistics in the U.S.S.R. and Eastern Europe* (translations of Soviet and Eastern European articles).

2. The Western view of optimal efficiency is presented in general in Abram Bergson, *Essays in Normative Economics* (Cambridge, Mass.: Harvard University Press, 1966). This view is applied to problems of central and decentralized planning in Benjamin Ward, *The Socialist Economy* (New York: Random House, 1967).

3. The specifics of linear programming are presented in elementary form in W. Allen Spivey, *Linear Programming: An Introduction* (New York: Macmillan Company, 1963).

4. A thorough presentation of linear programming is presented in Robert Dorfman, Paul Samuelson, Robert Solow, *Linear Programs and Economic Analysis* (New York: McGraw-Hill Book Company, 1958). An excellent application of linear programming to national planning problems is in Hollis B. Chenery and Paul G. Clark, *Interindustry Economics* (New York: John Wiley & Sons, 1959), Chapter 4.

5. Marxist approaches to optimum planning may be seen in Charles Bettelheim, *Studies in the Theory of Planning* (Bombay: Asia Publishing House, 1959); K. Porwit, *Central Planning — Evaluation of Variants* (New York: Pergamon Press, translated from Polish in 1967); and Janos

[14] Actual calculation of this solution is explained thoroughly in Dorfman, Samuelson, and Solow, *op. cit.*, Chapter 4.

Kornai, *Mathematical Planning of Structural Decisions* (Amsterdam: North Holland Publishing Co., 1967). A review of Kornai's book in the *American Economic Review* of September 1968 says that it "is a landmark in the history of planning and the application of mathematical techniques in socialist countries."

6. Discussion of relative investment criteria may be found in Amartya Kumar Sen, "Some Notes on the Choice of Capital Intensity in Development Planning," *Quarterly Journal of Economics*, Vol. 71 (Nov., 1957), pp. 561–584.

7. Two Soviet articles introducing the basic principles of linear programming are B. Finkelshtein, "Principles of Linear Programming," *Problems of Economics*, Vol. 5 (July, 1962), pp. 16–26; and A. Kaplan, "Application of Linear Programming Models in Soviet Transportation," *Problems of Economics*, Vol. 5 (June, 1962), pp. 27–31. A Western evaluation of present Soviet use of linear programming appears in Benjamin Ward, "Linear Programming and Soviet Planning," in Herbert Levine, ed., *Mathematical Techniques in Soviet Planning* (Yale University Press, 1967). Also see C. A. K. Lovell, "Profits and Cybernetics as Sources of Increased Efficiency in Soviet Planning," *Southern Economic Journal*, Vol. 34 (January, 1968).

8. The best single collection of modern liberal Soviet writing on planning problems is V. S. Nemchinov, ed., *The Use of Mathematics in Economics* (London: Oliver and Boyd, first published in Russian in 1959, translated under editorship of A. Nove in 1964). There is also a translation of the entire book by L. V. Kantorovich, *The Best Use of Economic Resources* (Cambridge, Mass.: Harvard University Press, 1966, first published in 1959, an expansion of his 1939 work). Also see B. Ward, "Kantorovich on Economic Calculation" *Journal of Political Economy* (December, 1960). The best Western history of the earlier Soviet debates is in Gregory Grossman, "Scarce Capital and Soviet Doctrine," *Quarterly Journal of Economics*, Vol. 67 (August, 1953), pp. 311–343. A typical Soviet article of more recent vintage is T. Khachaturov, "The Economic Effectiveness of Capital Investments," translated in *Problems of Economics*, Vol. 10 (September, 1967), pp. 3–12.

9. Recent Soviet theory is expertly described in Michael Ellman, "Optimal Planning — A Review Article," *Soviet Studies*, Vol. 20 (July, 1968), pp. 112–135.

PART FIVE

REFORMS AND COMPARATIVE EVALUATION

13

DECENTRALIZATION, 1965 AND AFTER

Socialism in the modern world has usually included central planning. What is the historical background of the decentralized or market form of socialism?

Sources of Decentralization Debate

Marx himself wrote very little about the details of socialist planning, always emphasizing that it would be utopian to discuss such details before the advent of an actual socialist economy. His few comments relating to this subject are clearly tangential and not directly to the point.

In his diatribe against Proudhon, he defends the large-scale economic unit, and attacks any idea of a return to very small-scale farming and artisan enterprises. He writes that:

> ... The automatic workshop wipes out specialists and craft-idiocy.
>
> M. Proudhon, not having understood even this one revolutionary side of the automatic workshop, takes a step backward and proposes to the worker that he make not only the twelfth part of a pin, but successively all twelve parts of it. . . . To sum up, M. Proudhon has not gone further than the petty bourgeois ideal. And to realize this ideal, he can think of nothing better than to take us back to the journeyman or, at most, to the master craftsman of the Middle Ages.[1]

Both here and in *Capital* Marx is clearly in favor of optimal size of units, even if the required size is 50 or even 100 percent of an entire

[1] Karl Marx, *The Poverty of Philosophy* (New York: International Publishers, n.d.), pp. 121–122.

305

industry. Nevertheless, planning within such units is still far from central planning.

With respect to another aspect of decentralization, Marx clearly envisioned socialism as a national phenomenon, quite distinct from the forming of local cooperatives. He wrote:

> That the workers desire to establish the conditions of cooperative production on a social, and first of all on a national scale in their own country, only means that they are working to revolutionize the present conditions of production, and had nothing in common with the foundation of cooperative societies with state aid. But as far as the present cooperative societies are concerned they are of value *only* insofar as they are the independent creations of the workers and not protegées either of the government or of the bourgeoisie.[2]

Certainly Marx did not see cooperatives as either the vehicle by which to reach socialism or as the necessary form of socialism. Yet the quote also shows that Marx did not rule out the use of the cooperative form as an improvement either under capitalism or socialism.

The final aspect of decentralization on which Marx seems to have written is the question of the "anarchy of production." There is certainly much in the works of Marx[3] indicating that he disapproved of the competitive or market mechanism under capitalism as being unplanned or anarchical and thereby allowing extreme fluctuations and instability in economic life. Engels — with Marx's approval — wrote that:

> . . . every society based on commodity production has the peculiarity that in it the producers have lost control of their own social relationships. . . . No one knows how much of the article he produces is coming on to the market, or how much demand there is for it; no one knows whether his individual product will meet a real need, whether he will cover his costs or even be able to sell it at all. Anarchy reigns in social production.[4]

It is clear that Marx and Engels disapproved of the planlessness of capitalism. In addition, they felt it to be an important cause of the periodic crises of depression or inflation. Nevertheless, this does not show that they would necessarily disapprove of the market device under socialism, since socialism provides a very different economic environment. The question turns on whether market socialism would be as prone to instability as market capitalism.

Soviet Experience. Lenin's words supporting the New Economic Policy (NEP) in the early 1920's are sometimes cited by Soviet writers in defense of decentralization. This is, nevertheless, an inappropriate citation since Lenin defended NEP only as a temporary meas-

---

[2] Karl Marx, "Critique of the Gotha Programme," *Selected Works*, Volume 2 (New York: International Publishers, n.d.), p. 576.

[3] See, Karl Marx, *Theories of Surplus Value* (New York: International Publishers, 1952), pp. 391–402.

[4] Frederick Engels, *Anti-Duhring* (New York: International Publishers, 1939, first published 1878), p. 297.

ure, not as a long-term policy. The experience of the NEP, however, can legitimately be considered relevant to a discussion of decentralization. During the NEP period, even large-scale Soviet industrial firms were made financially independent, and were allowed a high degree of autonomous decision-making. A positive evaluation of performance under NEP would emphasize that small-scale enterprises flourished and recovered even beyond prewar levels in the 1920's. On the other hand, its critics argue that under NEP Soviet heavy industry failed to accumulate much new capital for expansion beyond the prewar level.[5]

⭐ *Lange's Model.* In connection with the debate on the possibility of rational planning, mention was made of the decentralized socialism advocated by Lange.[6] This scheme not only played a role in that debate, but figures in the present debate on decentralization. Although Lange mentioned the possibility of price and output decisions by completely independent socialist firms, the more interesting variant today is his somewhat more centralized proposal. In brief, he proposed (1) that the central planners set some more or less arbitrary prices, basing them simply on the pre-socialist prices, then (2) that the planners should change them if, at those prices, there is excess demand as shown by long lines of unsatisfied consumers or excess supply as shown by goods left on the shelves. At the same time, (3) the managers would produce up to the point where their marginal cost equals the given price, that is, where profit is at a maximum. In long-run decisions, (4) industries would invest up to the point where their average cost is at a minimum. On the other side, (5) central planners would loan capital to firms at that rate of interest which would equalize firm demand with the supply of capital determined at the center. Finally, (6) households would have freedom of choice as to where to work and as to what consumer goods to buy with their wages. Although this model was long considered purely hypothetical (and was disowned by Lange as a practical proposal), it will be observed below that many of its assumptions are being approached in the current practice or proposals of Eastern Europe.

Yugoslav Experience. After it broke away from Stalin's control in 1948, Yugoslavia instituted within a few years a radically decentralized version of socialism. In theory, the workers in each enterprise could (1) elect the manager, (2) determine the production plan and the prices of outputs (in competition with other firms), and (3) with very few constraints, split the profits after taxes between wages and investment as they saw fit. Although Yugoslav practice was never quite this extreme, the Yugoslav experiment nevertheless shook Eastern Europe and the Soviet Union. At first, it was declared pure anathema and condemned as mere reversion to capitalism, but it has come more and

[5] For a view of the NEP as a successful experiment in market socialism, see V. N. Bandera, "The NEP as an Economic System," *Journal of Political Economy*, Vol. 71, No. 3.

[6] See Oskar Lange, *On the Economic Theory of Socialism* (New York: McGraw-Hill Book Company, 1964, first published 1938).

more to be considered a fruitful experience for study and partial imitation.

Changing Soviet Economic Conditions. It was noted in Chapter 11 that Soviet planning reforms may have been generated partly by the increasing complexity of the economy and partly by the shortage of labor. This at least is Dobb's argument,[7] which more generally contends that rational planning and decentralization are more necessary in relatively advanced countries than in less developed countries. Dobb emphasizes that technical innovation is now the most important Soviet goal, and that innovation depends mainly on "constant initiative . . . at the place of production." By contrast, he maintains, in the early Soviet Union the central problem was not technological improvement, but putting to work in industry the resources that were unemployed or less profitably employed in agriculture.

A more skeptical view of the relation between development and reform is taken by Wiles.[8] He argues essentially that it is even more important to make the correct planning decision in an underdeveloped country than in a highly developed one, because a wrong allocation decision can be catastrophic for a poor country (as seen perhaps in China's attempt at a "Great Leap Forward"). It would seem that in the less developed economy Dobb is more concerned about the proper ratio of investment to consumption, whereas Wiles is worried about how the investment is to be allocated. Dobb would admit the vital importance of investment allocation, but would say that these decisions are much simpler in the less developed country. He also argues that the total investment is more important than its allocation in the initial industrialization drive. Hence Dobb argues that economic efficiency and organization becomes more important in developed countries, whereas Wiles sees it as equally important at all stages of development.

History of the Liberman Proposals

The "Great Debate" on decentralization in the U.S.S.R. ostensibly originated with a 1962 article in *Pravda* by Kharkov economist Evsei G. Liberman,[9] proposing to revamp the existing incentive system for Soviet enterprises. The editorial board of *Pravda* footnoted the article with a request for written responses to the proposals; reactions were immediate. The discussion which followed was extended to include nearly every aspect of Soviet economic life, so that the participants could evaluate all of the implications as well as the specifics of Liberman's plan. In the press, in technical discussion groups, in the U.S.S.R. Academy of Sciences, and in the Central Committee of the Communist

[7] M. Dobb, *Soviet Economic Development Since 1917* (New York: International Publishers, 1966), p. 373.

[8] See, e.g., P. J. D. Wiles, *The Political Economy of Communism* (Cambridge, Mass.: Harvard University Press, 1964), Chapter 11.

[9] "Plan, Profit, and Bonuses," *Pravda*, September 9, 1962, translated in M. E. Sharpe, ed., *The Liberman Discussion* (White Plains, N.Y.: International Arts and Science Press, 1965), pp. 79–87.

Party, notables and newcomers both participated in an intensive debate about the present and proposed systems.

In 1963 and early 1964 there was a year of relative slack in open discussion, during which important experiments with reform ideas were implemented on a limited basis. Then, in 1964, a second round commenced again with a *Pravda* article inviting responses.[10] The winds of change grew even stronger during this phase of the controversy. The Soviet government ultimately responded with what some regard as a major alteration of state-enterprise relations: the September, 1965 Kosygin Reform. Each phase of the debate as well as the Reforms are worth examining in some detail.

Within the atmosphere of increased freedom for scientific inquiry after 1956, there arose a faction of economists whose approach was quite pragmatic. They analyzed organizational matters and very concrete issues of policy; they sought experiments and solutions to deal with limited problems. Criticism of the malfunctions of the enterprise incentive system during the 1950's flowed largely from their evidence and conclusions. Kharkov Professor E. G. Liberman was one of these critics. Liberman published three papers in Soviet journals during the 1950's.[11] He argued that specific problems created by existing success indicators could be overcome by appropriate changes in the operational constraints of enterprises. The scheme of reforms he advocated in the 1959 paper was essentially of the same kind as that which touched off the 1962 controvesry. However, until 1962 neither this man nor his recommendations were the subject of public focus or the attentions of other writers.

The debate was given urgency when the Soviet political leadership became alarmed over the retardation in growth rates apparent in the early 1960's. As already noted, these difficulties as well as the need for reform may both be due to the growing complexity and interdependence of Soviet allocations, which make it increasingly difficult to devise priority rankings and balance the plan. The opposite argument by some U.S. economists, that the problems may be purely temporary and unconnected with the level of development, has also been noted. These more non-economic factors would include poor weather, the enormous manpower losses of the Second World War, too much extravagance with foreign aid, and increased spending on military and space ventures.

At the same time, some of the leading economic theorists began to support the proposals for institutional reform. In April, 1962, the late academician V. S. Nemchinov gave pragmatist Liberman a first chance to influence important academic theorists by persuading the Scientific

[10] V. Trapeznikov, "For Flexible Economic Management of Enterprise," *Pravda*, August 17, 1964, translated in Sharpe, *op. cit.*, pp. 193–201.

[11] "Cost Accounting and Material Encouragement of Industrial Personnel," in *Voprosy Ekonomiki* (1955); No. 6 "Planning Industrial Production and Material Stimuli for Its Development," in *Kommunist* (1956); No. 10 and "Economic Levers for Fulfilling the Plan for Soviet Industry," in *Kommunist* (1959). No. 1 All are translated in Sharpe, *op. cit.*, pp. 3–64.

Council of the Academy of Sciences to hear the then obscure Kharkov professor. Despite the strong support of Chairman Nemchinov, the proposals were rejected by the Council. By September however, the Communist Party initiated a public discussion of the Liberman proposals.

The Essentials of the Liberman Plan[12]

The Kharkov incentive system (as Liberman calls his plan) openly calls for structural changes in the planning process, but only at the level of the firm. All the prices and outputs are to continue to be centrally planned. The relationship of the planning apparatus to the individual enterprise, however, is to be fundamentally changed.

To encourage greater flexibility and initiative, the large number of indicator targets presently passed down to the firm is to be streamlined to "key indices" only. Liberman recommends assigning enterprises just those targets which exclusively pertain to their final output mix: quantity and assortment of production, product destinations, and delivery dates. The *input* mix is to be determined by each individual firm: the planners will then presumably sum up all of the enterprise needs, and provide for them through the centrally planned system of material allocations (though this would be quite difficult).

How well an enterprise fulfills society's demand for maximum efficiency is to be assessed solely on the basis of "ultimate efficiency." Profitability — which is defined to be profits expressed as a percentage of total capital — is to serve as this inclusive evaluator, and is to be estimated in yearly plans submitted by all firms. Once the stated output goals are attained, the rate of profitability achieved becomes the sole determinant of the amount of bonus funds awarded to the firm and its employees. Liberman depicts the central planners as "relieved from petty tutelage over enterprises" and from "costly efforts to influence production through administrative measures rather than economic ones."[13]

Bonus payments to enterprises are to be computed by comparing the profitability rate of a particular firm with a "profitability norm" established for the branch of industry within which each firm is to be included. The attempt is to set a "single standard of profitability for enterprises in roughly the same natural and technical conditions." Norms also are to vary with the proportion of new products in a firm's production program — being raised, for example, when no new products are being introduced. Different incentive payment scales will then be set up for the different branches of industry. The bonus premiums earned by the firm under this system will be utilized — as the manager directs — to (1) pay salary bonuses to management and workers, (2) provide new

[12] Derived from the three 1962 Liberman articles: "Plan, Profits, and Bonuses," *Pravda* (September 9, 1962), translated in Sharpe, *op. cit.*, pp. 79–87; "Planning Production and Standards of Long-Term Production," *Voprosy ekonomiki* (1962), No. 8, translated in Sharpe, *op. cit.*, pp. 65–78; and "Reply to Critics of the Profit Proposal," *Ekonomischeskaya gazeta*, No. 46 (November 10, 1962), translated in *Current Digest of the Soviet Press* (1962), No. 45, p. 18.

[13] Liberman, in Sharpe, *op. cit.*, p. 79.

housing, nurseries, kindergartens and recreation facilities for worker families and (3) finance small, decentralized investments.

To motivate directors to attempt as ambitious a plan as their productive potential allows, Liberman advances three proposals. First, incentive premiums per ruble of capital invested are to rise as the rate of profit increases. Second, the firm is to benefit more from fulfilling its own profitability plan than from overfulfilling it, Third, the norms of profitability are to be established "for an extended period of time" (from 2 to 5 years or more). This will prevent the harmful practice of raising norms whenever a firm surpasses its planned targets. In this way, the firm directors can count on reaping benefits from successful innovations or particularly effective cost-saving programs. The concern for profitability is also supposed to stimulate the manager to search for cost reductions and to produce the output mix demanded by his consumers.

Western Evaluation of the Liberman Plan

Liberman would use "profitability" as the sole determinant of the manager's bonus, defining "profitability" as the percentage of profit to capital. Previously, profitability was only one of many indicators, and was defined as profit to current costs. Moreover, fixed capital was given free to the enterprise. There was thus no limit to the capital a manager wanted to use, and no reason for him to use it carefully — so it was often used very extravagantly and wastefully. Under Liberman's plan, the manager would not want to waste capital or use it at all unless it raises the rate of profit on capital.

According to Liberman, therefore, this indicator of profitability should act as a deterrent to the inefficient use of capital. Western economists note that in this respect the profitability indicator will act as the interest rate under capitalism. Several Western critics,[14] while agreeing that this is an important advance, contend that it is still far from the necessary establishment of an interest charge on capital. Only such an interest charge would really put on pressure for the efficient use of capital by managers, since their bonus depends on the profitability of their firm, and the interest would then be a cost that reduces the profitability. It will be seen that the current reforms have moved the Soviets far in this direction.

Another very positive feature of Liberman's system is the proposal to base "profit" calculation on actual sales of goods rather than on output. Under the old system of output targets, the manager's bonus depended on units produced, not units sold. The new sales requirement would make the manager sensitive to the market. It would presumably force him (1) to produce a higher quality and (2) to produce the assortment desired by his customers. Although Western critics agree that this is a forward step, they[15] insist that the assortment may still be far from the optimal as long as the price structure is largely arbitrary. The manager

[14] See, e.g., Harry G. Shaffer, "Ills and Remedies," *Problems of Communism* (May–June, 1963), p. 25.

[15] See, e.g., *Ibid.*, p. 26.

will strive for the most profitable sales mix, but this will be socially optimal only if the price structure is rational.

Moreover, most Western economists also agree that, in order to prevent contradictions between profitability and the desirable product mix from arising (even after a thorough price reform), prices must be made more flexible and responsive to change. How to allow this flexibility and still keep price-fixing a central responsibility, as Liberman desires, then becomes a vital issue for discussion. In fact, it has been argued[16] that there *must* be conflicts between the need for rapid price changes and centrally planned prices. The argument is that bureaucratic price changes take time both for receipt of information and for decision-making. The contention is therefore that the bureaucratic process takes too long compared to the rapid price changes necessary to balance the economy.

It is also worth emphasizing Liberman's excellent proposal to give higher bonuses for fulfilling the enterprise's own planned profitability than for overfulfilling a lower plan. This means that enterprises will no longer hold back and misinform planners by claiming to have less capacity than they really have. In this respect, Liberman's proposal is to make the rules more like contract bridge, where one gets a bigger bonus by bidding more, than like auction bridge, where one bids only as high as necessary to win the auction. This incentive to firms to state their full capacity would be reinforced by Liberman's proposal to guarantee long-term targets, which could not be increased by the planners after the plan begins.

Another incentive problem met by Liberman is how to give directors a positive inducement to undertake technological innovation. Liberman's scheme for judging by profitability over the long run should provide managers with incentive to invest in new equipment and technology in spite of the risks and temporary slowdowns incurred when the new machinery is installed. Furthermore, since the emphasis is on overall profitability rather than on premiums for specific innovations, we may conclude that the material interests of the director will be "rather well correlated with the interests of society at large."[17]

Western critics argue, however, that there is "bound to be trouble along the line (where) the centralized portion of the plan meets the decentralized plans concocted by the enterprises."[18] More specifically, output targets in the Liberman scheme are set by the central planners, but firms are supposed to set their own input mix. How can this work? Certainly it would be difficult. Yet, if firms now have the incentive to state truthfully their capacities and needs for inputs, perhaps planners could do a fair job of planning the outputs of each producer good so that there would be roughly the required amount of each good available. The general Western consensus seems to be that reforms like the Liberman scheme would be a great step toward maximum efficiency, but that

---

[16] Alec Nove, "The Liberman Proposals," *Survey* (April 1963), p. 117.
[17] Shaffer, *op. cit.*, pp. 25–26.
[18] Nove, *op. cit.*, p. 117.

many pitfalls remain, both at the enterprise level, and at the central planning level.

Soviet Controversy, 1962–1963

Both moderate and active supporters of the Liberman system in the Soviet Union agree that a "rational" price system is a necessary precondition for a profit-based index to serve as an effective evaluator of enterprise efficiency. Although Liberman himself has been somewhat indefinite about the changes in pricing methodology which would be necessary to achieve this "rationality," others (such as V. S. Nemchinov) have taken a strong stand for many years. Since profits derive from selling prices and cost prices, profitability will be a measure of real, and not merely of paper, efficiency only if prices reflect the relative values of all inputs into production. Consequently, one Soviet writer asserts that a substantial price deviation "above or below the socially necessary outlays, results, regardless of the operation of the enterprise, either in an unjustifiably low profitability, and even loss, or in excessive profitability."[19] Furthermore, the most advanced economists openly recognize capital (at least fixed capital) as a scarce factor of production, and conclude that interest rates must be set at levels reflecting this scarcity.[20]

One group of Soviet writers argued further that the existing material supply system was too complex and inflexible to give enterprises the freedom of input determination envisioned in Liberman's incentive scheme. Therefore, they advocated replacing administrative allocation with a system of "state trade," in which enterprises would negotiate independent agreements with suppliers and customers.[21] Nemchinov boldly argued that all planning of intermediate goods should cease; the State should decide only what final products it needs.[22]

The majority of responses to *Pravda's* 1962 request for discussion, however, were characterized by either total hostility to Liberman's scheme or considerable criticism. For example, Zverev, former Minister of Finance, denounced the theory he sees lurking behind Libermanism: that profit is created not only by the worker's labor, but also by fixed and variable capital. "It is hardly necessary to prove the erroneousness of such a theory."[23] Second, he argued against the premise that the central planners are less informed as to the capabilities of enterprises than the enterprise itself. They "are obligated to know, and actually do know, the production capacities of enterprises."[24] Third, he points to the profit-

---

[19] L. Gatovskii, "The Role of Profit in a Socialist Economy," *Kommunist*, 1962; translated in *The Soviet Review* (Summer, 1963), p. 20.

[20] For instance, see V. Nemchinov's article "Plan, Assignment, and Material Incentive," in *Pravda* (September 21, 1962), translated in Sharpe, *op. cit.*, pp. 107–113.

[21] See, e.g., L. Vaag and S. Zakharov, *Voprosy ekonomiki*, No. 4 (1963), No. 4.

[22] See Nemchinov, *loc. cit.*

[23] A. Zverev, "Against Oversimplification in Solving Complex Problems," *Problems of Economics*, April 1963, p. 18.

[24] *Ibid.*, p. 16.

ability "norms" to be established for branches of industry, asserts that they would not be objective for all firms in a grouping, and predicts that constantly changing technical conditions among firms would cause persistent pressure on any norm-setting government agency to revise the norm. The only way to keep the norms "fair," he concludes, would be to continuously revise them.[25]

Furthermore, a full measure of hostility was unleashed to attack the increase in decentralized investment likely to occur with the adoption of a Liberman scheme. Convinced that existing defects in "capital construction" are due to insufficient centralization, several writers emphatically decried the proposal to leave an increased number of investment decisions with enterprises. They claimed that enterprises are "ignorant of the various national economic interrelations," so that the effect would be to increase "parochialism" and to multiply "disproportions in the national economy."[26]

Professor Liberman's reply in 1962 to his critics made some interesting points. First, Liberman attempts to clear away the confused notion held by some that profitability alone would be the single index to regulate enterprise behavior. The production goals which society demands of enterprises, including the quantity and assortment of output, are still to be centrally planned and individually assigned to firms. Only after meeting the output targets does profitability take prime importance for the firm. Second, he counters the charge that successful enterprises will be able to rest on past efficiency achievements. He asserts that "even a small increase in incentive payments is of some interest" and that "every manufacturing enterprise must constantly introduce new production . . . or its incentive scale will drop."[27]

By May, 1963, however, controversy had died down considerably. The government gave no further indication of its readiness to alter the basics of its system of minutely detailed planning and supervision of enterprises. Yet during the lull in public debate which lingered through mid-1964, problems with unsold consumer goods became critical. It was apparently the unwanted inventory increases that precipitated the first Soviet experiments with profit incentives and direct ties to consumers.

Specifically, the drastic situation of soaring inventories of textile and clothing goods stirred the government in early 1964 to place two large garment manufacturing associations — the "Bolshevicka" in Moscow and the "Mayak" in Gorky — under the rules of a new system. This system has some of the characteristics of Liberman's scheme, at least in spirit, if not in detail. The two producers were to work out their own

[25] *Ibid.*, p. 18.

[26] K. Plotnikov, "E. G. Liberman: Right and Wrong," *Voprosy ekonomiki* (1962), No. 11, translated in Sharpe, *op. cit.*, pp. 161–165; also I. Kasitskii, "The Main Question: Criteria for Premiums and Indices Planned for Enterprises," *Voprosy ekonomiki* (1962), No. 11, translated in Sharpe, *op. cit.*, pp. 135–140.

[27] E. G. Liberman, "Reply to Critics of the Profit Proposal," *Ekonomicheskaya gazeta* (November 10, 1962), No. 46, pp. 10–11, translated in *Current Digest of the Soviet Press*, Vol. XIV, No. 45, p. 18.

output plans on the basis of orders from retail outlets, and their performance was to be judged by sales rather than output, though not by profit as in Liberman's scheme. They were to negotiate their own contracts with principal suppliers, and financial penalties were to be levied for failure to make deliveries according to contract. In spite of a number of predictable difficulties, especially difficulties with surrounding bureaucracy, both associations overfulfilled output and profit plans for the year. The U.S.S.R. Council of National Economy decided to extend the experiment to 400 associations in the textile, clothing, leather, and footwear industries during 1965. There were even trials of the new system among a few factories manufacturing producer goods.

The Resumption of Debate: 1964–1965

Shortly after this initial experimentation with greater incentives began public discussion was again requested by the editors of *Pravda*.[28] The inference is that desires for economic reform from within the Party had significantly grown in the interim. The party was probably influenced by the intensification of the Soviet economy's problems from 1962 to 1964, including the rapidly mounting inventories of consumer goods, the grain crop failures in 1963 and the declining growth rate. The Soviet Party was surely also influenced by the virtual stagnation of the Czech economy in 1963, the inception in 1964 of profit sharing and a charge on capital in Hungary, and the continued success of the decentralized Yugoslav system.

Another lead article by Liberman in *Pravda* in 1964 reiterated his position and, in addition, advocated a charge on capital. Within six months, the newspaper reported having received 600 articles and letters in response. The bulk of public communication at this time showed a substantial shift in mood from the 1962 controversy. The author of "Survey of Readers' Letters" in *Pravda* (February 17, 1965) concluded that the overwhelming majority of writers felt it necessary to

> intensify sharply the role of economic levers in the management of the national economy to expand the rights of enterprises, to enhance the importance of profit . . . and to put price formation in order.

Expressions of total hostility were practically nonexistent, while an expanded and vocal group of economists, research workers, and enterprise managers became increasingly insistent in their demands for the adoption of widespread change.

The degree of enterprise autonomy urged by some of the writers[29] now went considerably beyond the Liberman Plan and its 1962 extensions. Arguing that output plans should be based on orders from customers,

[28] Footnote to Academician V. Trapeznikov's article of August 17, 1964, *op. cit.*

[29] V. Belkin and I. Berman, "Independence of the Enterprise and Economic Stimuli," *Izvestia* (December 4, 1964), translated in Sharpe, *op. cit.*, pp. 225–230.

they asserted first, that enterprises "should be given the right to amend the output plan with the consent of the customer" and second, that when an enterprise is producing a product "with higher consumer properties than are stipulated by the standards, it should be given the right to fix the price with the agreement of the customer." One Soviet author[30] at that time even proposed to abolish central price-setting, and replace it by competition ruled by consumer demand.

The goals of most hopeful reformers, however, did not at first include changes which would decentralize price setting. Their main new demand was for the introduction of direct links with suppliers in order to supplant the unwieldy system of central supply allocations. They were also loud in demanding a price calculus with capital charges. Nevertheless, complete central control over national parameters (including prices) was still regarded as integral to the preservation of economic balances and a high rate of accumulation.[31] Only after the reforms actually began in 1966 and 1967 was considerable sentiment voiced for price decentralization as well as output decentralization.

Official Reforms

Although "economic experiments" were extended and given more varied trials during 1965, it was not until September of that year that the government responded with a major organizational reform in industry, which moved somewhat in the direction of the Liberman proposals. Adopted as law by the Supreme Soviet on October 2nd,[32] the stipulations of the Kosygin Reform were conservative and tentative, yet they did begin the process of reform. The section pertaining to the individual enterprise contained four significant new policies. First, and most important, managers' bonuses are to be paid for fulfillment of planned targets for sales, profit or profitability, and physical output. The scales of bonuses will be designed so as to provide relatively higher rewards for fulfillment of planned targets than for overfulfillment of targets. Moreover, to evaluate the amount of sales, the "gross value of output" indicator is to be replaced by "output sold." This change implies the necessity to produce what consumers desire. Numerous target directives will be eliminated, including the norms for labor productivity, number of workers and employees, and average wages.

Second, the enterprise will be permitted to retain and utilize a large proportion of profits (and some portion of depreciation allowances) for bonuses, welfare purposes, and decentralized investment. This may turn out to be a very significant measure, giving financial muscle to the decentralization reforms. Third, half of centralized investment is to be financed by repayable and interest-bearing loans from banks, and interest charges are to be levied (in the form of a tax) on all fixed and work-

[30] O. Volkov, *Pravda* (August 23, 1964).

[31] See, e.g., V. Trapeznikov, *loc. cit.*

[32] See, Text of laws in *Pravda* (October 3, 1965), translated in U.S. Congress, Joint Economic Committee, *New Directions in the Soviet Economy* (Washington, 1966), Part 4, pp. 1063–1066.

ing capital put at the enterprise's disposal.[33] Fourth, contracts between enterprises are to be more strictly enforced, prohibiting superiors from changing enterprise plans at will during the plan period. Incidentally, at the same time, Khrushchev's regional economic councils were abolished, and industrial direction was returned to about 20 central industrial ministries — but with provision for the now increased autonomy of individual enterprises.

Some of the reform measures do approach the spirit, if not the letter of Liberman's scheme. Attention to what has been left out of the Kosygin system, however, gives us a more pessimistic view of the possibility that the reform will implement the kind of changes which Liberman sympathizers have been proposing. For example, it has been pointed out numerous times that any attempt at a greater reliance on profitability criteria would be useless (or even harmful) without a rational price system. Yet the wholesale price reform has been very slow in coming, and has not made the more drastic changes requested by Soviet reformers. Furthermore, the new committee charged with price policy was told no more than that prices should reflect costs, a remarkably insufficient suggestion considering that economists and planners have been arguing the basic principles for at least ten years.

Moreover, the new economic system continues to maintain the method of direct materials allocation, though there are new reports of some attempts to replace or modify it by the introduction of large wholesale-warehouse type establishments in which enterprises can buy anything they need. As long as the system of direct materials allocation is continued, the reforms certainly will not result in the Liberman objective of enterprise freedom to vary inputs. Notice that the reformed system also keeps the central limits on total payrolls, and allows managers only to choose the labor mix within those limits. At the same time, the apparent intent to allow more decentralized investments may result in a significant decrease in central control over the determination of future output. Indeed, as we noted in describing this reform, the allowance of a large amount of decentralized investment may turn out to be one of the most important practical features of the reform.

On the other hand, it must be admitted that even these limited Soviet reforms have already run into bureaucratic obstruction and sabotage. Thus, by the beginning of 1967 only 673 industrial enterprises employing about 2.5 million workers had switched to the new system; whereas the original timetable had called for more than 10 million workers on the new system by that date. Perhaps more important in the long run, there have been numerous reports of continued extra-legal interference by government and Party organs in the day-to-day operations of enterprises, including those on the new system.

The undoubted difficulties of the new system will be resolved eventually either by retrogression or by further reform. Which direction is

[33] See discussion of this reform in I. Liberman, "Payments on Assets: Their Budgetary and Cost Accounting Functions," translated in *Problems of Economics*, Vol. 10, No. 6 (October, 1967).

taken will depend on many factors, including external ones such as peace in Vietnam, but the pressure and prestige of reform is now very strong. Unless drastic adverse changes in the international scene occur, it seems quite likely that the winds of progress and change will continue to blow strongly in the Soviet economy.

SELECTED REFERENCES

Most of the Soviet contributions to the debate are collected in M. E. Sharpe, editor, *The Liberman Discussion: A New Phase in Soviet Economic Thought* (White Plains, New York: International Arts and Science Press, 1965).

It is also worth examining the official discussion by A. Kosygin as well as the decisions of the Plenary Meeting of the C.P.S.U. Central Committee on September 29, 1965, translated in U.S. Congress, Joint Economic Committee, *New Directions in the Soviet Economy* (Washington: U.S. Government Printing Office, 1966), Part 4, pp. 1033–1066. A Soviet comment is translated in N. Federenko, "The Reforms in Industry," *Problems of Economics*, Vol. 10, No. 6 (October, 1967).

Western views may be found in the following articles:

1. Robert W. Campbell, "Economics: Roads and Inroads," *Problems of Communism* (Nov.–Dec., 1965), pp. 23–33. Also R. W. Campbell, "Economic Reform in the U.S.S.R.," *American Economic Review*, Vol. 58 (May, 1968), pp. 547–558.

2. B. J. McFarlane, and I. Gordijew, "Profitability and the Soviet Firm," *The Economic Record* (Dec., 1964), pp. 554–568.

3. Alec Nove, "The Liberman Proposals," *Survey* (April, 1963).

4. Harry G. Shaffer, "Ills and Remedies," *Problems of Communism* (May–June, 1963), pp. 27–32.

5. Vladimir Treml, "Revival of Soviet Economics and the New Generation of Soviet Economists," *Studies on the Soviet Union*, Vol. V, No. 2 (1965), pp. 1–22. Also V. Treml, "The Politics of 'Libermanism,'" *Soviet Studies*, Vol. 19 (April, 1968), pp. 567–572.

6. ———, "Soviet Economics in Flux," *The ASTE Bulletin* (Winter, 1964), pp. 3–15.

7. Alfred Zauberman, "Liberman's Rules of the Game for Soviet Industry," *Slavic Review* (December, 1963), pp. 734–744.

8. Marshall I. Goldman, "Economic Controversy in the Soviet Union," *Foreign Affairs* (April, 1963), pp. 498–512.

9. U.S. Congress, Joint Economic Committee, *New Directions in the Soviet Economy* (Washington, D.C.: U.S. Government Printing Office, 1966), contains three pertinent articles:

    a. Ruth V. Greenslade, "The Soviet Economic System in Transition," pp. 1–18.

    b. John P. Hardt, Dimitri M. Gallik and Vladimir G. Treml, "Institutional Stagnation and Changing Economic Strategy in the Soviet Union," pp. 19–62.

    c. Imogene Erro, "Economic Reform in the Soviet Consumer Industries," pp. 555–568.

10. A summary and tentative evaluation of the working of the reforms both in the Soviet Union and Eastern Europe may be found in the

Staff Report on "Communist Economic Reforms," and the reprint of Gregory Grossman, "Economic Reforms: A Balance Sheet," both printed in Committee on Banking and Currency, U.S. House of Representatives, *The Fiat-Soviet Auto Plant and Communist Economic Reforms* (Washington, D.C.: U.S. Government Printing Office, March 1, 1967).

11. Some Western books discussing efficiency both in central planning and in decentralized situations are: A. Balinsky, A. Bergson, J. Hazard, and P. Wiles, *Planning and the Market in the U.S.S.R.: the 1960s* (New Brunswick: Rutgers University Press, 1967); George R. Feiwel, *The Soviet Quest for Economic Efficiency* (New York: Praeger, 1967); and Jere L. Felker, *Soviet Economic Controversies, The Emerging Marketing Concept and Changes in Planning, 1960–1965* (Cambridge, Mass.: MIT Press, 1966). Also see articles in George R. Feiwel, ed., *New Currents in Soviet-type Economies: A Reader* (Scranton: International Textbook Co., 1968), pp. 296–404.

14

DECENTRALIZATION IN
EASTERN EUROPE

This chapter examines the course of reform and decentralization in the socialist economies of Eastern Europe. The comparison and contrast with the Soviet Union will be very instructive.

The Yugoslav Revelation

The Yugoslav experience revealed to the whole Communist world that an economy could be largely decentralized while remaining socialist. Although it was at first denounced with the usual Stalinist unanimity, later — when the anti-Stalinist tide began to rise — the Yugoslav economy became a model to investigate.

If the Yugoslav model were pursued to its logical extreme: (1) each enterprise would be completely free to make its own decisions on output and prices, constrained only by the pure and perfect competition of all the other enterprises; (2) the entire wages and profits (after taxes) would be available to the workers of each enterprise to dispose of as they see fit, either for reinvestment in the enterprise or for immediate distribution to the individual workers; and (3) taxes would be used by the central government for administration and to add investment up to the desired national level. Since logic, however, is usually far from actuality in economics, it is useful to begin by examining the actual course of events leading to the present Yugoslav economic system.

Background of Yugoslav System. The Cominform (or Communist Information Bureau) was formed in 1947 by Stalin primarily as a means of keeping Eastern Europe — and perhaps especially Yugoslavia — on a tight leash. In 1948, however, Yugoslavia broke with the U.S.S.R., and took a position advocating complete independence and equality for

320

all socialist nations. The Yugoslavs complained that the Russians had attempted to dominate their Army, to exploit their economy through joint companies, to use secret agents to investigate and blackmail important Yugoslavs, and to threaten the cutting off of all trade should Yugoslavia take any independent action. In reply, the Cominform excommunicated Yugoslavia, charging that Yugoslavia slandered the U.S.S.R. and that Yugoslavia was no longer Marxist because it had stopped pushing collectivization.

The Yugoslavs eventually answered that the U.S.S.R. had deviated further and further from socialist democracy toward bureaucratic over-centralization. As a concrete reaction, by 1950 the Yugoslavs began to decentralize their economy and create their own "socialist democracy." This focused on "workers' councils" in each factory, a form which seemed to implement some of the ideas of the syndicalist movements of the 19th Century. As a result of the drastic reorganization, the cutting off of all Soviet trade, and an increased need for military spending, Yugoslavia went through some years of very difficult economic troubles (though Western aid and trade largely offset the loss of Soviet and Eastern European trade).

During this period, the Yugoslavs advanced the economic theory that central or administrative planning may at first greatly help the progress of an underdeveloped or war-torn socialist economy. As the economy becomes more built-up, complex, and interrelated, however, such extreme central direction "turns into its opposite," and becomes a barrier to further progress. Some form of this theory has become the basis for the reforms in much of Eastern Europe and even the Soviet Union.

Additional Yugoslav theories, which round out their new world-view, emphasize first that all socialist nations including the Soviet Union are equal. Second, many forms and many roads to socialism may be equally good in different circumstances. The Yugoslavs at first even included the Scandinavian socialist forms. Later limitations of the doctrine, however, led to attacks on "social democrats," both foreign and internal — exemplified in the famous trial of Djilas, who advocated an end to the single-party system. The two doctrines of equality and different roads to socialism were heretical at first, but are now common currency in Eastern Europe. Third, the Yugoslavs claim that the state withers away and full democracy enters through the road of decentralization, beginning first in the economy and then spreading to the political sphere. This is opposite to the Soviet doctrine, which sees the withering-away as beginning with the abolition of police and armies, but retaining central planning indefinitely. Fourth, the most important form of economic decentralization is local workers' possession and *control* of the factories, though the nation still *owns* them.

On the purely political side, the Yugoslav central leadership under Tito keeps a tight rein, and their theory is correspondingly cautious. They allow criticism of a socialist government within socialist limits, but not anti-socialist criticism. The courts are supposed to protect individual rights, and to emphasize a socialist humanist approach. They hold that socialism does require some form of political democracy, but not the bourgeois form used in capitalist countries. They argue that bourgeois democracy is democratic only for the wealthy minority. One Yugoslav writer says that the multi-party system may be acceptable in principle, "but . . . in a comparatively backward country like Yugoslavia . . . such a system would inevitably destroy not only the socialist foundation of such a country but even its independence."[1] It is interesting that he correlates lack of democracy with economic backwardness, presumably with the implication that economic progress may set the stage for more political democracy.

Details of the Yugoslav Economic System. A discussion of the framework of the Yugoslav system as it has operated since 1950 is useful, even though many important changes have occurred within it since that date. These changes are discussed in the next section.

Farming in Yugoslavia after 1950 reverted to private ownership. There are few collectives today, though the goal of collectivization still remains. In fact, the government is very, very gradually buying up individual pieces of land as farmers retire. In addition to farming, there is also a private business sector in Yugoslavia, mostly in the areas of trade and handicrafts. Private businesses and farms may hire up to five persons, though this limit has apparently been exceeded in practice. Farmers may acquire land up to ten hectares. The private sector thus plays a very small role in industry, but constitutes almost the whole of the farming sector. Private enterprise also plays an increasing role in the catering and service sector.

In the socialist sector of industry each factory is run as a producer's co-operative, under the control of its own Workers' Council. The Workers' Councils are a feature unique to Yugoslav socialism. We shall see that many of the other Eastern European countries are slowly decentralizing their economies toward fully independent activity by each enterprise. Yet none of them presently intends to institute Workers' Councils as a basic feature of their economy, preferring control by government-appointed managers. Only the Yugoslavs consider Workers' Councils the most vital part of their economic structure. They not only praise its allegedly democratic aspects, but also claim that it motivates workers and managers to the highest efficiency. Some Yugoslavs have even asserted that the Workers' Councils are responsible for their high rate of growth, though skeptics attribute the high growth rate primarily to a high rate of investment.

How does the system of Workers' Councils operate? The workers elect a council. The manager is then appointed by the local government, but the workers' council has a veto power over the appointment of the manager. The council can also fire the manager; it sets wages, within limits set by the central government; it sets prices, also within limits set by central agencies; it sets production targets and determines technology;

[1] Quoted in Fred W. Neal and G. W. Hoffman, *Yugoslavia: The New Communism* (New York: Twentieth Century Fund, 1962), p. 170.

and may dispose of its profits after taxes through additions to wages, collective welfare projects, or reinvestment. The taxes going to the national government are used for financing of major investment projects, as well as defense and welfare.

Since all of the firms compete in the market, prices set will be "rational" from the viewpoint of welfare economics, provided that there is pure and perfect competition. Nevertheless, since a large percentage of investment is still under the central control, capital cannot freely flow to areas of higher profits. Therefore, this constitutes a barrier to entry of other firms, and may allow monopoly or oligopoly to arise in any area where the central government sets an optimum size of firms which is very high in relation to the total market. Since Yugoslavia is a small country, and the total market for many commodities is a limited one, there are many such industries where the optimum size of firm demands only one or a few producers. As the result of such monopolies, (1) price relationships are distorted away from the socially "rational" price, (2) resources are therefore allocated wrongly from the social viewpoint, and (3) consumers are exploited in the sense of paying higher prices to these particular firms.

Expansion and new investment by a particular firm also has some peculiar aspects under this system. If an entirely new firm is set up, then it has its own Workers' Council to look after the benefit of its own workers. New firms are often, but not always, set up by old firms. Even in that case, however, the new council does not return any profits to the old firm that set it up, though it is obligated to pay interest to the government on the capital that has been given to it. In a few cases, such new enterprises are treated legally as mere subsidiary parts of the old firm. In this case the additional profits are divided amongst the workers of both the old and new firm. In either case, the way that a Workers' Council looks at a new investment project outside of its own plant is far more complicated than the usual profit calculus of a competitive firm under capitalism. One would expect some tendency to limit projects to those that might be considered a legitimate part of the old firm.

In addition to these micro-economic aspects of investment, there is also something new in this system with respect to the question of aggregate investment. What is to keep the workers of a particular firm from deciding that all of their profits should go into current wages or welfare projects, rather than reinvestment and expansion of the productive base? Legally, the only constraint is that the firm must first pay its taxes to the central government. In practice, the central government does take a very large tax bite, and in the past has used much of these taxes for investment, and has achieved a very high rate of economic growth. The Yugoslavs also claim that the workers are generally very willing to make many large reinvestments, supposedly being willing to wait for the large future returns.

In practice, the Communist Party group within each enterprise also exerts a strong pressure toward socially-minded collective welfare projects and toward reinvestment for expansion of the productive base. The manager of the enterprise also exerts a somewhat independent pressure, in most cases advocating the expansion of the enterprise capital. Actually, it appears that the balance of power over the distribution of income between workers and managers and higher authorities varies from plant to plant as well as from year to year. For example, Yugoslav as well as Western economists agree that in 1961 workers' wages increased more than productivity, causing inflation in the consumer goods market. At present, the percentage of investment to national income is very high. Therefore, a large percentage of all investment, especially that going into new enterprises, must be and is still done by the central government, but an increasing percentage is coming under the control of existing firms and local governments.

It should be noted that the revenue of the enterprise must pay (1) interest on loans from the banking system, (2) depreciation allowances, (3) interest to the central government on the initial capital investment, (4) the turnover tax on sales, (5) miscellaneous taxes and fees, and (6) the income tax on profits. After the firm has paid these expenses, it is then free to divide the rest of the revenue between wages and new investment. Yet the workers still must pay an additional Social Insurance Tax on their wages. It is also required that of the investment funds, at least 24 percent must go to a housing fund and to communal investment projects, such as recreation centers. One further restriction lies in the fact that the government enforces a minimum wage for each worker.

It might be noted that the total of all the various taxes, including profit tax, turnover tax, and the interest on initial capital, has stayed about one-third of the gross national product. Of these government revenues, Yugoslavia in 1961 spent about 50 percent on defense, 35 percent on welfare, and 15 percent on investment. Nevertheless, when the central government, local government, and enterprise investment are all added together, in 1961 it was found that gross investment amounted to a full 35 percent of gross national product.

Central planning also removes some additional areas from the decision-making of the Workers' Councils at the enterprise level. Central planning is responsible (1) for all of the most important investment projects, (2) for most research and development, and (3) for the educational supply of skilled and professional workers.

Trends in the Yugoslav System. The initial Yugoslav move in 1950 — the institution of Workers' Councils in each enterprise — seems to have been more of a political gamble for popular support than a well-thought-out economic scheme. It is true that the steps toward economic decentralization followed this initial step quite rapidly, but in a piece-meal fashion. On the political level, the further measures toward decentralization were undertaken to give some real meaning to the Workers' Councils by allowing them to make important decisions. Economically, decentralization was necessary in order to remove the conflict between the decisions of the councils at the enterprise level and the continued flow of detailed plans from the central planning bureau. It was only in 1952 that it was explicitly stated that economic democracy means the "self-management" of the enterprise by all of the members in it.

Since 1950 the system has fluctuated several times between central planning and a market system of competition. There has been a general trend toward more decentralization, but with frequent retrogressions to more direct central control in particular aspects of wages, prices, or investment. A major series of reforms in 1961 ended several kinds of centralized planning and control, especially decentralizing the international trade of enterprises. In 1963 the current five-year plan was abandoned and, on principle, only a quite vague and general "guideline plan" was put in its place.

Then, in 1965, came the most radical Yugoslav decentralization move — perhaps to show they were still the leaders in spite of the rash of reforms announced that year in the Soviet Union and all over Eastern Europe. At any rate, a U.S. Congressional Subcommittee[2] reports that this time the Yugoslavs really

> . . . meant to do what in theory they had been doing since 1950. Briefly, it was proposed to liberalize imports as fast as the country could afford; to decentralize the banking system and make it the source of investment capital, free of governmental interference; to encourage the entry of foreign capital, with the management and technical skills which would accompany it; to free prices from administrative control as quickly as possible (while imposing a price freeze to prevent too rapid readjustments); in short, definitely to get the Government (and the party) out of business.

Another Western observer[3] even comments that, "At the present moment, the abandonment of national priority planning in Yugoslavia goes perhaps further than in most Western democracies . . ."

At the same time, there is an apparent contradiction between the trend toward more decentralization and the Yugoslav imposition of a price freeze "to prevent too rapid readjustments." In fact, the percentage of all internal prices legally under central control in the final analysis rose from 60 percent in 1964 to 90 percent in 1966.[4] Yugoslav economists claim that the imposition of controls is temporary; and designed merely to prevent inflation, not to interfere with price competition. It seems true that the Yugoslavs are not terribly worried about *relative* price levels, though their degree of monopoly in many industries should perhaps make them worry. They are, however, very concerned over the immediate problem of inflation or the *absolute* rise of the whole price level. Un-

---

[2] Subcommittee on International Trade, Committee on Banking and Currency, U.S. House of Representatives, *The Fiat-Soviet Auto Plant and Communist Economic Reforms* (Washington, D.C.: U.S. Government Printing Office, 1967), p. 46.

[3] Wolfgang Friedmann, "Freedom and Planning in Yugoslavia's Economic System," *Slavic Review*, Vol. 25 (December, 1966), p. 639.

[4] *Ibid.*, p. 633.

fortunately, as will be seen in the next section, there is some reason to believe that a tendency to inflation may be inherent in the wage-price policies of the Workers' Councils, and not merely a temporary phenomenon. But if inflationary pressure persists, when will price controls be lifted?

The 1965 reforms also instituted a major financial change. Until the reforms only about 25 to 30 percent of fixed investment funds came from the enterprises themselves, and even this was effectively controlled by the central planners. In that period, central funds financed 70 to 75 percent of the total investment. These central funds came mostly from taxes, whether administered by the government or by the banks. Thus, Yugoslavia's high rate of investment was largely tax-financed and centrally directed.[5] The reforms have drastically changed the situation by allowing more enterprise-directed investment from enterprise funds and from a highly decentralized banking system.

The new Investment Banking system of Yugoslavia is unique in that each bank is controlled by an "assembly," in which each member votes according to stock held, *but* no one member can have more than 10 percent of the votes. The bank itself can hold only 10 percent of the votes, sociopolitical organizations are limited to another 20 percent, and at least 70 percent of the votes must be held by individual enterprises (and other banks). These banks will supply most of the credit for investment and will make most of the final decisions on economic development. "It is the investment banks that decide on the award or refusal of credits, and against their decisions there is no legal or administrative appeal."[6]

Yugoslavia has made phenomenal progress under their system of market socialism, achieving growth rates well above the centrally planned economies of Eastern Europe and the Soviet Union or the private enterprise economies of Western Europe and the United States. Their official statistics show that from 1954 to 1964 their economy raced along at 9.4 percent increase per year in their "gross national product" (defined in the usual Marxist manner), 12.5 percent a year in industry, and even 5.0 percent a year in agriculture.[7] Obviously, even if outside observers would estimate rates a little lower, these data make the Yugoslav experiment look very attractive. They cannot, however, be taken as conclusive evidence of outstanding long-run performance of their type of system without a great deal more study over a much longer period.

The full effects of the 1965 reforms will not be known for some time. Their initial effect, however, has been to raise the level of unemployment, and to cause a temporary decline in living standards. The reason is that competition has been more cutthroat than before, while inefficient enterprises no longer have available to them an almost infinite supply of central credit. The less efficient enterprises have therefore had to cut back production or, at least, drastically limit expansion — exactly as in a pri-

---

[5] See the interesting discussion by Gregory Grossman, *Economic Systems*, (Englewood Cliffs, N.J.: Prentice-Hall, Inc., 1967), p. 104.

[6] Friedmann, *op. cit.*, p. 634.

[7] See data and discussion in Grossman, *op. cit.*, pp. 105–106.

vate enterprise economy. The question is whether in the long run the re-adjustment, however painful at the moment, will increase the growth rate of the average enterprises, even if it means the eventual merger and take-over of the failing and inefficient enterprises.

Some Problems of the Yugoslav System. Prices of products in Yugoslavia are set by the enterprises (to the extent allowed by government price control), and the enterprises have every reason for increasing prices at every opportunity. If output demanded does not fall proportionately, then higher prices can give the opportunity for the Workers' Council of the enterprise to pay out higher wages. Furthermore, as was noted, a small country like Yugoslavia inevitably has a large number of monopoly producers because a single large-scale optimum size enterprise takes such a huge slice of an industry. Partly, this problem is mitigated by foreign trade since foreign competition helps keep the monopolies in line. The result of the strong wage position and the monopoly structure of industry has been a chronic tendency toward price inflation. One interesting result of the monopoly pricing is that socialist Yugoslavia has passed an anti-monopoly law against combinations in restraint of trade or conpsiracies to raise prices.

In addition, the natural reaction of a central government with a planning tradition like Yugoslavia's was the imposition of a large number of price controls. It was noted above that by 1967 a large percentage of Yugoslavia's industrial sales were of price-controlled goods (though this is supposed to be a temporary situation). Firms either may set prices only within certain limits, or they must get agency approval for any price change. Bureaucracy thus returns to the price-setting stage via the back door, though the enterprises are still the formal sources of all prices. It is interesting that this system has much in common with a Lange-type system in which enterprises may set their output, but prices are centrally set.

Another Yugoslav problem has been the continuing importance of regional or national rivalries. This is especially significant in the investment process, in which the allocation is achieved partly by local and regional agencies. Some of the allocation is by central planners, but they themselves may be afflicted by regional biases. Moreover, it is not just a matter of regional rivalries — it is that the regions are in such vastly different stages of economic development. It is still necessary to ensure equal development by investing in Macedonia, for example, when the same project could do much better in one of the more advanced regions. This is a profound problem and causes, in the short run at least, a great loss from inefficient allocation of investment relative to what might be done if there were no extra-economic regional considerations.

There is also a problem arising from the attempt to give real local power to Workers' Councils over the specific plants and enterprises. This tends to result in the splitting up of industries into units of a small enough size for democratic participation. In this case, the political objective may conflict with the economic goal of achieving large enough enterprises to make use of all possible economies of scale. Thus, it is notorious that the railways of Yugoslavia have been divided up into a rather loose association of more than 160 autonomous enterprises. For a country the size of Yugoslavia, this seems to be far too many competing firms in an industry that requires much integration. Similarly, Yugoslavia has five factories each of which makes entire radios. Yet considerable economies of scale might be obtained by having each of the factories specialize in a single radio component. In actual fact, in recent years there has been a strong trend in some industries toward merger of enterprises, in spite of the obstacles presented by entrenched Workers' Councils.

Another problem which socialism was supposed to have avoided, but which is found in Yugoslavia today, is a certain degree of job insecurity and unemployment. It is theoretically possible that a system of market socialism like that of Yugoslavia might be subject to a certain degree of aggregate unemployment. In the past, this has generally been overcome by a sufficient amount of central investment, and by exportation of about 400,000 workers, mostly to West Germany. Nevertheless, there is a continuing real problem of frictional unemployment to the degree that inefficient enterprises are allowed to go bankrupt, though there is non-economic pressure against this. Moreover, there was a significant amount of aggregate unemployment in 1966 and 1967.

In addition to the regional biases mentioned earlier, investment allocation under the Yugoslav system is subject to certain distortions due to the limited outlook of individual enterprises, operating on purely profit criteria. Since workers are only attached to the firm for a limited time (at most during their lifetime) the Workers' Councils tend to neglect many long-run considerations in favor of short-run rapid returns. Furthermore, some individual Yugoslav firms — like those under a private enterprise system — tend to overlook the possible social benefits and possible social damages of their investments. For example, each firm does not consider fully the effects of creating smog in the community.

A quite different problem is posed by the continuing private nature of Yugoslav farming. Since it is not only private but also of low productivity in general, with low yields per worker, this private area of agriculture tends to conflict with the socialized and rapidly modernizing industries. The official Yugoslav remedy is that farming itself will eventually be socialized, but the lack of significant movement in this direction may leave one skeptical of the political feasibility of the move at any time.

Finally, consider the left-wing, Chinese criticism that the Yugoslav system will eventually revert to capitalism. This is based on the notion that workers and managers in particular plants are coming to have a vested economic interest in those plants. It is hard to see, though, how the workers of a given plant in the Yugoslav system can ever use their possession of the plant either to exploit other workers or to pass on their position as an inheritance to their children. The second left-wing criticism is the related one that the Yugoslav economic psychology is reverting to the bourgeois outlook of profit-making rather than one of social benefit. This may certainly be the case to some extent, but it is not easy to see that the central planning alternative produces less of a money-making psychology on the part of workers and managers. These very difficult problems are viewed from a comparative point of view in the next chapter.

The Polish Reforms

The Polish economy was largely devastated by the Second World War. Consequently, efforts immediately following this period were aimed at restoration. Emergency dictums and chaos characterized the years 1944 and 1945. At the end of 1945 the government inaugurated some partial planning, consisting merely of financial plans and indirect controls. Accordingly, even early socialization ventures were mainly an aftermath of war rather than the manifestation of Communist doctrine.

In 1947 the Poles made their first attempt at long range planning. The plan covered three years, and stressed increases in industrial output as well as an increase in the standard of living in the country. During these years the Central Planning Office was composed of a Socialist-Communist coalition whose members often disagreed markedly on economic matters. During this period, however, all sides accepted the fact that Poland was characterized by a three sector economy: state, cooperative and private. One faction, including Oskar Lange and Gomulka (the present Premier), desired to keep one sub-sector of the economy in private hands, and supported the adoption of a law encouraging private initiative. In addition, they favored the retention of a labor market to regulate wages, and advocated selling consumer goods at market-clearing prices. In 1946, for example, Lange

> . . . insisted that the fields of peasant farming, handicraft, and small and medium-scale industry should remain the terrain of private initiative. He specified that in order to assure a lasting basis for the development of democratic forms of social existence, the Polish economic structure must, among other things, prevent the concentration of economic power either in the hands of private capitalists and landed gentry or in the hands of the state bureaucracy. He was especially fearful of the latter. . . .[8]

The other faction, led by Hilary Minc, believed that the private and cooperative sectors of the economy were inhibiting the development of the state sector. Gradually, this faction discarded the notion of the three sector economy. Cooperatives, they contended, could lead to private enterprise, and the private sectors themselves should only be allowed to exist until the time they could be removed without disrupting the economy.

In 1948 the debate between the two factions crystallized. Minc charged the other faction with deviations from Marxist principles. He felt that the national income data had been constructed by bourgeois methods, and that the non-socialist sector of the economy enjoyed inflated importance. He declared that a rapid increase in the producer goods sector is the most

---

[8] Quoted in Thad Alton, *Polish Postwar Economy* (New York: Columbia University Press, 1955), p. 109.

vital goal in the long run. Minc supported detailed and ambitious plans, accompanied by restriction of present consumption to insure their fulfillment. Lange and Gomulka, on the other hand, advocated a more balanced pattern of growth and discouraged heavy sacrifices for doubtful future gains.

The immediate result was that many of the liberal faction were forced to resign their posts in 1948, and Gomulka was purged. Minc was placed at the head of the State Planning Commission, where he reigned as economic 'tsar' of Poland for many years. Thereafter, until the mid-1950's the Polish economy was closely patterned after the centralized Soviet model. The private sector declined markedly. Soviet experts served in important advisory capacities to the Polish planners. Moreover, Soviet methods of planning were adopted, stressing merely consistent plans based on technological data, with little account given to the calculation of economic efficiency based on prices or costs.

Plans and Criticisms of the Mid-1950's. The six-year plan of 1950 through 1955, resembling Soviet five-year plans, had various shortcomings but did achieve many of its goals. During the time span which it covered, Poland's output of producer goods nearly tripled. In addition, urban employment increased by close to 60 percent. However, reality drifted away from the six-year plan, as witnessed by the fact that in its later years only yearly governmental plans had any operational significance (as is usually also the case with Soviet plans). One Polish economist at the time called the whole plan a failure because real wages had risen only 13 percent during the period under consideration. A Soviet economist declared that many of the Polish problems with the plan stemmed from the fact that their allocation for defense was far too high. And in the later part of 1953 a Warsaw newspaper proclaimed that even the industrial gains made under the plan were 'mostly myths.'

The six-year plan was attacked primarily because it was unrealistic; the planners were accused of dogmatic optimism. The second main criticism of the six-year plan centered around the fact that it produced serious imbalances within the Polish economy. Attacked specifically was the growth of the heavy industrial sector at the expense of the consumer goods industry and agricultural production. Gomulka, who is now the Premier, was especially critical, and at many points found reason to attack the Soviet heavy industry thesis. In addition, it was argued that the schematic notions on planning held by the pro-Soviet group allowed very little room for the operation of material incentives. Furthermore, by dogmatically following the Soviet pattern, the pro-Soviet group had forced Poland to curtail production in areas where it possessed comparative advantage on the world market, thereby decreasing the efficiency of investment. Finally, over-centralization and bureaucratization were cited as two main evils incurred by following the Soviet example.

In June, 1956, soon after Khrushchev's attack on Stalinism, the Second Polish Congress of Economists was convened. The conference called for an immediate increase in the living standards in Poland, an improvement in the quality of both producer and consumer goods, and more efficient use of raw materials. In addition, they criticized the incentive system, claiming that it rewarded waste in materials, transportation, equipment, and labor; they called for increased initiative on the part of the managers in the enterprise. Participants in the conference concluded that there was no need to decrease investment, it must only be restructured. Investment funds should increasingly be directed towards raw material production, agriculture, and especially consumer goods.

The major suggestion resulting from this conference was that the economic bureaucracy in Poland be decentralized, thereby enabling the economy to develop along more suitable lines. One economist stated that, "The planners' role should amount to creating such economic conditions that the decisions of the enterprise would go in the direction suggested."[9] Another economist participating in the discussions of the conference noted that, "We became aware of the awful destruction caused by the bureaucratic central system of running the national economy, and to what degree these things had made people lose faith so that even the most trivial matter could not be settled without asking the central authorities."[10]

In accordance with this line of thought, it was suggested that the State Planning Commission be restricted to the elaboration of mutually consistent plans for the development of sectors, the balancing and distribution of certain crucial products, price setting and allocation of profits, and concentration on long-range economic problems.

Ferment and discussion of all aspects of Polish life rose to new heights after this conference in 1956. The public at large had some very sharp words about the weaknesses of the Polish economy. They complained that the economy was not consumer oriented enough, and that the quality of household goods had fallen considerably. After the economic conference, even *Trybuna Ludu* — the official newspaper of the Communist Party in Poland — ran a series of extremely critical articles on the state of the economy. The 7th Plenum of the Communist Party called for the liquidation of overly extensive central planning and limitation of central directives, for the institution of incentive schemes designed to eliminate waste, for improvement of the quality of goods produced, for the re-enforcement of the Enterprise Fund through a larger deduction for it from the profits of the enterprise, for easing of the supply situation, and for planners to base production on more realistic estimates of the capacity of the economy. Public grumblings reached a climax with the Poznan industrial riots, in which workers conducted an illegal, general strike against the government. The grievances of the workers were numerous. They included, on the economic side, complaints of overindustrialization with lack of concern for consumer desires, increasing prices, low purchasing power, and poor living standards.

Concrete Manifestation of Reform. In October, 1956, a bloodless revolution turned out the Stalinists, and put in power the liberal Communists — led by Gomulka. They felt that they had a popular mandate

[9] Quoted in Nicolas Spulber, *The Economics of Communist Eastern Europe* (New York: John Wiley & Sons, 1957), p. 157.

[10] *Ibid.*, p. 201.

for change, and high on the agenda was economic reform. In the spring of 1957 the Economic Council's Commission on the Economic Model, under the direction of Oskar Lange, finally drew up a new set of reform Theses. Although they allowed some change, they were a compromise, and were far more conservative than the nature of the criticisms would suggest.

Nevertheless, decentralization of the economic bureaucracy was begun. The scope of the directives of the central authorities was reduced. The State Planning Commission's function became essentially one of guidance. It was deprived of its quasi-legislative and managerial functions, and relieved of its executive functions. Its staff was cut almost in half. Its previous balancing and distributing functions were parceled out among the various Ministries and independent enterprises. In addition, the activities of the Provincial People's Councils, the City Councils, and the Worker's Councils in the enterprises were greatly enhanced.

The methods of formulating plans were reviewed at the same time, and several changes worth mentioning were consequently enacted. In order to render the plans more internally consistent, econometrics was to be utilized to a far greater extent than had previously been the case. In addition, the planners made significant theoretical advances in the recognition of mathematical techniques, some small number of which were actually used in the planning process. Likewise, the planners began to do more careful price planning and cost-price calculating, although the price system still did not reflect any notion of opportunity costs.

In addition, because of the poor record of socialized farming, agriculture was de-collectivized. Private farming was considered a painful one-step backward, but necessary as a basis for going "two steps forward" in the future. Furthermore, the volume of investment was decreased, and the planned growth rate of the economy was somewhat lessened, in order to concentrate on immediate production of high quality consumer goods. Investment was also diverted from heavy industry, and increased in the light industrial and agricultural sectors. According to one Polish economist, "the new economic policy at present aims for a considerable improvement of the material situation of the people. . . ."[11] Although the central planners still barely tolerated the private sector of the economy, an increase of investment funds available to the non-socialist sector was allowed. According to another Polish economist, "Certainly socialism will not tumble down if haberdashery, carpet slippers, little screws and tubes are manufactured by private concerns."[12]

Retreat. The trend toward decentralization and reform of the Polish economy reached a peak in 1957. Thereafter, the liberalizers came under increasing attack. Due to economic slow-down, pressures from Party bureaucrats in the economic ministries, inflation, a decline in real wages, and the failure of farm production to increase markedly, many of the reforms that had been undertaken in the previous two years

[11] Kazimierz Secomski, *Premises of the Five-Year Plan in Poland* (Warsaw: Polonia Publishing House, 1958), p. 9.
[12] Quoted in *Time* (February 25, 1957), p. 31.

were attacked as right-wing deviations. Critics accused the decentralizers of loosening the bonds that held the old economic order together before they were able to revive individual initiative, and of never actually developing a real system of local or provincial autonomy. Comparative anarchy, they argued, was the end result of the powers that had been granted to the districts and the provinces.

Finally, in 1959, Gomulka himself attacked the decentralization tendencies. Decentralization, he said, had gone too far with the result that a financial breakdown was in the offing, and the coordination of plans was decreasing. Living conditions, he noted, had improved, but at the expense of other more vital considerations. Investment in the capital goods sector, he warned, was lagging dangerously. He also told the country that it would be unwise to extend these liberal economic policies any further, and that it must hold to the criteria announced in 1957. He advocated stricter financial control, widening of the role of the State Planning Commission to again include executive functions, and increased investment in the heavy industrial sector. Thus, with the loss of influence of the liberal Economic Council, and the appointment of two prominent Stalinists as deputy premiers at the end of 1959, the decentralization trend was slowly halted and even rolled back.

The 1965 Polish Reforms.[13] After the Liberman debate opened in the Soviet Union, it was natural that a new round of debate was sparked in Poland. In July, 1965 the Polish government announced their new economic "model," which is scheduled to begin operation during the years 1966 to 1970. The new system presents several characteristics that may put it ahead of the Soviet reforms, but not by as much as might have been expected after the Polish events of the 1950's.

The indicators of industrial performance are to be drastically reduced and two synthetic indicators relating to profits are to be the main determinants of the bonus payments to firm managers. The two indicators are "rentability," or the ratio of profits to the cost of output sold; and "profitability," or the ratio of profits to assets. Rentability is to be most important in almost all industries, though the Polish (as well as Western) theoretical economists would mostly prefer the profitability criterion. Nevertheless, the top manager is free to set any other bonus criteria for sectional managers and workers within the enterprise.

The financial independence of the Polish firm is to be increased by its retention of a larger portion of profits in certain "funds" earmarked for specific purposes. These purposes include research and development as well as capital repairs.

On the other hand, these funds as well as the calculations of rentability and profitability — are also to be established at the "association" level. These "associations" include several firms, and have previously acted mainly as a transmission belt for plans and directives. Now it is promised that these associations will also have more independence from

---

[13] The author's thanks go to Professor Andrzej Brzeski for a clear interpretation of the new situation, though he bears no responsibility for the presentation made here.

central control. It might be noted, though, that greater power for such regional or industrial associations would not only reduce central planners' control, but, in practice, might also reduce the firm's independence.

Poland has scheduled a complete price reform for 1967–68. After this reform, relative prices will presumably be in more rational ratios to each other, so as to make profits a more meaningful figure for either firms or "associations." In addition, under the new system interest will be charged on the assets given the firm by the central government. Thus, cost calculations will henceforth include the price of fixed capital as well as current costs.

Just as in the case of the Soviet Union, it is impossible to predict the final degree of decentralization to be achieved by these reforms. In appearance, they seem to go further than the Soviet reforms, but only practical experience will delineate their real extent. As further difficulties are encountered, Poland could conceivably recentralize. On the other hand, there is very great pressure on the Communist Party in Poland — as in all Eastern Europe, except Albania — to continue to solve all economic problems by more and more radical decentralization.

Czechoslovakia's Economic Reforms[14]

On January 30, 1965, some six months before Poland, and some ten months before the U.S.S.R., Czechoslovakia announced a very radical set of reforms. When and if completed, these reforms would put it far along the Yugoslav road to a market socialist economy, leaving behind the old methods of Soviet central planning, but supposedly avoiding some of the extremes and mistakes of the Yugoslav system. The Czechs agree that a socialist economy needs an overall economic plan stating general means and ends for a given time period, but they also believe that a market mechanism is one necessary means to achieve plan fulfillment. They note that a market mechanism has always existed to some extent in every socialist economy, with the exception of the period of war communism in the Soviet Union. While they are extending the market mechanism, they contend that the real question is how to achieve a harmony of plan and market.

They do not consider the extension of the market and the attempt to harmonize the market with the plan to be a retreat from socialism, but an improvement in the process of achieving socialist aims. After all, under the new system the profits of socialist enterprises still do not go to a private entrepreneur; they can be used only for wages to workers, reinvestment in plant facilities, or for social consumption (such as workers' cafeterias). The workers in turn may use their wage income only for the purchase of consumer goods and services, and not for investment in productive facilities such as would bring private profit, private rent, or private interest.

[14] The economic analysis of this section relies with appreciation on the interpretations given in the unpublished lecture of Dr. Bedrich Levcik delivered at the University of California, Berkeley, in 1965.

Some History of the Czech Economic Development. The interesting questions about modern Czech economic history are: (1) why is an economic reform and an extension of the importance of the market especially needed in Czechoslovakia, and (2) why has Czechoslovakia been taking steps in this direction ahead of the other socialist countries? In fact, their practical reforms were initiated before the other countries, though the economic discussion in Czechoslovakia began later than the others, that is, in 1962 and 1963.

The Czech explanation begins with the point that rigid central planning did chalk up some achievements during the 1950's and early 1960's. The Czech national income in constant prices did increase at an annual compound rate of 7.4 percent in the period of 1948 through 1962. This era showed a vast increase of personal consumption, and even more striking advances in culture and education, in the free health service, and in a full-coverage social security scheme. As a result, Czechoslovakia continues to rank higher than any of the other socialist countries (except, perhaps, East Germany) in its average standard of living, and approaches or surpasses the Western European standard of living for its working class.

In 1963, however, Czechoslovakia was shocked to find that its centrally planned economy suffered an actual decline in industrial output and national income, which was the first time this had occurred in any Communist-run Eastern European economy in peacetime. Czech official data for 1963 reveal a half-percent decline in industrial output and a 2.2 percent decline in all national income produced. That decline pulled down the growth rate for the whole 1961–1965 period to a mere 1.9 percent a year, in spite of a recovery and rapid improvement in 1964 and 1965.[15] On the basis of this shock, an intensive debate raged for some years.

Czech economists now believe that the system of central planning, which had previously suited their needs fairly well, is definitely outmoded and a hindrance to further development. They point out that central planning was initiated at a period in Soviet development when the Soviet Union had large reserves of unused manpower, and when its economic backwardness called for the achievement of certain production targets *at any cost.* They argue that in 1950, when central economic planning became the general rule, Czechoslovakia similarly had unemployed manpower and unutilized output capacity.

In the 1960's, however, the Czech economists claim that Czechoslovakia is in a period of scarce resources and scarce manpower, which demands the utmost efficiency in their use. They add that this is especially true because of the increased burden of foreign aid to underdeveloped countries. The Czechs also point out that Czechoslovakia is the least backward and most industrialized of all the socialist countries.

[15] United Nations Economic Commission for Europe, *Economic Survey of Europe in 1965* (New York: United Nations, 1966), pp. 2–6.

Therefore, they believe that its higher degree of complexity and inter-relationship among industries especially makes detailed central planning impossible, and necessitates much use of the market. For example, it is asserted that a market mechanism would dictate that the Czech economy concentrate on its advantageous position in producing high *quality* steels, rather than the vast and costly production of the large quantity of all kinds of steel emphasized by central planning.

Perhaps the most serious misallocation problem of all was the attempt to invest in too many new projects at once. Shortages of all kinds of capital goods and raw materials led to hundreds of major unfinished projects. Statistically, this showed up in a vast lowering of the ratio of output per unit of capital employed. It also meant vast imbalance when the planned projects were not completed and did not produce their planned output.[16] These investment mistakes were largely due to lack of an interest rate as well as all the other problems of central planning enumerated earlier.

The Czech economists further argue that Czechoslovakia is coming to have such a wide variety of consumer goods that central planning is unable to achieve correct allocation of resources among all of these goods. Finally, it is argued that Czechoslovakia is highly dependent on foreign trade and so *must* increase its efficiency and the quality of its goods in order to procure the best terms of trade.

The more general ideological argument for a radical change in economic thinking is presented by the initiator of the Czech reforms, Ota Sik, who contends:

> Until recently, the connection between planning and the market was incorrectly understood and the concept of the market was applied to the socialist economy in a sort of shamefaced way. It was held, wrongly, that planned social coordination, planned management of production, was the absolute antipode of orientation on the market, of utilizing market levers . . . These tenacious theoretical premises brought much harm; because of them a system of planning and management was adhered to which meant that production could not be adequately geared to its proper aim . . . and consumers could not exert any direct influence on the producers. . . . Socialist planned production should consistently seek to satisfy market demand.[17]

In 1968 the struggle for reform spread over into the political arena. In January, a palace revolution ousted the old Stalinist leadership and substituted an extremely liberal or progressive faction of the Communist Party. The new progressive leadership, under Alexander Dubchek, allowed an extensive area of freedom of the press and instituted several new avenues of democratic participation in the political process. The political fight was apparently set off in part by the conflict over the

[16] See, e.g., Josef Goldman and J. Flek, "Economic Growth in Czechoslovakia," *Economics of Planning*, Vol. 6, No. 2 (1966), p. 125–137.

[17] Ota Sik, Czech economist, translated in *World Marxist Review*, Vol. 8 (March, 1965), p. 18.

economic reforms, since the old leadership was dragging its feet in implementing the economic reforms. As a result, it was expected the large-scale political reforms would speed up and widen the scope of the economic reforms.

In August 1968 all of the hopes and dreams of the Czechs were crushed by Soviet tanks. The Soviet invasion spelled a tragic end to this promising experiment in establishing an efficient and democratic system of socialism. The harshest restrictions, however, fell in the political sphere, including the exile of some of the leading political and economic reformers, including Ota Sik. At the time of this writing, it is not yet clear to what extent the economic reforms will be held back. Therefore, the following section on the details of the economic reforms — which was written before the Soviet invasion, has been left unchanged.

Details of the Czech Economic Reforms. Until the reforms, except for a very half-hearted decentralization experiment in 1961, the old-style Soviet kind of detailed central planning system was in full force in Czechoslovakia. Now, each enterprise determines its own current production plans on the basis of market conditions. The central plan is limited to the setting of a few aggregate proportions for the whole economy. The enterprise receives all of its income from sales, no longer eligible for government subsidies. From its total sales or revenue of any kind, it must first pay the cost of services and materials obtained from other industries. Second, it must pay a fixed rate of interest on the capital assets given it originally by the central government. Third, it must repay the principal and pay interest on any further loans. Then it must pay a fixed percentage of its profits in the form of a tax into the government budget. Finally, the enterprise must finance its own new investment. After these deductions, it has left under the management's control a "fund for remuneration" which it uses for (a) the payment of basic minimum wages and (b) the payment of all sorts of bonuses to managers and workers as the enterprise may decide.

This reform, which allows sizeable bonuses based upon profits and productivity, is especially important for Czechoslovakia. In addition to central planning, Czechoslovakia had an extremely narrow range of wages, regardless of skills or productivity. This greatly discouraged workers or foremen or even managers from exerting very much energy to increase production. Even under the new system, the bonuses paid by profitable plants cannot be more than 20 percent of wages. Moreover, wages in unprofitable plants cannot fall below 92 percent of the pre-reform level. Thus, Czechoslovakia will still continue to have more wage equality than any other country, except possibly China.

If the management is to produce an optimal product mix in the most efficient manner, price-setting will be crucial to the operation of this system. Whether to produce apples or oranges, whether to use coal or gas, is clearly based upon the relative price of the commodities. The Czechs are using three types of price systems. The first type of price-system uses *fixed* prices for a limited number of basic commodities, including some raw materials and some consumer good necessities. These few prices are centrally set and changed from time to time according to the central view of supply and demand conditions. By this means, the Czechs hope to avoid undue price-raising by monopoly enterprises.

The second price system involves central government setting of min-imum price *limits* for a large number of fairly standardized goods. Thus, in this group the enterprises are allowed some flexibility, but within centrally set limits. Special leeway is given to enterprises in setting prices for new and improved products.

Finally, the largest group of prices will eventually be the completely *unplanned* prices, set solely by the enterprises according to the supply and demand of firms and consumers. By the end of 1967, however, these unplanned prices were still only 5 to 10 percent of the total.

The central economic planners are thus left free from detailed day to day enterprise decisions and can concentrate on long-range macro-economic planning. The central plan is intended to assure a high rate of economic growth as well as the most important balances between ag-gregate supply and demand for all commodities and services, including the balance of international trade payments. In order to achieve these goals, the central plan can use not only the usual fiscal and monetary tools of capitalist countries, *but also continues to have the most impor-tant direct economic levers in its own hands.* Namely, it uses taxes to retain control over a large amount of resources for allocation in the most important new investment projects; so the central plan continues to al-locate about 60 percent of new investment, and the enterprises about 40 percent. Nevertheless, even central investments are supposed to be based on proposals initiated by the firms and implemented by the firms. The central plan also continues to set the educational quotas for students in different fields to ensure the correct number of skilled and profes-sional workers for each category.

East German Economic Reforms

East Germany not only began to discuss reform proposals very intensively as early as 1962, but also declared the establishment of a completely reformed "New Economic System of Planning and Lead-ing" as early as 1963. The most essential part of this new system was a shift in responsibility for planning and the execution of the plans from central planning agencies to a new intermediate organ known as the Association of State Owned Enterprises. All production was divided into approximately eight such Associations, each consisting of a large group of enterprises in the same industry group.

The Associations not only act as a conveyor belt for ideas upward from the enterprise and directives downward from the central planners, but themselves undertake a considerable new sphere of action. They concentrate especially on the execution of their part of the plan, the allocation of labor within their area of jurisdiction, the introduction of new technology in all of their plants, and the vital function of distribut-ing the profits among their plants. In order to make the profit calcula-tions more meaningful, there has also been instituted a large-scale price reform to establish rational prices of inputs and outputs, as well as a very thorough cost accounting system. Thus, prices have been revised especially in raw materials, an interest rate is charged on the fixed capital of enterprises (in the form of a "tax" on their initial "production-fund"), and a system of differential rents for land has been established according to differences in fertility, climate, and other conditions.

Of course, the decentralization to the Association level still leaves a highly centralized planning mechanism, and for the most part merely changes the locus of bureaucratic planning. The introduction of the Associations as autonomous entities is also not very different from the similar establishment of Associations in Poland. In neither country does this grouping amount to real economic decentralization, that is, the giving of decision-making power to the enterprise. Until 1965 the reforms were implemented only very slowly and in small doses. Only then was there some further increase in the powers of the enterprise as well as the Associations, between which the struggle for control is not yet settled.

In addition to the decentralization of planning down to the Association level and the prices reforms, East Germany introduced Liberman-type reforms in 1965. Under these reforms, managers are paid bonuses primarily according to the success of the enterprise in profit-making. Furthermore, retained profits are the sole source for large bonuses and highly differentiated wages for workers.

A Western reporter[18] interviewed the director of an East German manufacturing Association, and observed:

> . . . Within limits set by the national economic plan, he can hire and fire, shift labor from one plant to another, borrow money (at interest), allocate investment capital from earnings, distribute profits to himself and to other members of the concern, and deal directly with foreign and domestic customers — all without passing through a single ministerial anteroom . . . directors must, however, submit their production plans to one of the nine newly re-established industrial ministries in East Berlin, which also exercise ultimate financial control. The East German economy is still centrally planned. But, as . . . [this director] says, "If your plants make profits, you don't see the planning people for long stretches. They don't come around here very often, I can assure you."[19]

The same Western reporter claims[20] that these new industrial executives have the youngest average age in the world; and are instructed to be "business-like," "creative," and to think for themselves! This is surely a radical departure for formerly Stalinist East Germany, but it accurately reflects the new atmosphere in most of Eastern Europe. More concretely, in order to ensure popular backing, the East German workweek was reduced in 1966 from 48 to 44 hours, while the flow of consumer

[18] Welles Hangen, *The Muted Revolution: East Germany's Challenge to Russia and the West* (New York: Alfred Knopf, 1966), pp. 85–86.
[19] *Ibid.*
[20] *Ibid.*, p. 98.

goods has been considerably increased.[21] After a slowdown in 1963, its 1964 and 1965 industrial growth rates reached a respectable 6 to 7 percent (in official data).

Hungarian Economic Reforms

Hungary has progressed rapidly in the direction of more mathematical calculation of central plans. It has made a wide use of input-output methods and has begun to introduce linear programming wherever possible. In addition, for a short time after the Hungarian Revolution of 1956, it introduced a type of Workers' Council authority in local factories. This local authority, however, was drastically reduced in scope as soon as the revolution receded, and local initiative was again superseded by central planning. Hungary now is beginning again to institute extensive decentralization reforms, but at a very slow pace, to be completed in 1969. These reforms follow the Czech model for the most part, but actually go further than the Czechs with regard to decentralization of investment and in several other important economic respects (though Czechoslovakia has now gone much further with political reform). One U.S. writer,[22] who has carefully compared all of the Eastern European economic reforms, characterizes the Hungarian as "the most daring" of all of them.

The Hungarians advance the familiar argument that the increasing complexity of their economy makes necessary a further economic decentralization.[23] They add that consumers are becoming more selective, and now reject low-quality goods or unwanted substitutes. The Hungarians also contend that their low population growth and full employment make even more important the most economic use of available labor. They emphasize, finally, that they need decentralization in order to improve quality as well as output mix, especially in connection with the international trade of their enterprises. International trade is vital because Hungary's trade dealings, its exports plus its imports, constitute 35 percent of its national product. Hungarian economists[24] predict that in a few years there will be no more physical targets given to enterprises at all, though the market mechanism will still be complemented by central planning of most investment.

The Hungarian reform proposals reject Workers' Councils and continue to rely on directors who represent the central government. They argue that it is more democratic for the enterprises to be controlled by a central government (elected by all the people) than by local workers'

[21] Ibid., p. 90.

[22] Gregory Grossman, "Economic Reform: A Balance Sheet," reprinted in Committee on Banking and Currency, U.S. House of Representatives, The Fiat-Soviet Auto Plant and Communist Economic Reforms (Washington, D.C.: U.S. Government Printing Office, 1967), p. 60.

[23] See, e.g., R. Nyers, "The Comprehensive Reform of Managing the National Economy in Hungary," Acta Oeconomica, Vol. 1 (1966, published in English by Hungarian Academy of Sciences), pp. 19–37.

[24] E.g., ibid., pp. 20–21.

councils:[25] The goal of the enterprise is to maximize its profit rate on assets; the bonus of the manager (and the workers to some extent) is based on this profit rate. In this way it is hoped to "replace administrative by economic" controls; and to get the enterprises to meet their consumer demands to the best of their ability out of their own economic self-interest.

As in Czechoslovakia, the Hungarians have three groups of prices. The first group, basic raw materials and consumer necessities, continue to have centrally-set prices. The second group of especially important goods, including all monopolized goods, have only a maximum price set centrally. The third group, comprising all other commodities, have prices set solely by the competition of enterprises. Eventually, it is hoped to move more and more goods into the third category. As in all the countries now decentralizing, it is recognized that the price reform is a crucial condition of success. If the new price structure does not adequately reflect demand preferences as well as realistic supply costs, then the now independent decisions of the individual plant managers will lead them far astray.

Enterprises now determine all replacement and modernization investment. Central investment is concentrated mainly on infra-structural needs (such as transportation and communication) and public utilities. The central government continues to finance some part of the investment in new projects, and some part of the investment in expansion of existing enterprises, but the enterprises now do a large part of even this new net investment. In sum, it was announced in January, 1967 that 55 to 67 percent of all investment will be decentralized under the new plan.

There will no longer be targets of any kind fixed for collective farms. Their prices, outputs, and day-to-day operations will be guided only by economic levers with *no* administrative interference. They will finance most of their own investment from internal funds or from bank credit.

Finally, Hungary will move toward less equality of income, and toward assigning more importance to bonuses and differential wages. In the past, it is contended,[26] there was little incentive because incomes from different jobs and different levels of accomplishment were much too nearly equal.

Bulgarian Economic Reforms

In spite of a rather underdeveloped economy, Bulgaria has taken astonishingly rapid steps toward economic decentralization. In 1965, they instituted experiments in a very large number of factories of an extreme Liberman-type, with sole power for the manager to make many kinds of decisions, including many investment decisions. The degree of decentralization is much less than in the radical Czech and

---

[25] *Ibid.*, p. 23.
[26] *Ibid.*, pp. 36–37.

Hungarian reforms, but so far compares closely with the East German steps actually taken.[27]

Situation in Rumania

Rumania has proceeded very far in the direction of economic independence from the Soviet Union and the building of a self-sufficient economic base. Nevertheless, it appears that so far Rumania has retained strict centralized economic planning.

The Albanian View

Albania bases itself on the support received in materials and in ideology from China. It shares a very dim view of the current economic reforms in most of Eastern Europe, and condemns them as steps back toward capitalism. It has no intention of following this reform road — though there are reports of some small steps toward rationalization and decentralization of some administrative planning tasks.

Summary of Eastern European Reforms

It may be useful at this point to review very briefly the status of decentralization reform in all of the Eastern European economies. Reference is made here only to the three main dimensions of possible decentralization: short-run operational decisions, price setting, and investment planning.

Short-Run Operational Decisions. Short-run operational decisions include the choice of the current output mix and the choice of technology within the limits of presently available labor, capital, and raw materials. In Albania and Rumania these decisions are still made in very great detail at the central planning or intermediate level — with minimal decisions left to the enterprise, and bonuses based on meeting or overfulfilling output targets. In the Soviet Union and Poland there is still central planning of the major output decisions, but the current reforms give the enterprise manager a fairly wide range of choice in their implementation. The manager's bonus depends to a significant extent on a measure of profitability, and he can maneuver both the output and the input mixes to a considerable degree in accord with his view of the most profitable choice.

Bulgaria and East Germany also continue central planning of total amounts of each product, but the director is free to produce those outputs in any way he sees fit. Almost his sole criterion is profitability, though he must submit his production plans in advance to ensure some conformity to the national goals. Czechoslovakia and Hungary will go much further when the new reforms are complete. They intend to limit the national economic plan only to aggregate ratios, such as the ratio of investment to consumption, leaving all planning of current output mixes and technological choices to the enterprise manager. Enterprises can buy and sell as they will, while the manager is judged on how well he maximizes the enterprise profit.

[27] See Grossman, "Economic Reforms," *op. cit.*, p. 62.

Finally, Yugoslavia's national plan does not pretend to be a command, but only a guideline. Enterprises can make any kind of output and input decisions they wish, being limited only by general government fiscal and monetary controls, in addition to anti-trust legislation. Furthermore, Yugoslav enterprises are not directed by government-appointed managers, but rather by managers appointed and controlled (in theory, at least) by Workers' Councils.

Price Setting. In Albania and Rumania prices continue to be set by central authorities, while planning at all levels continues to be primarily in physical terms, with prices relegated to a very subordinate position. In the Soviet Union, Poland, Bulgaria, and East Germany price-setting also continues largely a function of central authorities. Yet relative prices are recognized in these countries as vital to both central planning decisions and managers' decisions — especially in Bulgaria and East Germany where the manager's range of choice is so wide. In all of these four countries, therefore, price reforms are under way to attempt to produce more rational prices. And in all four, voices are heard demanding far more decentralization of price-setting.

In Hungary and Czechoslovakia all prices have been revised into three groups. Some basic goods are still centrally priced; a second group of goods are priced by enterprises within centrally set limits; and many less important goods now have their prices set by the enterprise alone.

Finally, Yugoslav enterprises are supposed to be free to set any prices they wish within the limits of the competitive market for their goods. The latest available report, however, states that there is still in existence a "temporary" price control over 80 or 90 percent of all goods. This means that a government agency can veto or prohibit any price changes on these goods initiated by the enterprises.

Investment Planning. The third and last dimension of decentralization reform is the planning of investment or the long-run expansion of capacity to produce. Once again, in Albania and Rumania investment is almost all centrally planned. In this dimension, however, the rest of Eastern Europe is also reluctant to decentralize control to the enterprise level. In most of these countries, direction of investment remains the most vital lever of central planning to control their long-run economic evolution. Furthermore, it is argued that most important investment involves fairly large quantities of capital, so that it must continue quite centralized in practice. It is also maintained that new planning methods are quite sufficient to allocate it rationally, especially in an environment of decentralized and competitive current output and price decisions.

Under the reforms, the Soviet Union, Poland, and Bulgaria allow enterprises to invest from 14 to 20 percent of capital. Yet even that is considered a radical innovation, and is unlikely to be increased very soon. East Germany has apparently decentralized almost all investment to the Association level, but little or none to the enterprise level.

Even Czechoslovakia has decentralized only about 40 percent of investment, though enterprises are supposed to "suggest" or "initiate" all investment. Hungary, however, has announced that it will decentralize 55 to 65 percent of all investment under the reformed system. Finally, Yugoslavia claims that under its latest reforms almost all investment will be decentralized to enterprises. The important practical question in Yugoslavia, however, is the financing of the investment. Very little of the capital as yet comes from enterprise reinvestment; most of it comes from the banks. Whoever provides the capital really controls the investment pattern, but the Yugoslav enterprises are in turn *supposed* to predominate in the control of the banks. Only experience under the new systems will show in practice how real is the degree of decentralization of investment in Yugoslavia, Hungary, and Czechoslovakia.

Growth and Performance of Eastern Europe

A summary of the growth and performance of each of the Eastern European planned economies is limited here to the discussion of a few aggregate facts. Table 14–1 compares official growth rates with those estimated by the most comprehensive U,S. study. Albania and Yugoslavia are not included in this table, Albania because the U.S. study does not yet claim reliable data on it, Yugoslavia because it can no longer be called centrally planned. Albania and Yugoslavia are each separately discussed below.

The choice between the official Eastern European estimate, which shows an average rate of growth of 7.5 percent a year, and the U.S. estimate by Ernst, which shows an average rate of growth of only 5.1 percent

---

Table 14–1

Annual Average Growth Rates of Gross National
Product in Eastern Europe, 1950–1964

Country	Official Data on GNP Growth Rate for Each Country	U.S. Estimate of each Country's GNP Growth Rate
Bulgaria	8.7	5.9
Czechoslovakia	6.2	4.0
East Germany	6.1	5.1
Hungary	6.7	4.8
Poland	7.3	4.9
Rumania	9.7	5.7
Average	7.5	5.1

Sources and Notes: Official data are most conveniently found in United Nations Economic Commission for Europe, *Economic Survey of Europe,* annual issues for 1947 through 1965 (New York: United Nations, 1948–1966). The official data all record the Marxist definition of national income or national product, which differs in many respects from the Western concept of GNP. The U.S. estimates are by Maurice Ernst, "Postwar Economic Growth in Eastern Europe," in U.S. Congress, Joint Economic Committee, *New Directions in the Soviet Economy* (Washington, D.C.: U.S. Government Printing Office, 1966), pp. 873–916. Ernst adjusts official data himself and also relies on the publications of the Alton Project or "Research Project on National Income in East-Central Europe" at Columbia University.

a year, depends on one's evaluation of all the statistical problems listed in the Appendix to Chapter 5 — which need not be repeated here. In fact, Ernst also presents a weighted average for all of Eastern Europe of only 4.9 percent growth of Gross National Product a year (weighted by the estimated value of GNP in each of the countries).

If Albania is added to the Eastern European countries, with its officially reported 8.8 percent rate of growth of national income for the same period, this would somewhat raise the Eastern European average. Albania falls among the less developed East European economies, along with Bulgaria and Rumania, whose officially recorded growth rates of national product were 8.7 and 9.7 percent a year. On the other hand, the two most developed, Czechoslovakia and East Germany, officially claimed rates of only 6.2 and 6.1 percent a year. One should not, however, necessarily attribute the differences mainly to the level of development, since many other factors played a role.

How do the growth rates of the centrally planned Eastern European economies compare with other economies. First, the growth rate of Soviet national product was discussed in Chapter 5: for the period 1950 through 1963, its official claim was 8.8 percent a year, against a U.S. estimate of 5.8 percent. Since 1964 was a very good year for the Soviet Union, its record for the 1950–1964 period was clearly above the Eastern European average, and in the same range as Bulgaria and Rumania. Second, it may be useful to recall from the same chapter that the U.S. official claim for the rate of growth of GNP in the United States was only 3.5 percent a year for the 1950–1963 period, or considerably below the long-run Eastern European average. Third, it might be recalled from the section on Yugoslavia that its unique system of market socialism witnessed an officially claimed growth rate of national product of 9.4 percent a year in the period 1954 through 1964.

The study by Ernst also compares the planned Eastern European economies with the mainly private enterprise economies of Western Europe.[28] He finds that the average growth rate of GNP in nine selected Western European countries in the period 1950 through 1964 was 5.0 percent a year (or 5.4 percent in the weighted average). The nine countries are Austria, Belgium, Denmark, France, West Germany, Greece, Italy, Netherlands, and Norway. There is no question that these Western European countries had very high growth rates in this period (much above the U.S. rate), but whether their average was as high as the Eastern European average clearly rests on some very controversial statistical determinations. Among major developed private enterprise economies, one should also mention the very low growth rate (much below the U.S. rate) of the "old" and ailing economy of the United Kingdom; but also the very high growth rate of Japan in this period (well above the Soviet rate).

Returning to the six centrally planned Eastern European economies listed in Table 14–1, a more detailed examination of growth rates reveals some interesting facts, similar to Soviet phenomena. These tend-

[28] Ernst, *op. cit.*, p. 880.

encies are immediately obvious when the growth rate averages are broken down by time period and economic sector. First, both the official data and U.S. estimates agree that Eastern European growth rates suffered a decline in the early 1960's. Thus, Ernst finds a decline in his weighted average annual growth rate of Eastern European GNP from 5.7 percent in 1950–1955 to 5.2 percent in 1955–1960 to 3.6 percent in 1960–1964.[29]

Second, the official data and U.S. estimates both agree that Eastern European industry is comparatively very rapid in growth, while Eastern European agriculture is comparatively very slow in growth. Thus, Ernst finds that the average Eastern European industrial growth rate for the period 1950 through 1964 is 8.0 percent a year, or considerably higher than his estimate of 6.1 percent a year for Western Europe. Even using his weighted averages for the same period, Ernst finds Eastern European industry growing 7.6 percent a year while Western European industry grows at the slightly lower rate of 6.8 percent a year. Official Eastern European data show *much* higher industrial rates and, of course, make the contrast far more striking.

In agriculture, however, even the Eastern European regimes do not claim rapid advances. In this sector, Ernst's very conservative U.S. estimate puts the (unweighted) average rate of growth of Eastern European agriculture at only 1.8 percent a year from 1950–1953 to 1960–1963. This compares with an (unweighted) average growth rate of Western European agriculture of 2.1 percent a year from 1950–1953 to 1960–1963.

Finally, Ernst measures the productivity of capital in Eastern Europe versus the productivity of capital in Western Europe. This measure depends on the growth of output, which was just discussed, and the growth of capital stock, to which the analysis must now turn for a brief look. Table 14–2 shows the percentage of national product going into investment in each country.

This table shows a steadily rising percentage of investment to national product in every European country studied from 1950 to 1963. There is a wide range in the ratio from the low of 14.5 percent in East Germany in 1950–1954 to the high of 41.5 percent in Bulgaria in 1960–1963. Yet most of the ratios are generally in the 20 to 30 percent range. If this U.S. study is correct, then it is also generally the case that Eastern European investment ratios are above Western European. On the average for the whole period 1950 to 1963 (giving equal weight to each country and each year), this study finds that the ratio of gross fixed investment to GNP was 25.0 percent in the five selected Eastern European countries, against 21.3 percent in the eight selected Western European countries.

The reader may recall here that the growth rate equals by definition the marginal output-capital ratio times the investment ratio. Thus, if a country has a growth rate of 5 percent a year and its investment from GNP is 25 percent, its marginal output-capital ratio *must* be 20 per-

[29] *Ibid.*, p. 880.

Table 14–2

Gross Fixed Investment in Eastern and Western Europe
(as percent of GNP)

Country	1950–54	1955–59	1960–63
Bulgaria	23.7	27.7	41.5
Czechoslovakia	23.5	27.3	27.7
East Germany	14.5	19.4	23.6
Hungary	25.9	24.2	27.2
Poland	21.1	25.1	28.1
Eastern Europe *Average*	21.7	24.7	29.6
Austria	20.1	23.1	24.1
Belgium	no data	17.1	19.1
Denmark	17.2	18.6	22.5
France	18.1	20.3	21.7
West Germany	21.1	24.3	26.4
Greece	15.9	19.2	28.9
Italy	19.7	22.4	25.6
Netherlands	21.5	24.4	24.7
Western Europe *Average*	19.1	21.2	24.1

Source: Maurice Ernst, "Postwar Economic Growth in Eastern Europe," in U.S. Congress, Joint Economic Committee, *New Directions in the Soviet Economy* (Washington, D.C.: U.S. Government Printing Office, 1966), p. 890.

cent (because .05/.25 = .20). A marginal output-capital ratio of 20 percent means that five units of capital invested will increase output by one unit a year.

If Eastern Europe had growth rates no higher than Western Europe, while its investment ratio was higher, then its marginal output-capital ratio must be lower. In fact, Ernst found, as shown above, that Eastern European growth rates of GNP were not higher, but lower than Western European rates; so his figures must show a lower marginal GNP per unit of capital invested. More precisely, in the averages discussed here, Western European GNP weighted average growth rates were given by Ernst for the years 1950–1964 as 5.4 percent, and their investment ratio average (for 1950–1963) as 21.3 percent, so their marginal output-capital ratio must have been 25.4 percent. For Eastern Europe, in the same years he gives the weighted average growth rate as only 4.9 percent, and the investment ratio as 25.0 percent, so their marginal output-capital ratio must have been only 19.6 percent. This is a significant difference in productivity, though the difference would be much less using his unweighted averages.

On the other hand, it was observed that official Eastern European data placed their (unweighted) average growth rate at 7.5 percent. With an investment ratio of 25.0 percent, this implies a marginal output-capital ratio of 30 percent — or well above the Western European marginal output-capital ratio. Thus, as is usual in comparative economics, it can only be concluded that the result depends on whose figures are accepted. According to the pessimistic U.S. estimate of Eastern European growth rates, their marginal product per unit of capital was lower than the Western European — while according to the optimistic official data on Eastern European growth rates, their marginal product per unit of capital was higher than the Western European.[30]

SELECTED REFERENCES

On Yugoslavia

1. J. Marcus Fleming and Viktor R. Sertic, "The Yugoslav Economic System," *International Monetary Fund Staff Papers*, Vol. 9 (July 1962), pp. 202–223 (this article is a good general introduction).

2. Fred W. Neal and G. W. Hoffman, *Yugoslavia: The New Communism*, Twentieth Century Fund (New York: 1962).

3. Albert Waterson, *Planning in Yugoslavia: Organization and Implementation* (Washington: Economic Development Institute, International Bank for Reconstruction and Development, 1960). More recent is Svetozar Pejovich, *The Market-Planned Economy of Yugoslavia* (Minneapolis: University of Minnesota Press, 1966).

4. Rudolf Bićanić, "Economic Growth Under Centralized and Decentralized Planning in Yugoslavia: A Case Study," *Economic Development and Cultural Change*, VII, 1 (October 1957), pp. 63–74.

5. Wolfgang Friedmann, "Freedom and Planning in Yugoslavia's Economic System," *Slavic Review*, Vol. 25 (December, 1966), p. 639.

6. Radmila Stojanovic, editor, *Yugoslav Economists on Problems of a Socialist Economy* (New York: International Arts and Sciences Press, translated 1964).

7. Jaroslav Vanek, "Yugoslav Economic Growth and Its Conditions," *American Economic Review*, Vol. 53, No. 2 (1963), pp. 555–561.

8. M. Vućković, "The Recent Development of the Money and Banking System of Yugoslavia," *Journal of Political Economy*, Vol. 71, No. 4 (1963), pp. 363–377.

9. Benjamin Ward, "The Firm in Illyria: Market Syndicalism," *American Economic Review*, LXVI (September, 1958), pp. 566–589.

10. Benjamin Ward, "Workers' Management in Yugoslavia," *Journal of Political Economy*, LXV (October 1957), pp. 373–386. Also see B. Ward, "Political Power and Economic Change in Yugoslavia," *American Economic Review*, Vol. 58 (May, 1968), pp. 568–579.

11. B. Horvat and V. Rascovic, "Workers' Management in Yugoslavia," *Journal of Political Economy*, Vol. 67 (April 1959), pp. 194–198.

On Poland

1. Thad Paul Alton, *Polish Postwar Economy*, Columbia University Press (New York: 1955).

[30] The reader may decide which estimate is more probable after reviewing the list of problems of statistical comparison in the Appendix to Chapter 5.

2. John Kenneth Galbraith, *Journey to Poland and Yugoslavia* (Cambridge: Harvard University Press, 1958).

3. John Michael Montias, *Central Planning in Poland* (New Haven and London: Yale University Press, 1962).

4. Nicolas Spulber, *The Economics of Communist Eastern Europe* (New York: The Technology Press of MIT and John Wiley & Sons, Inc., 1957).

5. A. Erlich, "The Polish Economy after October 1956," *American Economic Review* (May, 1959).

6. John Michael Montias, "Unbinding the Polish Economy," *Foreign Affairs* (April, 1957).

7. Leon Smolinski, "Reform in Poland," *Problems of Communism* (July–August, 1966).

On Czechoslovakia

1. Alfred Zauberman, *Industrial Progress in Poland, Czechoslovakia and East Germany, 1937–1962* (Oxford University Press, 1964).

2. Jan M. Michal, *Central Planning in Czechoslovakia* (Stanford: Stanford University Press, 1960).

3. George J. Staller, "Czechoslovakia: The New Model of Planning and Management," *American Economic Review*, Vol. 58 (May, 1968), pp. 559–567.

4. Harry G. Shaffer, "Czechoslovakia's New Economic Model: Out of Stalinism," reprinted in Shanti S. Tangri, editor, *Command Versus Demand* (Boston: D. C. Heath and Co., 1967).

5. Vaclav Holesovsky, "Planning Reforms in Czechoslovakia," *Soviet Studies*, Vol. 19 (April, 1968), pp. 544–556.

6. Lida Urbanek, "Some Difficulties in Implementing the Economic Reforms in Czechoslovakia," *Soviet Studies*, Vol. 19 (April, 1968), pp. 557–566.

7. The official Draft Principles of the new reforms and several comments by Czech economists fill an entire issue of *Eastern European Economics*, Vol. 3 (Summer 1965), a very useful journal of translations from original sources, published by International Arts and Sciences Press, in White Plains, New York. A passionate defense of the reforms is made by its initiator, Ota Sik, "Czechoslovakia's New System," *Eastern European Economics*, Vol. 4 (Fall 1965), pp. 3–12.

8. One may also consult various issues of a journal published by the Czechs in English, *Czechoslovak Economic Papers*, edited by Bedrich Levcik, published by Publishing House of the Czechoslovak Academy of Sciences, in Prague.

On East Germany

1. Welles Hangen, *The Muted Revolution: East Germany's Challenge to Russia and the West* (New York: Alfred Knopf, 1966).

2. Wolfgang R. Stolper, *The Structure of the East German Economy* (Cambridge, Massachusetts: Harvard University Press, 1960).

3. Evelyn Anderson, "East Germany," *Survey: A Journal of Soviet and East European Studies*, No. 42 (June 1962).

4. Dorothy Miller and Harry G. Trend, "Economic Reforms in East Germany," *Problems of Communism* (March–April 1966).

5. Hans Boehme, "East German Price Formation under the New Economic System," *Soviet Studies*, Vol. 19 (January, 1968), pp. 340–358.

6. Some of the literature from East Germany has been translated in articles in the *Journal of Eastern European Economics*, Vol. 3, No. 2 (Winter 1965), entire issue; and also three articles in *Eastern European Economics*, Vol. 3, No. 3 (Spring 1965). Especially important is the article "Directives for the New Economic System of Planning and Managing the Economy," translated in *Eastern European Economics*, Vol. 3, No. 3 (Spring 1965), pp. 3–27.

On Hungary

1. There is an excellent issue of the journal, *Economics of Planning*, entirely devoted to Hungarian methods of planning written by Hungarian economists, *Economy of Planning*, Vol. 5, No. 3 (1965), entire issue.

2. A monograph by the Hungarian economist, Janos Timar, "Planning the Labor Force in Hungary," with an introduction by Lynn Turgeon, in *Eastern European Economics*, Vol. 4, Nos. 2 and 3 (Winter–Spring 1966), entire two issues.

3. There is also a new Hungarian quarterly journal written in English, called *Acta Oeconomica*, published by the Hungarian Academy of Sciences. The first volume of this journal contains one especially relevant article by R. Nyers, "The Comprehensive Reform of Managing the National Economy in Hungary," pp. 19–37.

On Bulgaria

1. The background of the Bulgarian economy is outlined by Bulgarian economists in *Eastern European Economics*, Vol. 3, No. 3 (Spring 1965).

2. A further discussion by Bulgarian economists may be found in some articles in *Eastern European Economics*, Vol. 3, No. 3 (Spring 1965).

3. A Western view is in J. F. Brown, "Reforms in Bulgaria," *Problems of Communism* (May–June, 1966).

On Rumania

For references on Rumania, see Chapter 11.

Summary on all Eastern European Reforms

1. Michael Garmarnikow, *Economic Reforms in Eastern Europe* (Detroit: Wayne State University Press, 1968).

2. Articles on reforms in particular countries and all of Eastern Europe in George R. Feiwel, ed., *New Currents in Soviet-type Economics: A Reader* (Scranton: International Textbook Co., 1968), pp. 405–629.

15

CENTRAL PLANNING VERSUS
DECENTRALIZED SOCIALISM

This final chapter begins the difficult job of comparison of the advantages and disadvantages of centralized socialism versus decentralized socialism, with brief references to private enterprise systems as another point of comparison. After investigating these differences one by one in terms of the basic criteria for comparison, it ends with a final section speculating on the possible convergence of central planning and decentralization.

Criteria for Comparison

In this book the main criterion for comparing centrally planned socialism with decentralized socialism will be, of course, an economic one. Which type of system has performed better and which may be expected to perform better in the future? Economic performance may best be indicated by the rate of economic growth, though the growth in output of consumer goods alone is more relevant to individual welfare. But then all other economic problems will be found to impinge upon and determine the rate of growth. Schematically, one may think of the rate of economic growth as being equal to the ratio of investment to output multiplied by the ratio of increased output from that investment. The factors in this scheme can then be listed one by one. First, we must examine the ratio of increased saving out of increased income, usually called the marginal propensity to save. Second, there is the question of whether all saving is in fact invested, that is, the question of the full use of capacity and, indirectly, the full employment of labor. Third, the analysis must consider the ratio of increased production to net investment.

351

This last ratio of marginal product to investment in turn depends upon (a) static efficiency or efficiency at a given time, and (b) technological improvements.

A further consideration in evaluating each economic system is the equity of its income distribution; that is to say, it is necessary to examine not only how big the pie is, but also how it is cut. In addition to the economic criteria, this comparison considers briefly what effect the different economic systems may have on political life, that is, which system is more conducive to political democracy and which is more conducive to political dictatorship. Finally, the analysis considers very briefly the effect of different economic systems upon the cultural and psychological behavior of society and the individuals in the society.

Growth and the Saving Ratio

If it is assumed that the economy is working as efficiently as possible, has a given rate of technological change, and is at full employment, then the sole determinant of the rate of economic growth could be considered to be the increment in saving each year. In a private enterprise economy, such as the United States (if the vast role of government is ignored), the ratio of additional saving to additional income will be determined for the most part by the voluntary action of all affluent individuals and all profitable businesses. Thus, each private or corporate investor presumably makes some decision dividing his income between its immediate consumption and its reinvestment for a private profit return in the future. Since private investors also ultimately determine the retention and reinvestment of corporate profits, one may think of the saving ratio as determined for all practical purposes by the decisions of private stockholders and their hired managers, who allocate corporate profits between consumption and saving. In practice, of course, much saving goes into the hands of banks, who then lend it back to businesses. In the United States the net investment ratio has run in the neighborhood of one-tenth of national income.

In the case of a centrally planned socialist economy, such as the Soviet Union, the saving decision is one which is generally made by the political leadership, and enforced through the central plan, regardless of household desires. The sources of saving in the Soviet Union are comprised of the several flows of funds into the central budget, primarily profits from government enterprises, sales taxes on the population collected through government enterprises, and taxes on collective farms and individuals. Since the political leadership is vitally interested in economic growth, has close control of the sources of saving, and takes a very long-run view of raising the level of consumer satisfaction, they ordinarily attempt and achieve a much higher saving ratio than under private enterprise. In fact, the Soviet Union has generally saved from a quarter to a third of its national product.

The marginal saving ratio of a market socialist economy is not as simple to predict, and depends upon several crucial details of its economic organization: Does the enterprise have full control of all current price and output decisions? Who makes most investment decisions, the enterprise or the government? Who controls the enterprise, a "Workers' Council" or a government-appointed manager?

If the central government makes investment decisions directly or indirectly, then a high saving and investment ratio may be expected, regardless of the extent of decentralization in other respects. Yugoslavia, for example, has in the past generally collected high taxes ("forced saving") from its enterprises, and has achieved thereby a very high saving-to-income ratio. If, however, the Workers' Council in the enterprise really controls its own managers and the distribution of its own gross income, then the result might be expected to be more like that arrived at by private stockholders in the United States. The Yugoslavs, however, claim that — when they are given the choice — the Workers' Councils freely elect to reinvest a large ratio of net income, rather than distribute it in wages. If Yugoslavia goes through with the announced reforms that would decentralize almost all investment decisions to the level of the Workers' Councils (or banks controlled by them), it will be very interesting to see whether their rate of investment remains as high as it has been.

Saving and Investment (Full Employment)

Under private enterprise, the saving ratio may be very high, but it will not lead to much growth if very little of the saving is actually invested. Investment depends on expectations of profit. If there is no expectation of profit, there will be little or no investment, and the excess saving will be "hoarded" or not spent. This is the basic reason for fluctuating rates of growth and periodic absolute declines or depressions under private enterprise.

A centrally planned economy is not subject to this periodic lack of investment demand. Its economy may slow up, or even fluctuate periodically, but it will not be due to excess saving. In fact, the Soviet Union has always had a "shortage" of saving, even though it saved a quarter to a third of national income. This "shortage" is caused by the unlimited demand of the central planners for more capital investment. Centrally planned economies have generally achieved reasonably full employment of both labor and capital, and this constitutes one reason for their high rates of growth.

It is still difficult at this time in history to say whether a market socialist economy could be subject to cyclical unemployment, though there has been some evidence of unemployment in Yugoslavia in 1962, 1966, and 1967. Again, it would largely depend on whether investment were centrally controlled or controlled by local enterprise Workers' Councils. If most investment is in reality centrally controlled (as in Yugoslavia in the past), then full employment should be assured just as under central planning. If the Workers' Council in each enterprise really makes the investment decision, then — just as under private enterprise — they might all periodically have expectations of little or no profit yield. In this case, if there were no central intervention, the result could be periodic lack of investment, leading to periodic unemployment of men and capital. Nor would fully decentralized market socialism be able to resist the secondary consequences of swings in output and prices as easily as central planning does.

Efficiency of Resource Allocation

If an economy is saving a constant proportion of its output, and is fully investing the capital thus saved, then its rate of growth will depend on the rate of growth of its productivity. Leaving dynamic questions aside till the next section, productivity reduces to the question of static efficiency, or how well an economy allocates capital, labor, and natural resources — specifically, how well does it allocate its resources among different possible technologies and among different possible output mixtures.

Under private enterprise, each firm chooses its technology and its output mix according to its view of the best way to maximize its profits. With pure and perfect competition, the most profitable technological solution is determined by the objective technical possibilities and the market prices of inputs; while the most profitable output mix depends on the prices of outputs and the pattern of consumer demand. All prices are automatically determined by supply and demand in the market places. *If* there is pure and perfect competition, both the technological decisions and the output mixture should be optimum in terms of consumer desires, given the existing rate of growth of total national product and its distribution.

Of course, if — as in the United States — there is neither pure nor perfect competition, but a very high degree of monopoly as well as limited knowledge and limited mobility of resources, there will *not* be an optimal distribution of resources. A private enterprise system characterized by monopoly, imperfect competition, and imperfect knowledge can usually be accused of: (1) waste and duplication because of trial and error methods; (2) irrational long-run decisions based on temporary short-run situations; (3) the large wastes of irrational buying due to persuasive advertising and other sales expenditures; (4) monopolistic restriction and distortion of outputs away from the preferred consumer pattern; and (5) monopolistic higher prices and profits, which change income distribution and further distort the pattern of consumer effective demand. For the purposes of this discussion, it is not necessary to evaluate these points.[1]

Central planning, on the other hand, is sometimes held to be inefficient even if it works as perfectly as a pure model of it could in theory. Von Mises argues that planned socialism could not work at all because the lack of an automatic market mechanism would lead to irrational prices. Hayek admits that planned socialism could work, in theory, through the solution of a very large number of equations. Hayek argues, however, that it will not work efficiently in practice because too much

[1] See, e.g., the evaluation in John K. Galbraith, *The New Industrial State* (Boston: Houghton Mifflin, 1967).

information plus too many calculations must go into the solution of this multitude of equations. Yet Soviet experience has shown that centrally planned socialism can not only work, but can work with some limited degree of efficiency. The Soviet Union does manage to maintain a high and improving level of productivity in spite of many obvious inefficiencies.

All of this is not to say that centrally planned socialism necessarily works more efficiently than private enterprise. Hayek's point, that central planners cannot know or do everything, finds plentiful support in the recent hue and cry for reforms in the U.S.S.R. and Eastern Europe. Moreover, the fact that the Soviet growth rate has been higher than the U.S. rate can *not* be attributed to greater static efficiency in the Soviet economy. On the contrary, although the evidence is fragmentary, the Soviet economy seems to reveal somewhat less static efficiency than the U.S. economy. For example, the study by Bergson cited in Chapter 5 shows that Soviet product per worker is far lower than U.S. product per worker. He also found that Soviet product per unit of capital is roughly equal to or a little higher than U.S. product per unit of capital, but the net result is still a considerably lower Soviet product per unit of capital-and-labor. Even with all the qualifications to Bergson's conclusions listed in that chapter, this and other evidence pointing to lower Soviet static efficiency seems quite strong.

The higher Soviet growth rate must therefore be explained mainly in terms of (1) the high ratio of saving to income, (2) the investment of all saving and the full employment of all workers, and (3) a good record of dynamic efficiency expressed mostly in a high rate of growth of education, research, and technological innovation. These latter factors, considered in detail in Chapter 9 and reviewed in the next section, are now considered by most economists to be the most important factors determining economic growth.[2]

The evidence in Chapter 9 also shows why future Soviet growth rates can *not* merely be assumed to be the same as past rates, since some part of the higher Soviet growth rate of past may have been due to some special advantages. These included (1) the advantages of backwardness, such as the ability to borrow more advanced technology, (2) the large supply of labor available from agriculture, and (3) the concentration in the prewar period on a few relatively easy products to produce, such as steel and oil, compared with the more complex and difficult product mix of today.

Turning to the alleged advantages of central planning, it may be argued that central planners should be able to (1) have more information available on long-run and aggregate facts than plant managers, (2) make use of higher quality scientists for the few central planners than are available for the thousands of planning positions in all of the individ-

[2] See, e.g., E. D. Domar, "On the Measurement of Technological Change," *Economic Journal*, Vol. 71 (December, 1961), pp. 709–729; also R. M. Solow, "Technical Progress, Capital Formation, and Economic Growth," *American Economic Review*, Vol. 52 (May, 1962), pp. 76–86.

ual plants, and (3) more quickly correct aggregate imbalance by increasing or reducing investment. On the other hand, a more decentralized system presumably would have the advantages that: (1) local plant mangers may be expected to have a better feel for (micro) details concerning short-run and enterprise conditions, (2) complete decentralization would eliminate large numbers of bureaucrats and bureaucratic wastefulness, and (3) decentralized price-setting in a competitive market would result in more rational prices (provided there is no monopoly).

It might be noted in this connection, that while the Soviet economy has been highly centralized in theory, at least until the 1965 reforms, it has always been somewhat more decentralized in practice as a result of the behavior of Soviet managers. Nevertheless, it has had vast problems under central planning in obtaining masses of detailed information, in processing the many calculations necessary for planning, and in getting managers to execute the Plan in the prescribed manner.

Even Lange's more decentralized scheme, whereby central planners only set prices while managers set outputs, has also been criticized on the grounds that it would have a lower level of efficiency than a perfectly competitive system. Thus, Hayek[3] argues that in reality Lange's model would adjust to supply and demand changes very slowly because all of the information for changing prices would have to flow up and down through a vast bureaucracy.

Secondly, Hayek argues that there would be an additional problem in getting managers to follow the correct rules for optimal input and output mixtures. Specifically, if the manager is merely supposed to maximize the profit of the enterprise, then under conditions of monopoly, he would make decisions contrary to social optimization. The manager of a monopolistic firm will not maximize profit by merely setting his output at the point where marginal cost equals prices, but at the point where marginal cost equals marginal revenue. This is a somewhat technical way of saying that a monopoly will restrict output to a lower level in order to set higher prices and make higher profit. Furthermore, Hayek argues that a central planning board will not automatically correct the situation because the lower supply relative to demand merely tells it to continue to raise prices. Presumably, the planning board does not know the marginal cost curve of the enterprise, and it would destroy the simplicity of Lange's scheme if they tried to discover marginal costs for all enterprises.

In the case of market socialism, where the enterprise sets both prices and outputs and makes most investment decisions, several concrete problems may be expected to arise (and most of these have shown up to some extent in Yugoslavia). Many of the efficiency problems will be identical to those allegedly present under competitive private enterprise. Thus, one would again expect to find (1) competitive waste and duplication, (2) irrational long-run decisions based on very temporary

[3] See, F. von Hayek, "Socialist Calculation: The Competitive 'Solution,'" *Economica* (May, 1940).

short-run situations, (3) wasteful advertising and other expenses directed solely at making more sales, (4) monopolistic restriction of output by some enterprises contrary to consumer preferences, and (5) higher prices and profits by some monopoly enterprises.

In addition, in an economy where enterprises are run by Workers' Councils on the Yugoslav model, other types of inefficiencies may also be expected. For example, there is the fact that the desire for democratic participation of workers in the councils may lead to much smaller scale enterprises than would be dictated by the purely economic criteria of the economies of scale. The tendency would be to limit enterprise size because democratic control becomes much less meaningful for an enterprise with hundreds of thousands of workers. Workers' Councils may also be hesitant to spend the profits of their enterprise to set up a new related enterprise, even though the investment might be very profitable, simply because the new enterprise may then be split off from the old to form a new Workers' Council.

The strongest argument in favor of the Workers' Council system is that it provides more incentive for the workers. Central planning not only provides less personal involvement, but the workers know that extra profits are retained by the government, so a production drive is often considered to be a "speed-up" by the workers in a centrally planned economy.

Growth and Technical Progress

The efficiency of the system will be determined not only by how well it allocates the resources at a given moment under given technological conditions, but also how well it succeeds in the discovery and introduction of new technology. In a private enterprise economy new technology is developed by private researchers, presumably all working for the prospect of expected profit from the discoveries. In practice, in the United States today, most non-governmental research on industrial applications of science is conducted by individuals and groups working for large corporations. Since it is only the corporation which directly benefits from a discovery, there is some question as to how much economic incentive for discovery exists for the individual researcher. In addition, some scientific investigations are today so large in scale that they cannot be conducted by any private enterprise, especially since private enterprise tends to take a very short-run view of the returns to research. Even in the United States, because of the large scale and the long time required for research to pay off, the bulk of basic research is today being carried out under government control or sponsorship.

In addition to scientific discovery, another problem of technological progress is the actual use of such discoveries in industry, which use is called "innovation." Innovation involves the further problem that patent rights have traditionally been considered necessary to motivate innovation by a private enterprise, but that these rights exclude the use of the innovation by other enterprises. Furthermore, enterprises may keep secret some of their new processes, and such trade secrets obviously restrict the spread of knowledge. Moreover, enterprises may sometimes withhold inventions that would destroy most of their market, for example, the discovery of a razor blade that could never get dull. Finally, it is notorious that in practice many important inventions are kept off the market during periods of depression, since innovation requires investment, and there is little investment during depression periods.

Under centrally planned socialism the incentive situation for individual research is much the same as under the conditions of large corporate or governmental research in the private enterprise system. In the case of centrally planned socialism, the individual obviously has no necessary and direct stake in the final use of his invention (that is, no monopoly by a patent right). Nevertheless, he will be paid wages and wage bonuses — and perhaps given a promotion — for any new invention he produces. It is even possible to give individual scientists continuing royalty payments from their productions. In point of fact, the Soviet Union, like the United States, has put a tremendous amount of money into scientific research; and has paid its scientists an even higher relative wage than the United States. It appears that the percentage of the labor force in research, and especially in basic research, is higher in the Soviet Union than the percentage in the United States.[4]

When the question of industrial innovation is examined, at first glance everything appears to be to the advantage of centrally planned socialism. In the first place, there are no exclusive patents granted to keep other enterprises from using the innovation; and in the second place, there are presumably no trade secrets kept from other enterprises. This situation should guarantee the widest *dissemination* of the knowledge of new technology (though it may also be argued that the lack of patents and private profit opportunities lowers the incentive to *discovery*). Moreover, central planners themselves presumably do everything possible to spread information on innovations as widely as possible, and to insure that all enterprises use the latest available innovations. The main problem that arises under central planning, however, is that managers are very hesitant to take the risk of introducing an innovation. The manager is generally paid his bonus on the basis of each month's performance, and is subject to frequent transfers to different enterprises. Therefore, the manager may well be afraid that an innovation will lower his performance record in the short run, and that he will not be around in the long run when the innovation proves helpful to his present enterprise. Moreover, there is always the risk that any particular innovation may prove a failure even in the long run.

Furthermore, the Soviet manager has also been subject to a form of "speed-up." That is, if he substantially over-fulfills the plan because of a newly adopted innovation, or even if he is *expected* to substantially over-fulfill a plan because of newly adopted innovations, his planned

[4] See, e.g., N. De Witt, "High Level Manpower in the U.S.S.R.," U.S. Congress, Joint Economic Committee, *New Directions in the Soviet Economy* (Washington, D.C.: U.S. Government Printing Office, 1966), pp. 789–817.

target itself may be raised, thus providing him with a more difficult goal to meet. Liberman's proposals in the Soviet Union attempt to deal with this problem by allowing the plants to submit their own plans, by giving a much higher bonus for the fulfillment of that plan than for over-plan fulfillment, and by guaranteeing that the plan remains unchanged for a period of three to five years (unless the plant itself wishes to raise the targets). The Soviet Union is moving in the direction of assuring long-run rewards to the manager for successful innovation, but whether those assurances will be real enough in practice to convince the managers is still debatable.

Under the system of decentralized or market socialism, the inventor must still work for some larger economic unit, since that is necessary for all large scale scientific work in our modern world. In fact, the necessary scale of most research is now becoming so large that the enterprise itself will normally be too small for the most efficient scope of research and development. This has apparently been recognized by Czechoslovakia, where the new decentralized system preserves central direction and finance of most research and development.

If market socialism is to reward an enterprise for being first with an innovation, then it would also seem necessary for it to introduce exclusive patenting in order to prevent other competitive enterprises from immediately copying the innovation. Perhaps it could require licensing at a reasonable fee to all applicants who wish to use the patent. This may be one of the reasons why countries such as Czechoslovakia still require that new major investment projects be made by the central plan, rather than being left to existing enterprises. Finally, notice that an enterprise under market socialism might hestitate to spend for innovations, as well as any other types of new investment, if its profit-making outlook appears bleak.

The Equity of Income Distribution

Under private enterprise, there is a very wide range of income distribution, including large numbers of individuals with very low incomes, and a few with extremely high incomes. This is condemned by those whose ethical viewpoint calls for a complete equality of incomes as a goal in itself. Nevertheless, from Marx to Marshall, most economists who have thought and written on the problem would argue that, at our present level of economic development and of individual psychology, it is necessary to have a wide range of income distribution as an incentive for the individual to produce more. The real question comes when we ask exactly how wide this spread must be, and what are the sources and methods of obtaining income by the different recipients.

Under private enterprise the many small incomes are earned for the most part by wage and salary workers, while the relatively few very large incomes are received in the form of private profit, rent, or interest on capital. The contention of Marxists is, of course, that the incomes of the holders of capital and other property are obtained through the "exploitation" of the wage worker, that is, that the worker produces the product and the owner of capital receives the income from it. No attempt is made to resolve this question here.

Under centrally planned socialism there is, of course, only wage income, and no return to private individuals for the ownership or use of capital and property rights. Although income in the Soviet Union is almost all composed of wages and salaries, it is important to note that the income distribution *among wage earners* is probably as wide in the Soviet Union as in the United States. On the other hand, because of the existence of property incomes, U.S. income distribution as a whole is far less equal than the whole Soviet distribution.

The wide range of Soviet wage distribution was introduced by Stalin as a device to encourage the most possible production by workers. Considering wages only, one must then compare in terms of one's ethical values the goal of increased national production versus the goal of increased equality of income. Stalin's successors emphatically claim to be reducing the amount of income inequality both by reducing wage differentials and by increasing the percentage of free public goods provided by the government. They argue that this is now possible because of a higher level of economic development achieved in the Soviet Union. Their announced goal is the free distribution of all goods to the consumer, or at least of all "basic" goods; but they are proceeding in this direction more than cautiously, at a very slow snail's pace.

Yugoslavian market socialism and all of the new proposals for decentralized socialism in Eastern Europe provided for very wide wage differentials, to be based in part upon the profit record of the enterprise. In the Yugoslav case, the workers in fact have the legal right to distribute all profits above taxes in the form of wage payments. The Chinese, on the other hand, have strongly condemned such profit-based bonuses, and have argued for a wider use of revolutionary ideological and nonmaterial rewards. Of course, no one in Eastern European enterprises receives private profit for himself as a return on a capital investment. On the other hand, under any system of profit-based bonuses or profit-sharing by workers, it is true that two workers with the same occupation and same skills may no longer earn the same income, since their incomes will in part be based on the profits of two differently situated enterprises.

Political Democracy

The main political problem deriving from private enterprise arises from the inequality of economic ownership and income. The socialist critics argue that the concentration of economic wealth leads to the concentration of political power. They further argue that such political power is achieved by the owners of private enterprises regardless of the formal political structure, whether it be a fascist dictatorship as in Spain or a two-party political democracy as in the United States. Their argument is that the owners of great wealth can easily control the means of propaganda, such as newspapers and television. The wealthy are also supposed to be able to control both political parties, either by buying the delegates to conventions or by the financing of political campaigns, since these campaigns require such great amounts of financial resources. Finally, the socialist critics allege that the process of control of politics is greatly aided by the ability to give lucrative jobs or to black-list anyone, from a retired general to a non-conformist playwright.

The main problem for political democracy under a system of centrally planned socialism wears a very different aspect. It is not the holders of private wealth, but the top bureaucracy which controls all of the economic levers of society. Thus, the top Soviet leaders fully control all media of communication by virtue of government ownership. They are also in a position to give jobs and promotion or demotion to all working members of the society. The Soviet Union has largely ignored this problem, and has suffered all the evils of political dictatorship. It is certainly possible in theory, however, to curb such a bureaucracy even in a centrally planned economy through the use of a multi-party election process, and various institutionalized means for the opposition to make its own propaganda. For example, the opposition might be alloted a certain amount of time, as it is on the government-owned B.B.C. in England; or it might be allowed to form a non-profit cooperative venture, such as some of the listener-sponsored radio stations in the United States.

The fact remains that Stalin exercised a long and bloody dictatorship in the Soviet Union, and that the Communist Party is still the only legal party in that country. What is not yet proven is whether this dictatorship was due to the socialist economic system *or* to the existence of particular historical circumstances, such as the extreme economic backwardness of Tsarist Russia. Many socialists argue that it was the economic, political, and social backwardness of the Soviet Union that gave rise to Stalinist dictatorship. They argue that the only way to eliminate economic backwardness rapidly is to impose heavy investment burdens on the population. Yet these necessary burdens would not be accepted by a democratic vote, but could only be imposed by dictatorial decree. They argue further that the socialist economic system actually tends to work against personal dictatorship; and that to the degree that the Soviet Union is freeing itself from economic backwardness, it has slowly begun to liberalize its political activities.

The Soviet invasion of Czechoslovakia was a striking case of retrogression to Stalinist methods. It set back the development of democracy in both the Soviet Union and Eastern Europe by several years. It is possible, of course, that the wave of revulsion against repressive methods may be so strong that it will spread from Eastern Europe into the Soviet Union itself. Thus, in the long-run the invasion might help cause the defeat of the present Soviet leadership and a considerable advance toward political democracy. That is pure speculation, however, and no one can predict how long it will be before such progress occurs in the Soviet Union — but the present evidence seems to indicate quite a long time.

Finally, there is the case of market socialism. Its advocates, such as the Yugoslav Communist Party, argue that full decentralization of economic power to local Workers' Councils eliminates most of the bureaucracy as well as all bureaucratic power of the top leadership. They also argue that the cooperative form of workers' management allows only relatively small income differentials, based upon the ability of the group of workers in each enterprise; and that it prohibits any striking concentration of private wealth. In view of the fact, however, that Yugoslavia has been subject to political dictatorship during its period of market socialism, one may be permitted some skepticism about these claims.

Some observers deny that there is much real workers' participation or democratic content in the Workers' Councils[5] and believe that they are rather dominated by the local Communist Party in nominations to the councils as well as in the performance of their duties. At any rate, Yugoslavia has not achieved anything like complete decentralization and therefore still maintains a large bureaucracy under the direction of the Central Committee of the Yugoslav Communist Party and President Tito. Once again, it may perhaps be argued that this political dictatorship does not stem from the form of market socialism, but from the historical conditions of war devastation and guerrilla discipline during the Second World War, plus the economic backwardness and rigid central planning of the immediate postwar period.

Cultural and Psychological Behavior

If the preceding section on political democracy was quite speculative, this section on the cultural and psychological effects of different economic systems must be even less firmly based. Thus, in a general way, the critics of private enterprise allege that its system produces an intense concentration by individuals upon their own private gain and the acquisition of money, without regard for other social or cultural values. They argue that it produces an extremely antisocial and individualistic psychology, family splits expressed in divorce fights over property, and highly commercialized art forms, catering to the lowest possible tastes in order to make the most money.

The criticisms of the cultural and psychological behavior of individuals under centrally planned socialism, as seen in the Soviet Union, are quite different, though no less critical. The Soviet Union has been characterized by all of the negative aspects of a political dictatorship. According to the critics, this political dictatorship has necessarily led to a highly conformist and unthinking psychology for the average citizen. Political dictatorship has only allowed art forms expressing political propaganda, with little artistic content, though there has been some

---

[5] See, e.g., Benjamin Ward, "Workers Management in Yugoslavia," *Journal of Political Economy*, LXV (October, 1957), pp. 373–386. Ward, himself, later changed his tune in his article in *American Economic Review* (May, 1965); and a strong positive evaluation is given in B. Horvat and V. Rascovic, "Worker's Management in Yugoslavia," *Journal of Political Economy*, Vol. 67 (April, 1959), pp. 194–198.

considerable improvement in recent years in the wake of political liberalization.

Lastly, the Chinese have violently criticised the U.S.S.R. and Eastern Europe (and especially Yugoslavia) from the opposite point of view: that these countries are becoming too lax and non-revolutionary. They cite the new Soviet emphasis on consumer goods and the new economic reforms which stress profits. They contend that Soviet citizens are becoming fully dedicated to the bourgeois value of money-making, because of the very wide wage differentials used as a tool to insure the incentive to produce. Both China and Cuba among the socialist countries argue strongly in favor of the extensive use of non-material and ideological (or propagandistic) incentives for work. This they consider will produce a more communist and socially oriented psychology and culture. Obviously, the present book is not the place to investigate further either these arguments or the social mileiu of these countries.

Convergence of Central Planning and Market Socialism

Chapter 12 of this book discussed the attempts of Soviet reformers, such as Novozhilov, to arrive at a more perfect method of calculation for central planning. Chapters 13 and 14 considered the attempts of Liberman and the other Soviet and Eastern European economists to decentralize planning, so that decision-making would focus primarily on the enterprise manager. The manager would make his decisions on the basis of market supply and demand. The question arises of the relationship between these two sets of reforms.

The most extreme version of Libermanism is a picture of the invisible hand of the market operating so that each socialist firm must act out of its own self-interest so as to bring about the best interests of socialist society. On the other hand, the vision of Novozhilov is one of information pouring into central calculating machines, programmed so that they will turn out a plan which gives an optimal choice of technology as well as the output mix. If it is true that programming can solve all of the problems of allocation of resources, then why not use only central planning — and merely give the results as direct orders to each enterprise? Why should the market mechanism play any further role once optimal programming has been perfected?

In fact, in the Soviet Union today the conservatives, to the degree that they accept Novozhilov's vision of more perfect calculation, argue that the better methods and electronic calculators make continued central planning the best road to follow, and make it unnecessary to decentralize.[6] On the other hand, Novozhilov himself and many others believe that rational prices are merely the necessary basis for decentralization. These Soviet writers insist that rational prices for use by managers in decentralized decision-making must stem from an optimal output plan,

[6] See, e.g., the dogmatic defense of central planning in I. Rusinov, "Prospects in the Development of Planning of Agricultural Production," translated in *Problems of Economics*, Vol. 10 (September, 1967), pp. 25–32.

based in turn on demand preferences and on the objectively existing supply conditions.[7] On the basis of centrally calculated rational prices, managers at the enterprise level could then make all output and input decisions more efficiently. The enterprise managers could act with more detailed information, and with a more "democratic" content (based on workers' and consumers' preferences), than could the central planners.[8]

Specifically, modern methods of programming do theoretically allow planners to calculate the correct inputs and outputs for each enterprise. But the staggering amount of data and calculation work required to accomplish this job make it somewhat infeasible in practice. The contrary suggestion, now emerging from Soviet and Eastern European practice as well as theory, is to have the central planners calculate rational prices from a more limited amount of data. This can be done with modern methods just as easily as the calculation of all inputs and outputs. These centrally calculated prices, usually called shadow prices, would then be given to the enterprise managers as the data with which the managers must operate. The managers would go ahead on the basis of these prices to reach their own decisions on input and output mixtures. In addition, these writers propose to charge interest and rent as the prices of fixed capital and internal resources, which will then complete the necessary price information upon which managers must act.

The managers will thus make their decisions upon the basis of their own knowledge of the technical conditions in the firm, as well as the prices given them by the central planners. As noted in the previous two chapters, the tendency does exist for central planners to set prices, while managers are receiving more freedom in decisions of technological methods and output mixtures. The end result would be a mixed system wherein the enterprise managers would make all of the current and short-run decisions concerning the use of available labor, raw materials, and capacity; while the central planners would be free of this detail, so that they could concentrate on long-run macro-economic investment planning for the expansion of capacity and the introduction of new technology. While some such converging trend between central planning and market socialism may be discerned in the Soviet Union and Eastern Europe, it is still not clear where on the spectrum these countries will finally be found.

SELECTED REFERENCES

1. A full-scale attack on the inefficiency of central planning compared to the private enterprise market mechanism is in Abram Bergson, *The Economics of Soviet Planning* (New Haven: Yale University Press, 1964).

[7] See, e.g., the quite clear exposition in N. Fedorenko, "Price and Optimal Planning," translated in *Problems of Economics*, Vol. 10 (October, 1967).

[8] For an extensive discussion of the new developments and some of their relationships, see Egon Neuberger, "Libermanism, Computopia, and Visible Hand: The Question of Informational Efficiency," *American Economic Review*, Vol. 56 (May, 1966), pp. 131–144.

2. An evaluation by several Western economists with several articles concentrating on the relative advantages of central planning versus decentralization is to be found in Gregory Grossman, editor, *Value and Plan* (Berkeley: University of California Press, 1960).

3. The viewpoint in favor of central planning and against decentralization is most ably expressed by a Western Marxist in Charles Bettelheim, *Studies in the Theory of Planning* (Bombay: Asia Publishing House, 1959), Chapter 1.

4. The Eastern European reformer's viewpoint is perhaps best expressed in Ota Sik, *Problems of Socialist Commodity Relations* (New York: International Arts and Sciences Press, translated 1967).

5. The history and defense of the special Yugoslav concept of decentralization and Workers' Councils is presented in a very sophisticated form in Branco Horvat, *Towards a Theory of Planned Economy* (Belgrad: Yugoslav Institute of Economic Research, first published 1961, translated 1964).

6. The most sophisticated version of the Chinese attack on Yugoslav market socialism is presented in Paul Sweezy and Leo Huberman, "Peaceful Transition from Socialism to Capitalism," *Monthly Review*, Vol. 15 (March, 1964), pp. 569–590.

INDEX

367